OXFORD EARLY CHRISTIAN STUDIES

General Editors

GILLIAN CLARK   ANDREW LOUTH

THE OXFORD EARLY CHRISTIAN STUDIES

Series includes scholarly volumes on the thought and history of the early Christian centuries. Covering a wide range of Greek, Latin, and Oriental sources, the books are of interest to theologians, ancient historians, and specialists in the classical and Jewish worlds.

TITLES IN THE SERIES INCLUDE:

Fallen Angels in the Theology of St Augustine
Gregory D. Wiebe (2021)

Jerome's Commentaries on the Pauline Epistles and the Architecture of Exegetical Authority
Andrew Cain (2021)

Tatian's Diatessaron
Composition, Redaction, Recension, and Reception
James W. Barker (2021)

Clement and Scriptural Exegesis
The Making of a Commentarial Theologian
H. Clifton Ward (2022)

Dorotheus of Gaza and Ascetic Education
Michael W. Champion (2022)

Spiritual Direction as a Medical Art in Early Christian Monasticism
Jonathan L. Zecher (2022)

The Library of Paradise
A History of Contemplative Reading in the Monasteries of the Church of the East
David A. Michelson (2022)

The Cult of Stephen in Jerusalem
Inventing a Patron Martyr
Hugo Méndez (2022)

The Metaphysics of Light in the Hexaemeral Literature
From Philo of Alexandria to Gregory of Nyssa
Isidoros C. Katsos (2023)

Patriarch Dioscorus of Alexandria
The Last Pharaoh and Ecclesiastical Politics in the Later Roman Empire
Volker L. Menze (2023)

Origen of Alexandria and the Theology of the Holy Spirit
Micah M. Miller (2024)

The Interpretation of Kenosis from Origen to Cyril of Alexandria
Dimensions of Self-Emptying in the Reception of Philippians 2:7
Michael C. Magree (2024)

Christology and the Logic of Grace in Fifth-Century Gaul

DONALD FAIRBAIRN

Great Clarendon Street, Oxford, OX2 6DP,
United Kingdom

Oxford University Press is a department of the University of Oxford.
It furthers the University's objective of excellence in research, scholarship,
and education by publishing worldwide. Oxford is a registered trade mark of
Oxford University Press in the UK and in certain other countries

© Donald Fairbairn 2025

The moral rights of the author have been asserted

All rights reserved. No part of this publication may be reproduced, stored in a retrieval
system, transmitted, used for text and data mining, or used for training artificial
intelligence, in any form or by any means, for commercial purposes, without the
prior permission in writing of Oxford University Press, or as expressly permitted by law,
by licence or under terms agreed with the appropriate reprographics rights organization.
Enquiries concerning reproduction outside the scope of the above should be sent to
the Rights Department, Oxford University Press, at the address above.

You must not circulate this work in any other form
and you must impose this same condition on any acquirer

Published in the United States of America by Oxford University Press
198 Madison Avenue, New York, NY 10016, United States of America

British Library Cataloguing in Publication Data

Data available

Library of Congress Control Number: 2024942590

ISBN 9780198936190

DOI: 10.1093/9780198936220.001.0001

Printed and bound by
CPI Group (UK) Ltd, Croydon, CR0 4YY

To Abigail, the newest Fairbairn,
who married our son Trey
as this book was in production

Preface

This book has been on my mind for more than two decades. When I began collecting materials in 2003 to translate the sixth-century correspondence between Fulgentius of Ruspe and the Scythian monks on Christology and grace, I intended that set of translations to be a first step towards a book on the relation between those themes among all the participants in the 'Semi-Pelagian' controversy. My tenure as an administrator delayed that translation work, and it was not published until 2013 (Fathers of the Church, vol. 126). Another stint in academic administration put the book that I ultimately hoped to write on hold as well, and when I finally took up the project in earnest in 2021, both the scope and what I had to say about the subject had changed. Rather than surveying all the participants, I had decided that it would be fruitful to concentrate on the southern Gallic writers, and only those of the fifth century, since the Christological writings of these writers had received little attention. I will leave it to the reader to decide whether the narrowing in focus prompted by my thinking during the years of delays turned out to be a good thing!

In the meantime, the book benefitted from the encouragement and suggestions of many people. My wife Jennifer has been my sounding board for this and all my writing projects, as have our children Trey and Ella once they were old enough to take an interest in them. Augustine Casiday has long applauded the idea of this project and encouraged me to see it through. My students Anthony Catri and Thomas Hill have discussed the ideas at length with me and urged me to put them into writing, from their days as my research assistants a decade ago up to the present time. Kurt Jaros and I have had stimulating conversations about the Gallic writers, and he has kindly given me a copy of his dissertation, which is cited often in this book. Once I began work on the book, our son Trey (by this time a German specialist, unlike his father, who is more at home with the Romance and Slavic languages) helped me make sure I correctly understood secondary literature in German.

I would like to thank the series editors, Gillian Clark and Andrew Louth, as well as the two anonymous readers of the manuscript, for their affirmation, encouragement, and especially their invaluable critiques that have made this a much better book. I only hope the revisions I made in response have done some justice to the quality of their suggestions. I would also like to thank Tom Perridge, Aimee Wright, and the production staff at Oxford University Press. Their kindness and professionalism have been as great as ever.

viii   PREFACE

In spite of the sharp eyes that have read this book, no doubt mistakes remain. In particular, there may be places where my view of the Gallic monks misrepresents them or views them without proper nuance. I take full responsibility, and I invite the criticisms and corrections that will no doubt come from other scholars. It is a privilege to be a part of the ongoing scholarly discussion of the patristic understanding of Christ, grace, and salvation.

Donald Fairbairn
Wilmore, Kentucky, USA
29 February 2024
(The feast of St. John Cassian in the Eastern Church)

Contents

Note on Citations	xi
List of Abbreviations	xiii
Introduction	1
1. Setting the Stage: Christology and Grace in Augustine's Later Writings	22
2. Leporius: A Crypto-'Pelagian', Proto-'Nestorian'?	49
3. John Cassian: 'Nestorius', Grace, and the Monastic Life	68
4. Vincent of Lérins: 'Nestorius', Christian Orthodoxy, and Grace	100
5. Prosper of Aquitaine: Grace, 'Nestorianism', and God's Salvific Will	135
6. Faustus of Riez: 'Nestorianism' and *Prima Gratia*	170
Conclusion	202
Bibliography	207
General Index	219
Scripture Index	223

Note on Citations

Throughout this book, I cite patristic sources by abbreviations of the standard Latin titles and quote them from published English translations whenever possible. When I modify a published translation, I indicate as much. In the footnotes, I cite each patristic work by the book and paragraph number in keeping with the divisions found in the best edition of the text, followed by the page number of the modern edition I am using (in parentheses), and then the page number of the translation I am using, if any [in brackets]. If no published translation is indicated, the translation in the text is my own. Section one of the bibliography gives fuller information about the editions and translations of the patristic works cited and quoted.

Within patristic quotations, I often include material in either parentheses or brackets. Parentheses enclose noteworthy portions of the Latin text behind the translation. (In contrast, parentheses enclosing English writing are the translator's explanatory glosses, not my own.) Brackets enclose explanatory material I have added, such as a phrase that is implied but not stated in the text. When a patristic quotation includes a quotation from or clear allusion to a biblical passage, I italicize the biblical quotation and indicate the reference of the biblical text either in brackets within the patristic quotation or in my discussion of the passage.

For the sake of brevity, citations of editions and translations of patristic texts and of secondary literature use abbreviations whenever it is practical and advantageous to do so. A list of abbreviations follows.

Abbreviations

ABenR	*American Benedictine Review,* New York, 1950–.
ACO	*Acta conciliorum oecumenicorum,* ed. E. Schwartz, Berlin, 1914–40.
ACW	Ancient Christian Writers, ed. Quasten and Plumpe, Westminster, MD, 1946–.
ANF	*The Ante-Nicene Fathers,* ed. Alexander Roberts and James Donaldson, New York, 1885–87.
AugSt	*Augustinian Studies,* Villanova, PA, 1970–.
CCist	*Collectanea Cisterciensia,* Forges, 1934–.
CCSL	Corpus Christianorum Series Latina, Turnhout, 1954–.
CD	*La Ciudad de Dios* (at various times called *Revista Agustiniana* and *Religión y Cultura*), Madrid, 1881–.
CistS	*Cistercian Studies,* Barryville, VA, 1962–.
CSEL	Corpus Scriptorum Ecclesiasticorum Latinorum, Vienna, 1866–.
DR	*The Downside Review,* Bath, 1880–.
DTC	*Dictionnaire de théologie catholique*, Paris, 1902–72.
E.T.	English Translation
ETL	*Ephemerides Theologicae Lovaniensis,* Louvain, 1924–.
FC	The Fathers of the Church, Washington, DC, 1947–.
Fr.T.	French Translation
JEH	*The Journal of Ecclesiastical History,* London, 1950–.
JTS	*The Journal of Theological Studies,* Oxford, 1899–1949 (old series); 1950– (new series).
l.	Line
Lat.V.	Latin Version
ll.	Lines
MGH:AA	Monumenta Germaniae Historica: Auctores Antiquissimi, Turnout, 1819–.
NPNF[1]	A Select Library of the Nicene and Post-Nicene Fathers of the Christian Church, first series, ed. Philip Schaff, New York, 1886–89.
NPNF[2]	A Select Library of the Nicene and Post-Nicene Fathers of the Christian Church, second series, ed. Philip Schaff and Henry Wace, New York, 1890–1900.
n.s.	New Series
OECS	Oxford Early Christian Studies, Oxford, 1993–.
OECT	Oxford Early Christian Texts, Oxford, 1971–.
OSHS	Oxford Studies in Historical Theology, 1997–.
OTM	Oxford Theological Monographs, 1983–.
PCBE	*Prosopographie chrétienne du Bas-Empire, Vol. 4: La Gaule chrétienne (314–614),* ed. Luce Pietri and Marc Heijmans, Paris, 2013.
PG	Patrologia, series graeca et latina, ed. J.P. Migne, Paris, 1857–66.

xiv ABBREVIATIONS

PL	Patrologia, series latina, ed. J.P. Migne, Paris, 1841–64.
PMS	Patristic Monograph Series, 1976–.
ProEccl	*Pro Ecclesia,* Northfield, MN, 1993–.
RAM	*Revue d'ascétique et de mystique,* Tolouse, 1921–.
REAug	*Revue d'études augustiniennes et patristiques,* Paris, 1955–.
RevSR	*Revue des sciences réligieuses,* Strasbourg, 1921–.
RechSR	*Recherches de science réligieuse,* Paris, 1910–.
RTAM	*Recherches de théologie ancienne et médiévale,* Louvain, 1929–.
SC	Sources chrétiennes, ed. Lubac and Daniélou, Paris, 1941–.
SJT	*Scottish Journal of Theology,* Edinburgh, 1948–.
StPatr	*Studia Patristica,* Berlin (vols. 1–16) and Oxford (vols. 17ff.), 1957–.
SVigChr	Supplements to *Vigiliae Christianae*: Texts and Studies of Early Christian Life and Language, ed. J. Den Boeft et al., 1987–.
Syr.V.	Syriac Version
TS	*Theological Studies,* Woodstock, MD, 1940–.
TTH	Translated Texts for Historians, Liverpool, 1987–.
TU	Texte und Untersuchungen zur Geschichte der altchristlichen Literatur, Berlin, 1883–1976.
VigChr	*Vigiliae Christianae,* Amsterdam, 1947–.
WS	*Woodbrooke Studies: Christian Documents in Syriac, Arabic, and Garshūni Edited and Translated with a Critical Apparatus,* ed. Alphonse Mingana, Cambridge, 1927–34.
WSA	The Works of Saint Augustine: A Translation for the 21st Century, Brooklyn, NY, 1990–.

Introduction

In Christian history, one of the more unfortunate names for a theological dispute is the moniker 'Semi-Pelagian Controversy' to refer to the on-again, off-again conversation in southern Gaul and North Africa from the late 420s to the late 520s. The term 'Semi-Pelagian' was unknown for most of Christian history and seems to have first emerged in Protestant polemics in the middle of the sixteenth century as a way to refer to the Roman Catholic Church's alleged view of grace and human action, with no reference to any ancient Christian controversy or heretical group. By the end of the sixteenth century the term was being used in Roman Catholic circles as well and began to be applied to the southern Gallic writers of the fifth and early sixth centuries.[1] By the early seventeenth century, 'Semi-Pelagian' was the common way of referring to the grace-related discussions of the fifth and sixth centuries.[2]

That term grew out of and carried with it a particular understanding of the discussion, one that took its categories from Augustine's earlier opposition to Pelagianism and assumed the primary issue was how much emphasis a writer gave to divine and human action in the process of salvation. Within this framework, scholars then classified patristic writers who seemed to fall between Augustine and Pelagius on a spectrum as 'Semi-Augustinian' or 'Semi-Pelagian'. Scholars in the late nineteenth century and much of the twentieth adopted the name 'Semi-Pelagian' at least in part because they embraced this basic understanding of what the discussion was about and how its proponents should be categorized. But as the twentieth century rolled on and gave way to the twenty-first, new scholarship identified additional factors affecting the discussions and thus increasingly questioned the usefulness of the term 'Semi-Pelagian' to describe

---

[1] See Irena Backus and Aza Goudriaan, ' "Semipelagianism": The Origins of the Term and its Passage into the History of Heresy', *JEH* 65 (2014), 35–46.

[2] See Mannes Jacquin, 'A quelle date apparaît le term "semi-pélagien"?' *Revue des sciences philosophiques et théologiques* 1 (1907), 506–8; Émile Amann, 'Semi-Pélagiens', *DTC* 14/2 (1939), 1796; Donato Ogliari, *Gratia et Certamen: The Relationship Between Grace and Free Will in the Discussion of Augustine with the So-Called Semipelagians* (Leuven: Leuven University Press, 2003), 5–6; Alexander Y. Hwang, *Intrepid Lover of Perfect Grace: The Life and Thought of Prosper of Aquitaine* (Washington, DC: The Catholic University of America Press, 2009), 2–3.

Christology and the Logic of Grace in Fifth-Century Gaul. Donald Fairbairn, Oxford University Press.
© Donald Fairbairn 2025. DOI: 10.1093/9780198936220.003.0001

2 CHRISTOLOGY AND THE LOGIC OF GRACE

figures such as Cassian of Marseilles (*c*.360–*c*.435),[3] Vincent of Lérins (died *c*.450),[4] and Faustus of Riez (*c*.404–*c*.490).[5]

With this shift in scholarly opinion has come a bit of a quandary about how to label the so-called 'Semi-Pelagians'.[6] Given that the proponents of a collection of views in partial opposition to Augustine all lived in southern Gaul, the geographic descriptor 'Gallic' is (re-) emerging as a useful way of naming both the theologians involved and the controversy itself.[7] To some degree, the long discussion pitted monastic leaders from southern Gaul against thinkers from outside the region—Italy, North Africa, and even as far away as Scythia Minor.[8] In fact, if one categorizes Prosper of Aquitaine (*c*.390–*c*.455)[9] by his later writings rather

---

[3] Of the many works on Cassian's life and monastic endeavours, three that may justly be called classics are Jean Claude Guy, *Jean Cassien: vie et doctrine spirituelle*, Théologie, pastorale et spirtualité, recherches et syntheses 9 (Paris: P. Lethiellieux, 1961); Owen Chadwick, *John Cassian: A Study in Primitive Monasticism*, second edition (Cambridge: Cambridge University Press, 1968); Columba Stewart, *Cassian the Monk*, OSHS (Oxford: Oxford University Press, 1998). See also 'Cassianus 2', in *PCBE* 4 (2013), 430–7. On Cassian's birthplace (probably Scythia Minor), see Ionuţ-Alexandru Tudorie, 'Cassianus, Natione Scytha: Revisiting an Old Issue', *Revue d'histoire ecclésiastique* 115 (2020), 5–33. I should mention that Panagiotes Tzamalikos, *The Real Cassian Revisited: Monastic Life, Greek Paideia, and Origenism in the Sixth Century*, SVigChr 112 (Leiden: Brill, 2012), xii, makes the striking claim that '"John Cassian", the alleged "father of Western monasticism", is only a figment fabricated by means of extensive blatant Medieval forgery'. Tzamalikos's work is primarily concerned with establishing the existence and brilliance of Cassian the Sabaite, a Greek monk of the sixth century whose work on monastic rules in the East and Egypt, Tzamalikos contends, is the basis from which the Cassianic corpus was translated and expanded. Tzamalikos's argument is unpersuasive for a variety of reasons. For a response re-asserting the more universal view that the Sabaite's writing was a Greek translation and abbreviation of Cassian's longer works (and thus that Cassian of Marseilles did in fact exist), see Columba Stewart, 'Another Cassian?' *JEH* 66 (2015), 372–6. See also the review of Tzamalikos's work by Augustine Casiday in *The Journal of Medieval Monastic Studies* 3 (2014), 119–25.

[4] For Vincent's life and significance, see Thomas G. Guarino, *Vincent of Lérins and the Development of Christian Doctrine*, Foundations of Theological Exegesis and Christian Spirituality (Grand Rapids, MI: Baker Academic), 2013. See also 'Vincentius 4', in *PCBE* 4 (2013), 1978–80.

[5] For Faustus's life and legacy, see Gustave Weigel, *Faustus of Riez: An Historical Introduction*. Philadelphia: Dolphin Press, 1938; Rossana Barcellona, *Fausto di Riez interprete del suo tempo: un vescovo tardoantico dentro la crisi dell'impero* (Soveria Mannelli, Italy: Rubbettino, 2006). See also 'Faustus 1', in *PCBE* 4 (2013), 734–44.

[6] Ogliari, *Gratia et Certamen*, 7–9, points out that the designation 'Semi-Pelagianism' gives the false impression of a unified movement connecting Africa with Gaul, and also gives rise to the idea that the monks agreed with Pelagian ideas on grace and free will. Among alternative proposals, he claims that 'Semi-Augustinianism' fails to take into account the fact that the Gallic monks were working with a pre-Augustinian, traditional view, not a partly Augustinian one indebted to him. And 'Anti-Augustinians' is accurate only if one considers it to mean opposition to certain of Augustine's views, not to Augustine's thought as a whole. Similarly, Rebecca Harden Weaver, Introduction to *Grace for Grace: The Debates after Augustine and Pelagius*, ed. Alexander Hwang et al. (Washington, DC: The Catholic University of America Press, 2014), xvii, comments: 'The foci of scholars have become narrower with the result that the complexity of events and positions has been illuminated . . . One result, however, is the loss of any simple way to name or characterize the "controversy".'

[7] Hwang, *Intrepid Lover of Perfect Grace*, 2–6, recommends '*doctores Gallicani*'—a phrase that originated with Gennadius, *De uir. illust.* 59 (60) (PL 58.1092) [*NPNF*[2] 3.395].

[8] This assertion is perhaps an oversimplification, because it is possible that the Gallic writers' views were shaped in opposition more to predestinarian views within Gaul than to Augustine himself. See Augustine Casiday, *Tradition and Theology in St John Cassian*, OECS (Oxford: Oxford University Press, 2007), 17–42.

[9] For Prosper's life and significance, see Hwang, *Intrepid Lover of Perfect Grace*; Jérémy Delmulle, *Prosper d'Aquitaine contre Jean Cassien: Le* Contra Collatorem, *L'Appel à Rome du parti Augustinien*

than his earlier ones and does not rank him as a strong Augustinian, then all the ardent Augustinians in the discussion—Augustine himself, the Scythian monks, and Fulgentius of Ruspe—were from outside southern Gaul, whereas all the writers later branded as 'Semi-Pelagians', as well as Prosper who has never been so branded but came increasingly to agree with them—were Gallic. In this book I shall use 'Gallic' as a purely geographic designation to refer collectively to the writers from southern Gaul.

As helpful as recent scholarship has been in expanding our understanding of the contours of the discussion, there is an aspect of the charitological debate that has still received little attention. This is the connection between Christology and grace in the thought of the fifth-century southern Gallic writers, and in particular, the connection between their understanding of what the Nestorian heresy consisted of and the ways they articulated the role of divine grace in salvation. Of course, Cassian—whose *Conlatio* 13 occupies a prominent position in the controversy—also wrote a lengthy treatise in opposition to Nestorius and even linked Nestorian thought to Pelagian ideas. But most scholars have regarded his Christological work as being of little value, have discounted the connection between Christology and grace (at least the way Cassian articulated it), and have given that work little positive attention. It is also well known that in the sixth century, the Scythian monks saw a connection between Christology and grace and that they were able to convince both the future Emperor Justinian and Fulgentius of Ruspe of that connection.[10] But the fact that Vincent, Prosper, and Faustus all wrote against Nestorianism as well as writing on grace has received less scholarly attention. When one places the works of these three figures alongside those of Cassian, there is a small but significant body of Gallic writing from the fifth century dealing with both Christology—especially Nestorianism—and grace. Might these two themes be more closely connected than we typically admit? And if so, might the Gallic views of Christology and grace need to be placed alongside the African/Scythian views in our estimation of the controversy and its resolution at the Second Council of Orange in 529?

In this book I shall argue that these questions should be answered affirmatively. Giving attention to the anti-Nestorian Christology of these Gallic writers is valuable in two ways. First, it can provide a bit of corroborating evidence for the broader question of whether Latin Christology was Antiochene in character— that is, whether it saw Christ as a combination of two subjects, the Word and the

---

dans la querelle postpélagienne, Textes et Études du Moyen Âge 91 (Rome: Fédération Internationale des Instituts d'Études Médiévales, 2018), xxii–xxx. See also 'Prosper 1', in *PCBE* 4 (2013), 1553–6.

[10] For the correspondence between the Scythian monks and Fulgentius, see FC 126.

4 CHRISTOLOGY AND THE LOGIC OF GRACE

man, who could be considered at least quasi-separately[11]—as many scholars in the past century maintained. Second, such attention is warranted because Christology may have contributed to the way the Gallic writers construed what I shall call the 'logic of grace', by which I mean the sequence with which one reasons theologically between the concepts of hamartiology, Christology, charitology, and soteriology. This book is an exploration of fifth-century Gallic thinking about the relation between Christology and the logic of grace, with Nestorianism as a significant catalyst for that thinking.

As I introduce this book, I shall give a summary of scholarship on the grace-related controversies, beginning with those scholars who have seen the issue primarily as the amount of emphasis one gave to grace and to human action, and then turn to scholars who have identified other aspects as being important in the discussions. This summary will serve to underline the relative lack of attention to Christology in scholarly literature on the 'Semi-Pelagian Controversy'. I shall then mention the opinions of the few scholars who have brought Christology into the picture, and we shall see that the relation between Christology and grace in this controversy needs more attention. Then I shall briefly outline the connections between Christology and grace in Theodore's and Nestorius's thought that may stand behind the Gallic writers' opposition to Nestorianism. Finally, I shall briefly explain how I shall use key words and phrases that will become terms in this study: Nestorianism, Pelagianism, Semi-Pelagianism, Antiochene, Augustinian, logic of grace. By doing these things, I hope to prepare the way for my consideration of Christology and the logic of grace in the southern Gallic writings of the fifth century.

Scholarly Views Focused on Degrees of Emphasis

In the middle of the nineteenth century, Philip Schaff encapsulated the traditional scholarly interpretation of the grace-related controversy by delimiting between Augustine and Pelagius two other positions: Semi-Pelagianism and Semi-Augustinianism. Of the former he writes: 'It proceeded from the combined influence of pre-Augustinian synergism and monastic legalism. Its leading idea is, that divine grace and the human will jointly accomplish the work of conversion and sanctification, and that ordinarily man must take the first step.'[12] Schaff justifies

---

[11] McWilliam helpfully characterizes 'Antiochene' Christology as a Christology that emphasizes a moral union between the man and the Word and sees in Christ a humanity that could have existed apart from the Word, even though it never did (Joanne McWilliam Dewart, 'The Influence of Theodore of Mopsuestia on Augustine's *Letter 187*', *AugSt* 10 (1979), 113. See also Camillus Hay, 'Antiochene Exegesis and Christology', *Australian Biblical Review* 12 (1964), 21.

[12] Philip Schaff, *History of the Christian Church, Vol. 3: Nicene and Post-Nicene Christianity from Constantine to Gregory the Great, A.D. 311–590* (New York: Charles Scribner's Sons, 1867 [Reprint of 5th edition, revised, Peabody, Mass.: Hendrickson, 1996), 858.

both the idea of a spectrum of views and the placement of Semi-Pelagianism in the middle of the spectrum by arguing that it rejected the Pelagian understanding of human moral soundness and grace as a merely external aid, while also disagreeing with Augustine's teaching on the sovereignty and irresistibility of grace, and thus on predestination. He asserts: 'The union of the Pelagian and Augustinian elements thus attempted is not, however, an organic coalescence, but rather a mechanical and arbitrary combination, which really satisfies neither the one nor the other, but commonly leans to the Pelagian side.'[13]

Towards the end of the nineteenth century, Adolph von Harnack concurred in seeing Semi-Pelagianism as an amalgamation of Pelagian and Augustinian elements. Unlike Schaff, however, Harnack insists that Semi-Pelagianism was the ancient doctrine of the church and that the surprise was not that a protest arose against Augustinianism, but that the church was compelled to submit to the African bishop's teaching.[14] Harnack writes, 'It is usual to condemn "Semi-Pelagianism." But absolute condemnation is unjust. *If a universal theory is to be set up, in the form of a doctrine, of the relation of God to mankind (as object of his will to save), then it can only be stated in terms of "Semi-Pelagianism" or Cassianism.*'[15] Cassian, Harnack asserts, declined to probe the mystery of predestination, but 'demanded that so far as we affirmed anything on the subject, we should not prejudice the universality of grace and the accountability of man, *i.e.*, his free-will'.[16]

Although Harnack's portrayal largely treats grace-related discussions as independent of Christology, he does hint at a connection when he writes: 'As Pelagianism had formerly amalgamated with Nestorianism, to which it gravitated, and had thus sealed its doom, so semi-Pelagianism did not escape the fate of being assailed by the dislike which orthodoxy influenced by Monophysitism cherished against all "that was human".'[17] Here, we see that for Harnack, both in Christology and in grace-related questions, the issue is one of relative emphasis between divine and human initiative. Pelagianism 'gravitated' towards Nestorianism in that both of them profoundly emphasized human action in salvation. Likewise, both 'monophysitism' and the orthodoxy influenced by it disliked human initiative, and thus found the Semi-Pelagians suspect. For Harnack, even when there is a connection between Christology and grace, that connection should be understood in terms of the degree of emphasis given to divine and human action—both in the Incarnation and in individual Christian life.

For much of the twentieth century, scholars often adopted the same basic approach as Schaff and Harnack, dividing fifth-century writers according to where

---

[13] Ibid.

[14] Adolf von Harnack, *History of Dogma*, vol. 5, trans. from vol. 3 of the 3d German edition by J. Millar (London: Williams & Norgate, 1898. Reprint, New York: Russell & Russell, 1958) [German 1st edition, *Lehrbuch der Dogmengeschichte*, vol. 3, 1889. German 3d edition, vol. 3, 1897], 245.

[15] Ibid., 249, italics his.

[16] Ibid.

[17] Ibid., 255.

6 CHRISTOLOGY AND THE LOGIC OF GRACE

they fell on a spectrum between the extremes of Pelagianism (excessive emphasis on human action in salvation) and Augustinianism (strong—and maybe excessive—stress on divine action).[18] This interpretative trend was accompanied by a corresponding tendency to place Christology and grace in separate categories and to see the controversies about them as unrelated disputes.

Scholarly Views Elucidating Other Aspects of the Controversies

In partial contrast to the trend we have seen above, scholarship since about 1980 has focused on other factors in the grace-related discussions. A brief look at some of these factors will inform this study, even as it will also illustrate that Christology continues to receive little attention from scholars of the controversy.

Writing in 1989, Ralph Mathisen detailed the prominent role factional church politics played in fifth-century Gaul. He claims that the great fifth-century controversies occupying the attention of the imperial government were of little interest in Gaul.[19] By this he presumably means the Christological controversies, and this assertion serves to remind us that scholars do not regard Christology as being germane to the discussions over grace in Gaul. Mathisen argues further that the Gallicans were primarily concerned about rivalry and strife between their sees, and he suggests that anti-Pelagian sentiment in southern Gaul was the result of regional rivalries as much as doctrinal ones. Two Gallican bishops, Heros of Arles and Lazarus of Aix, were both deposed from their sees about the year 412 as a result of factional conflict, and they spent time in self-exile in the East. They may have arrived in Palestine at about the same time Pelagius did and could have known him personally. At any rate, in 415 they wrote a letter to the Synod of Diospolis, which exonerated Pelagius, and in 416 they wrote to the Council of Carthage, which condemned him. Pope Zosimus, who was initially favourable to Pelagius, attacked Heros and Lazarus in several letters in 417, but Augustine praised the two ex-bishops.[20] Mathisen believes that Heros and Lazarus got their anti-Pelagian sympathies from their factional affiliations back in Gaul before they arrived in Palestine, and he suggests: 'It is just possible, therefore, that Gallic anti-Pelagianism

---

[18] See, e.g., Émile Amann, 'Semi-Pélagiens', in *DTC* 14/2 (1939), 1796; Justo L. González, *A History of Christian Thought, Vol. II: From Augustine to the Eve of the Reformation* (Nashville, Abingdon Press, 1971), 55–6; Jaroslav Pelikan, *The Christian Tradition: A History of the Development of Doctrine, Vol. 1: The Emergence of the Catholic Tradition (100—600)* (Chicago: University of Chicago Press, 1971), 331.

[19] Ralph W. Mathisen, *Ecclesiastical Factionalism and Religious Controversy in Fifth-Century Gaul* (Washington, DC: The Catholic University of America Press, 1989), xi.

[20] Ibid., 37–9. See also William J. Collinge, Introduction to *Saint Augustine: Four Anti-Pelagian Writings*, trans. John A. Mourant and William J. Collinge, in FC 86.95.

was at least in part another manifestation of Gallic anti-Italian sentiment; if influential Italians were going to favor Pelagianism, all the more reason for many Gauls to oppose it.'[21]

Mathisen goes on to argue that anti-Pelagianism was a unifying sentiment among the contentious Gallic clergy: accusing outsiders of Pelagianism, usually without naming names, was a common rhetorical device. Mathisen concludes: 'Affirmations of anti-Pelagian sentiments were to become in Gaul a means of establishing consensus among the often-contentious Gallic bishops: it was one view upon which they all could agree. In this, the Gauls of the later fifth century were the spiritual heirs of the tyranophiles Heros and Lazarus.'[22] Mathisen's analysis is important for our purposes because it should lead us to be very cautious about taking at face value a charge of Pelagianism made by Gallican clergy. We shall need this caution when we consider the case of Leporius in chapter 2.[23]

Similarly, in 1990 Thomas Smith stressed the influence of the chaotic political and social situation of fifth-century Gaul on the discussions of grace. Many people attributed the disintegration of the late antique Roman social order to God's judgement on their sins and were impelled towards repentance and moral earnestness. In such a climate, a predestinarian theology was inevitably understood as undermining moral striving, and Smith concludes: 'A theology that could be perceived as enjoining passivity, even indolence, would appear to be both novel and repugnant to a theological culture whose heroes and leaders pursued virtue through ascesis and offered themselves as human barter to barbarian kings.'[24]

In an important survey published in 1996, Rebecca Harden Weaver explored three major perspectives on the grace-related controversies: first, she argues that the need to safeguard the relation between human action and divine agency determined the Semi-Pelagian position, and the need to safeguard the sovereignty of grace determined the Augustinian position. Second, different social contexts (monastic vs. congregational) affected the issues raised and the positions taken. Third, different traditions were appealed to: 'The Semi-Pelagian heritage derived from the Eastern, Origenist tradition of the desert fathers; the Augustinian tradition was new, Western, and almost entirely self-constructed.'[25] Weaver's study shows that the discussion was not so much about different positions on a spectrum of views,

---

[21] Ibid., 40. The 'influential Italians' Mathisen has in mind include Pope Zosimus.

[22] Ibid., 41.

[23] For a summary of the little that we know about Leporius's life, see 'Leporius', in *PCBE* 4 (2013), 1150–1.

[24] Thomas A. Smith, De Gratia: *Faustus of Riez's Treatise on Grace and Its Place in the History of Theology* (Notre Dame, IN.: University of Notre Dame Press, 1990), 59–60.

[25] Rebecca Harden Weaver, *Divine Grace and Human Agency: A Study of the Semi-Pelagian Controversy*, PMS 15 (Macon, GA: Mercer University Press, 1996), ix–x.

8 CHRISTOLOGY AND THE LOGIC OF GRACE

but rather a clash of competing concerns, with each side seeing the other's view as a threat to its own context and emphases.[26]

Very much in keeping with Weaver's analysis is the work of Smith and Ogliari at the beginning of the twenty-first century. Writing in 2001, Smith argues that we should look at the flare-ups of resistance to Augustine in the 430s and 470s not in terms of their theological disagreements per se, but in terms of what lay beneath them. He writes: 'These late moments of awkward discomfort over grace were not simply contests over metaphysics and theology; they were, perhaps more directly and viscerally, confusions over a controlling metaphor, confusions that persisted even despite substantial theological agreement. For Augustine's doctrine of grace bore within it an image, a metaphor, that deeply vexed its Gallic audience, however well-disposed that audience might have been toward his person and teaching.'[27] Smith perceptively recognizes that differences in Christian imagination between Gaul and Augustine's Africa could not easily be overcome, in spite of substantial doctrinal agreement. And in a 2003 work, Ogliari considerably advances the arguments proposed by Weaver and Smith. He claims: 'The ascetic/monastic perspective of the anti-Augustinian party played a major role in the so-called Semipelagian controversy. We believe that the debate between Augustine and the African and Gallic monks was not so much affected by theoretical premises or pre-suppositions about the relationship between grace and free will as by the attempt to define the potentialities and/or limits of human effort within the framework of the Christian "struggle" for perfection.'[28]

A major collaborative work on the grace-related controversies was published in 2014,[29] with chapters on the Gallicans, Cassian, Vincent, Prosper, Faustus, and Caesarius, as well as on the Africans, Augustine and Fulgentius of Ruspe. These chapters cover the thought of the Gallic writers on an impressive array of issues— original sin,[30] prevenient grace,[31] pneumatology in relation to grace,[32] God's

---

[26] See also Rikus Fick, 'Die Intensiteit van die Semi-Pelagiaanse stryd in die Galliese Kerk van die vyfde en sesde eeu', *In die Skriflig/In Luce Verbi* 41 (2007), 601–15. Fick argues that the monastic and ecclesial context of the Gallic discussion was the decisive factor in the less contentious character of the Semi-Pelagian Conroversy in comparison to the earlier Pelagian Controversy.

[27] Thomas A. Smith, 'Agonism and Antagonism: Metaphor and the Gallic Resistance to Augustine', in *StPatr* 38 (2001), 283–4.

[28] Ogliari, *Gratia et Certamen*, 15.

[29] Alexander Hwang et al., eds., *Grace for Grace: The Debates after Augustine and Pelagius* (Washington, DC: The Catholic University of America Press, 2014).

[30] Nestor Kavvadas, 'An Eastern View: Theodore of Mopsuestia's *Against the Defenders of Original Sin*', in *Grace for Grace*, 271–93.

[31] Ralph W. Mathisen, 'Caesarius of Arles, Prevenient Grace, and the Second Council of Orange', in *Grace for Grace*, 208–34.

[32] Thomas L. Humphries, Jr., 'Prosper's Pneumatology: The Development of an Augustinian', in *Grace for Grace*, 91–113.

universal salvific will,[33] and especially the degree to which one may speak of separate Gallic and African traditions.[34] For our purposes, though, it is striking that only one chapter—by Augustine Casiday—makes reference to Christology in connection with the discussions about grace.[35] I shall return to that chapter in the next section of this Introduction.

Still more recently, T. Kurt Jaros argues in 2020 that a key to the controversies was the concept of original sin and makes a compelling case that the Gallic writers affirmed an understanding of the connection between Adam's sin and ours that was much more like that of the Eastern Christian tradition than like Augustine's view. In this 'Eastern' (or one might say 'pre-Augustinian patristic') understanding, mortality and the propensity towards sin are somehow inherited from Adam, but any notion that we inherit Adam's guilt is explicitly rejected.[36]

These newer studies elucidate many previously underappreciated factors that contributed to the controversies over grace in fifth-century southern Gaul and considerably enhance our understanding of the discussions. It is significant, though, that so few of them make any particular point of examining the role of Christology in the grace-related controversies. Ogliari recognizes that the Incarnation (as the gratuitous assumption of humanity by the Word) is central to Augustine's doctrine of grace, and he laments perceptively of Augustine: 'We cannot help but be unfavourably struck by the fact that the place and role of Christ as Mediator and Saviour of mankind and, as a consequence, that of the Church (his mystical body and "sacrament" of salvation) do not appear to be decisive, as if they were "preempted" by God's eternal decrees.'[37] But Ogliari does not develop these Christological themes in the Gallic writers, and he virtually disregards Cassian's *De incar. Dom.* The connection between Christology and grace remains an understudied aspect of the grace-related controversies.

---

[33] Roland J. Teske, '1 Timothy 2:4 and the Beginnings of the Massalian Controversy', in *Grace for Grace*, 14–34.

[34] Alexander Hwang, '*Pauci Perfectae Gratiae Intrepidi Amatores*: The Augustinians in Marseilles', in *Grace for Grace*, 35–50; Boniface Ramsey, 'John Cassian and Augustine', in *Grace for Grace*, 114–30; Matthew J. Pereira, 'Augustine, Pelagius, and the Southern Gallic Tradition', in *Grace for Grace*, 180–207.

[35] Augustine Casiday, 'Vincent of Lérins's *Commonitorium, Objectiones,* and *Excerpta*: Responding to Augustine's Legacy in Fifth-Century Gaul', in *Grace for Grace*, 131–54.

[36] T. Kurt Jaros, 'The Relationship of the So-Called Semi-Pelagians and Eastern Greek Theology on the Doctrine of Original Sin: An Historical-Systematic Analysis and its Relevance for 21st Century Protestantism', Ph.D. Dissertation, University of Aberdeen, 2020.

[37] Ogliari, *Gratia et Certamen*, 357.

Scholarship that Indicates a Connection between Christology and Grace

Nevertheless, a few scholars have given significant attention to the role Christology played in the Western discussions of grace and have seen the Christological/charitological issues through a different lens than simple degrees of emphasis on divine and human action. As long ago as 1943, Agustín Trapé claimed that the metaphysical naturalism of the Antiochene School led to Arianism, Nestorianism, and Pelagianism. In an article on Leporius, he argues that while the Antiochene exegetical method had important strengths, the school's focus on historical investigation and practical morality led it to reject metaphysics. This in turn produced a naturalistic tendency inclined towards rationalism, and once this tendency was applied to humanity, it produced Pelagianism; once it was applied to Christ, it produced Nestorianism. Trapé further claims that the Antiochene School significantly influenced the Gallic monks, since Cassian brought Eastern monasticism to the region.[38] This analysis is probably too sweeping to be particularly credible, and Trapé offers no explanation for his claim that Cassian (who was opposed to Leporius's 'Nestorianism') could be a historical link between Antioch and southern Gaul. Nevertheless, other scholars would make similar pronouncements about a connection between Christology and grace.

Jean Plagnieux began a 1956 study with the fact that both Cassian and Prosper saw a complicity between Nestorianism and Pelagianism, however little those heresies seemed to have in common on the surface.[39] After a careful consideration of the connections Augustine drew between Christology and grace, Plagnieux asserts that Augustine, Cassian, and Prosper, in opposing Pelagianism, all showed a deep awareness of the specificity of Christianity, a specificity most clearly shown in the soteriological angle of its Christology. He concludes, 'Therefore, from a strictly historical point of view, such points of contact [between Nestorianism and Pelagianism] can seem to be false because they are anachronistic, as if they are abusively retroactive or simply anticipatory. But from a doctrinal point of view, this connection plunges to the heart of the Christian mystery and should be greeted as a decisive improvement.'[40] This is a tantalizing potential connection of ideas, even if it is not strictly accurate to speak of any historical dependence between Nestorian-style Christological mistakes and Pelagian-style mistakes on grace. At the same time, Plagnieux's claim, while more precise than Trapé's somewhat similar contention, is still rather vague and undeveloped.

---

[38] Agustín Trapé, 'Un caso de nestorianismo prenestoriano en Occidente resuelto por San Agustín', *CD* 155 (1943), 61–4.

[39] Jean Plagnieux, 'Le grief de complicité entre erreurs nestorienne et pélagienne: d'Augustin à Cassien par Prosper d'Aquitaine?' *REAug* 2 (1956), 392.

[40] Ibid., 402. My translation.

Some three decades later, in 1984, Michael Azkoul expressed yet another similar opinion, claiming that Pelagius was a secularist who thought all we needed was re-education, not resurrection, and he found sympathy among the Nestorians. Azkoul claims, 'Indeed, their congeniality was the issue of a, perhaps unconscious, yet common christology.'[41] Azkoul elaborates on this point using the language of Chalcedon and later Christology when he argues that salvation depends on the synergy between divine and human wills, both in the person of Christ and in the sanctification/deification of a Christian. Nestorian Christology, he insists, breaks down the synergy of the two wills of Christ by refusing to allow that the divine assumed humanity, so there can be no deification, no participation in divinity. Pelagius's soteriology is also based on the determination of one will, the human, and this also negates the Incarnation by denying the need for it. At the same time, Azkoul claims, Augustine's monergism is the implicit affirmation of a monophysite Christology: it denies the human cooperation with the divine in salvation. Azkoul concludes: 'Speaking plainly, both the Pelagian-Nestorian and Augustinian-Monophysite heresies, monergistic heresies, oppose the synergistic orthodoxy of Chalcedon. . . . Put another way, Pelagius argued against the "assumption" of the human by the Divine and the doctrine of Augustine implies not "assumption" but absorption. In either case, the divine Economy is scuttled.'[42] In contrast to all these mistakes, Azkoul declares that God in Christ accomplished what humankind could not and divine fiat would not accomplish. The human being is not a passive creature who is declared innocent by the selective will of God.[43]

Azkoul's article, like those of Trapé and Plagnieux, includes little specific evidence and should be regarded as a bird's-eye view. Nevertheless, taken together these three scholars point to connections between Christology and grace and imply that speaking accurately of salvation, Christology, and grace is not just a matter of achieving the right balance between divine and human aspects in the life of the Savior and of the believer. Instead, all three scholars see absolute mistakes—not just mistakes of emphasis—in the Pelagian assertion that human beings need simply to learn what is required for us to rise up to God, and Azkoul sees absolute mistakes in the Augustinian implication that divine fiat (predestination) is the decisive factor in salvation. Likewise, all three see absolute mistakes—again, not just mistakes of emphasis—in Nestorian Christology that denies the assumption of humanity by the Logos, and Azkoul sees absolute mistakes in so-called monophysite Christology that refuses to see two wills and operations in the incarnate Lord. According to all three scholars, there is a crucial conceptual link between a Pelagian 'soteriology' (actually anthropology) and a Nestorian Christology, and

[41] Michael Azkoul, 'Peccatum originale: The Pelagian Controversy', *The Patristic and Byzantine Review* 3 (1984), 45–6.
[42] Ibid., 46.
[43] Ibid., 50.

12 CHRISTOLOGY AND THE LOGIC OF GRACE

according to Azkoul there is likewise a connection between an Augustinian so-teriology/anthropology and a 'monophysite' Christology. In spite of the fact that Trapé and Plagnieux do not share Azkoul's assessment of Augustine, all three believe that Christology and grace are related, and that in particular, Nestorianism and Pelagianism share logical connections.

In contrast, in the late twentieth century Joanne McWilliam drew parallels between Christology and grace in a quite different way. She regards Augustine's Christology as one in which the man Christ is a unique recipient of the grace of the Word, and it is precisely his receiving grace that makes him the source of grace for us. In this way, Augustine's Christology and charitology are not only similar to that of Nestorius, but are actually dependent on Nestorius's teacher, Theodore of Mopsuestia.[44] Writing in 1982, McWilliam summarizes: 'His [Augustine's] Christology proceeded in step with his theology of grace. For Christ, as for all human persons, it is grace which strengthens and confirms the will in virtue. And in *On Predestination* and *On the Gift of Perseverance* it is the man, Jesus Christ, who affords the paradigm of predestination.'[45] The force of this claim emerges very clearly as McWilliam asks poignantly whether Augustine's Christology could have survived the Council of Ephesus. She continues: 'Could he, at that bitterly divided meeting, have remained faithful to his conviction that Christ the man was mediator and saviour, the paradigm of grace received? Such a christological stance would not have been well received by Cyril and his followers.'[46] This last assertion is certainly correct, but is McWilliam right about Augustine's Christology and charitology? She effectively places him as far removed from Azkoul's assessment as possible, and she clearly sees a Theodorean/Nestorian understanding of both Christ and grace as attractive, in contrast to all three of the scholars I have considered just above. I shall return in chapter 1 to the question of how to interpret Augustine's Christology, and the remainder of this book will address how his thought relates to the Christology of the southern Gallic writers.

Writing in 2003, I sought to probe the connections between grace and Christology in a way different from McWilliam and similar to the vaguer claims of Plagnieux (although somewhat less similar to Trapé's and Azkoul's views). In a study of Cassian's monastic writings and especially *De incar. Dom.*, I argue that the latter work is worth more attention than it normally receives and that its critique of Nestorianism is not as theologically maladroit as many scholars think. Cassian's Christological terminology is indeed sloppy, and his claim that Nestorius sees Christ as *solitarius homo* is surely false on the surface. But if one digs deeper, one can see that Cassian's critique of both Nestorius and Pelagius grows out of

---

[44] See Joanne McWilliam Dewart, 'The Influence of Theodore of Mopsuestia', 113–32; Joanne McWilliam Dewart, 'The Christology of the Pelagian Controversy', in *StPatr* 17 (1982), 1221–44.
[45] Ibid., 1239.
[46] Ibid., 1241.

a fundamental difference between himself and the two of them. I argue that for Nestorius, like Theodore before him, salvation is primarily the human task of rising from the first age to the second, and Christ is a man who is uniquely indwelt by the Son, uniquely graced by God, so that he can be our leader in the march to the second age.[47] In stark contrast, Cassian sees salvation as the gift of divine fellowship to mankind, a gift that requires the personal descent of the Word through the assumption of human nature into his own person. Beneath Cassian's muddy terminology lie clear connections between grace and Christology, connections that are very different from those drawn by Theodore, Nestorius, and Pelagius.[48]

My work in 2003 was developed further by Augustine Casiday, who writes in 2007 that Cassian's critique of Nestorianism is based on a rejection of the Pelagian idea that Christ is merely a role model for Christians. Cassian holds a dim view of the capacity of the human will and argues that the Word's assumption of humanity is crucial in the healing of the will.[49] Casiday writes, 'Because Cassian taught these things about the will, there was no common ground for him and the Pelagians. Even if both parties were keen to promote moral reform (as they indubitably were), their respective messages were fundamentally unlike.'[50] Discussing Cassian's Christology itself, Casiday asserts: 'Cassian teaches that the Logos took on human nature and so lived a human life.... He did so without loss to the Glory that is appropriate to the divine Nature. The affirmation that the Logos is the Person of Christ ... is the cornerstone of his Christology.'[51]

Casiday also extends the ideas he and I have discerned in Cassian to another Gallican, Vincent of Lérins. Writing in 2014, he criticizes the common view that places the southern Gallic writers on a spectrum between Augustine and Pelagius and argues that this approach cannot do justice to Vincent's respect for Augustine's Christology and clear dislike of his teaching on predestination. Casiday concludes: 'Not only does Christology open up a fresh vantage on grace and predestination, but the fact that a monk wrote a distinctly theological work enables us to compare like with like rather than fretting over how to extract content from a treatise and from an exhortation for purposes of comparison.'[52]

In 2020, Jaros examined Vincent's use of Augustine's connection between Christology and grace but saw more difference between Vincent and Augustine

---

[47] Donald Fairbairn, *Grace and Christology in the Early Church*, OECS (Oxford: Oxford University Press, 2003), chap. 2. I shall return to these ideas later in this Introduction.
[48] Ibid., chaps. 5–6.
[49] Casiday, *Tradition and Theology*, 111–12.
[50] Ibid., 112.
[51] Ibid., 235. See also the brief but similar treatment in Jaros, 'The Relationship of the So-Called Semi-Pelagians', 202–3.
[52] Augustine Casiday, 'Vincent of Lérins's *Commonitorium, Objectiones,* and *Excerpta*: Responding to Augustine's Legacy in Fifth-Century Gaul', in *Grace for Grace: The Debates after Augustine and Pelagius,* ed. Alexander Hwang et al. (Washington, DC: The Catholic University of America Press, 2014), 141–2.

14 CHRISTOLOGY AND THE LOGIC OF GRACE

than Casiday alleged. Specifically, Jaros distinguishes between what he calls *historia salutis* (the events in time, culminating in the life, death, and resurrection of Christ, through which God works to effect the salvation of people) and *ordo salutis* (the steps of God's work in the salvation of a particular human being). He argues that for Augustine, the predestination of the assumed humanity of Christ is strictly paralleled by the predestination of each Christian. For Vincent, in contrast, the distinction between *historia salutis* and *ordo salutis* means that the predestination of the assumed humanity does not imply the predestination of the Christian in an Augustinian way.[53] Jaros also points out that Faustus affirms Augustine to be orthodox on Christology but not on other points, which suggests that Faustus as well as Vincent connects Christology and grace differently from Augustine.[54]

Thus, in these works from the last two decades, Casiday, Jaros, and I have enumerated some potential connections between Christology and grace that others had previously noted more generally, and we have explored them in the writings of Cassian, Vincent, and to a much more limited degree, Faustus. But many aspects of the connections remain understudied. We have not explicitly spelled out the differences between the way Cassian draws the connections and the way Augustine does. Casiday and I have not dealt specifically with Cassian's *Conlat.* 13, and Jaros has addressed that Conference from the vantage point of grace, not Christology.[55] Casiday has explored Vincent only briefly, and even Jaros's treatment is relatively short. Finally, we have barely touched on these questions in the writings of Prosper and Faustus. There is room for a more substantial study of Christology and grace among the southern Gallic writers in the light of connections suggested in this section, and this work attempts such a study.

Connections between Nestorian Christology and Charitology

It is well known that Nestorius's Christology involved a concept called 'prosopic union', according to which the Logos and the man Jesus are two πρόσωπα or persons in their own right, but each one makes use of the πρόσωπον of the other, so there is a conjunction between the two πρόσωπα such that they can count as a single 'πρόσωπον of union'.[56] Given this level of technicality, one may well ask what such a Christology could possibly have to do with charitology. Answering that question involves recognizing that the idea of prosopic union is not so much the heart of Nestorius's Christology as it is an attempt to solve a problem created by his

---

[53] Jaros, 'The Relationship of the So-Called Semi-Pelagians', 240–9.
[54] Ibid., 265.
[55] Ibid., 169–88.
[56] See the extensive discussions of prosopic union in Nestorius, *Lib. Her.* 1.3 (Nau, 127, 137, 147) [Driver/Hodgson, 143, 154, 165–6], 2.1 (Nau, 195, 233) [Driver/Hodgson, 220, 262], etc.

INTRODUCTION   15

Christology—the problem that the Logos and the man Jesus seem to be separate persons. Nestorius's Christology is actually based on and supports a particular understanding of soteriology and grace inherited from his teacher Theodore. These soteriological and charitological bases of Nestorius's Christology are the points of contact that will concern us in this study, and they require some general explanation here.

The foundation of Theodore's thought is his concept of the two ages, the first of which is an age of mortality, imperfection, and sin, and the second of which is characterized by immortality and perfection.[57] Human beings are called to rise from the first age to the second with the help of divine grace, with Christ as our leader or trailblazer. Thus, salvation is largely a human task, one for which human beings need a leader on an upward march of progress, and in which grace is primarily divine aid or cooperation in that task. Such a view also depends on a robust understanding of human capacity. In a lost work whose contents can be pieced together from later sources, called *Contra defensores peccati originalis*, Theodore seems to take his understanding of the issues in the Pelagian Controversy from Julian of Eclanum's depiction of Jerome's and Augustine's thought as Manichaean. In fact, the fifth-century Latin anti-Pelagian Marius Mercator (one of our main sources for the lost work of Theodore) actually claims that Theodore's ideas found their way to Rome through a Syrian theologian named Rufinus, that Pelagius directly borrowed from them, and thus that Theodore was the father of Pelagianism. Mercator argues further that Julian spent some time in Mopsuestia and that Theodore harboured him there for a time before having him condemned at a synod in Cilicia.

Whatever truth there may be in these historical claims, it does appear that in the lost work, Theodore criticizes the Augustinian idea of original sin and instead argues that human beings were created mortal (although called to overcome that mortality as they advanced to the second age), and he rejects the idea that God might punish the whole human race for the sin of a single representative. A particular issue in the understanding of the lost work is how, for Theodore, mortality can be both a created condition and the result of each person's sin. There is no easy answer to that question, precisely because Theodore looks at the world not from the vantage point of humanity's first sin and its effects, but from the perspective of the second age. From

---

[57] See Theodore, *Hom. cat.* 1.3 (Tonneau/Devreese, 5) [*WS*, 5.19], 10.17 (Tonneau/Devreese, 271) [*WS* 5.113]; 14.28 (Tonneau/Devreese, 459–61) [*WS*, 6.69]. For scholarly judgements on the centrality of the two ages in Theodore's thought, see Robert Devreese, *Essai sur Théodore de Mopsueste* (Vatican City: Biblioteca Apostolica Vaticana, 1948), 21; Richard A. Norris, Jr., *Manhood and Christ: A Study in the Christology of Theodore of Mopsuestia* (Oxford: Clarendon Press, 1963), 160. See also Rowan A. Greer, *Theodore of Mopsuestia: Exegete and Theologian* (Leighton Buzzard: Faith Press, 1961); Rowan A. Greer, 'The Analogy of Grace in Theodore of Mopsuestia's Christology', *JTS*, n.s., 34 (1983), 82–98.

16   CHRISTOLOGY AND THE LOGIC OF GRACE

that perspective, it is clear that his overall view of the drama of redemption focuses on human advance in moral virtue under the tutelage of God's grace.[58]

As a result, Theodore sees Christ as a man who receives grace from the indwelling Logos, and with the help of this grace the man advances to the second age and provides the paradigm for us to do so as well (with the help of the Holy Spirit indwelling us).[59] Thus, Theodore distinguishes sharply between the indwelling Logos and the indwelt man (whom he calls the λημφθείς ἄνθρωπος, a phrase that comes into Latin as *homo assumptus*), and he ascribes the human actions of Christ—including most notably the crucifixion—to the man, not to the Logos.[60] Indeed, protecting the Logos from involvement in the human experiences of Christ is a central concern for Theodore, a concern that goes hand-in-glove with his understanding of salvation as an upward march of humanity rather than a divine descent. Therefore, Theodore interprets the Creed's second paragraph to refer to two distinct persons. It is the Logos who is true God from true God, ὁμοούσιος with the Father, and it is the man who was incarnated, suffered, died, and rose for our salvation.[61] Theodore also feels keenly the accusation that such a Christology amounts to a denial of Christ's unity (before him, Diodore had been directly criticized on that point by Athanasius and Gregory of Nazianzus), and he develops the idea of prosopic union as a way of addressing this problem; he emphasizes that there is a single Christ because the word 'Christ' refers to both the Logos and the man.[62] Again, prosopic union is the solution to a problem, not the actual heart of this Christology.

Nestorius follows his teacher Theodore in virtually all aspects of his thought. He distinguishes sharply between the Logos and the *homo assumptus*,[63] he adopts the same interpretation of the Creed,[64] and he uses the word 'Christ' to refer to the Logos and the man considered collectively.[65] In the extant writings of Nestorius, however,

---

[58] For excellent discussions of the complexities involved in reconstructing and interpreting this lost work, see Norris, *Manhood and Christ*, 157–86; Kavvadas, 'An Eastern View: Theodore of Mopsuestia's *Against the Defenders of Original Sin*', in *Grace for Grace*, 271–93; Giulio Malavasi, 'The Involvement of Theodore of Mopsuestia in the Pelagian Controversy: A Study of Theodore's Treatise *Against Those who Say that Men Sin by Nature and not by Will*', *Augustiniana* 64 (2014), 227–60.

[59] See, e.g., Theodore, *Hom. cat.* 5.18 (Tonneau/Devreese, 125) [*WS* 5.44], 6.2 (Tonneau/Devreese, 133) [*WS* 5.63], 7.9 (Tonneau/Devreese, 175) [*WS* 5.78]; Theodore, *De incar.* 12.2 (Swete 2.304).

[60] See, e.g., Theodore, *De incar.* 5 (Swete 2.292–3); Theodore, *Hom. cat.* 6.5–6 (Tonneau/Devreese, 139–41) [*WS* 5.65–6].

[61] See, e.g., Theodore, *Hom. cat.* 3.6 (Tonneau/Devreese, 61) [*WS* 5.37]. See also Joanne McWilliam Dewart, 'The Notion of "Person" Underlying the Christology of Theodore of Mopsuestia', in *StPatr* 12 (1975), 199–207.

[62] See, e.g., Theodore, *De incar.* 5 (Swete 2.292–3).

[63] See, e.g., Nestorius, *Ser.* 5 (Loofs, 234–5), *Ser.* 9 (Loofs, 252), *Ser.* 14 (Loofs, 287).

[64] See especially Nestorius, *Ep. II ad Cyr.* 2–6 (*ACO* 1.1.1.29–30) [*TTH* 72.123–4]. This is part of Cyril's and Nestorius's famous correspondence about the right way to understand the Creed. For an extended explanation of the differences between the way Theodore and Nestorius on one hand interpret the Creed and the way Cyril (along with Cassian) does so, see Mark S. Smith, *The Idea of Nicaea in the Early Church Councils, AD 431–451*, OECS (Oxford: Oxford University Press, 2018), 28–34.

[65] See, e.g., Nestorius, *Ser.* 10 (Loofs, 275).

INTRODUCTION   17

we find less on the two ages[66] and a lot more on the more technical idea of prosopic union.[67] Thus, the charitological and soteriological aspects of Nestorius's thought are more assumed than stated, but there is agreement among scholars that he sees salvation in the same way Theodore does: as a human task accomplished with the help of grace, in which Christ is our leader.[68] In modern times, these Theodorean/ Nestorian emphases regarding grace and salvation, and especially this way of understanding the person of Christ as a conjunction of the Logos and the assumed man, are often regarded as 'Antiochene', and it is sometimes argued that these emphases were common to many in Syria—thus that there was a widespread and fairly uniform 'Antiochene School'. Hence arises the modern question of whether Western patristic Christology was Antiochene—a question that will recur throughout this book.

Where Nestorius differed from Theodore, however, had to do with the title *Theotokos* ('bearer of God') for Mary. Theodore agreed to use this title, although he interpreted it to mean not that the Son Mary bore was genuinely God, but that Mary bore God in the sense that God indwelt the man whom she bore.[69] After Nestorius became bishop of Constantinople in 428, he publicly preached against the title *Theotokos* and argued instead for the title *Christotokos*, since in his thought the word 'Christ' could refer to both the Logos and the man Jesus conjoined to him.[70] This public opposition to a widespread and revered title for the Virgin was the initial spark for the Nestorian Controversy.[71] Nestorius was understood both in the capital and elsewhere as denying the divinity of Christ, an understanding that was not technically accurate because for him, the word 'Christ' referred to both the Logos and the man, so his affirmation of the full divinity of the Logos meant, in his mind, that he affirmed the divinity of Christ. Arguably, though, Nestorius's thought amounted to a denial of Christ's divinity, since the man Jesus Christ who lived among us on earth was someone else than the Logos and thus not truly God in and of himself.

From 428 to 430, information about Nestorius's teaching made its way to the West through two means.[72] Most importantly, Nestorius himself wrote several letters to Pope Celestine, in which he made the severe tactical mistake of

---

[66] We do, however, see the idea of the two ages without the nomenclature in Nestorius, *Ser.* 9 (Loofs, 257–9).

[67] See the passages cited above: Nestorius, *Lib. Her.* 1.3 (Nau, 127, 137, 147) [Driver/Hodgson, 143, 154, 165–6], 2.1 (Nau, 195, 233) [Driver/Hodgson, 220, 262].

[68] See, e.g., Turner's confident conclusion in Henry E.W. Turner, *Jesus the Christ* (London: A.W. Mowbray & Co., 1976), 39: 'If Christ was to be our "athlete" and the redemption which he brought was to speak to our condition, his victory must be his own with the assistance of the grace of God which is also available to us, and not an act of God the Logos.'

[69] See Theodore, *De incar.* 15 (Swete 2.310).

[70] See Nestorius, *Ser.* 9 (Loofs, 252).

[71] For the course of the Nestorian Controversy leading to the Council of Ephesus, see TTH 72, which includes outstanding introductions by Thomas Graumann, translations of the most relevant documents before and during the council by Richard Price, and references to the locations of the Greek and Latin texts of those documents in *ACO* 1.

[72] See Émile Amann, 'L'affaire Nestorius vue de Rome', *RevSR* 23 (1949), 5–37, 207–44; 24 (1950), 28–52, 235–65.

18   CHRISTOLOGY AND THE LOGIC OF GRACE

voicing concerns about some followers of Pelagius who had sought refuge in Constantinople. Nestorius implied to Celestine that he thought the West had condemned them unjustly and that the case should be re-opened.[73] This effectively turned the West against Nestorius and led Western writers such as Cassian to assume Nestorius agreed with the Pelagians and thus to posit a connection—genuine or not—between Nestorianism and Pelagianism. A second vehicle for conveying Nestorius's ideas to the West was a dossier that Cyril of Alexandria compiled and sent to Rome with the deacon Posidonius.[74] This dossier supplemented the information available to Cassian as he finalized *De incar. Dom.* in the spring and summer of 430, and that work in turn likely became the basis for the way other Gallic and Western writers understood Nestorius. On the basis of the information provided by Cyril and Cassian's report, Nestorius came to be understood in the West as affirming that Jesus Christ was a man united to God the Word by virtue of his merits, a Christology that seemed to fit with the belief that Pelagianism affirmed all human beings can be united to God by virtue of our merits. On the basis of such an understanding of Nestorius's Christology, he was condemned at a Roman synod led by Celestine in August of 430, and he was given ten days to recant and affirm the faith of Rome and Alexandria.

Back in the East, however, the case of Nestorius was not so easily resolved. Cyril of Alexandria muddied the waters considerably by writing twelve anathemas to which Nestorius had to subscribe in order for the Roman condemnation to be reversed. These anathemas were strongly worded and easy to misinterpret, and they led many in Syria to stop worrying about Nestorius and to start being suspicious of Cyril. When the Council of Ephesus finally met in the summer of 431, it devolved into two competing councils—a larger one led by Cyril that condemned Nestorius's thought, and a smaller one headed by John of Antioch that included Nestorius and deposed Cyril. Cyril's council was eventually deemed to be the legitimate ecumenical council,[75] and it is worth noting that the papal representatives who joined Cyril's council ensured that that council would condemn Pelagius and his follower Caelestius, as well as Nestorius.[76] It is likely that no discussion went into this condemnation of the Pelagians, but it is significant that an ecumenical council implied a connection between Christology and grace by rejecting both Nestorianism and Pelagianism. On the other hand, the very fact that competing councils were held has led many modern interpreters to label Cyril's council 'Alexandrian' and John's 'Antiochene'—thus adding to the modern perception that there were competing schools with competing Christologies, and again bringing

[73] See Nestorius, *Ep. I ad Cael.* 1 (*ACO* 1.2.12) [TTH 72.98].

[74] The dossier included Latin translations of Cyril's correspondence with Nestorius, some of Nestorius's sermons, and other writings. See *ACO* 1.5.55–60.

[75] The technical name for John's council is the *Conciliabulum* or 'place of assembly'.

[76] See the acts of the session of Cyril's council that met on 10–11 July 431 (*ACO* 1.1.3.53–9) [TTH 72.368–75].

to prominence the question of which Eastern Christology the thought of the West resembled.

If one steps back from modern questions about technical Christology and looks at Nestorius and Theodore through a broader lens, the impression one gains is that their soteriology was one of human ascent with the help of divine grace. Thus, the foundations of Nestorius's thought—although not the presentation issues such as prosopic union and the denial of the title *Theotokos*—bore significant similarities to the thought of Pelagius and his followers, who also saw salvation in terms of human ascent, following the example of Christ, with the help of grace. (These similarities may explain Theodore's and later Nestorius's favourable attitudes toward Pelagians who found their way to Syria and Constantinople.) Many in the fifth-century church, both in the East and West, regarded this soteriology of human ascent as fundamentally unacceptable and insisted on a soteriology of divine descent: the Logos had to come down personally to earth to accomplish human redemption. Along with this insistence was a corresponding stress on maintaining the absolute priority of divine grace and divine action in salvation. Thus, in Gaul the Nestorian Controversy provided one of the key catalysts for fifth-century Western reflection on Christology and grace. The other key catalyst, of course, was the aftermath of the Pelagian Controversy itself, and especially the teaching of the later Augustine on grace and Christology in response to Pelagianism. The way or ways that Gallic writers interacted both with Augustine's thought and that of Nestorius will be our concern in this book.

Terminological Conventions to be Used in This Book

As we consider how southern Gallic writers understood the relation between Christology and grace, we need to recognize that both catalysts mentioned just above lay far outside Gaul—in Constantinople and in Latin North Africa. The Gallic monks' understanding of both disputes was necessarily somewhat limited and perhaps inaccurate. As a result, it will be important for us to keep in mind the differences between what the people in question actually wrote or meant and the way they were perceived in fifth-century southern Gaul. I shall attempt to maintain the reader's awareness of these differences through particular terminological conventions:

- I shall normally place 'Nestorius' and 'Nestorianism' in inverted commas when discussing the Gallic writers' perception of Nestorianism. Part of the purpose of this book will be to build a picture of 'Nestorianism' as the monks of southern Gaul understood and responded to it. I shall argue that 'Nestorianism' was not as far removed from the actual teaching of Nestorius as one might think, but our main focus will be the Gallic writers' responses to 'Nestorianism'.

20 CHRISTOLOGY AND THE LOGIC OF GRACE

- Likewise, I shall normally enclose 'Pelagianism' in inverted commas when discussing the Gallic writers' understanding of Pelagianism. We shall have little occasion to deal with what Pelagius himself actually believed. Instead, 'Pelagianism' as the Gallic writers perceived it and responded to it will be our concern.
- The Gallic monks' attitudes towards Augustine and his followers will be a key part of this book. As a result, we shall need to distinguish being *anti-Augustine* (that is, directly and explicitly opposed to the teaching of the bishop of Hippo himself) from being *anti-Augustinian* (that is, opposed to what the Augustinians in Gaul were saying). We shall also need to distinguish being *anti-Augustinian* from being merely *non-Augustinian* (that is, differing with Augustine and/or his followers on particular points, especially predestination, without actually considering Augustine's teaching or that of his followers to be heretical).

In addition to these conventions that highlight the ways the fifth-century Gallic writers perceived and understood others in their time, it will also be important for us to recognize the potential differences between the ways we today tend to understand the writers of the fifth century and what they may have actually meant, in two ways:

First, there is no doubt that Theodorean/Nestorian Christology is vastly different from that of Cyril of Alexandria and others. But as we have already seen, when modern scholars call Theodorean/Nestorian Christology 'Antiochene', they are in effect assuming that such Christology was common in the fifth century and perhaps even that it was legitimate and non-heretical. To remind readers that such word usage reflects a value judgement different from that of the historic church (which regarded Theodorean/Nestorian Christology as both rare and heretical), I shall place 'Antiochene' in inverted commas. When I discuss so-called Antiochene Christology without assuming it was widespread, I shall generally call it Theodorean/Nestorian Christology. Likewise, when modern scholars call Cyrillian Christology 'Alexandrian', they may be assuming that this Christology was merely that of one school, rather than that of the church as a whole. I shall generally refer to this Christology as 'Cyrillian/Chalcedonian' in order to reflect the historic church's belief that Chalcedonian Christology was largely consistent with that of Cyril of Alexandria,[77] and I shall argue that the Christology of all writers in this study was broadly Cyrillian/Chalcedonian, not Theodorean/Nestorian.

---

[77] On the fact that the church, and especially the delegates at Chalcedon, understood the Chalcedonian Definition as substantially Cyrillian, see, e.g., Lionel Wickham, Introduction to *Cyril of Alexandria: Select Letters*, OECT (Oxford: Oxford University Press, 1983), xi–xliii; Richard Price, 'General Introduction, Part V: The Theology of Chalcedon', in *The Acts of the Council of Chalcedon*, TTH 45 (Liverpool: Liverpool University Press, 2005), 1.56–75. See also Donald Fairbairn, 'Interpreting Conciliar Christology: A Survey in the Service of Analytic Theology', *Journal of Analytic Theology* 10 (2022), 363–81.

Second, we have already seen that when modern scholars call the southern Gallic writers 'Semi-Pelagians', this nomenclature derives from the assumption that the proper way to view the discussions about grace is to place writers on a spectrum between Pelagius and Augustine, in terms of their relative emphasis on divine and human action. The terminology also tends to reflect the assumption that Augustine's thought is the norm and that of others is an aberration from that norm, or to say it differently, that the 'Semi-Pelagians' did not sufficiently emphasize the priority of divine action and divine grace in salvation. In order to remind the reader of the value judgement associated with this terminology, I shall normally place 'Semi-Pelagian' in inverted commas when I use the phrase at all. My non-pejorative phrases for those writers will be 'Gallic writers', 'Gallic monks', or 'southern Gallic writers'.

One final term that will loom large in this study is 'logic of grace'. I shall argue that the Gallic writers were united by a common logic: beginning with the inability of fallen humanity to accomplish salvation, they reasoned from the Fall to the Incarnation. On the basis of this reasoning they used the Incarnation itself as the means to establish the priority of divine grace in salvation, and they emphasized the universal effects of the Incarnation on all, as well as the particular effects on individual Christians. This logic (from the Fall, to the Incarnation, to the general and particular aspects of grace) stands in partial contrast to a more Augustinian logic that proceeds from the Fall to predestination, and uses predestination as the means to establish the utter gratuity of grace. This Augustinian logic then turns to the particular aspects of grace in the lives of the elect, with little attention to more general aspects of grace. I shall argue further that the difference between these two kinds of logic derives not from different Christologies, but from when (in a logical sequence) and how different writers bring the Incarnation into their logical reflections on grace. In a sense, Augustine and the Gallic writers shared the same anti-'Pelagian' and anti-'Nestorian' focus on the priority of divine grace and action in salvation, and they shared the same Cyrillian/Chalcedonian Christology of divine descent. But their common Christology functioned differently because of Augustine's upholding predestination as the proof of divine priority, in contrast to the Gallic monks' upholding the Incarnation itself as the demonstration of divine priority.

It is now time to turn to the fifth century. In the body of this book, I shall set the stage for the Gallic discussions of grace by looking at connections between Christology and the logic of grace prior to the rise of Nestorianism—in the later writings of Augustine (chapter 1) and in the case of the Gallic monk Leporius (chapter 2). Then I shall devote chapters 3–6 to Cassian, Vincent, Prosper, and Faustus, and shall examine what each writer considers the error of 'Nestorianism' to be, whether he also takes note of Eutychianism if he wrote after the late 440s, and whether and how that understanding of Christological error affects his positive Christology and his articulation of charitology.

1

Setting the Stage

Christology and Grace in Augustine's Later Writings

The beginning of the Gallic discussions of grace, the so-called 'Semi-Pelagian Controversy', slightly predated Nestorius's arrival in Constantinople (428), so obviously the Gallic discussions did not initially involve Nestorius or his Christology. Instead, it was the arrival in Gaul in 427 of Augustine's *De corrept. grat.* (originally written to a group of monks at Hadrumetum in North Africa) that either prompted or at least fanned the flames of the local discussion.[1] Nevertheless, Christology was significant at the very beginning of the conflict, because in that work, Augustine famously writes of Christ the man as the supreme example of grace, and he repeats and elaborates on that claim in the treatise he subsequently addresses directly to the Gallic monks, *De praed. sanct.*[2] (as well as in the unfinished work *Con. Iulian. opus imperf.*[3]). In a sense, Augustine's thought set the stage for the Gallic discussions by providing a clear articulation of one way of connecting Christology and grace, a way of reasoning that I shall explore in this chapter.

These writings at the very end of Augustine's life are not the only places where he connects Christology and grace. There are a few passages in his earlier anti-Pelagian writings in which he turns his attention from grace as it operates in individual people to grace in connection with the Incarnation and person of Christ,[4] and he makes a similar connection in *Enchir.* as well. The way Augustine writes of Christ in his letters and treatises from the time of the grace-related controversies has been variously interpreted. He uses the word *homo* to describe Christ the man in a way that some have regarded as 'Antiochene', as if one could conceive of the man separately from the Word who assumed him. Other scholars have insisted that Augustine intends the word *homo* in the sense of *humana natura* and that his point is that the Word assumed a human nature, not a quasi-independent man.

---

[1] We should remember the possibility, mentioned in the Introduction, that the Gallicans were reacting to a local predestinarianism, not just to Augustine himself.

[2] For most of Christian history, book two of *De praed. sanct.* has circulated as a separate work, *De don. pers.* It is likely, though, that Augustine intended the two books as a single work. Prosper indicates as much in *Resp. excerp. Gen.* praef. (PL 51.187) [ACW 32.49], and it is presented as a single work in CSEL 105 and in this book.

[3] See Augustine, *Con. Iulian. opus imperf.* 1.138–40 (PL 45.1138--9) [WSA I/25.145–7], 4.84 (PL 45.1386) [WSA I/25.450–1].

[4] Jean Plagnieux, 'Le grief de complicité entre erreurs nestorienne et pélagienne: d'Augustin à Cassien par Prosper d'Aquitaine?' *REAug* 2 (1956), 397, points out that as early as 412, Augustine was already connecting Christology and grace in the same way he would do at the end of his life.

Christology and the Logic of Grace in Fifth-Century Gaul. Donald Fairbairn, Oxford University Press.
© Donald Fairbairn 2025. DOI: 10.1093/9780198936220.003.0002

These questions about Augustine's Christology play a major role in broader scholarly discussions about whether Latin Christology as a whole should be regarded as 'Antiochene'.

Accordingly, in this chapter I shall first address general questions about Augustine's Christology in relation to the issues of the Nestorian Controversy that would soon arise to the East. Then I shall examine representative Christological assertions from the time of the Pelagian Controversy (412–418) and from *Enchir.* (*c.*420), paying careful attention to the relatively few places where Augustine draws connections between Christology and grace. Finally, I shall turn to the writings that came directly to the attention of the Gallic monks and shall examine the three places in those writings in which Augustine describes the man Christ as an example of grace (and predestination). As we shall see, Augustine's Christology would meet the approval of the Gallic monks, but his understanding of grace (and especially predestination) would not.

Questions about Augustine's Christology

In an important article published in 2020, Alexander Pierce summarizes more than a century of scholarship on Augustine's Christology by outlining two broad categories of scholars, those who see Augustine as basically 'Antiochene' (I should prefer to call this 'Theodorean/Nestorian') and those who see him as 'Chalcedonian' (I should prefer to add 'Cyrillian'). The first group of scholars has seen 'the uniqueness of Jesus to be based upon his unique receptivity to God's presence, not on any concrete union of distinct realities.'[5] Pierce points out that Dorner and Harnack were earlier representatives of this Antiochene/Theodorean group[6] and that Joanne McWilliam has been a noteworthy later proponent: in a 1979 article she actually claims that Augustine's mature Christology is directly dependent on Theodore.[7] The second group, Pierce asserts, 'associates the increasing

---

[5] Alexander H. Pierce, 'At the Crossroads of Christology and Grace: Augustine on the Union of *Homo* and *Verbum* in Christ (*c.*411–430),' *Augustinianum* 60 (2020), 455. Pierce builds on an earlier summary: Joanne McWilliam, 'The Study of Augustine's Christology in the Twentieth Century', in *Augustine: from Rhetor to Theologian*, ed. Joanne McWilliam (Waterloo, ON: Wilfrid Laurier University Press, 1992), 183–205. McWilliam's terms 'revisionists' and 'defenders/traditionalists' correspond approximately to Pierce's categories of those who see Augustine as 'Antiochene' and those who see him as 'Chalcedonian'.

[6] See August Dorner, *Augustinus, Sein theologisches System und seine religionsphilosophische Anschauung* (Berlin: Verlag von Wilhelm Hertz, 1873), 87–107, who argues that while Augustine affirms unity in Christ, the thrust of his Christology points towards distinction between the Word and the man, not identity. See also Adolf Harnack, *History of Dogma*, vol. 5, trans. from the 3d German edition by J. Millar (London: Williams & Norgate, 1898, reprint, New York: Russell & Russell, 1958),125–38.

[7] McWilliam Dewart, 'The Influence of Theodore of Mopsuestia on Augustine's *Letter 187*', 113–32. One could also place Studer in this group. See Basil Studer, '*Una Persona in Christo*: Ein augustinisches Thema bei Leo dem Grossen', *Augustinianum* 25 (1985): 487, who believes that for Augustine, the one person of Christ is the result of the union of Word and man, not the person of the Word himself.

24   CHRISTOLOGY AND THE LOGIC OF GRACE

technicality of Augustine's description of Christ's ontological union both with the later definitions of Chalcedon and with the Neoplatonic background of his notion of union,[8] and Pierce includes Scheel and Portalié as early scholarly representatives of this group.[9] Others who largely fall into the same category include van Bavel, Diepen, Grillmeier, and Verwilghen.[10] Also noteworthy are Maxwell, Williams, and Casiday.[11]

Pierce also describes two recent approaches to Augustine's Christology that fall somewhat outside the earlier dichotomy. John McGuckin, writing in 1990 in response to McWilliam, believes she is correct that Augustine speaks of a 'moral union' between the Word and the man, but insists that this is not the only model of the Incarnation he employs; he also uses an ontological model as well.[12] As Pierce aptly summarizes, 'By *moral union* McGuckin refers to God's indwelling presence, which both Christ and those under grace experience—albeit in differing degrees. By *ontological union* he means the composition of one Christ out of two distinct realities: the Word and a human being.'[13] Because of the presence of an ontological model in McGuckin's view of Augustine, I should prefer to place McGuckin within

---

[8]   Pierce, 'At the Crossroads', 455–6.

[9]   See Otto Scheel, *Die Anschauung Augustin über Christi Person und Werk* (Tübingen: Drack von H. Laup Jr., 1900), 26–54. See also Eugène Portalié, 'Augustin (Saint),' *DTC* 1/2 (1909), 2363–4, who stresses the continuity between Augustine's Christology and that of Cyril of Alexandria and points out that he explicitly rejected the idea of an indwelling of the Word in the man Jesus by grace. Cf. Eugène Portalie, *A Guide to the Thought of Saint Augustine*, trans. Ralph J. Bastian, Library of Living Catholic Thought (Chicago: Henry Regnery Company, 1960), 153–61.

[10]   See Tarsicius J. van Bavel, *Recherches sur la christologie de Saint Augustin: L'humain et le divin dans le Christ d'après Saint Augustin*, Paradosis 10 (Fribourg: Éditions Universitaires, 1954), 39, who argues that the idea of a moral union is completely strange to Augustine; H.M. Diepen, 'L'*Assumptus Homo* patristique,' *Revue Thomiste* 63 (1963), 231, who argues that even when Augustine uses *homo*, he intends *humanitas*, the human nature of Christ; Alloys Grillmeier *Christ in Christian Tradition. Vol. 1: From the Apostolic Age to Chalcedon (451)*, trans. John Bowden (London: Mowbrays, rev. ed. 1975), 408–9, who argues that in his mature Christology, Augustine excluded any language hinting that God was merely indwelling Christ; Albert Verwilghen, *Christologie et Spiritualité selon Saint Augustin: L'Hymne aux Philippiens*, Théologie historique 72 (Paris: Beauchesne, 1985), 482.

[11]   See David R. Maxwell, 'What Was "Wrong" with Augustine? The Sixth-Century Reception (or Lack Thereof) of Augustine's Christology', in *In the Shadow of the Incarnation: Essays on Jesus Christ in the Early Church in Honor of Brian E. Daley, S.J.* (Notre Dame, IN: University of Notre Dame Press, 2008), 217–18, who argues that Augustine's Christological formulations and use of *homo* appear to be Theodorean/Nestorian when viewed from an anti-Nestorian lens, but they were not actually intended in that way; Rowan Douglas Williams, 'Augustine's Christology: Its Spirituality and Rhetoric', in *In the Shadow of the Incarnation*, 185–6, who claims that Augustine rejects the Antiochene tendency to distribute the actions of Jesus between the Word and the man, on the grounds that it is only because the Word chose to become human that Jesus acts in a human way; Augustine Casiday, 'Vincent of Lérins's *Commonitorium, Objectiones,* and *Excerpta*: Responding to Augustine's Legacy in Fifth-Century Gaul', in *Grace for Grace: The Debates after Augustine and Pelagius*, ed. Alexander Hwang et al. (Washington, DC: The Catholic University of America Press, 2014), 146, who writes, 'Despite the initial associations that Augustine's preference for speaking in terms of an 'assumed man' might elicit in modern scholars, Augustine clarifies that the person of Christ Jesus is the singular and exceptional instance of human nature (common to all humans) being assumed by God the Word in the Word's own person without thereby generating a fourth divine person.'

[12]   John A. McGuckin, 'Did Augustine's Christology Depend on Theodore of Mopsuestia?' *The Heythrop Journal* 31 (1990), 39–52.

[13]   Pierce, 'At the Crossroads', 458–9, italics his.

the Chalcedonian/Cyrillian camp rather than as an outlier to either group. Pierce also notes Dominic Keech's provocative 2012 work in which he 'takes Augustine furtively to affirm an Origenian account of the preexistence of souls united in Adam wherein Adam and his stock sinned and fell with the exception of the soul of Christ to whom Adam's sin was never communicated.'[14] Pierce does not find Keech's case persuasive and largely agrees with McGuckin, and the purpose of his article is to elaborate on the way the moral and ontological models of the Christological union interact in Augustine's later thought.[15] In the light of this helpful taxonomy, we should do well to interact in a bit more detail with McWilliam's view of an Antiochene/Theodorean Augustine, with McGuckin's view of a Chalcedonian/Cyrillian Augustine (but with an important qualification), with Keech's view of an Origenian Augustine, and with Pierce's own proposals later in his article.

As we saw in the Introduction, McWilliam means by 'Antiochene' a Christology that emphasizes a moral union between the man and the Word and that sees in Christ a humanity that could have existed independently of the Word, even though it never did.[16] McWilliam argues that Augustine's Christology moved in an increasingly 'Antiochene' direction and that by 412 he was writing of the Christological union itself as being one of grace, just as Theodore had done earlier.[17] McWilliam claims that in *Ep.* 187 (written in 417), Augustine breaks new ground, writing 'that God is present to Christ not substantially nor by operation, but by love and grace, and that this gracious presence differs from the divine presence to the just in general in its fullness and because it brings about a personal union between the Word and the man in Christ'.[18] Based on a comparison between Augustine's letter and the extant fragments of Theodore's *De incar.*, she argues that Augustine had seen that work and had found it to be congenial. Both patristic writers, she claims, see the Christological union as one of grace, although she admits that Augustine's vision of the role of the *homo assumptus* in maintaining the grace of the union is less active than Theodore's.[19] McWilliam sees Augustine's de-emphasis on the role of the man as being a result of the Pelagian Controversy: he was forced to underplay his own earlier stress on free will.[20]

McGuckin, writing in direct response to McWilliam, describes three stages in the development of Augustine's Christology. First he sought to remove any vestiges of subordination of the Son to the Father, then he began to identify the historical Christ and the mystery of his body, the church. Finally, beginning with

---

[14] Ibid., 460.

[15] Ibid., 460–1.

[16] McWilliam Dewart, 'The Influence of Theodore of Mopsuestia', 113.

[17] Ibid., 116–17. Cf. my fuller discussion of Theodore's Christology, interacting with McWilliam and others, in Donald Fairbairn, *Grace and Christology in the Early Church*, OECS (Oxford: Oxford University Press, 2003), 28–52.

[18] Ibid., 117–18.

[19] Ibid., 119–29.

[20] Ibid., 130–1.

26 CHRISTOLOGY AND THE LOGIC OF GRACE

the Pelagian Controversy, he started to write of Christ as the man perfectly endowed with God's grace. It is in this latter phase that Augustine bears similarities to Theodore.[21] In *Ep.* 187, Augustine's overall point is that there are degrees of God's presence, and the Christological question is whether he is working with an ontological or a grace-centered model of the Christological union. McGuckin argues (as Pierce later acknowledges) that Augustine actually uses both and does not see the two models as being mutually exclusive.[22] Furthermore, McGuckin rejects McWilliam's claim that Augustine had read Theodore's *De incar.*, on the grounds that he would not have been able to read the work in Greek, and we have no evidence that it was translated into Latin by that time. Instead, he suggests, it is more likely that Augustine's idea of degrees of God's presence comes from Porphyry and the Neoplatonists.[23]

Keech takes an entirely different angle on Augustine's Christology and thus stands outside of the debate between McWilliam and McGuckin. He argues that Augustine's view is best expressed through the phrase *homo dominicus*, the 'lordly man' whom the Word assumed at the Incarnation, and he claims that for Augustine, this *homo* was not merely a quasi-independent man who could have lived apart from the Word, but actually a pre-existent man. In this way, the *homo assumptus* becomes—in Keech's Augustine—the unfallen human soul of Jesus which, alone among the pre-existent rational souls, remained firm in its devotion to the Word. But after Rufinus's Latin translation of Origen's *De princ.* became available in *c.*395, Augustine had to be much more careful about identifying himself with Origen than he had been previously, and he stopped using the phrase *homo dominicus*.[24] Keech resolves the conflict between McWilliam and McGuckin by arguing that both of them miss the central problem: 'A person cannot have merits without first being a person; natures cannot deserve blessing or punishment. Christ's "human nature", therefore, has some kind of existence before it is taken into union with the Word.'[25] Keech concludes that in Augustine's early Origenian Christology, 'the human soul of Jesus is elected to become Incarnate precisely because of its foregoing goodness and love, on account of which he can assume the "likeness of the flesh of sin" without subsequent defilement. Expediently moving away from only half this formulation in his own Christology, Augustine's mature theology would remain permanently disjointed, offering an incomplete Christ to a race condemned and incapable of its own salvation.'[26]

---

[21] McGuckin, 'Did Augustine's Christology Depend on Theodore of Mopsuestia?' 42.

[22] Ibid., 45–8.

[23] Ibid., 49–50.

[24] Dominic Keech, *The Anti-Pelagian Christology of Augustine of Hippo, 396–430*, OTM (Oxford: Oxford University Press, 2012), 208–13.

[25] Ibid., 229.

[26] Ibid., 235.

SETTING THE STAGE   27

Keech's reconstruction is certainly ingenious, and if its purpose is to break the horns of the dilemma posed by McWilliam and McGuckin, it clearly succeeds in laying out an alternative possibility. The problem is that Keech's view requires more subterfuge on the part of Augustine than most scholars are willing to tolerate. At the beginning of the Pelagian Controversy, Augustine angrily rejects the idea of pre-existence of souls: 'Or are we perhaps supposed to hold that exploded and rejected theory that souls first sin in their heavenly dwelling and gradually and slowly come down to bodies corresponding to their merits and suffer more or less bodily afflictions for the life they previously lived?'[27] The rationale for his rejection is the fact that Paul's point in Rom. 9:11–12 is precisely that Esau and Jacob had no prior merits on the basis of which God chose the latter rather than the former.[28] Keech treats angry outbursts such as this one as smokescreens designed (consciously or not) to hide what Augustine actually thinks. But considering that the later Augustine's favourite expression would be *nullis praecedentibus meritis*, it is more credible to think that he believes what he writes here: neither Christ nor the believer has done anything ahead of time to deserve grace. An Origenian account of Augustine's Christology simply will not do.

We are back, then, to the disagreement about whether the Christological union is purely moral (McWilliam et al.) or primarily ontological with a moral element as well (McGuckin). Pierce agrees with McGuckin and advances his argument considerably. He asserts, 'For Augustine, then, the ontological union of the two distinct realities in a single person is not mutually exclusive with God's indwelling presence [i.e., moral union], but is itself the greatest inflection of divine presence. . . . God's indwelling of Christ is not only greater by degrees but qualitatively different in that God's presence in Christ is intrinsic to his person while it can only ever be extrinsic for all other human persons.'[29] Pierce concludes succinctly, 'It is by being situated as an ontological mediator that Christ is able to provide moral mediation for human sin.'[30]

To Pierce's argument I should like simply to add a terminological nuance. Much of the debate has to do with what Augustine means by the word *homo*, as applied to the man Christ, and scholars disagree about whether Augustine is akin to Theodore in using that word in the sense of *homo assumptus*, or whether he

---

[27] Augustine, *De pecc. mer. rem.* 1.31 (CSEL 60.28) [WSA I/23.50]. See also *De grat. Christi* 2.36 (CSEL 42.195) [WSA I/23.453], where Augustine rejects the idea that the soul of an infant could have sinned prior to this life and could be judged for that sin committed in a pre-existent state.

[28] One should remember that this biblical passage was central to Origen's reflections on the pre-existence of souls. So strongly did he believe divine favour had to be the response to human merit that, faced with the fact that Jacob and Esau had done nothing in this world by which to earn favour or disdain, he postulated that they must have pre-existed and acquired virtue or sin prior to their human conception. See Origen, *De princ.* 3.1.21–2. (Behr, 360–70). In contrast, Augustine takes the passage much more at face value, as a statement that in fact Jacob and Esau had no preceding merits or demerits, in this life or in a hypothetical previous one.

[29] Pierce, 'At the Crossroads', 474–5.

[30] Ibid., 477.

28 CHRISTOLOGY AND THE LOGIC OF GRACE

means it in the sense of an assumed human nature. But we need to remember that these are not the only possibilities. *Homo* can, of course, also refer to the human race as a whole, and there are some Christological passages where it is possible that Augustine shifts from speaking of Christ to speaking of the human race while still using the same word, *homo*. Also important is the possibility that for Augustine *homo* can and sometimes does mean 'the Word considered *qua homo* after the incarnation'. As we shall see, while McGuckin and Pierce correctly argue for a 'moral model' of the Incarnation in some passages, the reason such a model can succeed is that Augustine is treating the Word-made-flesh as man, rather than considering the same Word as God. The 'as God/as man' distinction is a classic patristic way of describing Christ that predated by several centuries the nature/person distinction.[31] Indeed, the 'as God/as man' distinction accomplishes something that is at least slightly obscured in the later nature/person distinction: the ability to think of the same person—God's eternal Son—living in two different ways at the same time. He lives in a divine way as he always has, but after the Incarnation he also lives in a human way, as a man dependent on grace.[32] I believe that when we recognize the possibility that for Augustine *homo* can mean 'the incarnate Word considered as a man', much of the fog surrounding his Christology dissipates: it is the incarnate Word considered as a man who is indwelt by his own grace.

Accordingly, it is now time to look at some Christological passages from the Pelagian Controversy, focusing on what Augustine means by *homo* in each use of the word and how his varying usages of *homo* enable him both to distinguish Christ from Christians and yet link him to us in grace. In order to help the reader sort out possible translations of *homo* in these passages, I shall need to modify existing English translations by rendering *homo* with anarthrous 'man', until I am able to discuss the possible renderings and to explain how I think the word should be understood in each context.

Christology and Grace in Augustine's Anti-Pelagian Writings and *Enchir.*

During the years 412–418 when the main portion of the Pelagian Controversy took place, Augustine's major treatises include a few references to Christology in connection with grace, and at the same time he wrote several significant letters

[31] For a Latin example from the turn of the third century, see Tertullian, *Adu. Prax.* 26 (CSEL 47.285) [*ANF* 3.626], where Tertullian asserts that 'the Son died not indeed after the divine substance, but after the human (*filium ... non enim ex diuina, sed ex human substantia mortuum)*'. As we shall see, Augustine normally makes this point using the phrases *secundum deum* and *secundum hominem*, which makes him more ambiguous and prone to misinterpretation than Tertullian is in this passage.

[32] In contrast, the nature/person distinction might incline one to attribute divine and human actions and experiences to natures, rather than to the single person, the Word-made-man.

dealing primarily with Christology. It is important to consider these writings together in order to recognize the shape of his Christology in relation to his teaching on grace and predestination.

De pecc. mer. rem.

Augustine's first writing from the Pelagian Controversy, *De pecc. mer. rem.*, dates to about 412, and in book one of that work, he deals with the transmission of mortality and guilt to Adam's posterity. Near the end of that long discussion, Augustine quotes Jn. 3:1–21 in its entirety and paraphrases Jesus as saying that earthly human beings can become heavenly ones only through rebirth as members of Christ's body. The key verse in Augustine's interpretation is Jn. 3:13 (no one ascends into heaven except the one who came down from heaven), and he writes: 'Hence, all who need to be transformed and raised up must come together into the unity of Christ (*in unitatem Christi . . . concurrant*), so that the Christ who has come down may himself ascend. He does not regard his body, that is, his Church, as something distinct from himself (*aliud . . . quam se ipsum*).'[33] After quoting Jn. 3:13 again, Augustine continues, 'For, though he became the Son of Man on earth, he did not think it inappropriate to use the title Son of Man, of his divinity, by which he remained in heaven, when he came down to earth. After all, he did not want us to understand two Christs, one God and the other man (*ne quasi duo Christi accipiantur, unus deus et alter homo*), but one and the same Christ, both God and man (*se unus atque idem deus et homo*).'[34] For Augustine, as for the church fathers more broadly, 'Son of Man' is a title that the Word assumed at the Incarnation when he assumed humanity. Although he *became* Son of Man, he did not *become* in an absolute sense; that is, he did not begin to exist. Instead, the one who always existed as Son of God became Son of Man in addition, so that one may use 'Son of Man' even when speaking of him in terms of his deity, or 'Son of God' even when speaking of him in terms of his humanity. Thus, Augustine can say that the Son of Man was in heaven and the Son of God walked on the earth.[35]

This passage describes the drama of redemption as a downward movement of God's Son in order to raise human beings up to himself by uniting them to himself as his body. Considering this movement from the angle of grace, one can say that it is not enough for God to help us accomplish what is needed for our elevation. We cannot elevate ourselves, so we need God to come down. From the vantage point of Christology, then, Christ cannot be simply a man whose connection to God enables him to rise up and thus to lead us up as we follow. He must be God the Son

---

[33] Augustine, *De pecc. mer. rem.* 1.60 (CSEL 60.60) [WSA I/23.69].
[34] Augustine, *De pecc. mer. rem.* 1.60 (CSEL 60.60-1) [WSA I/23.69, translation slightly modified].
[35] Augustine, *De pecc. mer. rem.* 1.60 (CSEL 60.61) [WSA I/23.69-70].

30 CHRISTOLOGY AND THE LOGIC OF GRACE

who descends from heaven to earth (alone) and then ascends back to heaven (with us, the members of his body). Broadly speaking, a view of the inability of fallen humanity to save itself goes hand-in-glove with a view of Christ as the eternal Son himself, rather than as a man who is indwelt or empowered by God. As we shall see, Augustine often uses language that might seem to imply that the humanity of Christ is a quasi-independent man, but that language needs to be understood in the light of controlling themes such as this one from Jn. 3:13.

Later in the same work, Augustine makes this implicit connection between Christology and grace explicit by contrasting the humility of the Incarnation with human pride. He writes: 'God came humbly out of mercy, revealing his grace with wondrous clarity (*gratiam claram manifestamque commendans*) in that man whom he assumed (*in ipso homine, quem ... suscepit*) with such great love before his companions. After all, he who was in that way united to the Word of God (*ipse ita uerbo dei coniunctus*) did not bring it about by any preceding merits of his will that the one Son of God also became the one Son of Man as a result of that union.'[36] In this passage one might well think that Augustine is writing of a man conjoined to the Word: the verb is *coniungo*, and the relative pronoun *quem* is masculine. But the overall thrust of the passage is the downward motion of God to come to us in humility, not the upward ascent of a man. The grace Augustine describes here is not that of the Word's elevating an assumed man, but that of the Son of God becoming Son of Man, that of divine descent. So, in this passage *homo* seemingly refers to an assumed human nature, not an assumed quasi-independent man.

Letters from 412 to 415

At about the same time (also *c*.412) Augustine wrote a long letter to a pagan intellectual named Volusian to answer various questions that had arisen about the Incarnation.[37] In response to Volusian's questions,[38] Augustine primarily emphasizes that the Word of God did not cease to fill heaven and earth when he became human, nor did he cease carrying out his divine functions. At one point in the letter, he explains the Incarnation by emphasizing that divine power is never constrained. He writes: 'That same power joined to itself a rational soul and through it also a human body (*ipsa sibi animam rationalem et per eandem etiam corpus*

[36] Augustine, *De pecc. mer. rem.* 2.27 (CSEL 60.99–100) [WSA I/23.98].

[37] John Thomas Newton, Jr, 'The Importance of Augustine's Use of the Neoplatonic Doctrine of Hypostatic Union for the Development of Christology', *AugSt* 2 (1971), 3, argues that this letter, *Ep.* 137, marked the point at which Augustine began to use Neoplatonic teaching to elucidate a doctrine of hypostatic union.

[38] Augustine summarizes Volusian's questions as whether the Lord of the universe filled the Virgin, whether she bore him in the normal manner while remaining a virgin, whether the Lord of the universe actually was a tiny baby, grew up, etc., and whether he abandoned his throne and his providential care of the world while he was on earth. *Ep.* 137.2 (CSEL 44.98) [WSA II/2.213].

humanum) and absolutely whole man (*totumque omnino hominem*) that would be changed for the better without itself being changed for the worse (*in melius mutandum nullo modo in deterius mutate*).[39] Here the crucial question is how to interpret the word *homo* in the phrase *totumque omnino hominem*. In the translation quoted above, Teske apparently takes it to refer to an assumed man, so that the sense is that the divine power joined to itself a rational soul, a human body, and an 'absolutely whole man' in order that the man would be changed for the better without the divine power being changed for the worse.[40] This rendering makes good grammatical sense of the suffix -*que* that seemingly links *hominem* to the preceding *corpus humanum,* but it makes little conceptual sense. For starters, it was common to refer to a whole human being as 'rational soul and body', but it would have been very strange indeed to refer to a whole human being as 'rational soul and body and absolutely whole man'. Moreover, if this phrase is about an alleged *homo assumptus*, then in what sense can the *homo* be changed for the better through the Incarnation, since he did not exist previously? In contrast to Teske's rendering, Parsons takes this instance of *homo* to refer to the human race as a whole and renders the phrase 'and chose to better all mankind without suffering any diminution itself'.[41] It seems to me that Parsons's interpretative decision is preferable, since *totumque omnino hominem* is part of a gerundive phrase describing what needed to be changed, namely, *hominem* or the human race. While one might have wished for a more causal connective than the mere -*que*, the sense is most likely that the reason the divine power joined to itself both rational soul and body was that mankind as a whole (not just the material or immaterial component in isolation) needed transformation. Accordingly, I believe we should modify Teske's translation to something like the following (consistent with that of Parsons): 'That same power joined to itself a rational soul and through it also a human body, since mankind as a whole needed to be changed for the better without itself [the divine power] having been changed for the worse.'

This passage is indicative of the problems that vex translators of Latin Christological texts. For Augustine and others, the word *homo* stands for several different realities, often more than one in any given passage. But the passage is also illustrative: if Parsons and I are correct, Augustine's thought moves from humanity in the sense of a complete human nature (body and rational soul) to humanity in the sense of the human race as a whole. Perhaps the progression of thought would have been clearer if he had used *humanitas* for 'human race as a whole' instead of *homo*. But he did not, and as we shall see, almost no Latin writers of the fifth century demonstrated that kind of terminological precision. We must attend carefully to the flow of thought in any given passage to be confident about how Augustine or

---

[39] Augustine, *Ep.* 137.8 (CSEL 44.107) [WSA II/2.217, translation slightly modified].
[40] WSA II/2.217.
[41] FC 20.24.

32 CHRISTOLOGY AND THE LOGIC OF GRACE

another Latin writer is using *homo* to describe the relation between the man Christ and mankind.

Another passage later in the letter is also illustrative. Augustine emphasizes that the Word is present everywhere, but he 'assumed man (*suscepit hominem*) in a far different way from that in which he is present to other creatures, and he made from himself and that entity the one Jesus Christ (*seque et illo fecit unum Iesum Christum*), the mediator of God and human beings. He is equal to the Father according to his divinity (*secundum diuinitatem*) but less than the Father according to the flesh, that is, according to man (*secundum carnem, hoc est secundum hominem*).'[42] Here again, Teske renders *homo* as 'the man',[43] giving the distinct impression that Augustine is talking about an assumed man. But notice two important things about the passage. First, Augustine does not repeat *homo* in the clause *seque et illo fecit unum Iesum Christum*. While Teske renders this as 'made from himself and that man the one Jesus Christ',[44] Augustine here means that whatever *homo* referred to in the previous clause, the Word made one Jesus Christ from 'that' and from himself. Second, at the end of the quoted passage, the phrase *secundum hominem* is directly contrasted to the earlier phrase *secundum diuinitatem* (not *secundum deum*) and directly parallel to the phrase *secundum carnem*. It is thus virtually certain that in this passage Augustine means *homo* in the sense of *caro* or *humana natura*, not in the sense of a quasi-independent man. The idea is that the Word assumed a human nature and made from himself and that entity (the assumed human nature) the one Jesus Christ. He is thus equal to the Father according to his divinity but less than the Father according to his humanity.[45]

As the Pelagian Controversy continued, Augustine's letters began to show a concern to make clear that the Incarnation did not introduce a fourth person into the Trinity. If the Word had assumed a complete (quasi-independent) man to himself, that would have implied—according to both Augustine and others later as they opposed Nestorius—that the Trinity had become a quaternity. Writing in about 415 to his childhood friend Evodius, Augustine describes several events from the Gospels and sums them up by writing, 'But because all these things were done in order to set free this nature (*ipsam naturam*), only man was joined to the unity of the person of the Word of God (*solus homo ... in unitatem personae uerbi dei ... coaptatus est*), that is, of the only Son of God, by a marvelous and singular assumption....'[46] Here we find Augustine using *natura* to refer to the human race or human nature as a whole, and *homo* to refer to that which the Word assumed, language that suggests the assumption of a quasi-independent man. Yet Augustine continues by writing, 'For the number of persons was not increased by the assumption of

---

[42] Augustine, *Ep.* 137.12 (CSEL 44.111) [WSA II/2.219, translation slightly modified].
[43] WSA II/2.219.
[44] Ibid.
[45] Cf. FC 20.27, which generally concurs with my interpretation.
[46] Augustine, *Ep.* 169.7 (CSEL 44.616) [WSA II/3.110, translation slightly modified].

man (*homine adsumpto*); rather, the same Trinity remained. For just as in any man (*in homine quolibet*)—apart from the one who was assumed in a singular manner (*praeter unum illum, qui singulariter susceptus est*)—soul and body are one person (*anima et corpus una persona est*), so in Christ the Word and man are one person (*ita in Christo uerbum et homo una persona est*).'[47] In this passage, Augustine certainly appears to have in mind an assumed man: notice in particular the masculine forms *qui* and *susceptus est* in the statement that *homo* was assumed by the Word. Passages such as this lend credibility to the Antiochene/Theodorean reading of Augustine's Christology. But this assertion is preceded by the insistence that the assumption of *homo* did not add a new person to the Trinity, and it concludes with the concurring assertion that in Christ the Word and *homo* are one person. In that context, this passage must mean either that the *homo* is not really brought into the unity of the Trinity or that *homo* means 'human nature' rather than 'quasi-independent man'. There is no hint of the first possibility here or anywhere else in Augustine's writings, so the second must be correct. Thus, the masculine forms *qui* and *susceptus est* should be taken simply as grammatically masculine, not as indications that *homo* refers to a person. While the use of *homo* is more jarring in this passage than in others I have considered, even here, the context strongly suggests that Augustine means by *homo* something other than 'assumed man'.

Ep. 187 from 417

As the Pelagian Controversy was nearing its resolution, Augustine wrote a long letter to Dardanus, a prefect of Gaul, to answer questions about Jesus's statement that the thief on the cross would today be with him in paradise [Lk. 23:43]. The issue is how the repentant thief could be with Christ in paradise, since Jesus himself would not be in paradise that day. Augustine sets up the question as follows: 'If, then, we think that the phrase, *Today you will be with me in paradise* was written in terms of man whom God the Word assumed (*secundum hominem, quem uerbum deus suscepit*), paradise ought not to be thought to be in heaven on the basis of those words. For on that very day the man Jesus Christ (*homo Christus Iesus*) was not going to be in paradise but in the underworld in terms of his soul (*secundum animam*) and in the tomb in terms of his flesh (*secundum carnem*).'[48] Here again we find a use of the word *homo* that might lead one to envision a quasi-independent man, especially since again we find the masculine relative pronoun *quem* used to describe the one whom God assumed. Notice that the rest of the passage concentrates on *homo Christus Iesus* and describes him as being in two places at once, in the underworld *secundum animam* and in the grave *secundum carnem*.

---

[47] Augustine, *Ep.* 169.8 (CSEL 44.617) [WSA II/3.110, translation slightly modified].
[48] Augustine, *Ep.* 187.5 (CSEL 57.84) [WSA II/3.233, translation modified].

34 CHRISTOLOGY AND THE LOGIC OF GRACE

Thus, he is discussing two ways of considering a single person—according to his soul and according to his body. Just as any recently departed person may be considered to be in the underworld in terms of her or his soul and in the grave in terms of his or her body, so it is with the man Jesus whom the Word assumed. Again, we find that Augustine's language gives ample fodder for an Antiochene/Theodorean interpretation.

Nevertheless, as Augustine continues his long explanation, it becomes clear that this is not what he means. He writes:

> And yet when we call Christ the Son of God we do not exclude man (*hominem separamus aut*), nor when we call the same Christ the Son of Man do we exclude God (*separamus deum*). For as man (*secundum hominem*) he was on earth, not in heaven where he is now . . . though as the Son of God he was in heaven, as the Son of Man he was still on earth and had not yet ascended into heaven. Similarly, according to that by which he was the Son of God (*secundum id, quod filius dei erat*), he is the Lord of glory, but according to that by which he is the Son of Man (*secundum id autem, quod est filius hominis*) he was crucified. . . . And for this reason the Son of Man as God (*secundum deum*) was in heaven, and the Son of God as man (*secundum hominem*), was crucified on earth. Consequently, just as he could correctly be called the Lord of glory when he was crucified, though that suffering pertained to his flesh alone (*cum ad solam carnem illa passio pertineret*), so he could correctly say, *Today you will be with me in paradise*, though as regards his lowly human condition (*iuxta humanam humilitatem*) he was going to be in the tomb in terms of his flesh and in the underworld in terms of his soul on that day. But in accord with the divine immutability (*iuxta diuinam uero immutabilitatem*) he had never left paradise because he is always everywhere.[49]

In this passage, we again see the use of *homo* and *deus*, but here the focus throughout lies on a single person considered in different ways, not on a quasi-independent man and a quasi-separate Word of God. Augustine writes of Christ both *secundum deum* and *secundum hominem*, and he provides greater specificity about each of these expressions as he goes along. To think of Christ *secundum deum* is to think of him *secundum id, quod filius dei erat*, according to that by which he is the Son of God. It is to think of him *iuxta diuinam uero immutabilitatem*, according to his divine immutability. The neuter expression *id, quod* and the mention of a quality—divine immutability—indicate that *secundum deum* does not refer to the Word somehow separate from an alleged assumed man, but to a quality, his divinity that he possesses because he is God's eternal Son. Likewise, to consider Christ *secundum hominem* is to consider him *secundum id autem, quod est filius*

---

[49] Augustine, *Ep.* 187.9 (CSEL 57.88–9) [WSA II/3.235, translation modified].

hominis, according to that by which he is the Son of Man. It is to consider him *iuxta humanam humilitatem,* according to his human lowliness. Again, the neuter expression *id, quod* and the mention of a quality—human lowliness—indicate that we should take *secundum hominem* in the sense of 'according to his humanity', not in the sense of 'pertaining to a quasi-independent man'.

The latter portion of this long letter is an extended discussion of different ways in which God may be said to be present with creatures, a discussion that seems to bear some resemblances to Theodore's *De incar.* and that therefore leads scholars such as McWilliam to assert that Augustine's Christology is Antiochene, and even influenced by Theodore himself. However, at the end of this discussion, Augustine draws a very sharp distinction between Christ and Christians, a distinction that shows he is thinking about divine presence in a different way from Theodore. He writes:

> We believe that there is this difference between the head and the other members—that in any member, however eminent, such as some great prophet or apostle, although the divinity dwells in him, *all the fullness of divinity* [Col. 2:9] does not dwell in him as it does in the head, which is Christ. . . . Or, apart from the fact that *the fullness of divinity* dwells in that body as in a temple, is there another difference between that head and the excellence of any member? There clearly is, because the singular assumption of that man formed one person with the Word (*quod singulari quadam susceptione hominis illius una facta est persona cum uerbo*). . . . No saint by any excellence of grace has received the title 'the Only-Begotten' in the same way that he who was the very Word of God before all the ages bears this same title after assuming man (*quod est ipsum dei uerbum ante saecula, hoc simul cum adsumpto homine diceretur*). That assumption, then, is singular, nor can it in any way be shared by some human saints, no matter how outstanding in wisdom and holiness. Here we have a clear and evident proof of God's grace. For who would be so sacrilegious as to dare to say that some soul could bring it about by the merit of his free choice that he be another Christ? How, then, would one soul alone have merited to belong to the person of the only-begotten Word through free choice, which is naturally given to all in common, unless a singular grace had bestowed this?[50]

In this passage, as in so many others, Augustine begins as if he were treating *homo* as a quasi-independent man,[51] but as always, the progression of the passage makes

---

[50] Augustine, *Ep.* 187.40 (CSEL 57.116–17) [WSA II/3.249, translation slightly modified].

[51] Joanne McWilliam takes this very passage as an indication that Christ the man is united to the person of the Word by grace and sustained by grace, not by his own free will. Her interpretation implies that Augustine's Christology is Theodorean—something she explicitly claims elsewhere, as we have seen—and contrasts sharply with my own reading of the same passage. See McWilliam Dewart, 'The Christology of the Pelagian Controversy', 1232.

clear that this is not what he means. This time, the clue to his intention lies in the fact that he treats the personal subject of Christ as the incarnate Word, not as the *homo*. He begins by contrasting *homo* with Christians, but when he reaches the central point of the contrast, he does not write that no Christian has been united to the Word in such a way as to be called only-begotten. (*That* would be Theodorean!) Instead, he writes that no Christian has been called only-begotten as the Word who bore that title from all eternity is called even after the Incarnation. The Incarnation is not 'grace' in the Theodorean sense that the Word unites a man to himself because of that man's worthiness in his sight, or even in an Origenian sense that the soul of Jesus clung steadfastly to the Word so as to be worthy of such union. Instead, the Incarnation is grace in the sense that the Word united humanity to himself, through no preceding merits of either that humanity (the '*homo*') or the human race as a whole. Here Augustine anticipates the connection between Christology and grace that he will draw more explicitly in his latest writings, which I shall consider later in this chapter.

De grat. Christi

In Augustine's final treatise from the main portion of the Pelagian Controversy, *De grat. Christi* [c.418], he forges a more direct link between Christology and grace by reflecting on the Adam/Christ typology.[52] He writes: 'They [the Pelagians] try to separate the righteous people of old from the grace of the mediator, as if the man Jesus Christ were not the mediator between God and those people, because he was not yet a man, inasmuch as he had not yet assumed flesh in the womb of the virgin (*quia nondum ex utero uirginis carne suscepta homo nondum fuit*), when those righteous people lived.'[53] In this passage we see clearly that Augustine centres Christ's person around the Word. The 'he' whom we call Jesus Christ is the same 'he' who was the Father's Son even before he became man. This 'he', this Word, took flesh at the Incarnation so as to become the man Jesus Christ. As Augustine continues these reflections, he stresses that the person—God the Son—mediates between God and the human race not through his divinity, but through his humanity, as man:

> But he is not mediator because he is equal to the Father; in that respect he is as distant from us as the Father is. And how is he to be the middle ground (*medietas*),

[52] Mathijs Lamberigts, 'Competing Christologies: Julian and Augustine on Jesus Christ', *AugSt* 36 (2005), 174, helpfully summarizes: 'While Adam did not really play a role in the Pelagian scheme of salvation history, he was a major figure in the framework of Augustinian thought. It would not be unfair to claim that during the Pelagian controversy, Augustine's whole view of history could be reduced to the stories of two individuals: Adam and Christ.'

[53] Augustine, *De grat. Christi* 2.31 (CSEL 42.190) [WSA I/23.450].

when he is equally distant? ... He is, then, the mediator by the fact that he is man; he is inferior to the Father in terms of that by which he is closer to us; he is superior to us in terms of that by which he is nearer to the Father. This is clearly stated as follows: He is inferior to the Father in the form of the servant (*inferior patre, quia in forma serui*); he is superior to us because he is without the stain of sin (*superior nobis, quia sine labe peccati*).[54]

Here again, we see that Augustine thinks of Christ as a single person, the Word, who should be understood as living in two ways after the Incarnation: as God and as man, according to the form of God by which he is equal to the Father, and according to the form of a servant by which he is inferior to the Father. In contrast to Theodore, who interprets the form of God and the form of a servant in Phil. 2 as references to the Word and the *homo assumptus*,[55] Augustine takes the form of God and the form of a servant to refer to two ways of thinking about the one person, the incarnate Word.

This passage sits in the midst of a discussion of Adam and Christ, which itself comes in a longer treatment of original sin. It is original sin that links us to Adam's sin and thus makes us in need of the Incarnation and the Son's consequent living as a man for our salvation. For those under original sin, there is no room for worthiness or merit. We cannot and do not have any merit by which we might approach God. It is necessary for God's Son himself, living as a man, to bridge the gap between himself and the sinful human race. While he does not say so directly in this passage (as he has done in *Ep.* 187 previously), Augustine implies that the Incarnation is grace for the purpose of bringing the human race as a whole to God, just as much as the work of the Holy Spirit is grace for the purpose of bringing an individual to faith.

Enchir.

As Augustine writes to his friend Laurentius about the faith [*c*.420], he devotes *Enchir.* 34–36 to a discussion of Christ the mediator, and during this discussion he describes Christ the man as the supreme example of grace, just as he will do later in his final writings. Prior to describing Christ in that way, he makes clear, as always, that when he speaks of the *homo*, he does not mean a quasi-independent man. Augustine writes:

Insofar as he is God (*in quantum deus est*), he and the Father are one (*unum*) [cf. Jn. 10:30], and insofar as he is man (*in quantum homo est*), the Father is greater

---

[54] Augustine, *De grat. Christi* 2.33 (CSEL 42.193) [WSA I/23.451].
[55] See, e.g. Theodore, *Hom. cat.* 6.5–6 (Tonneau/Devreese, 139–41) [WS 5.65–6].

than he [cf. Jn. 14:28]. But since he is the only Son of God, by nature and not by grace, he became also the Son of Man that he might be full of grace (*plenus gratia*) as well.... But he is different as Word and as man (*aliud est propter uerbum, aliud propter hominem*): as Word he is equal, as man lesser; one and the same is Son of Man and Son of God (*unus dei filius, idemque hominis filius*); there are not two sons of God, divine and human, but one Son of God, God without beginning, man from a certain beginning in time (*deus sine initio, homo a certo initio*), our Lord Jesus Christ.[56]

In this passage, we see again that Augustine's use of masculine and neuter pronouns clarifies his potentially ambiguous use of the word *homo*. The one person can be thought of in two ways, *in quantum deus est* and *in quantum homo est*, and these are not different persons (that would be *alius... alius*), but instead different things (*aliud... aliud*), different realities or states. One can think of the Son in two ways—as God and as man, without beginning and with a beginning, one with God and less than God—but nevertheless, it is the same person who is thought of in both ways. In this passage, Augustine is thus using *homo* in the sense of 'the Word/ Son considered as a man'.

Immediately afterwards, Augustine holds up the *homo* in Christ as the supreme example of grace. He writes:

Here the grace of God is made clearly and abundantly plain. For what did human nature in Christ the man (*natura humana in homine Christo*) do to deserve being assumed in a unique way into the unity of the person of the one Son of God (*in unitatem personae unici filii dei*)? What good will (*bona uoluntas*), what care for carrying out good intentions, what good works went before, that that man (*iste homo*) might be worthy to be one person with God (*una fieri persona cum deo*)? Was he man (*homo*) before, and was the unique benefit of being worthy of God offered to him alone? Certainly from the moment when he began to be man he began to be nothing other than the Son, the only Son, of God, and because of God the Word, who on assuming him became flesh, he was certainly God, so that, just as any human being is one person, that is, a rational soul and flesh, so Christ is one person, Word and man. Whence can human nature (*humanae naturae*) have received such great glory, which is without doubt a free gift, given without preceding merit?[57]

Here the phrase *natura humana in homine Christo* certainly makes it seem as if the man is a quasi-independent human being, a different person from the Word, since on the surface it seems hard to say that *homo* refers to 'human nature' when the

---

[56] Augustine, *Enchir.* 35 (CCSL 46.69) [WSA I/8.295–6, translation slightly modified].
[57] Augustine, *Enchir.* 36 (CCSL 46.69-70) [WSA I/8.296, translation slightly modified].

same phrase describes the human nature in that *homo*. We should remember, however, that just before this passage, Augustine has used the word *homo* to mean 'the Word considered as a man', so it is likely that he means the same thing here. When one considers the Word as a man, there is in him a human nature. Furthermore, the Word certainly did not exist *as a man* prior to the Incarnation, and therefore there was no *bona uoluntas* on the basis of which the union of divine and human might have occurred. The assumption of humanity by the Word such that he could be thought of as God and as man must have been purely by grace, not by any preceding merits. This grace then becomes the basis for the grace by which God extends salvation to sinful human beings.

As a result, we see that in all these Christological passages from Augustine's writings during the Pelagian Controversy and *Enchir.*, expressions that might be taken to imply that *homo* means a quasi-independent assumed man are more plausibly understood in context as referring to an assumed humanity or to the one Son considered as a man in terms of his humanity. The letters I have cited are not directly related to the controversy and thus do not address grace-related issues in any detail, but nevertheless, Augustine does hint at a connection between the grace by which the Word assumed humanity to save an unworthy human race and the grace by which God snatches an unworthy individual human being from perdition in order to save him or her. He also hints at this connection in Christological passages from writings that are directly connected to the Pelagian Controversy and whose primary foci lie on issues of grace and human incapacity. Neither in the case of Christ nor in the case of Christians is God's grace given in response to human worthiness, as Theodore had indicated previously. While Nestorius has not yet appeared on the scene, Augustine stands in contrast to the proto-'Nestorianism' of Theodore.

Christ as the Supreme Example of Grace in Augustine's Last Writings

At first glance, Augustine's depictions of Christ as the supreme example of grace and predestination in *De corrept. grat.* and *De praed. sanct.* appear to establish a strict parallelism between Christ and believers. The man Christ Jesus was predestined and graced to be united to the Word through no preceding merits of his own, and in the same way, believers are predestined to be united to God through no preceding merits of our own. Such strict parallelism would have been possible if Augustine had affirmed a Theodorean view of Christ as a quasi-independent man united to the Word by grace. But since—as we have seen—this is not the way Augustine views Christ, we may suspect that the relation between the predestined man Christ and predestined believers is more nuanced than this. We need

40 CHRISTOLOGY AND THE LOGIC OF GRACE

to look carefully at these three passages to discern the contours of the relation he is describing.

De corrept. grat.

In the middle of this treatise to the monks at Hadrumetum, Augustine emphasizes that Adam had a great grace, but of a different sort than that which we need. Before the Fall he was filled with joy, without struggle against himself, such as we now endure. Augustine continues:

> Hence, these saints do not now need a grace which is more filled with joy for the present, but a more powerful grace, and what grace is more powerful than the only-begotten Son of God (*quae potentior quam dei unigenitus filius*), equal to, and coeternal with the Father (*aequalis patri et coaeternus*), who became man for them (*pro eis homo factus*) and who without any sin of his own, either original or personal, was crucified by human sinners?[58]

Here we see that the Son of God is himself the more powerful grace that human beings need in our post-Fall condition. The thrust of the passage is that the Incarnation and crucifixion of one who is equal to and co-eternal with the Father constitute God's giving us this grace, giving us himself. For Augustine, Christ is not just an example of the gratuity of grace, even though that is the broader point of the extended passage. In addition, he, the Son of God, is the source of the grace that consists of himself. Notice that Augustine writes this before he considers the man Christ who had no preceding merits by which to deserve union with the Word. The subsequent discussion of Christ the man as the supreme example of grace is controlled by this prior statement that Christ is the Son of God who gives himself to humanity in grace. Furthermore, the subsequent use of *homo Christus* is controlled by Augustine's statement here that the eternal Son was made *homo*.

Augustine then quotes Rom. 8:31–2, stressing that God who gave his Son up for us all has also given us all things with him.[59] In doing so, he draws further attention to the fact that God has given us grace through his past action of giving us the Son through the Incarnation. Although his major point in the extended passage is that the predestination of the man Jesus parallels that of the saints, Augustine focuses not just on the fact that the Word has become the man he was predestined to be, but even more on the fact that the Incarnation was a unique event, one that has given grace to the predestined saints. He continues:

---

[58] Augustine, *De corrept. grat.* 30 (CSEL 92.254) [WSA I/26.129].

[59] In the Greek text, the final verb is future (χαρίσεται), and this is followed by most manuscripts of the Vulgate. Some Latin manuscripts have the perfect form *donauit*, which Augustine follows here.

God, therefore, assumed our nature (*naturam nostram*), that is, the rational soul and the flesh of Christ, the man (*hominis Christi*), and he assumed it in a singularly marvelous and marvelously singular manner. For, without any preceding merits of his own righteousness (*nullis justitiae suae praecedentibus meritis*), Christ was the Son of God from the first moment he began to be man (*filius dei sic esset ab initio quo esse homo coepisset*) in such a way that he and the Word, who is without beginning, might be one person (*ut ipse et uerbum quod sine initio est, una persona esset*).[60]

The second half of this passage, taken in isolation, certainly appears to assert the presence of an independent man to whom the Word was united. But this cannot be what Augustine means, because not only has he previously focused on the Word's action of becoming man, and not only has he quoted a biblical text that focused on God's giving his very Son, but even in this passage itself, he begins by stating that God took *naturam nostram*. Thus, the union was not between the Word and a quasi-independent man, but between the Word and the components that make up humanity. In this way, the Word became man and could begin to be called 'Christ the man'. Thus, when Augustine does not use the word *homo* to mean *humana natura*, it seems that he uses it to mean *Verbum qua homo*, the Word considered as a man. One could even suggest that the final phrase, *ut ipse et uerbum quod sine initio est, una persona esset*, means not that the Word and the man somehow count as a single person (as in Theodorean Christology), but that the Word and the man are the same person, because it is the Word who is now living as man.

It is from this base that Augustine builds his argument about the gratuity of grace. No human merits preceded the union of the Word and human nature in the Virgin's womb. He writes:

That birth which was, of course, gratuitous, united man to God, the flesh to the Word, in the unity of the person (*in unitate personae*). Good works followed upon this birth; good works did not merit it. For there was no reason to fear that the human nature assumed (*natura human suscepta*) in this ineffable way into the unity of the person by God the Word (*in unitatem personae a uerbo deo*) would sin by free choice of the will. This assumption, after all, was such that the nature of man, a nature assumed by God in that way (*natura hominis a deo ita suscepta*), would admit in itself no impulse of an evil will. Through this Mediator God has shown that he transforms those whom he redeemed by his blood from evil persons into persons who will thereafter be good for eternity, for he assumed this mediator in such a way that he never was evil (*quem sic suscepti, ut nunquam esset malus*) and that he never became good after being evil.[61]

---

[60] Augustine, *De corrept. grat.* 30 (CSEL 92.254) [WSA I/26.129, translation slightly modified].
[61] Augustine, *De corrept. grat.* 30 (CSEL 92.255) [WSA I/26.130, translation slightly modified].

42 CHRISTOLOGY AND THE LOGIC OF GRACE

Once again, Augustine writes in the second half of the passage in a way that might suggest that the mediator, the *homo Christus*, is an independent man conjoined to the Word. But again, a clear statement earlier in the passage controls the way the second half should be read. The assumption of man to God means the assumption of human nature to the Word. Thus, as awkward as it is for Augustine to write of the assumption of the mediator, this must mean that the assumption of human nature caused the Word to be now man as well as God, and thus he could function as mediator as man. The broader point, of course, is that the human nature could not have accrued any preceding merits since it did not exist before the Incarnation, so the Incarnation was thus gracious. In a similar but certainly not identical way, Augustine argues that believers have no preceding merits on the basis of which they are brought to God. This too is by grace.

Having established that the incarnate Word himself is the greater grace that human beings need after the Fall, Augustine elaborates on the word 'greater'. Whereas the grace given to Adam was governed by his free will in that he could remain in it or leave it, 'this second grace is so much greater, for it is not enough that a human being recovers by it his lost freedom; again, it is not enough that without it he cannot attain the good or remain in the good, even if he wills to, unless this grace also makes him will to'.[62] With this in mind, Augustine reiterates his well-known set of distinctions between *posse non peccare/mori* (the ability not to sin/die), *non posse non peccare/mori* (the inability not to sin/die), and *non posse peccare/mori* (the inability to sin/die).[63] It is crucial to recognize that in this iteration, these distinctions follow closely upon his description of Christ himself as the greater grace needed in the post-Fall world. The grace that turns fallen human beings who cannot fail to sin into saints who cannot sin is not merely a more intense grace of the form Adam initially received. It is greater precisely in that it is the grace of Christ, the grace that consists of Christ himself.

Shortly thereafter, Augustine summarizes the difference between the grace given to Adam and that given to Christians:

The first man, then, who had received in that good state in which he had been created upright the ability not to sin, the ability not to die, the ability not to abandon the good, was given the help toward perseverance, not the help which made him persevere, but the help without which he could not persevere by free choice. But now the saints who have been predestined to the kingdom of God by the grace of God are not given such a help toward perseverance, but a help by which they receive perseverance itself, not only so that they cannot persevere without this gift, but also so that by this gift they cannot fail to persevere.[64]

---

[62] Augustine, *De corrept. grat.* 31 (CSEL 92.257) [WSA I/26.131].
[63] Augustine, *De corrept. grat.* 33 (CSEL 92.259) [WSA I/26.132].
[64] Augustine, *De corrept. grat.* 34 (CSEL 92.260) [WSA I/26.132–3].

Here one might have hoped that Augustine would make explicit the connection between Christ as grace and the greater grace given to Christians. He does not do so, and we are left to wonder whether he means that because of the believer's union with Christ, it is Christ who is actually persevering for him or her, whether she or he is participating in Christ's own perseverance as man. But even though Augustine does not explain, the course of the passage has made clear that there is such a connection. Christ considered as man is more than simply the greatest example of grace and predestination: he is the giver of the greater grace to the predestined. Christ and the Christian are parallel yet not *strictly* parallel in Augustine's illustration.

De praed. sanct., Book 1

In the first book of his treatise written directly to the Gallic monks, Augustine brings up the common objection that there will be no incentive to live piously if salvation is based on predestination. After admitting that in the case of adults, who have had occasion to use their free choice, the objection does create a difficulty, he continues:

> But when we come to the little ones and to the very mediator between God and human beings, the man Jesus Christ, every claim to human merits preceding the grace of God collapses (*omnis deficit praecedentium gratiam dei humanorum assertio meritorum*). For those little ones are not set apart from the rest by any good merits so that they belong to the deliverer of human beings, nor was he made the deliverer of human beings by any preceding human merits (*nec ille ullis humanis praecedentibus meritis*) since he too was man (*cum et ipse sit homo, liberator factus est hominum*).[65]

Augustine discusses the case of baptized infants in paragraphs 24–9 and then turns his attention to Christ as the example of grace and predestination in paragraphs 30–2:

> There is also the most brilliant beacon of predestination and of grace, the savior himself, the very *mediator between God and human beings, the man Jesus Christ* [1 Tim. 2:5]. By what preceding merits of his, either of works or of faith, did the human nature which is in him (*natura humana, quae in illo est*) obtain such a dignity? Please reply! How did this man (*ille homo*) merit to be assumed by the Word coeternal with the Father into the unity of his person and to be the only-begotten

---

[65] Augustine, *De praed. sanct.* 1.23 (CSEL 105.199) [WSA I/26.168, translation slightly modified].

44 CHRISTOLOGY AND THE LOGIC OF GRACE

Son of God? What did he do beforehand, what did he believe, what did he ask for that he attained this ineffable excellence? Did this man not begin to be the only Son of God from the moment he began to be because the Word created and assumed him (*Nonne faciente ac suscipiente uerbo ipse homo, ex quo esse coepit, filius dei unicus esse coepit*)? Did not that woman who was full of grace conceive the only Son of God? Was not the only Son of God born of the Holy Spirit and the Virgin Mary....[66]

Here we should notice that Augustine moves from writing of the Saviour as a whole to mentioning *natura humana, quae in illo est*. In this case, 'the man Jesus Christ' must be the Word considered as a man, because if the man were the human nature, Augustine would not immediately write of the human nature within him. Accordingly, in the next sentence, *ille homo* may still refer to the Word considered as a man, although it is possible that Augustine here shifts to thinking of *ille homo* as the assumed human nature. At any rate, by the end of the passage, *homo* certainly refers to the assumed human nature. But just as in *De corrept. grat.*, so also here in *De praed. sanct.*, Augustine first writes precisely—using *humana natura* to refer to that which the Word assumed at the Incarnation—before sliding (perhaps unconsciously) into traditional usage of *homo*. In all cases, the clear statements should govern our interpretation of the ambiguous uses of *homo*: Augustine means by *homo* either human nature or the incarnate Word considered as a man.

After stressing that Christ the man did not merit the grace of being united to the Word, Augustine uses the biblical image of Christ as head of the church, his body, to turn his discussion to Christians:

> In our head, then, let this foundation of grace (*fons gratiae*) be seen from which he pours himself out (*se . . . diffundit*) through all his members according to the measure of each. Each human being becomes a Christian from the beginning of his faith by the same grace by which that man became Christ from his beginning. Each person is reborn by the Spirit by whom he was born. The same Spirit produced in us the forgiveness of sins who brought it about that he had no sin.[67]

Here, as in *De corrept. grat.*, we see that Augustine treats Christ as the source and content of grace: he pours himself out on our behalf. Thus, this passage begins with the differences between Christ and Christians—he, the head, pours himself out through the members of the body. Then the passage turns to the similarity between Christ and Christians: by grace he became Christ and we become Christians; by the Spirit he was sinless and we are forgiven of sins. In order to put the two parts of this passage together, one must assume that the passage is referring to Christ *qua*

---

[66] Augustine, *De praed. sanct.* 1.30 (CSEL 105.205) [WSA I/26.173–4, translation slightly modified].
[67] Augustine, *De praed. sanct.* 1.31 (CSEL 105.206) [WSA I/26.174].

homo. The Word is the source of grace, and he gives grace to his own humanity (or, to himself considered as a man), in order thereby to give grace to believers, the members of his body.

Augustine concludes by emphasizing that just as the man Jesus (that is, the Word considered as a man) was predestined to be the head of the body, so we are predestined to be the members. Again, just as in *De corrept. grat.*, the overarching purpose of Augustine's discussion is to defend his view of predestination using the man Christ as the supreme example. In the process, though, he also delineates important differences between Christ and Christians. While that delineation is not as clear as one might like, it is clear enough to show that in Augustine's view, God's grace given to the predestined saints originates with the Word (and the Spirit) and moves through the incarnate Word's own humanity (Christ as man is the head of the body) to the church as body and the individual members of that body.

De praed. sanct., Book 2

Augustine concludes *De praed. sanct.* by insisting that the man Christ was predestined to be united to the Word. He writes:

> There is, I repeat, no more illustrious example of predestination than the mediator himself. Let any believer who wants to understand it well pay attention to him, and let him find himself in him. I mean: a believer who believes and confesses in him a true human nature (*in eo ueram naturam credit et confitetur humanam*), that is, our nature (*id est nostram*), though raised up to the only Son of God by God the Word who assumes it (*suscipiente deo uerbo*) in a singular manner, so that he who assumed it (*qui suscepit*) and what he assumed (*quod suscepit*) is one person in the Trinity. For, when man was assumed (*homine assumpto*), a quaternity was not produced, but there remained a trinity, since that assumption ineffably produced the truth of one person in God and man (*personae unius in deo et homine*).[68]

Notice here that in the second half of the paragraph, Augustine uses *homo* to refer to the humanity of Christ, but prior to using that word, he uses *natura humana* to refer to that humanity, and even more strikingly, he uses a masculine relative pronoun *qui* to refer to the Word who assumed, and a neuter pronoun *quod* to indicate what the Word assumed. It is crystal clear that in this passage, Augustine envisions the Incarnation as the Word's taking a human nature into himself, not conjoining a quasi-independent man with himself. We should also notice that Christ's human

---

[68] Augustine, *De praed. sanct.* 2.67 [= *De don. pers.* 67] (CSEL 105.270) [WSA I/26.236, translation slightly modified].

46   CHRISTOLOGY AND THE LOGIC OF GRACE

nature is our human nature (*id est nostram*), which means that his humanity is the link between the Incarnation and our salvation.

Augustine continues by denying Manichaean, Photinian, and Apollinarian errors and then affirming positively:

> We say that Christ is true God, born of God the Father without any beginning of time and that same one (*eundemque*) is true man (*hominem uerum*) born of a human mother (*de homine matre*) at a certain fullness of time. Nor did this humanity by which he is less than the Father (*humanitatem, qua minor est patre*) lessen something of his divinity by which he is equal to the Father (*diuinitati, qua aequalis est patri*).[69]

Here Augustine makes clear that he sees the one who is born of the Father as the same one (*eundemque*) who is born of Mary. Strikingly, he refers to Mary's humanity with the word *homo*: 'born of a man as mother'! Clearly, then, the use of *homo* does not imply an independent man, since the word can be used of a woman's humanity. In the latter part of this passage, Augustine sets up a classic way of thinking of the incarnate Son as God in one sense and as man in another sense. Considered in terms of his humanity (*humanitatem*), he is less than the Father, but the same person, considered in terms of his deity (*diuinitati*), is equal to the Father.

Then Augustine turns one final time to the head/body imagery to explain the relation between Christ and Christians:

> He, then, who causes that man (*illum hominem*), without any preceding merits of that man, neither to contract by his origin nor to commit by his will any sin which might be forgiven him, causes people, without any preceding merits of theirs, to believe in him, and he forgives them every sin. He who makes that one (*fecit illum*) such that he never had and never will have an evil will makes a good will from an evil will in this one's members (*ipse facit in membris eius*). And he predestined both him and us, because he foreknew not our merits, but his future works both in him in order that he might be our head and in us in order that we might be his body.[70]

With these words—among the last that he ever wrote—Augustine stresses the priority of divine action, undergirded by divine predestination. Again he links the predestination of the man Christ with the predestination of Christians. Again he links Christ as head to Christians as members of the body. Again he emphasizes

---

[69] Augustine, *De praed. sanct.* 2.67 [= *De don. pers.* 67] (CSEL 105.270) [WSA I/26.236, translation slightly modified].
[70] Augustine, *De praed. sanct.* 2.67 [= *De don. pers.* 67] (CSEL 105.270–1) [WSA I/26.236–7, translation slightly modified].

that the grace by which Christ had no sin is also the grace by which believers are forgiven their sins. And in this passage Augustine also denies that predestination could have been enacted on the basis of foreseen human works. When God fore-knows good works, he foreknows his own works, not ours.

Conclusions on Christology and Grace in
Augustine's Latest Treatises

In the preceding discussion, I have pointed out the differences Augustine sees between Christ and believers,[71] even as I have stressed that his overall point has been to elaborate on the basic similarity—Christ considered as man, and men and women who believe in him, are both predestined with no preceding merits of their own. If one accepts Augustine's Christology as basically Chalcedonian/Cyrillian, then one is left with a logical progression. God who has predestined that his Son would give himself in grace to his own humanity so that he (considered as man) should be head of the church, has also predestined those men and women to whom the Son would give himself so that they should be the members of Christ's body, the church.[72] This predestination, in the case of Christ, cannot have been on the basis of any preceding merits of the man Jesus, because there was no man Jesus (that is, the Son had not yet become a man) before the Incarnation. So too in the case of the members of the body, there can be no preceding merits, or even fore-known merits, on the basis of which he has predestined the saints.

Furthermore, it is important to notice not only the connection Augustine draws between the predestination of Christ and that of Christians, but also the logical se-quence in which he draws it. If we step back from the comparisons themselves that I have analyzed and remember the context in which they come, we recognize of course that Augustine's point in his latest treatises is to explain the predestination of Christians to believe and to persevere. His logic of grace begins with the Fall, which makes the entire human race into one *massa damnata*, then moves to the predestination of the elect, and then justifies that predestination by describing the predestination of the humanity of Christ to be united with the Word. As a result,

---

[71] See Donato Ogliari, 'The Role of Christ and of the Church in the Light of Augustine's Theory of Predestination', *ETL* 79 (2003), 350, who argues that the reason Christ is an example of grace has to do not merely with the fact that he and Christians are both predestined, but with the hypostatic union by which God gives grace through his humanity to us. Similarly, Gérard Rémy, 'La christologie d'Augustin: cas d'ambiguïté', *RechSR* 96 (2008), 422, argues that one cannot symmetrically equate the predestining of an existing person to salvation and the predestining of Christ's humanity to be united to the Word. Augustine, he argues, understood this difference but was too quick to effect a seeming equa-tion of the two kinds of predestination.

[72] See Rebecca Harden Weaver, *Divine Grace and Human Agency: A Study of the Semi-Pelagian Controversy*, PMS 15 (Macon, GA: Mercer University Press, 1996), 57–8, who points out that the pre-destination of Christ's humanity to be united with the Word follows the same pattern as the predestin-ation of Christians to be the members of Christ's body.

for Augustine at the end of his life, what establishes the ultimate priority of divine grace in the salvation of human beings is not his Christology, even though it is a Christology of divine descent in connection with human incapacity to rise to God. Instead, what establishes that divine priority is the doctrine of predestination. This sequence and the corresponding centrality of predestination determine how Christology functions in Augustine's last writings. By placing the Incarnation after predestination in a logical sequence, the later Augustine sets himself up to focus on the particular effects of the Incarnation and redemption in the lives of the elect, not on any general or universal aspects that might apply to (or be offered to) all human beings. In a sense, at the end of Augustine's life his Christology functions in the service of his doctrine of predestination, and so he considers the effects of the Incarnation not in the human race as a whole, but primarily (or even only) in the predestined. To state this point even more directly, for the later Augustine the Incarnation does not accomplish a salvation that will be offered to all; instead, predestination logically predominates, and as a result, the Incarnation leads to faith and perseverance in the elect. For Augustine at the very end of his life, predestination drives the discussion of the spiritual life, just as it drives his discussion of Christology. As a result, it is not so much the case that his Christology leads to his understanding of grace as that his view of predestination controls the way he describes both Christology and grace.

Once one recognizes that for Augustine, the means to establishing the priority of grace is the teaching on predestination and that this priority dictates the way he connects Christology and grace, important questions arise about the Gallic monks and others who opposed his understanding of predestination. They certainly rejected the claim that there can be no preceding or foreseen merits related to grace. But was their disagreement limited to this point? Or did they disagree on this point because they held to a different Christology, one from which Augustine's logic of grace need not emerge? Or did they hold to a fundamentally similar Christology but reason with a different logic in establishing divine priority and linking Christology to grace and soteriology? (In other words, did a similar Christology function differently in their thought?) We saw in the Introduction that most discussions of the Gallic writers assume that their opposition to Augustine was unrelated to Christology, and thus that the answer to the first question above was 'yes' and the answers to the other two were both 'no'. But is this correct? Given that Augustine's doctrine of predestination led to objections in southern Gaul, we need to turn our attention to Marseilles and pay attention to Gallic Christology (or Christologies, as the case may have been).

2

Leporius

A Crypto-'Pelagian', Proto-'Nestorian'?

While it was Augustine's teaching on predestination that drew the fire of the Gallic monks and started (or at least inflamed) the long·fifth-/sixth-century discussion on grace, his link between the predestined believers and Christ the predestined man was not the only logical connection—or at least purported logical connection—between Christology and grace that lay in the background to the 'Semi-Pelagian Controversy'. In the second decade of the fifth century,[1] a monk in Marseilles by the name of Leporius[2] wrote a letter (not extant today)[3] that contained certain Christological mistakes. Leporius was rebuked by Proculus (bishop of Marseilles) and Cillenius (a bishop from elsewhere in Gaul) and was banned from the region. He wound up in Latin North Africa, where Augustine and three other African bishops (Aurelius of Carthage, Florentius of Hippo Diarrhytus, and Secundus, a bishop in Numidia) corrected him. Leporius then published a document, *Lib. emend.*,[4] in which he explains his previous mistake and professes his current understanding of Christ's person. At about the same time, Augustine wrote to Proculus on behalf of the African bishops to explain the situation, and he urged them to receive Leporius back into fellowship.[5]

For our purposes, three aspects of this case are important. First, the Christology for which Leporius was expelled from Gaul, which he later recanted under the tutelage of Augustine and others, offers a window into what was considered

---

[1] Scholars date these events as early as 410 and as late as 428. The consensus is 418, and I shall discuss the significance of the dating later in this chapter.

[2] Leporius may have originally been from Trier (Trêves) in what is today western Germany near the border with Luxembourg and France. Cassian refers to the Leporian Christological error as having sprung up *ex maxima Belgarum urbe*. See Cassian, *De incar. Dom.* 1.2 (CSEL 17.238) [*NPNF²* 11.552]. Cf. Roland Demeulenaere, Preface to 'Leporii, *Libellus emendationis*', in CCSL 64.97. On the other hand, Torsten Krannich, *Von Leporius bis zu Leo dem Großen: Studien zur lateinischsprachigen Christologie im Fünften Jahrhundert nach Christus*, Studien und Texte zu Antike und Christentum 32 (Tübingen: Mohr Siebeck, 2005), 14–18, argues that the text of that passage from Cassian is corrupted and that he is actually referring to Constantinople.

[3] Leporius mentions this letter three times, in *Lib. emend.* 2, 8, and 9 (CCSL 64.112, 119, 120).

[4] Found in CCSL 64.111–23. There is a German translation in Krannich, *Von Leporius bis zu Leo dem Großen*, 213–31. R. Weijenborg, 'Leo der Grosse und Nestorius: Erneuerung der Fragestellung', *Augustinanum* 16 (1976), 353–98, argues that the author of *Lib. emend.* was actually Leo, then archdeacon of Rome. For a detailed defence of Leporian authorship, see Krannich, *Von Leporius bis zu Leo dem Großen*, 20–42.

[5] *Ep.* 219 (CSEL 57.428–31) [WSA II/4.69–71].

Christology and the Logic of Grace in Fifth-Century Gaul. Donald Fairbairn, Oxford University Press.
© Donald Fairbairn 2025. DOI: 10.1093/9780198936220.003.0003

50   CHRISTOLOGY AND THE LOGIC OF GRACE

unacceptable in both Gaul and Africa and may also indicate possible connections of ideas with later Nestorianism. Second is the question of whether Leporius's Christological errors were connected to grace-related mistakes, possibly even to 'Pelagianism' itself. Third, Leporius's Christology after his correction can help to clarify our understanding of the state of Latin Christology in the early fifth century. In this chapter, I shall consider these issues.[6] As I do so, I shall rely on Leporius's *Lib. emend.*, Augustine's *Ep.* 219 to the Gallic bishops urging them to accept Leporius back into fellowship, Cassian's treatment of the Leporian case at the beginning of *De incar. Dom.*,[7] and the brief paragraph about Leporius written at the end of the fifth century by Gennadius of Marseilles in *De uir. illust.* Before I consider these three aspects of the Leporian case, I shall need to address briefly the question of when *Lib. emend.* was written.

The Date of *Lib. emend.*

Early twentieth-century scholarship tended to place the case of Leporius in the mid-420s or even as late as 428.[8] However, in 1965, Maier conclusively demonstrated that a date in the 420s was not possible by showing that Augustine's Sermon 396—a funeral oration for Bishop Florentius of Hippo Diarrhytus, one of the signers of *Lib. emend.*—was preached on 17 April 419. Maier argues that the date

---

[6] It is worth noting that somewhat later than the affair of Leporius, a similar case arose in Spain. There exists a letter, *Ep. Vit. Const.* (PL 53.847–9), dating to about 431, from two Spanish monks, Vidal and Tonancio (Vitalis and Constantius in Latin), to Bishop Capreolus of Carthage. The letter claims that certain unnamed people in Spain refuse to say God was born. Instead, they believe that Christ was born from the Virgin Mary as a mere man, and afterwards God dwelt in him. In contrast, Vidal and Tonancio affirm that God himself was in Mary's womb, that he was himself made man, and that he was born as true God and true man whom he assumed for the salvation of the human race. Capreolus responds with his second letter (PL 53.849–58); his first had been addressed to the Council of Ephesus and had been read out at the council (*ACO* 1.1.2.52–4) [TTH 72.278–9]. Capreolus links the view of the unnamed Spanish heretics with Nestorianism, which has by this point recently been condemned at the Council of Ephesus. He argues further that while God certainly dwelt in the patriarchs, prophets, apostles, and saints, this indwelling was not the same as the way the fullness of deity dwelt in Christ. In the other cases, the indwelling was that of another and from the outside, whereas in Christ the indwelling was that of his own divinity, since he was Son of God who became Son of man. See the discussion of this correspondence in Angel C. Vega, 'Vidal y *Tonancio* o un caso de nestorianismo en Espana', *CD* 152 (1936), 412–20. See also Palémon Glorieux, 'Prenestorianisme en Occident', in *Monumenta Christiana Selecta* 6 (Tournai: Desclée, 1959).

[7] George A. Bevan, 'Augustine and the Western Dimensions of the Nestorian Controversy', *StPatr* 49 (2010), 350, argues that Cassian 'deliberately misrepresents Leporius' views' to make them sound closer to Nestorius, so as to be able to tie Nestorius to Pelagius, with whom Leporius has already been associated. Bevan regards Augustine's *Ep.* 219 as a better indication of Leporius's views, but he does not indicate how *Ep.* 219 gives a different picture of Leporius than Cassian does. It is simpler to accept that Leporius, Nestorius, and Pelagius do in fact have some general ideas in common, as we shall see in this chapter and the next one.

[8] For a list of scholars, articles, and dates assigned to the case, see Jean-Louis Maier, 'La Date de la rétractation de Leporius et celle du "Sermon 396" de Saint Augustin', *REAug* 11 (1965), 40.

of the *Libellus* was in April or May of 418.[9] In 1985, Roland Demeulenaere pronounced a date of 418 or perhaps early 419 as definitely established.[10]

However, in 1989, Mathisen made a very different suggestion, starting from the oddity that Pelagius is not mentioned in *Lib. emend.* but that Cassian later gives great emphasis to a Leporian/Pelagian connection at the beginning of *De incar. Dom.* Mathisen suggests that this oddity can best be explained by assuming that the case of Leporius actually took place before Pelagius was known in Latin North Africa. If the case occurred *c.*410–413, Mathisen argues, Augustine would have been responding to Christology alone, the only aspect of Leporius's belief that he found objectionable. But later, Cassian—attuned to 'Pelagianism'—would have emphasized both the Nestorian/Leporian connection and the Pelagian/Leporian link.[11] Mathisen's proposal is very intriguing, but a potential problem with it is that Cassian is not known to have been in Marseilles in the early 410s. In *De incar. Dom.*, he comments that Leporius was 'admonished by us' (*a nobis admonitus*),[12] giving the impression that Cassian himself was part of the group of Gallic leaders who rebuked and excommunicated Leporius. This assertion could be merely a rhetorical flourish or even a careless comment, but if we may tentatively assume it is a statement of fact, then the date Cassian arrived in Marseilles becomes relevant to the dating of *Lib. emend.* Scholars place his arrival anywhere from 409 to 419, and the consensus seems to be between 415 and 417.[13] This consensus fits well with a date of 418 or early 419 for *Lib. emend.*, but it makes Mathisen's suggestion of 410–13 impossible if Cassian was involved in the rebuke of Leporius. I believe we need to retain a date of 418 or 419 for *Lib. emend.*, and thus we should assume that at the time Augustine corrected Leporius, the Pelagian Controversy was at the forefront of his mind. As a result, the lack of reference to Pelagius in *Lib. emend.* must be explained in another way, and I shall return to that question later in this chapter as I consider a possible connection between Leporius's Christological mistake and 'Pelagianism'.

---

[9] Maier, 'La Date de la rétractation de Leporius', 40–2.

[10] Demeulenaere, Preface to 'Leporii, *Libellus emendationis*', in CCSL 64: 99. See also Krannich, *Von Leporius bis zu Leo dem Großen*, 18–20.

[11] Ralph W. Mathisen, *Ecclesiastical Factionalism and Religious Controversy in Fifth-Century Gaul* (Washington, DC: The Catholic University of America Press, 1989), 128.

[12] Cassian, *De incar. Dom.* 1.3 (CSEL 17.241) [*NPNF*² 11.553].

[13] See Henri Irénée Marrou, 'Jean Cassien à Marseille', in *RMAL* 1 (1945), 5–26. See also Rebecca Harden Weaver, *Divine Grace and Human Agency: A Study of the Semi-Pelagian Controversy*, PMS 15 (Macon, GA: Mercer University Press, 1996), 77, esp. n.16.

52 CHRISTOLOGY AND THE LOGIC OF GRACE

Leporian Christology prior to His
Correction—Proto-'Nestorianism'?

In a lengthy treatment of Leporius published in 1964, Francis De Beer showed that at the root of the monk's Christological mistakes lay a pious and profoundly orthodox concern for divine majesty. A genuine incarnation might seem to place divine transcendence in peril, and Leporius was reticent about affirming that God might take upon himself a condition characterized by infirmities, by the need to eat, to grow, and so forth.[14] This admirable starting point pushed Leporius to describe the person of Christ in a way that amounted to a denial of a genuine incarnation. Early in *Lib. emend.*, Leporius himself explains:

> Although we did not deny that Christ, the Son of God, was born from the holy Mary, as we ourselves remember, yet by attending only minimally to the mystery of the faith, we said not that God himself was born as a man (*non ipsum Deum hominem natum*), but that a complete man was born with God (*sed perfectum cum Deo natum hominem*), because we were surely afraid of assigning the human condition to the divinity (*diuinitati conditionem assignaremus humanam*). O foolish wisdom! As if God would not despise being born with man (*cum homine ... nasci*), he who had himself dismissed, because of his status, the possibility of being born as a man (*nasci homo*), or that he could do the former, but as it turns out, he could not do the latter.[15]

Here we see that for Leporius, the issue in Christological orthodoxy was not simply the affirmation of divine and human in Christ or the degree of emphasis placed on divinity and humanity. Instead, the issue was the identity of the one who was born from Mary, the one who lived through the human experiences and therefore the one to whom we ascribe the *conditio humana*. In what the later Leporius calls 'foolish wisdom', the earlier Leporius spoke not of God the Word being born as a man himself (*ipsum*), but of the birth of a complete man with God. Why was this way of speaking foolish? Because it did not actually succeed in protecting the dignity of God. If it had been beneath God's dignity to be born *as* a man, it would also have been beneath his dignity to be born *with* a man.

Shortly afterwards, Leporius explains his earlier thought more fully:

> Therefore, since we so poorly recognize this power of God and consider ourselves wise in our minds and our own understanding, and fearing lest it seem that God was doing something unworthy of himself, we state that a man was born with God

---

[14] Francis De Beer, 'Une Tessère d'orthodoxie. Le "Libellus Emendationis" de Leporius' (Vers 418–421)', *REAug* 10 (1964), 150–4. See also Trapé, 'Un caso de nestorianismo prenestoriano', 51.
[15] *Lib. emend.* 2 (CCSL 64.113). All translations from *Lib. emend.* are my own.

(*hominem cum Deo natum esse*), so that we may ascribe what belongs to God separately solely to God (*ut seorsum quae Dei sunt soli Deo demus*) and may render what belongs to man separately solely to the man (*seorsum quae sunt hominis soli homini reputemus*). In doing so, we most obviously introduce a fourth person in the Trinity and we begin to make of the one Son not one but two Christs. May Christ our Lord and God himself now deliver us from this.[16]

In this passage it becomes clear that Leporius's purpose for the language of 'a man born with God' was so that he might treat the man and the Word separately, ascribing the characteristics of each one solely to that one. The post-correction Leporius claims that this constituted adding a fourth person to the Trinity and making of the one Son two Christs. We should remember from the previous chapter that during the mid-410s, Augustine began to be explicitly concerned to guard against the idea of turning the Trinity into a quaternity,[17] and this issue was a significant part of Augustine's argument as he corrected Leporius.[18] (The fact that Augustine turned to this concern in the middle of the decade provides additional evidence against a date of 410–13 for *Lib. emend.*)

But why would one think that affirming a man born with God might constitute adding a fourth person to the Trinity? If the Son is fully God, one of the persons of the Trinity, and the man Jesus is completely separate, not divine in any way, then the Trinity remains intact. But basically no one in the early church would admit such a complete separation between the Word and the man. On the other hand, if the man Jesus *is* the eternal Son, then again—in an utterly different way—the Trinity remains fixed at three persons. However, if one says—as Leporius did at first—that a quasi-independent man was born with God the Son, such that there is enough identity between the man and the Son that Christ the man can be called divine in some sense, yet not enough identity that the man Christ can be said to be the Son himself, then one could be heard as implying that there are four persons in the Godhead. Whether it is fair to draw such an inference from anyone's Christological thought is not the question; instead, the issue is whether such an inference could be imagined at all. Evidently it could be imagined and was so drawn, because Augustine felt compelled both to defend himself against such charges *c*.415 and, a few years later, to lead Leporius away from expressions that might tend in that direction.

For our purposes, the question at this point is whether Leporius's early mistake amounted to proto-'Nestorianism'. Of course, Cassian saw his thought as Nestorian, and I shall examine Cassian's argument in some detail in the next chapter of this

---

[16] *Lib. emend.* 3 (CCSL 64.113–14).
[17] See Augustine, *Ep.* 169.7–8 (CSEL 44.616) [WSA II/3.110], discussed in chapter 1.
[18] See Augustine, *Ep.* 219.1 (CSEL 57.428–9) [WSA II/4.69], where he explains that Leporius did not see that he was introducing a fourth person into the Trinity.

54   CHRISTOLOGY AND THE LOGIC OF GRACE

book. But most scholars deny the connection Cassian draws. Krannich argues that Cassian placed his own (mis-)understanding of Nestorius onto Leporius.[19] Similarly, Teske comments, 'Though Leporius taught certain views that are similar to those of Nestorius, there is no clear evidence that he was a Nestorian before Nestorius.'[20] But opinions such as these beg the question of what 'clear evidence' would look like, given that one is trying to assess whether an obscure monk held to the same heresy as a famous heresiarch who had not yet appeared on the scene. There could not be any evidence linking Leporius to Nestorius by name—in c.418 Nestorius was just as obscure as Leporius was, and some 2,700 kilometres away. Likewise, there would not be any evidence from the slightly later Eastern church linking Nestorius to Leporius—the Gallic monk was never well enough known in the East for such a link to occur to anyone. Any explicit connection could come only from someone close enough to the situation in Marseilles to know who Leporius was, yet conversant enough with the great debate later waged to the East (in Greek, no less) to see potential connections. In short, Cassian was the only one who could have made a direct connection by name, and if we are going to regard his evidence suspiciously, then we have no option but to conclude that there is no 'clear evidence' of a direct connection.

Much more important than any sort of direct, named connection, however, is a genuine link between the ideas of the early Leporius and the slightly later Nestorius. On this point, Émille Amann argued that *Lib. emend.* provides evidence in the West of an initial Nestorian work, quickly corrected by the vigilance of the Gallic bishops and the lucidity of Augustine.[21] On the other hand, De Beer insists that Leporius should be relieved of any suspicion of Nestorianism, even at the level of ideas. Leporius, De Beer claims, never thought in terms like those of Nestorius (or Pelagius) but rather that he was a monk 'tout pénétré du sentiment de la majesté divine'.[22] Grillmeier sides with Amann but gives much more specificity, as he argues that Leporius's theological doubts were the same as those of Nestorius later: Leporius did not agree with the *communicatio idiomatum* and was perplexed by references to a born and crucified God. He wanted to protect the traditional dogma of Christ's deity from doctrines that supposedly confused the natures. In fact, Grillmeier suggests that Augustine's tact and skill in handling the Leporian case was a significant factor preventing that case from becoming a major scandal as the case of Nestorius did later.[23] Augustine, Grillmeier argues, taught

---

[19]   Krannich, *Von Leporius bis zu Leo dem Großen*, 57.

[20]   Roland Teske, Introduction to Augustine, *Ep.* 219, in WSA II/4.69n.2.

[21]   Émile Amann, 'Léporius', in *DTC* 9/1 (1926), 439.

[22]   De Beer, 'Une Tessère d'orthodoxie', 184.

[23]   Alloys Grillmeier, *Christ in Christian Tradition, Vol. 1: From the Apostolic Age to Chalcedon (451)*, trans. John Bowden (London: Mowbrays, rev. ed. 1975), 464–6. It is also worth noting that in a similar opinion, Brian Daley describes Leporius's early difficulty as 'a scruple about the Christian notion of a genuinely incarnate God—a scruple shared at the time by a number of Greek theologians who belonged to what we know today as the "school of Antioch"'. See Brian E. Daley, *God Visible: Patristic Christology*

Leporius to refer the Incarnation to the person of the Son, not to the divine nature as a whole, and thus to distinguish the natures while still seeing the person of Christ as the Word himself. He continues, 'Under the guidance of Augustine, Leporius learnt the right grasp of the subject of the incarnation. The incarnation is the "descent of the Logos" and not a gradual "ascent of a mere man". There is *one person* in Godhead and in manhood, and so both the human and the divine can be predicated of this one person.'[24]

Is Grillmeier right on this point? We should remember that protecting the Logos from human experiences was a major motivating factor in Nestorius's thought as well that of Leporius. Nestorius reacted viscerally to the idea that God could be born, nurse, or grow up, and in particular, he insisted that divine impassibility made it impossible for the Logos to suffer and die. Moreover, for Nestorius, as for Theodore before him, the drama of salvation was primarily about the ascent of humanity—first the man Jesus ascended as our trailblazer, and then we follow him in ascent as well. One could also say of Nestorius and of Theodore before him that they too, like Leporius, were monks 'completely penetrated with the sentiment of divine majesty', in De Beer's memorable phrase. One could reasonably conclude that such concern for the impassible majesty of God, coupled with a soteriology of ascent in which there was less felt need to focus on divine descent, led all of them to describe the incarnate Christ in a way that kept the Word far removed from experiences they considered unworthy of him. I believe we can conclude that at the level of ideas, there was a strong connection between the concerns that undergirded Theodorean/Nestorian Christological thought and the thought of the early Leporius. To investigate this tentative conclusion more fully, we need to do two further things—first, to look for hints of an understanding of grace and salvation focusing on divine ascent in the earlier Leporius, and second, to look for confirmation in Leporius's statements of what he believes after his correction. I turn now to the first of those tasks.

Reconsidered, Changing Paradigms in Historical and Systematic Theology (Oxford: Oxford University Press, 2018), 156.

[24] Grillmeier, *Christ in Christian Tradition, Vol. 1*, 466. Grillmeier goes on to argue on 466–7: 'In the East, however, the basic presuppositions which helped to resolve the case of Leporius with so little friction were available neither to Nestorius nor to his opponents. To be an Augustine to the Patriarch of Constantinople would surely have been a difficult, though a useful task. Unfortunately, there was no such person even in Rome when his case was initiated there.'

56 CHRISTOLOGY AND THE LOGIC OF GRACE

The Early Leporian Understanding of Grace and Salvation—Crypto-'Pelagianism'?

Cassian not only linked Leporian thought to Nestorianism: he also linked the Gallic monk's pre-correction teaching to Pelagianism, and in the process linked Nestorianism to Pelagianism. Near the beginning of *De incar. Dom.*, Cassian writes that Leporius's mistakes sprang from Pelagianism, and he continues:

> In saying that Jesus Christ had lived as a mere man without any stain of sin, they actually went so far as to declare that men could also be without sin if they liked. For they imagined that it followed that if Jesus Christ being a mere man was without sin, all men also could without the help of God (*sine dei adiutorio*) be whatever he was as a mere man without participating in the Godhead (*ille homo solitarius sine consortio dei esse potuisset*), could be. And so they made out that there was no difference between any man and our Lord Jesus Christ, as any man could by effort and striving obtain just the same as Christ had obtained by His earnestness and efforts.[25]

Here Cassian makes two charges that are surely unfair: that Leporius and Pelagius see Christ as a mere man (he makes the same unfair charge against Nestorius, and I shall return to this charge later), and that they see both Christ and Christians as being able to obtain sinless perfection apart from grace. But if we grant the unfairness of the accusations and acknowledge the hyperbolic language, I suggest that the gist of Cassian's criticism is that Leporius, like Pelagius (and like Nestorius as well), saw salvation as a human action of ascending to perfection, rather than as a divine descent enabling human participation (*consortio*) in God. This charge, although exaggerated, concurs well with Grillmeier's assessment of Leporius's earlier thought as an idea of the ascent of mankind rather than the descent of the Word. In Cassian's mind, Leporius's early thought amounted to crypto-'Pelagianism'.

Writing at the end of the fifth century, Gennadius of Marseilles likewise argued that Leporius's Christological mistakes grew out of 'Pelagianism'. He writes: 'Because he relied on that purity of life (*praesumens de puritate vitae*) that came through his own great free will and effort (*quam arbitrio tantum et conatu proprio*), he did not rely on obtaining for himself the help of God (*non Dei se adjutorio obtinuisse crediderat*), and thus he began to follow the Pelagian doctrine (*Pelagianum dogma coeperat sequi*).'[26] It is reasonable to assume that Gennadius is relying largely, if not completely, on Cassian for this assessment.

---

[25] Cassian, *De incar. Dom.* 1.3 (CSEL 17.239–40) [*NPNF*[2] 11.553].
[26] Gennadius, *De uir. illust.* 59 (60) (PL 58.1092) [*NPNF*[2] 3.395]. This is my translation, not the one in NPNF.

Of course, most scholars have denied the validity of Cassian's (and Gennadius's) charge. In an illustrative assertion, Amann points out that there is no direct reference to Pelagius in *Lib. emend.*,[27] and at that date (*c.*418), if there had been any suspicion of a Pelagian connection, Augustine would surely have made him explicitly renounce Pelagianism.[28] This omission has convinced virtually all scholars. Perhaps most striking is the comment of Charles Brand that Cassian's link between Leporius and Pelagius was an attempt to deflect attention away from the accusation that *he himself* was a Pelagian.[29] Similarly, Grillmeier, who does entertain a connection of ideas between Nestorianism and Leporian thought, admits no such connection with Pelagianism.[30] More recently, Krannich points out that Leporius was thought of as a Pelagian by those in fifth-century Gaul but argues that there is no proof Leporius actually was a Pelagian.[31]

Another opinion comes from Mathisen, who as we have already seen interprets the silence about Pelagius in *Lib. emend.* to mean that the work was written early in the 410s, before Augustine became aware of Pelagius.[32] More generally, we saw in the Introduction to this work that Mathisen understands anti-Pelagianism in Gaul as a rhetorical device to unify the Gallic clergy who are at odds with each other on non-theological matters.[33] This interpretation blunts the force of Mathisen's willingness to grant Cassian's connection between Leporius and 'Pelagianism'. If one is going to argue that the link is real but is more rhetorical than genuinely theological, that amounts to the same thing as saying that the link is of little consequence for our Christological and charitological concerns in this book.

Thus, the general scholarly consensus is that if there had been any connection between Leporian thought and 'Pelagianism', Augustine could not have failed to direct Leporius to condemn Pelagius in *Lib. emend.* Mathisen's alternate suggestion—that *Lib. emend.* was written earlier, before Augustine knew of Pelagius—should be regarded as a concurring opinion rather than an opposing one, because Mathisen still sees the Leporian/Pelagian connection as more rhetorical than theologically significant. But are these the only options? I suggest not. Instead, I suggest that 'Augustine's' silence about Pelagius (that is, the failure of *Lib. emend.* to mention him by name) could have resulted simply from Augustine's

---

[27] The list of heretics Leporius renounces near the end of the work contains the following names: Photinus, Arius, Sabellius, Eunomius, Valentinus, Apollinaris, and the Manichees. There is no mention of Pelagius. See *Lib. emend.* 10 (CCSL 64.122).

[28] Amann, 'Léporius', in *DTC* 9/1 (1926), 437. See also Amann, 'L'affaire Nestorius vue de Rome', in *RevSR* 23 (1949), 229–30.

[29] Charles Brand, 'Le *De Incarnatione Domini* de Jean Cassien: Contribution à l'étude de la christologie en Occident à la vielle du concile d'Éphèse', Ph.D. Dissertation, Université de Strasbourg, 1954, 155. For my response to Brand's contention, see Donald Fairbairn, *Grace and Christology in the Early Church*, OECS (Oxford: Oxford University Press, 2003), 171.

[30] Grillmeier, *Christ in Christian Tradition, Vol. 1*, 465.

[31] Krannich, *Von Leporius bis zu Leo dem Großen*, 55–60.

[32] See Mathisen, *Ecclesiastical Factionalism and Religious Controversy in Fifth-Century Gaul*, 128.

[33] See Ibid., 37–41.

ignorance of the Pelagian underpinnings to Leporius's Christology, even though such underpinnings may have been there. Augustine and the other North African bishops who corrected Leporius had relatively little information to work from: a letter of Leporius (non-extant today) and whatever Leporius himself told them about his situation. It is hardly unreasonable to suppose that Leporius would have withheld from the African bishops some of the backstory. If the letter that got Leporius into trouble dealt primarily with Christology, and if the condemnation by the Gallic bishops likewise focused on Christology, then Augustine (and thus *Lib. emend.*) would have focused more or less exclusively on Christology, as we see to be the case. But if the Gallic writers knew from personal experience and/or other sources that there was also a grace-related problem with Leporius's thought, they might well have emphasized that problem in their own later summaries of the affair. In fact, at least Cassian, and perhaps also the Gallic bishops, knew Leporius personally and were in a very good position to know whether he had crypto-'Pelagian' tendencies as well as proto-'Nestorian' ones.

This suggestion is, of course, not provable. Even if the Leporian letter that started the dust-up were to be rediscovered, and even if it were in fact found to be silent on Pelagius, that silence could be understood by saying there is no connection between Leporian Christology and Pelagianism just as easily as by saying that there was a connection, but Augustine did not know of it. What this suggestion does accomplish, however, is to break the seemingly ironclad link between *Lib. emend.*'s silence on Pelagius and the assertion that there can be no connection between Leporian thought and 'Pelagianism'. The common scholarly opinion amounts to arguing against what Cassian and Gennadius *directly* assert—that Leporius's mistakes began with grace-related, 'Pelagian'-style problems—because of an assumption about what Augustine *must have done* if such a link were present. If there were such a link, the scholarly consensus assumes, Augustine would have known about it, and he would have acted accordingly. But it is simply not true that Augustine *must have known* about such a connection if it were genuinely present, and thus it is not true that the absence of an expected reaction from Augustine proves that no such connection was present. It proves only that Augustine did not know of such a connection.

Therefore, I argue that my alternative explanation—admittedly not proven—should lead us to take the Gallic assertions about Leporius's Pelagian past with at least some seriousness. My suggestion surely accounts for the known facts better than Brand's ingenious but implausible claim that Cassian is manufacturing a Leporian/Pelagian connection to hide his own Pelagian sympathies, and it arguably accounts for the presence of Cassian's claim better than simply saying he was wrong. On the face of it, one should admit that it is plausible to suppose that Leporius *did* have 'Pelagian' tendencies, that the Gallic bishops (and Cassian) knew of them, and that Leporius not surprisingly did not divulge those ideas as he spoke to Augustine and others after his expulsion from Gaul.

Even if one will grant the possibility of my suggestion, is there any positive evidence in its favour? I believe there is. Although *Lib. emend.* does not name Pelagius and does not emphasize grace-related ideas, the document does not ignore such ideas altogether. Late in the document, in the last of the three passages in which Leporius mentions his previous letter, he admits grudgingly that he has made another error in addition to the Christological ones he has previously described:

> In addition, I suppose I should acknowledge briefly that in the same letter in which I deviated, I added by a similar error, that as Christ our Lord fulfilled all things related to his passion, he as a complete man was not helped by divine aid in anything (*in nullo quasi perfectus homo a diuinitatis auxilio iuuaretur*), for I obviously wanted to consider Christ a complete man (*hominem . . . perfectum*), so that I might protect the Word of the Father from his sufferings (*et alienum ab his passionibus Verbum Patris assererem*), and I was trying to affirm that man alone, in and of himself (*solum per se hominem*), accomplished all these things by means of the capacity of his mortal nature (*possibilitate naturae mortalis*), without any kind of divine help (*sine aliquo deitatis adiutorio*).[34]

Much of this passage concerns Christological problems that Leporius has enumerated earlier—his previous desire to protect the Word from suffering and his corresponding belief that God assumed a quasi-independent man. But here we also see something else: a 'similar error' to the effect that the man Christ was 'not helped by divine aid in anything' as he underwent the passion.

The language here is strikingly similar to the way Cassian and later Gennadius describe Leporius's earlier belief—so striking, in fact, that it is worth placing the three comments side by side.

Leporius, *Lib. emend.* 9	Cassian, *De incar. Dom.* 1.3	Gennadius, *De uir. illust.* 59
I was trying to affirm that man alone, in and of himself (*solum per se hominem*), accomplished all these things by means of the capacity of his mortal nature (*possibilitate naturae mortalis*), without any kind of divine help (*sine aliquo deitatis adiutorio*).	For they imagined that it followed that if Jesus Christ being a mere man was without sin, all men also could without the help of God (*sine dei adiutorio*) be whatever he was as a mere man without participating in the Godhead (*ille homo solitarius sine consortio dei esse potuisset*).	Because he relied on that purity of life (*praesumens de puritate vitae*) that came through his own great free will and effort (*quam arbitrio tantum et conatu proprio*), he did not rely on obtaining for himself the help of God (*non Dei se adjutorio obtinuisse crediderat*).

---

[34] *Lib. emend.* 9 (CCSL 64.120).

60 CHRISTOLOGY AND THE LOGIC OF GRACE

The passage from Leporius himself admits that he saw Christ as a man accomplishing the passion without help from God. The passage from Gennadius claims that Leporius and the Pelagians relied on themselves to accomplish salvation without help from God. Cassian attributes both ideas to Leporius—that Christ could accomplish salvation without God's help, and that we can do so as well. The crucial point, of course, is the link between the assertion about Christ and the assertion about the human race as a whole. In Leporius's own work, he does not make such a link,[35] but Cassian explicitly makes the link as he accuses Leporius of having been a Pelagian. Indeed, at the level of ideas, this is arguably the crucial link between Nestorianism (which focuses on the assumed man as the one who achieves salvation in general) and Pelagianism (which focuses on the capacity of the individual human being to accomplish salvation).

As much as we may dislike Cassian's invective and propensity for overstatement, we should not discount this potential link altogether, and the fact that Leporius himself *does* write something akin to what Cassian claims should make us wonder whether the pre-correction Gallic monk did hold to something like a crypto-'Pelagianism'. Perhaps Cassian's assessment of Leporius should be taken more seriously than it normally is. With this possibility in mind, it is time to turn our attention to Leporius's post-correction thought, which takes up most of *Lib. emend.*

Leporius's Thought after His Correction

After Leporius's most lengthy explanation of his previous belief in *Lib. emend.* 3 (discussed above), he turns in the same paragraph to an equally detailed description of what he believes now:

> Therefore, we confess Jesus Christ our Lord and God, the unique Son of God, who was born from the Father before the ages, and in the last time he, God, was made man and was born (*factum hominem Deum natum*) from the Holy Spirit and the ever-Virgin Mary. And while we confess each substance of the flesh and of the Word (*utramque substantiam carnis et Verbi*), we uphold with a pious faithful belief that he is one and the same, God and man inseparable (*unum eundemque Deum atque hominem inseparabilem*). And so we say that from the time of his assumption of flesh (*ex tempore susceptae carnis*), all things pertaining to God passed to man (*omnia . . . quae erant Dei transisse in hominem*), and all things

---

[35] It might be conceivable to say that Leporius does in fact make this link. If one were to take *homo* in the second half of the passage quoted above as a reference to the human race as a whole, not to Christ the man, then Leporius would in effect be claiming that both Christ and we can achieve salvation without the help of grace. But this is a very unlikely interpretation of *homo* in this passage. The subject throughout is Christ, and thus it is nearly certain that everywhere in this passage, the word *homo* is referring to Christ (most likely to the Word considered as a man), not to the human race as a whole.

pertaining to man came to God (*omnia quae erant hominis in Deum uenirent*). And it was in this sense that the Word was made flesh, not that by transformation or change (*conuersione aut mutabilitate*) he began to be something he was not, but that by the power of the divine economy, the Word of the Father, without in any way departing from the Father, deigned to be made genuine man (*homo proprie fieri dignaretur*), and the Only-Begotten became incarnate by that secret mystery that he himself knew. For it is ours to believe; his to know![36]

In this passage we see three major Christological emphases. One is a focus on what could be called 'verbal symmetry', so common in Latin Christology. Leporius affirms that 'all things pertaining to God passed to man, and all things pertaining to man came to God'. This sort of verbal symmetry might lead one to believe that Leporius (and the many others who use this sort of literary device) are primarily concerned with affirming and appropriately stressing deity and humanity in Christ. A second emphasis is the distinction between the two substances in the incarnate Christ (*utramque substantiam carnis et Verbi*). This distinction, coupled with the consistent use of the word *substantia* to indicate each of the realities in the incarnate Christ, is a major strength of Latin Christology at this time when the Greeks were using the word φύσις in various confusing ways. In fact, the clarity that comes from this use of *substantia* largely overcomes the ambiguity that derives from the Latin use of *homo* in a variety of different ways.[37] Simply put, the reason we can recognize that the post-conversion Leporius is using *homo* to mean *caro* or *humana natura*—not to mean a quasi-independent man—is because his use of *substantia* controls his use of *homo*.

The other major Christological emphasis in this passage is the insistence that the person, the subject to whom all the human events happen, is none other than the Word, the eternal Son of God. Leporius declares that Jesus Christ is 'our Lord and God, the unique Son of God, who was born from the Father before the ages', not simply a man born with a unique connection to the Son of God, as he previously believed. He uses the phrase *unum eundemque* in the accusative case, which shows unambiguously that it is masculine and thus refers to a single *person*: the Son is one and the same as a person—the same person he has always been—even though now he has two substances after the Incarnation. Leporius concludes by asserting that it was the Only-Begotten who became incarnate, deigning to become genuine man without ceasing to be who he was as God. Clearly, Leporius's new Christology does not merely balance divine and human with appropriate emphasis given to each, but also locates the two substances in the single person of the Word. In this way, he

---

[36] *Lib. emend.* 3 (CCSL 64.114).
[37] Krannich, *Von Leporius bis zu Leo dem Großen*, 63, argues correctly that Leporius uses *homo* as a synonym for *caro* and *humana natura*. All three expressions refer to the assumed human nature, not to a quasi-independent man.

62 CHRISTOLOGY AND THE LOGIC OF GRACE

is able to speak of a true Incarnation, a genuine descent of the Word to the human sphere so as to bring the human race to salvation.

Leporius continues immediately:

> And thus God the Word himself, by receiving everything that belongs to man (*totum suscipiens, quod est hominis*), is made man (*homo sit*), and assumed man (*assumptus homo*), by receiving everything that belongs to God (*totum accipiendo, quod est Dei*), cannot be anything other than God. But although he is said to be incarnate and unmixed (*incarnatus . . . et inmixtus*), we must not allow any diminution of his substance. For God knows how to communicate himself without suffering any corruption, and yet truly to communicate himself. He knows how to receive into himself without himself being in any way increased, just as he knows how to impart (*infundere*) himself without himself suffering any loss.[38]

Here, as in Augustine's writings, we see the potentially ambiguous phrase *assumptus homo*, but in context, there can be no uncertainty. Leporius states that the way the Word was made man and assumed man was 'by receiving everything that belongs to man'. He also stresses that it was the Word himself who was made man. So, in this passage, *assumptus homo* must mean that the Word assumed a human nature, that is, a nature characterized by everything that belongs to mankind. Furthermore, the Word was made man without 'any diminution of his substance'. The Word was not turned into a man (ceasing to be God), nor was he merely with a man (as Leporius had previously thought). He became human by taking into himself all that pertains to humanity, without ceasing to be God or abandoning his divine substance. The potential ambiguity that could have resulted from the verbal symmetry of the previous passage or the use of the phrase *assumptus homo* in this one evaporates when these expressions are read together. The Incarnation was a downward movement of the Word by taking *humana natura* upon himself.

In par. 4 of *Lib. emend.*, Leporius turns to more technical Christological terminology. He writes:

> Therefore the flesh entered into the Word and not the Word into the flesh; and yet the Word was certainly made flesh. But as we have said, this properly happened only according to person (*personaliter*) and not according to nature with the Father and the Holy Spirit (*non cum Patre aut cum Spiritu Sancto naturaliter*), since the only-begotten God, true God who is one with the Father and the Holy Spirit in nature (*in natura*), is other in person (*alter est in persona*). For we do not say that the Father himself is who the Son is (*quem Filium*), nor again do we

---

[38] *Lib. emend.* 3 (CCSL 64.114–15).

say that the Son is the same one as the Father (*eundem Filium . . . quem Patrem*), nor again do we call the Holy Spirit the Father or the Son. But distinguishing the persons by what is proper to each (*in suis proprietatibus*), we call God the Father properly 'Father', and we say God the Son is properly 'Son', and we confess the Holy Spirit is properly 'God the Holy Spirit'. And when we say three times 'God and God and God', we believe not that there are three gods but that there is one perfection in his omnipotent Trinity.[39]

This passage begins by contrasting two ways of looking at the Incarnation. Leporius affirms that 'flesh entered into the Word', that is, that the Word assumed human nature into himself. Leporius rejects the idea that 'the Word enter into flesh', that is, that the Word indwelt a quasi-independent man. Then he builds on the use of *substantia* to distinguish deity and humanity in Christ by adding the synonymous word *natura*, and equally important, by clearly contrasting the concepts of substance/nature and person. We should recognize, of course, that *naturaliter* is contrasted with *personaliter*. (In grace-related discussions in Latin, the common usage is to distinguish what is by nature from what is by grace.) The taking of flesh was an event that happened to only one person, the Word, even though one may say that the entire Trinity was involved in the Incarnation. If the Incarnation were *naturaliter*, that would have meant that the Father and the Spirit also became incarnate. As Grillmeier has aptly summarized, 'It [*Lib. emend.*] states that the incarnation is to be regarded as a conjunction of human nature with the *person* of the Word, and not with the divine *nature*.'[40]

In par. 5 of *Lib. emend.*, Leporius addresses the completeness of Christ's two natures:

> Therefore, for us the Son of God was properly born from the Holy Spirit and the ever-Virgin Mary as the God-man Jesus Christ. And so the Word and the flesh became one in each other, so that although each substance remained naturally in its own completeness (*in sua perfectione naturaliter*) and without any diminution of its own, the divine [substance] might be communicated to the human [substance] (*humanitati diuina communicent*), and the human might participate in the divine (*diuinitati humana participent*). There is not one (*alter*) who is God and another one (*alter*) who is man, but the same God himself (*idem*) who is also man, and on the other hand, man who is also God (*homo qui et Deus*) is called and truly is Jesus Christ the only Son of God. And therefore, we must always take care to believe and not to deny that our Lord Jesus Christ, the Son of God (whom we confess to be true God who from before the ages has always been with the Father and equal to the Father) was the very one who received flesh and was made the

---

[39] *Lib. emend.* 4 (CCSL 64.115–16).
[40] Grillmeier, *Christ in Christian Tradition, Vol. 1*, 465, emphasis his.

64   CHRISTOLOGY AND THE LOGIC OF GRACE

God-man. We must believe not that over time he gradually advanced to the point of being God and thus held one status before the resurrection and another status after the resurrection, but that he always held the same fullness and power.[41]

This passage further clarifies any potential ambiguity surrounding the earlier symmetric language stating that everything belonging to man comes to God and everything belonging to God passes to man. Here, Leporius specifically states that in Christ there is not one person (*alter* is masculine) who is God and another person who is man. The distinction is at the level of natures/substances. Notice also the different verbs used to describe the exchange of properties between the substances. The divine is *communicated* to the human, but the human *participates* in the divine. Again, this is not a symmetric exchange. Rather, the movement is downward, from God to man: the Word communicates his divine nature to himself considered as a man, so that just as he (considered as a man) participates in his own divine nature, so we who are men and women may participate in his divine nature as well. Leporius contrasts this downward communication of divinity with the idea of an upwardly ascending Christ who advanced to the point of being God.

One could reasonably suggest that this statement implies a rebuttal of 'Pelagian' charitology/soteriology as well. If it is not possible for Christ to ascend from being man to being God, then it is surely not possible for anyone else to do so either. Human salvation requires the downward movement of God to communicate himself by grace to humanity. Just as a brief statement from later in *Lib. emend.* (discussed above) may indicate a connection between Leporius's earlier belief and 'Pelagianism', so also a brief statement here may indicate that in his post-correction thought, Leporius rejects the idea of the ascent of humanity to God. In neither case is the connection spelled out, because in both passages the subject is Christ, not the individual Christian. But it is possible that a connection is present.

In the following paragraph, Leporius returns to the fact that it was the Son, not the Father or Spirit, who became man, and he elaborates the implications of this truth:

For it was not God the Father who was made man, nor the Holy Spirit, but the Only-Begotten of the Father. So we must accept that there is one person (*una persona*) of the Word and flesh, so that we may believe faithfully and without any doubt that one and the same God the Son was always undivided and was spoken of as a giant of two-fold substance (*geminae substantiae etiam gigantem*). In the days of his flesh he also bore all things that belong to man (*omnia quae sunt hominis*), and he truly and always possessed the things that belong to God, *for he was crucified in weakness, but he lives by the power of God* [2 Cor. 13:4]. For this

---

[41] *Lib. emend.* 5 (CCSL 64.116).

reason we are not afraid to say that God was born from a human being (*ex homine natum Deum*), that God suffered as man (*secundum hominem Deum passum*), that God died (*Deum mortuum*), etc. But we are proud to say that God was born (*Deum natum*) and the same God suffered as man (*eundemque secundum hominem Deum passum*). *For I am not ashamed of the gospel*, says the Apostle, *for it is the power of God for the salvation of everyone who believes* [Rom. 1:16]. So it is the power of God to believe that God died as man (*secundum hominem credere Deum passum*).[42]

Throughout this passage, the 'he'—the subject who acts in Christ's life and to whom the human events happen—is God the Son. Affirming one person of a two-fold substance does not mean that the one person began to exist at the Incarnation. Rather, the person who was born, suffered, and died, was God.[43] He died *secundum hominem*, in terms of his humanity, but nevertheless, it was the eternal Second Person of the Trinity who died.[44]

These passages from *Lib. emend.* indicate that after his correction, Leporius explicitly rejects the idea of the Incarnation as a simple indwelling of the Word in the man Jesus. He instead sees the Incarnation as a downward movement of the Son to the human sphere by taking all that pertains to humanity into his own person.[45] In the process, Leporius makes a clear distinction between *substantia/natura* on one hand and *persona* on the other, and this terminological distinction helps to resolve

---

[42] *Lib. emend.* 6 (CCSL 64.117).

[43] Indeed, this is the thrust of the Ambrosian hymn *Veni, Redemptor Gentium*, which is likely the source of Leporius's language here. Verse 3 calls the one born from Mary *Deus* and verse 4 labels him *geminae gigans substantiae*. See Herman Adalbert Daniel, *Thesaurus Hymnologicus* (Leipzig: J.T. Loeschke, 1855), 1.12.

[44] Cf. Leporius's confession of faith in *Lib. emend.* 10 (CCSL 64.121–2): 'Therefore, I believe and confess according to the great mystery of piety that just as my Lord and God was born in the flesh (*in carne natum*), he also suffered in the flesh, died in the flesh, was raised in the flesh, ascended in the flesh, and was glorified in the flesh. I believe further that he himself is truly coming in the same flesh (*ipsum proprie in eadem carne*) to judge between the living and the dead. . . .' It is worth noting that Bernard Green, *The Soteriology of Leo the Great*, OTM (Oxford: Oxford University Press, 2008), 47, argues that the post-conversion Leporius believes the identity of Christ is the Word but that the *persona* of Christ is the union of divinity and humanity in the incarnate Word. It is not clear what Green means by this distinction, but it is possible that he intends something akin to what I mean when I write of the Word considered as a man after the Incarnation. The Word who before the Incarnation was simple—merely divine—has become complex—divine and human—but the acting subject is still the Word.

[45] David Maxwell summarizes Leporius's thought very similarly: 'The question of whether the man Christ accrues merit by natural human powers stands or falls on the question of whether there is an independent human subject in Christ. Leporius's insistence on the unity of Christ eliminates the possibility of viewing Christ as a paradigm of meriting salvation because talk of merit is nonsense when it is applied to a divine, omnipotent subject. Second, Leporius's rejection of the role of merit in the case of Christ brings with it a concern to maximize the distinction between Christ and the saints. Third, the recognition that God-made-man is the subject of all Christ's actions shifts Leporius's view of the Incarnation from primarily the ascent of the human to the divine to primarily the descent of God for the sake of human salvation.' See David R. Maxwell, 'Christology and Grace in the Sixth-Century Latin West: The Theopaschite Controversy' (Ph.D. Dissertation, University of Notre Dame, 2003), 41.

66   CHRISTOLOGY AND THE LOGIC OF GRACE

the ambiguity that results from his using the word *homo* in different, potentially confusing, ways.

Conclusions on Leporius, Augustine, and the Gallic Monastic World

Augustine's *Ep.* 219 indicates, of course, that he and other North African bishops corrected Leporius, and the letter's brief explanation of the issues concurs exactly with the longer exposition in *Lib. emend.* Augustine identifies the reason Leporius initially denied that the Word became man as 'fear, that is, that there would ensue a change or corruption of the divine substance, by which he is equal to the Father'.[46] Augustine also describes Leporius's post-correction thought the same way *Lib. emend.* does: 'But after he recognized that the Word of God, that is, the only-begotten Son of God, had become Son of Man in such a way that neither was changed into the other (*neutrum in alterum uersum*), but that, with each remaining in its own substance, God endured human sufferings in man in such a way that he retained in himself his divinity unimpaired, without any fear he confessed Christ as God and man'.[47] It is likely that Augustine not only spearheaded the correction of Leporius but also helped him write *Lib. emend.*, or even wrote it for him.[48]

At this point, we should notice that *Lib. emend.* is not only similar to Augustine's *Ep.* 219, but also remarkably consistent with the Chalcedonian/Cyrillian interpretation of Augustine's Christology as a whole. Both Leporius and Augustine use *homo* in varied ways, and indeed it is the use of *homo assumptus* in Augustine's writings that gave rise to the Antiochene/Nestorian interpretation of Augustine's Christology (and perhaps also of Latin Christology more generally). But Leporius's fuller discussions resolve any ambiguity that might have arisen from his use of *homo*. He sees the person of Christ as the Word himself and the Incarnation as a downward movement of the Word. I argued in the previous chapter that Augustine's Christology should be understood this way as well, and in fact, the clarity of *Lib. emend.* strengthens the case for a Chalcedonian/Cyrillian interpretation of Augustine. Since this is what Leporius wrote under Augustine's correction, surely it is also what Augustine himself meant in his own writings from the same time period that have been taken in various ways.

In spite of the congruence of Leporius's and Augustine's Christology, we do not have any indication of how Leporius's thought on grace might have connected

---

[46]   *Ep.* 219.1 (CSEL 57.428–9) [WSA II/4.69]. Cf. the elaboration in *Ep.* 219.3 (CSEL 57.430) [WSA II/4.70–1].

[47]   *Ep.* 219.3 (CSEL 57.430–1) [WSA II/4.71, translation modified].

[48]   But we should remember Weijenborg's claim that Leo was the author of *Lib. emend.* and Krannich's persuasive defence of Leporian authorship, mentioned in fn. 4 earlier in this chapter.

to Augustine's. The positive statement of Leporius's post-correction Christology has no direct mention of grace-related issues at all, nor does Augustine's *Ep.* 219. We have only the assertions of Cassian and Gennadius that Leporius had been a 'Pelagian'. Nevertheless, the prominence in *Lib. emend.* of the idea that the Incarnation was a downward movement of God suggests a framework for understanding grace in which any salvific human action must be preceded by that downward movement. Of course, there is no hint of whether the post-correction Leporius might have agreed with Augustine's logical link between the predestined man Christ and the predestined Christians. Thus, we have no way of knowing whether he might have reasoned from the Fall to predestination to grace (thus using predestination as the vehicle for asserting the priority of the divine in salvation), as the later Augustine did, or some other way.

Likewise, we have little evidence of how Leporius's later thought was received in Gaul. Augustine's *Ep.* 219 urging the Gallic bishops to receive Leporius back into communion did not elicit any response that is extant today, and Leporius remained in North Africa, rather than returning to Gaul. Cassian indicates that Leporius's later Christology concurred with that of Gaul,[49] and by linking Leporius's earlier Christology to 'Pelagianism,' Cassian also seems to imply that the resolution of his Christological problems also resolved his charitological mistakes. But beyond this, we have nothing to go on. Nevertheless, Leporius, like Augustine, stands in the background to the discussions that would soon publicly occupy the monastic world of Marseilles. It is now time to turn directly to Cassian, the first Masillian to link Christology to grace, to tie 'Nestorianism' to 'Pelagianism', and to connect Leporius to the entire complex of Christological and charitological ideas.

---

[49] In *De incar. Dom.* 1.6 (CSEL 17.245) [*NPNF*[2] 11.555], he writes, 'This confession of his therefore, which was the faith of all Catholics, was approved of by all the Bishops of Africa, whence he wrote, and by all those of Gaul, to whom he wrote (*et omnes Gallicani, ad quos scribebat*).'

3

John Cassian

'Nestorius', Grace, and the Monastic Life

The argument for calling Cassian a 'Semi-Pelagian' is based on the assumption that in his monastic corpus, and especially in *Conlat.* 13, Cassian seeks to balance his emphasis on divine and human action in salvation, and thus deserves to be placed somewhere between Pelagius and Augustine on a spectrum of emphases. This interpretation of Cassian is plausible only if one assumes that there is no particular connection between Cassian's Christology and his charitology, because his Christology, as evidenced in *De incar. Dom.*, is emphatically not a Christology of balanced emphasis on divine and human action.[1] But the assumption that there is no connection between Christology and grace in Cassian's mind is itself implausible, since Cassian is the one who most insistently connects Christological mistakes (those of Leporius and 'Nestorius') to charitological ones ('Pelagianism'). He above all others needs to be seen as affirming a connection, some sort of logic by which he moves from speaking of Christ to speaking of Christians and our salvation. If there is such a connection in Cassian's thought, it is certainly not the logic of Augustine, in which the predestination of both the man Christ and Christians links Christology and grace in a direct and seemingly monergistic way. So, what is the connection? What kind of logical move does Cassian make from his Christology to his understanding of grace and salvation? This is the question I shall tackle in this chapter. In order to address this question, I shall first consider what Cassian believes Nestorius's error consists of, then how he responds to it, relying on *De incar. Dom.* to address both issues. Then, acknowledging of course that *Conlat.* was written before Nestorius appeared on the scene, I shall turn back to *Conlat.* 13 to examine the way he writes of grace in connection to his Christology.

Cassian's Christology in *De incar. Dom.*

Given that Cassian's *De incar. Dom.* was the only Latin contribution to the Nestorian controversy of any significant length at all, one might have expected the work to garner a great deal of scholarly consideration. This has not been the case, and when

---

[1] Cassian's treatment of Christ's humanity is embarrassingly meagre. See Donald Fairbairn, *Grace and Christology in the Early Church*, OECS (Oxford: Oxford University Press, 2003), 187–8.

Christology and the Logic of Grace in Fifth-Century Gaul. Donald Fairbairn, Oxford University Press.
© Donald Fairbairn 2025. DOI: 10.1093/9780198936220.003.0004

the work has received attention, most of it has been negative. Nevertheless, it is important for our purposes to understand how Cassian perceived Nestorius's thought and how he formulated his own Christology in response to it.

De. incar. Dom. in Modern Scholarship

Cassian's *De incar. Dom.* has received far more condemnation than praise from modern scholars. One could adduce numerous examples, but let us be content here with two of the most famous and succinct. First, in his magisterial work on patristic Christology translated into English in 1975, Grillmeier laments, 'It is amazing how little Cassian, who probably came from Scythia Minor, the present Dobrogea, and had long remained in the East, could sympathize with Eastern theology. He himself is no great theologian.'[2] A quarter of a century later, in a work that overall is immensely favourable towards Cassian, Columba Stewart is even terser: 'A great work of Christology this is not.'[3]

There are numerous reasons for such dismissive attitudes, but foremost among them is the general scholarly opinion that Cassian has badly misunderstood Nestorius and treated him with gross unfairness. As far back as 1912, Jugie insisted that Cassian attributes to Nestorius doctrines that Nestorius expressly denied: that Christ is a mere man, that there is no difference between Christ and Adam, and that Christ was assumed by the Word later than at his conception.[4] Writing in 1950, Owen Chadwick contended, 'It makes pathetic reading, this passionate refutation of doctrines which his antagonist condemned as vigorously as he did. There would be piquant irony in it, if there were not tragedy.'[5] Writing in 1954, Amann declared that the polemical part of *De incar. Dom.* indicates that Cassian did not take the trouble to reconstruct Nestorius's thought and that the central argument—that Nestorius makes Christ to be a mere man who was elevated to divine status because of his merits—could be disproved from the sermons of Nestorius that Cassian certainly possessed.[6] In 1983 Karl-Heinz Kuhlman argued that 'Nestorianism' as Cassian represents it is not found in Nestorius himself.[7] In 1993 Vannier claimed that Cassian's work is based entirely on the premise that by denying the title

---

[2] Alloys Grillmeier, *Christ in Christian Tradition, Vol. 1: From the Apostolic Age to Chalcedon (451)*, trans. John Bowden (London: Mowbrays, rev. ed. 1975), 468.

[3] Columba Stewart, *Cassian the Monk*, OSHS (Oxford: Oxford University Press, 1998), 23.

[4] Martin Jugie, *Nestorius et la controverse nestorienne*, Bibliothèque de théologie historique (Paris: Beauchesne, 1912), 197–9.

[5] Owen Chadwick, *John Cassian: A Study in Primitive Monasticism* (Cambridge: Cambridge University Press, 1950), 157. This sentence is not present in the second edition from 1968, but Chadwick's assessment is no less bleak there.

[6] Émile Amann, 'L'affaire Nestorius vue de Rome', *RevSR* 23 (1949), 237–8.

[7] Karl-Heinz Kuhlmann, 'Eine Dogmengeschichtliche Neubewertung von Johannes Cassianus *De incarnatione Domini contra Nestorium libri 7*' (Th.D. Dissertation, University of South Africa, 1983), 172.

70   CHRISTOLOGY AND THE LOGIC OF GRACE

Theotokos, Nestorius is denying the deity of Christ and making him a mere man (*homo solitarius*) and that his defence of orthodoxy is riddled with errors.[8] Then in 1999 she elaborated on this by asserting that Cassian criticizes Nestorius unjustly for identifying Christ with Adam and for separating the man and the Son of God in Christ, for making two christs by not sufficiently uniting deity and humanity in the Saviour,[9] and she even suggested that Cassian's bitterness towards Nestorius may have stemmed partly from personal rancour towards a successor of Chrysostom in the see of Constantinople who opposed a group to which Cassian belonged, the fans of the previous bishop.[10] In 2003, Ogliari argued that instead of addressing the Christological questions, Cassian wrote a pamphlet intended to ruin Nestorius, and Ogliari also echoed Vannier's suspicions about Cassian's personal grudges.[11] Similarly, in 2005 Krannich argued not only that Cassian has misunderstood Nestorius, but that his own arguments are repetitive, circular rather than linear, and generally unconvincing.[12] And in 2008, Bernard Green called Cassian's accusations against Nestorius 'wild', labelled his link between Nestorius and Leporius a 'travesty', and concluded: 'Cassian found the heresies he expected to find in Nestorius; that probably led him to turn back to Pelagius and find the heresies he expected to find there.'[13]

These scholars certainly seem justified in criticizing Cassian for misrepresenting Nestorius. In *De incar. Dom.*, Cassian uses the phrase *solitarius homo* nearly forty times to describe Nestorius's teaching,[14] and perhaps most infamously of all, he cites Jesus's temptation by the devil and insists that the devil suspected Jesus was God even though he was also man. Cassian turns to Nestorius and inveighs: 'Learn then, you wretched madman, learn, you lunatic, you cruel sinner, learn, I pray, even from the devil, to lessen your blasphemy. He said: "If you are the Son of God." You say, "You are not the Son of God." You deny what he asked about. No one was ever yet found but you, to outdo the devil in blasphemy.'[15] It is certainly not true

---

[8] Marie-Anne Vannier, 'Jean Cassien a-t-il fait oeuvre de théologien dans le *De incarnatione Domini?*' *StPatr* 24 (1993), 351–2.

[9] Marie-Anne Vannier, Introduction to Jean Cassien, *Traité De L'incarnation Contre Nestorius: Introduction, traduction du latin et annotation par Marie-Anne Vannier*, Sagesses chrétiennes (Paris: Les Éditions du Cerf, 1999), 58.

[10] Ibid., 32.

[11] Donato Ogliari, *Gratia et Certamen: The Relationship Between Grace and Free Will in the Discussion of Augustine with the So-Called Semipelagians* (Leuven: Leuven University Press, 2003), 123–4.

[12] Torsten Krannich, *Von Leporius bis zu Leo dem Großen: Studien zur lateinischsprachigen Christologie im Fünften Jahrhundert nach Christus*, Studien und Texte zu Antike und Christentum 32 (Tübingen: Mohr Siebeck, 2005), 82–105, esp. 99.

[13] Bernard Green, *The Soteriology of Leo the Great*, OTM (Oxford: Oxford University Press, 2008), 28–35. The concluding quotation is on 33.

[14] E.g. *De incar. Dom.* 1.2 (CSEL 17.239) [*NPNF²* 11.552], 1.3 (CSEL 17.239–40) [*NPNF²* 11.552], 2.5 (CSEL 17.257) [*NPNF²* 11.561], 2.6 (CSEL 17.258–9) [*NPNF²* 11.561], 5.1 (CSEL 17.301–2) [*NPNF²* 11.580–1], 6.14 (CSEL 17.341) [*NPNF²* 11.598], 6.16 (CSEL 17.343) [*NPNF²* 11.599], 7.6 (CSEL 17.363) [*NPNF²* 11.608], 7.17 (CSEL 17.373) [*NPNF²* 11.613].

[15] *De incar. Dom.* 7.12 (CSEL 17.367–8) [*NPNF²* 11.610, translation slightly modified].

that Nestorius asserts of Christ, 'You are not the Son of God', that he claims Christ is *solitarius homo*, or that he believes Christ was adopted into deity at some point subsequent to his conception. Scholars can be forgiven for thinking that Cassian's invective is directed at a blatant caricature of what Nestorius actually teaches.[16]

Amidst this longstanding and broad chorus of dismissive scholarly voices, there have been at least two dissenters over the last couple of decades, Augustine Casiday and me. We have used different but complementary arguments to suggest that Cassian may not have misunderstood or misrepresented Nestorius as badly as most scholars assume, and it is worth recalling our arguments here. Writing in 2003, I argued that Cassian is not so naïve as to think that Nestorius actually says Christ was a mere man who was later adopted to sonship with God. Instead, Cassian believes that Nestorius's thought amounts to that, if one pushes that thought to its logical conclusions. I contend that the force of Cassian's charge that Nestorius sees Christ as adopted into sonship is not blunted simply by pointing out that Nestorius sees the union as beginning at Christ's conception. It is not merely the timing but the cause of the union that is Cassian's concern. If the Christological union is a simple conjunction of the *homo assumptus* with the Word based on the former's merits, Nestorius's thought still fails to pass muster with Cassian.[17] I conclude: 'If Christ is merely a man united to the Logos, and if this union depends, even to some degree, on the man's (foreseen) virtue, then the incarnation is no longer purely God's act of giving himself to us.'[18]

A few years later (2007), Casiday argued that Cassian's Christology in general and his portrayal of Nestorius in particular were caught up in the aggressive rehabilitation of Nestorius by scholars in the late nineteenth century and throughout the twentieth.[19] The discovery and publication of Nestorius's *Liber Heraclidis* led scholars to claim that the previously known writings and fragments of Nestorius were misleading, that his articulation of the Christological union was acceptable, and that his condemnation had little to do with his Christology and far more to do with ecclesiastical politics.[20] As it became common for scholars to argue that Nestorius's thought was actually unobjectionable, it also became seemingly necessary to argue that Nestorius could not have affirmed and did not affirm what

---

[16] Regarding the nature of the invective itself as a set of classical and patristic tropes for belittling an opponent, see Gerard Bartelink, 'Die Invektiven gegen Nestorius und seine Häresie in Cassianus' *De Incarnatione*', in *Heretics and Heresies in the Ancient Church and in Eastern Christianity: Studies in Honour of Adelbert Davids*, ed. Joseph Berheyden and Herman Teule, Eastern Christian Studies 10 (Leuven: Peeters, 2011), 275–91.

[17] See *De incar. Dom.* 5.1 (CSEL 17.301–2) [NPNF^s 11.580–1], and 7.8 (CSEL 17.364) [NPNF 11.609], both of which I quote and explain in Fairbairn, *Grace and Christology*, 180–2.

[18] Fairbairn, *Grace and Christology*, 182.

[19] Augustine Casiday, *Tradition and Theology*, OECS (Oxford: Oxford University Press, 2007), 216–26.

[20] For an especially strong statement—more recent than Casiday's work—of the idea that Nestorius was condemned purely for political reasons, see George A. Bevan, *The New Judas: The Case of Nestorius in Ecclesiastical Politics, 428–451 CE.* Leuven: Peeters 2016.

72 CHRISTOLOGY AND THE LOGIC OF GRACE

Cassian claimed he did, and therefore to accuse Cassian of incompetence, deliberate distortion, or culpable carelessness. Casiday summarizes his case by writing provocatively, 'Cassian's reputation has suffered since his treatise *Incarnation* was repeatedly battered by the tides of revisionist scholarship on Nestorius and Nestorian theology in the early twentieth century.'[21]

At this point, it is helpful to recognize the way these two arguments reinforce each other. The attempts to rehabilitate Nestorius centred around—and indeed must centre around—very technical questions of Christological terminology. In order to argue that Nestorius does not deny the deity of Christ, one has to understand that (as we saw in the Introduction) for Nestorius, the word 'Christ' is a collective term that refers to both the Logos and the *homo assumptus*. Likewise, in order to see Nestorius's Christ as a unity, rather than two separate persons (Logos and man), one has to dive deeply into the differences between the two πρόσωπα or φύσεις from which the one Christ was formed, on the one hand, and the resulting πρόσωπον of union, on the other. Scholars who are invigorated by such deep terminological complexities are profoundly disappointed by Cassian's muddled and inconsistent terminology, and it is easy for them to see Nestorius as a philosophical and linguistic genius and Cassian as an ignorant and befuddled fool railing at one whose brilliance he cannot understand. But what the terminological complexities may obscure is that Nestorius basically treats the φύσεις/πρόσωπα as persons, and so the Logos and the *homo assumptus* are—or at least can legitimately be seen as being—separate persons connected by a gracious conjunction, a moral union that does not negate the moral autonomy of the *homo assumptus*. Because of the centrality of the assumed man's moral autonomy to his picture of how salvation is accomplished, Nestorius's teaching is in fact about grace, not just about technical Christological terminology.

Such a characterization of Nestorius's thought cannot be a mere caricature, because as we saw in the Introduction, sympathetic scholars of Nestorius argue that this is precisely how Theodore and Nestorius understood Christ and salvation. But here is the rub: such a picture of Christ and salvation is acceptable to many modern scholars (hence the attempts to rehabilitate Nestorius), but it is emphatically not acceptable to Cassian. To him it amounts to a shocking denial (in effect, if not in words) of the deity of Christ and of the need for divine descent in redemption, and he thus rails against it with a vehemence that he has never previously shown against anyone. The fact that he is shocked reveals that Cassian's Christological

---

[21] Casiday, *Tradition and Theology*, 228. It is also worth pointing out that a recent opinion—largely concurring with that of Casiday and me, but argued with much less detail—comes from Peter Smith, whose main concern is to argue that Cassian seeks to avoid extremes on both sides of the Christological question, but who nevertheless insists, 'Cassian's royal road of Christology consisted of a divinity that was of one substance with the Father and a humanity that was of one substance with Mary. The Logos was the Person of Christ united to human form at conception, a human form that included passions and a will.' See Peter J. Smith, 'John Cassian's Royal Road: Discretion, Balance, and the Tradition of the Fathers', *DR* 139 (2021), 150–1.

and charitological concerns are very different from those of either Nestorius or the modern scholars who applaud Nestorius. Therefore, he must mean by 'deity' something different from what Nestorius means.

Perhaps the scholars who find Cassian's Christology unimpressive are asking for something he never intended to write—a dispassionate discussion of Christological terminology by which to achieve a balanced emphasis on deity and humanity (whether in the way Nestorius does or in some other way). If we are expecting that—and even more so if we uncritically accept Nestorius's way of emphasizing deity and humanity through his concept of πρόσωπον of union—we are likely to miss what Cassian is concerned about and thus the significance of the points he emphasizes. As a result, I ask the reader to take Cassian's *De incar. Dom.* seriously on its own terms. What does he think is wrong with Nestorius's thought? Why does it shock him so much?

The Problems with Nestorius's Thought, as Cassian Sees It

Cassian begins *De incar. Dom.* with the classical image of a hydra as an analogy to Christian heresies: as soon as one cuts off one head, two others emerge to take its place. With this image in mind, he names the heresies of Sabellius, Arius, Eunomius, Macedonius, Photinus, Apollinaris, and the new heresy that has sprung up *ex maxima Belgarum*, that is, the thought of Leporius.[22] Then, as we have seen in chapter 2, he links Leporius's thought with both 'Pelagianism' and the still newer heresy of Nestorius. According to Cassian, what all three of these heresies have in common is that they see Christ as a mere man who was rewarded for his virtue by being united with the Word, and thus that Christ is merely our example, not our redeemer through his death and resurrection.[23]

Cassian initially states these connections in *De incar. Dom.* 1.3. In our consideration of Leporius in chapter 2, we saw that in that passage, Cassian claims that Leporius and Pelagius saw Christ as a man who was rewarded for his virtue. For our present purposes, what is crucial is the implication Cassian draws from this assertion: He claims that both Leporius and the Pelagians . . .

. . . broke out into a more grievous and unnatural madness, and said that our Lord Jesus Christ had come into this world not to bring redemption to mankind (*non ad praestandam humano generi redemptionem*) but to give an example of good works (*sed ad praebenda bonorum actuum exempla*), to wit, that men, by

---

[22] *De incar. Dom.* 1.1–2 (CSEL 17.237–9) [*NPNF*[2] 11.551–2].

[23] My explication of Cassian's view of 'Nestorianism' presented here is similar to, but much more detailed than, the one presented briefly in Jaros, 'The Relationship of the So-Called Semi-Pelagians and Eastern Greek Theology on the Doctrine of Original Sin: An Historical-Systematic Analysis and its Relevance for 21st Century Protestantism', Ph.D. Dissertation, University of Aberdeen, 2020, 202–3.

74 CHRISTOLOGY AND THE LOGIC OF GRACE

following His teaching, and by walking along the same path of virtue (*eandem uiam uirtutis*), might arrive at the same reward of virtue (*uirtutum praemia*): thus destroying, as far as they could, all the good of His sacred advent and all the grace of Divine redemption (*omnem diuinae redemptionis gratiam*), as they declared that men could by their own lives obtain just that which God had wrought by dying for man's salvation.[24]

Here we should note the striking statement that Leporius's/Pelagius's view destroys the benefit of the Incarnation and the death of Christ. If the only thing people needed were an example, then the death of Christ—and perhaps the Incarnation as well—would have been unnecessary. Whether or not this is fair to Pelagius is not the issue; what we seek to understand here is how Cassian understood the implications of Pelagius's and Leporius's thought.

After quoting four passages from Leporius's *Lib. emend.* (discussed in chapter 2), Cassian turns his attention directly to Nestorius: 'And so you say, O heretic, whoever you may be, who deny that God was born of the Virgin, that Mary the Mother of our Lord Jesus Christ ought not to be called Theotocos, i.e., Mother of God, but Christotocos, i.e., only the Mother of Christ, not of God.'[25] Of course, looking at the controversy in hindsight as we do, one could object that this is not a fair starting point, because eventually Nestorius did, in fact, agree to call Mary *Theotokos*. But Cassian was writing in the summer of 430, before John of Antioch's autumn letter to Nestorius in which he would urge Nestorius to accept that title for Mary[26] and thus before Nestorius's reluctant acquiescence to do so.[27] Nestorius's prior refusal to grant the Marian title in 428 was the main source of his scandalous notoriety, and in the summer of 430 there was as yet no evidence that he would back down from that stance. With a proper recognition of what was happening at precisely that time, we should hardly be surprised that the *Theotokos* was Cassian's starting point and the source of his outrage towards Nestorius, nor that what follows in *De incar. Dom.* is a long, passionate, tedious defence of the deity of Christ, from biblical, creedal, and patristic sources.

In the midst of this long defence of Christ's deity, Cassian repeats summaries of 'Nestorius's thought in numerous places, three of which are especially significant. First, near the end of book 3 he quotes Thomas's confession, *My Lord and my God* [Jn. 20:28], and asserts:

---

[24] *De incar. Dom.* 1.2 (CSEL 17.240) [*NPNF*[2] 11.552–3].

[25] *De incar. Dom.* 2.1 (CSEL 17.246) [*NPNF*[2] 11.556].

[26] John of Antioch, *Ep. ad Nes.* 4 (*ACO* 1.1.195) [TTH 72.179]. For the significance of this letter, see Donald Fairbairn, 'Allies or Merely Friends? John of Antioch and Nestorius in the Christological Controversy', *JEH* 58 (2007), 383–99.

[27] Nestorius, *Ep. ad Ioh.* 3 (*ACO* 1.4.5) [TTH 72.181].

He surely touched the body of his Lord and answered that He was God. Did he make any separation between man and God (*discretionem aliquam hominis et dei*)? Or did he call that flesh *theodochos*, to use your expression, i.e., that which received Divinity (*susceptricem deitatis imaginem*)? Or did he, after the fashion of your blasphemy, declare that He whom he touched was to be honoured not for His own sake (*non propter se*), but for the sake of Him whom He had received into Himself (*propter eum quem in se receperat*)? But perhaps God's Apostle knew nothing of that subtle separation (*subtlitatem discretionis*) of yours, and had no experience of the fine distinctions (*elegantiam ac differentiam*) of your judgment. . . .[28]

Here we should notice the masculine pronouns *aliquam*, *eum*, and *quem*. Cassian is accusing Nestorius not simply of too strong a separation between deity and humanity, but of seeing Christ as a *man* who received some*one*—God as a separate person—into himself. This is fundamentally different from seeing Christ as *God* who received some*thing*—humanity—into his own person so as to be the same person before and after the Incarnation. Cassian's sarcastic reference to Nestorius's alleged subtlety and fine distinctions bolsters a significant point: such distinctions obscure but do not remove the problem of claiming Christ is not the Word-made-man, but a man indwelt by the Word.

The second significant reiteration of the problems with 'Nestorianism' comes at the beginning of book 5, as Cassian makes the alleged Pelagian/Nestorian connection even more explicit by returning to his claim that Nestorius regards Christ as having been born a mere man and then having attained to deity. Once again, we should acknowledge that on the face of it, this charge is not correct. But Cassian is concerned not merely with *when* Christ became God (at conception in the Virgin's womb or later in life), but with maintaining the difference between Christ and Christians. He writes that if one were to say that Christ achieved deity by his merits, and thus severed from him 'the honour of His sacred origin (*sacrae originis dignitate*),' that would mean asserting 'that all men could by their good life and deeds (*per bonorum actuum conuersationem*) secure whatever he had secured by His good life. A most dangerous and deadly assertion, indeed, which takes away what truly belongs to God, and holds out false promises to men. . . .'[29] As far as we

---

[28] *De incar. Dom.* 3.15 (CSEL 17.280) [*NPNF*[2] 11.571, translation modified]. The NPNF translator, Edgar Gibson, has *Theotocos* for 'theodochos' here. Whether the mistake is his or belongs to the edition of the text from which he was working, *theodochos* must be the correct reading, since *Theotocos* makes no sense in the context. *Theotokos* was a title for Mary, but his subject here is the humanity of Christ. Cf. the longer discussion in *De incar. Dom.* 5.2 (CSEL 17.303-4) [*NPNF*[2] 11.581–2], in which Cassian argues that if Christ were merely one who had received God (*theodochos*), he would have been no different from prophets and other holy ones, who may all be called *theodochi*.

[29] *De incar. Dom.* 5.1 (CSEL 17.302) [*NPNF*[2] 11.581]. See also *De incar. Dom.* 7.6 (CSEL 17.362–3) [*NPNF*[2] 11.608], in which Cassian accuses Nestorius of saying that Christ has no more than Adam did before the Fall.

76   CHRISTOLOGY AND THE LOGIC OF GRACE

know from Nestorius's extant writings, he never claims that all people could obtain by their good deeds that which Christ obtained by his, although he does take great pains to emphasize the similarities between Christ and us. But for Cassian, it is essential to emphasize the differences between Christ and us, not just the similarities. He was not a man who rose up to God so as to be able to lead us up. He was God who came down to do as man for us what we could not do for ourselves. If we acknowledge that Cassian is unjust to Nestorius in claiming that he affirmed a strict equality between Christ and Christians, nevertheless Cassian's concern is valid. A mere example is not a saviour, and the mere granting of a perfect example does not constitute redemption. Again, Cassian is addressing what Nestorius's thought implies, not what he actually writes, but the implication points to an important difference between Cassian's and Nestorius's Christology and charitology.

A third major reiteration of the problems with 'Nestorius's thought comes in book 6, as Cassian again equates 'Nestorianism' with 'Pelagianism'. He claims:

> If Christ who was born of Mary is not the same one as he who is of God (*idem Christus ex Maria est qui ex deo natus*), you certainly make two Christs; after the manner of that abominable error of Pelagius, which in asserting that a mere man was born of the Virgin, said that He was the teacher rather than the redeemer of mankind; for He did not bring to men redemption of life but only an example of how to live, i.e., that by following Him men should do the same sort of things and so come to a similar state.[30]

In this crucial passage, the new element (what we have not seen in the selections we have considered from books 1, 3, and 5) is the direct insistence that 'Pelagius' and 'Nestorius' make two Christs. Again, in Nestorius's case this is not technically true, because he uses the word 'Christ' to refer to the πρόσωπον of union between the Logos and the *homo assumptus*. But for Cassian, what is central is not that we find some way to affirm 'one Christ', but that the one Christ be the same person as the one who was eternally begotten from God.[31] Notice that the form *idem* could be masculine or neuter ('the same one' or 'the same thing'), but in this case, it must be masculine because *qui* and *natus* are masculine. If the *homo assumptus* is someone else besides the eternal Son of God, then such a one can be no more than an example of how to live, not an actual redeemer.

From these three passages in which Cassian returns to and builds on his claims about what 'Nestorius' implies, we see that he thinks both 'Pelagius' and 'Nestorius'

---

[30]   *De incar. Dom.* 6.14 (CSEL 17.341) [*NPNF*[2] 11.598, translation slightly modified].

[31]   Also noteworthy is the emphasis Cassian places on the Holy Spirit as the one who points Christians to the truth about who Christ is. In *De incar. Dom.* 2.6 (CSEL 17.259) [*NPNF*[2] 11.261], he claims that even the Holy Spirit cries out against Nestorius for his refusal to declare that Christ is God. See Thomas L, Humphries, Jr. *Ascetic Pneumatology from John Cassian to Gregory the Great*, OECS (Oxford: Oxford University Press, 2013), 6–13.

offer merely the possibility of human ascent to God in imitation of Christ, not the certainty that God has come down to us through the life, death, and resurrection of Christ. Christ could be our example based merely on a similarity to us—if Jesus has received God the Son into himself as we receive God the Holy Spirit into ourselves, then in both cases, God indwells and helps us, and the divinely indwelt man Jesus would be a splendid example. But as Cassian sees it, Christ could not be a genuine redeemer unless he is more than an example, which requires that he also be different from us as well as similar, and this requirement rules out a Christology of indwelling. Put simply, to be a redeemer as well as an example, Christ has to be God's eternal Son made human, not a human being in whom God the Son dwells.

This raises another question, however: If Nestorius never directly writes that Christ and Christians both advance to God by our own effort and merits, why is Cassian so sure that he implies it? In chapter 2, we saw that this is exactly what Cassian accuses both Pelagius and Leporius of claiming,[32] that Gennadius later makes the same accusation,[33] and most importantly, that Leporius himself admits that this is what he thought prior to his recantation.[34] We should also remember that Cassian knew Leporius personally and unlike Augustine, may very well have had first-hand knowledge of Leporius's crypto-'Pelagianism'. We need not assume that just because Nestorius never claims Christ and Christians obtain salvation by our merits, that must mean that Cassian is making up the accusation out of thin air. More likely, it seems, is that Cassian knows enough about Leporius to be confident that this is what *Leporius* meant in his charitology, that he finds in Nestorius a Christology that seems similar to that of the pre-recantation Leporius, and that he concludes this is what Nestorius meant as well. Perhaps the 'Nestorius' whom Cassian condemns is actually an amalgamation of Nestorius's stated highly-technical teaching with similar but more familiar grace-related ideas in Leporius— a 'Leporianized Nestorius', if you will.

In fact, both Bruno Morel and Torsten Krannich see Cassian as conflating Nestorius's thought with that of Leporius.[35] Where I differ from the two of them is that they see such a conflation as unjustified and indicative of Cassian's theological incompetence, whereas I suggest that it is plausible and gives a window into Cassian's own theological concerns. We must again remember that if Nestorius's Christology does in fact grow out of Theodore's charitology/soteriology—as sympathetic interpreters agree—Cassian is not necessarily wrong here. He has westernized their thought by using the word *merita*, but Theodore and Nestorius do see salvation as the upward movement of humanity by following the trail blazed

---

[32] Cassian, *De incar. Dom.* 1.3 (CSEL 17.239-40) [*NPNF²* 11.553].
[33] Gennadius, *De uir. illust.* 59 (60) (PL 58.1092) [*NPNF²* 3.395].
[34] Leporius, *Lib. emend.* 9 (CCSL 64.120).
[35] Bruno Morel, 'De Invloed van Leporius op Cassianus' Weerlegging van het Nestorianisme', *Bijdragen* 21 (1960), 31–52; Krannich, *Von Leporius bis zu Leo dem Großen*, 104–5.

78 CHRISTOLOGY AND THE LOGIC OF GRACE

by the *homo assumptus* who is indwelt by and aided by the Logos. A Leporianized 'Nestorius' may not be overly remote from the real Nestorius on this point.

Cassian's General Response to 'Nestorius' in *De Incar. Dom.*

Cassian believes 'Nestorius's' thought (possibly an amalgamation of Nestorian and Leporian ideas) implies that Christ is a mere man, possessing no more than we do through the indwelling of the Holy Spirit, and who can thus be a mere example for us, rather than a genuine redeemer. Cassian is shocked about this, and his outrage both accounts for the length of his defence of Christ's deity and the vitriolic tone that pervades it. This defence is organized into three parts: the marshalling of biblical evidence for Christ's deity in books 2–5, a discussion of the baptismal symbol of Antioch (which Nestorius himself presumably recited at his own baptism) in book 6, and a collection of statements from well-known church fathers in book 7. As he presents evidence from these sources, Cassian focuses on three main themes, with each theme woven into all three parts of the work. First, he insists that Christ is God, not a man indwelt by God. Cassian interprets Is. 7:14 and 9:6 to mean that the Christ would be God, and he takes Mal. 3:8 to mean that the Christ would be God even in his crucifixion.[36] He takes Peter's and Thomas's confessions in Mt. 16:16 and Jn. 20:28 as confirmation of God the Father's own confession at Jesus's baptism [Mt. 3:17] that he is God.[37] And in the infamous passage I have already cited above, he asserts that even the devil knows Christ is God.[38] Second, Cassian asserts that Christ is a unity, with no separation between the Word and the man. He affirms that the titles 'Son of God' and 'Son of man' apply to the same person, God the Son.[39] He insists that one cannot separate Christ into one person of the Son of God and another of the Son of man.[40] Third, Cassian emphasizes that Christ is the Word, not merely a man united to the Word. He quotes from Hilary, Ambrose, Jerome, Augustine, Gregory of Nazianzus, Athanasius, and John Chrysostom in order to show that all of them affirm the unity of Christ in the person of the Word.[41]

[36] *De incar. Dom.* 2.3 (CSEL 17.250–3) [*NPNF*[2] 11.557–9].
[37] *De incar. Dom.* 3.12–16 (CSEL 17.277–83) [*NPNF*[2] 11.570–2].
[38] *De incar. Dom.* 7.12 (CSEL 17.367–8) [*NPNF*[2] 11.610].
[39] *De incar. Dom.* 4.5 (CSEL 17.290) [*NPNF*[2] 11.575].
[40] *De incar. Dom.* 6.22 (CSEL 17.348) [*NPNF*[2] 11.602].
[41] *De incar. Dom.* 7.24–30 (CSEL 17.382–9) [*NPNF*[2] 11.617–20]. For more detail on these three major points, see Fairbairn, *Grace and Christology*, 180–7. Augustine is the only one of the church fathers whom Cassian names but does not honour with an encomium. The omission of an encomium is not necessarily a subtle swipe at Augustine but may be simply because Augustine is the only one still alive at the time Cassian writes. The more remarkable feature is not the lack of an encomium, but the presence of a living person among the quoted fathers. See Augustine Casiday, 'Cassian, Augustine, and *De incarnatione*', *StPatr* 34 (2001), 45–7. See also Boniface Ramsey, 'John Cassian and Augustine', in *Grace for Grace: The Debates after Augustine and Pelagius*, ed. Alexander Hwang et al. (Washington, DC: The Catholic University of America Press, 2014), 115.

As Cassian makes these points, he writes a great deal that is sloppy from the point of view of later Christological terminology. He frequently uses *homo* to refer to Christ's humanity in a way that might be read as implying a separation between the Word and the *homo assumptus*, were it not for the fact that he expends so much ink insisting that there is no such separation. Rather, it seems that like Augustine and most of the Latin church prior to Leo's *Tome*, he is using *homo* either to refer to the *humanitas* of Christ or to describe the incarnate Son considered as a man.[42] On the other hand, in a few passages he appears to assert that Christ's humanity was absorbed into his deity.[43] Cassian certainly does not evince anything like terminological precision or even consistency, and it is no surprise that so many scholars have dismissed *De incar. Dom.* At the same time, what is perfectly consistent in Cassian's work, as we have already seen, is his insistence that salvation cannot be achieved by human merit but must come by grace. Even if he is not right in attributing to Nestorius the idea that both Christ (as a man indwelt by the Word) and Christians (as women and men indwelt by the Holy Spirit) achieve salvation through merit, even if he is conflating 'Nestorius' with a Leporian idea to which Nestorius does not hold, his way of arguing against such an idea is striking and deserves our attention.

Redemption as More than Mere Example in *De. Incar. Dom.*

In what ways, then, does redemption involve more than merely giving an example? Cassian answers this question by focusing on three major aspects of redemption that cannot be subsumed into the category of 'example'. First, he insists that salvation is fundamentally a matter of adoption, and that only one who is the Son by nature can make people sons and daughters by grace/adoption. In a telling passage from book 5, Cassian sharply distinguishes Christ from prophets and other servants of God:

All, then, whether patriarchs, or prophets, or apostles, or martyrs, or saints, had every one of them God within him, and were all made sons of God (*filii dei facti sunt*) and were all receivers of God (*theodochi*), but in a very different and distinct way. For all who believe in God (*omnes credentes deum*) are sons of God by adoption (*per adoptionem*); but the only begotten alone is Son by nature (*per naturam*): who was begotten of His Father, not of any material substance, for

---

[42] See my discussion of the use of *homo* in Augustine in chapter 1. Also significant is the concurring opinion in David R. Maxwell, 'The Christological Coherence of Cassian's *On the Incarnation of the Lord*', StPatr 43 (2006), 430–1. Maxwell argues that Cassian's starting point is Christ the man (or, as I would prefer, 'the Son considered as a man') and that his major point is that this man is God.

[43] See *De incar. Dom.* 3.3–5 (CSEL 17.264–6) [*NPNF*[2] 11.564–5], as well as my discussion in Fairbairn, *Grace and Christology*, 195–7.

80   CHRISTOLOGY AND THE LOGIC OF GRACE

all things, and the substance of all things exist through the only begotten son of God—and not out of nothing, because He is from the Father. . . .[44]

Notice here that Christians are *theodochi*—receivers of God. If Christ himself were a *theodochos*—as we have seen Cassian accuse 'Nestorius' of saying—then he would be fundamentally like us but *not* also fundamentally different, and in Cassian's mind, the fundamental difference is just as crucial as the fundamental similarity. The reason for this is that redemption consists in *making* people daughters and sons of God, not merely in giving them an example so that they may make themselves such. Adoption is not something one can do for oneself: it is something one does to another, and an adopted son cannot adopt someone else into the family. One must be a natural member of the family to bring others in through adoption. The centrality of adoption in Cassian's soteriology is thus the source of the urgency with which he insists throughout *De incar. Dom.* that Christ had to be the same person before and after the Incarnation, that the one born from Mary had to be the one who had been eternally begotten from the Father.

A second aspect of Cassian's concept of redemption that cannot be subsumed into 'example' is closely related to the first. Just as Christ has to be the Son by nature to make us sons and daughters by adoption, so also he has to be the Son by nature to give us grace as well. During a discussion of Jn. 1:17, Cassian equates grace with divine power and largesse, and he asserts: 'If Christ is a mere man, how did these [grace and truth] come by Christ? Whence was there in Him divine power (*unde in eo diuina uirtus*) if, as you say, there was in Him only the nature of man? Whence comes heavenly largesse (*unde caelestis largitas*), if his is earthly poverty? For no one can give what he has not already. As then Christ gave Divine grace, He already had that which he gave.'[45] Here the idea is that if divine grace/power is given to one from the outside, that person is not able to pass the gift on to others. Only the source of divine power—God—can give that power to people.

A third way Cassian's concept of redemption goes beyond example is that it is fundamentally based on the downward movement of God to humanity, not on the ascent of men and women to God. As Cassian discusses the Antiochene baptismal symbol, he paraphrases the line that proclaims the Incarnation itself: 'He then, who is Very God (*deus uerus*), who is of one substance with the Father (*qui homousios patri*), who is the Maker of all things, He, I repeat, came into the world (*uenit in mundum*) and was born of the Virgin Mary.'[46] Cassian then explains this line of the symbol in relation to Gal. 4:4 (which he quotes), and concludes:

---

[44]   *De incar. Dom.* 5.4 (CSEL 17.305) [*NPNF²* 11.582].
[45]   *De incar. Dom.* 2.5 (CSEL 17.257) [*NPNF²* 11.561]. Cf. a similar argument regarding divine power in *De incar. Dom.* 7.20 (CSEL 17.378) [*NPNF²* 11.615].
[46]   *De incar. Dom.* 6.8 (CSEL 17.334) [*NPNF²* 11.595].

JOHN CASSIAN 81

You see then how by the word 'coming (*aduentus*)' it is shown that He who came was already in existence (*fuisse antea … adueniens*): for He only had the power to come, to whom there could be the opportunity of coming, from the fact that he was already existing. But a mere man was certainly not in existence before he was conceived, and so had not in himself the power to come. It is clear then that it was God who came (*deum ergo uenisse certum est*): to whom it belongs in each case both to *be*, and to come. For certainly He *came* because He *was*, and he ever *was*, because he could ever come.[47]

Here we see Cassian insisting again that it was God the Son himself who came and thus who became human; it was not merely the case that a man was born with a connection to God.[48] This assertion is important because it directly conflicts with Nestorius's own interpretation of the Creed. As we saw in the Introduction, Nestorius understands the second paragraph of the Creed to be naming the terms 'Lord', 'Jesus', 'Christ', and 'Only-Begotten' that apply to both the deity (the Logos) and the humanity (the *homo assumptus*), and then first describing the Logos as being 'God from God' and 'ὁμοούσιος with the Father', and then depicting the man as being born, suffering, and being raised.[49] Nestorius strikingly fails to mention the very point Cassian pounces on—that the one who was born, suffered, and was raised is the same one who had always been ὁμοούσιος with the Father. However much Cassian may be conflating 'Nestorius' with Leporius overall, here he has his finger on a point that certainly comes from the real Nestorius himself and that he regards as unacceptable.

Part of the reason this focus on the downward motion of the Word (and thus on the personal continuity between the Word and the incarnate Christ) is so important to Cassian is that the descent culminates in the death of Christ, without which there can be no redemption. Cassian claims that at his baptism, Nestorius would have recited the Creed and thus confessed that God was born, God suffered, and God rose again. Now, however, Cassian asserts that Nestorius is shocked at the idea that God was born and died: '"Can it possibly be," you [Nestorius] say, "that He who was begotten before all worlds, should be born a second time, and be God?" If all these things cannot possibly be, how is it that the Creed of the Churches says that they did happen? How is it that you yourself said that they did?'[50] Here Cassian is not specific about how exactly Christ's death accomplishes redemption, although elsewhere he asserts that the passion destroyed the devil's power over us.[51] But he is crystal clear in this passage that he believes that it had

---

[47]   *De incar. Dom.* 6.8 (CSEL 17.335) [*NPNF²* 11.595–6].
[48]   Cf. Casiday, *Tradition and Theology*, 233, who writes: 'The enduring stability of the Second Person of the Trinity before, during and after His Incarnation is of the utmost importance to both Leporius [after his correction, that is] and Cassian.'
[49]   See Nestorius, *Ep. II ad Cyr.* 2–6 (*ACO* 1.1.1.29–30) [*TTH* 72.123–4].
[50]   *De incar. Dom.* 6.9 (CSEL 17.336) [*NPNF²* 11.596].
[51]   *De incar. Dom.* 7.13 (CSEL 17.368–9) [*NPNF²* 11.611].

82   CHRISTOLOGY AND THE LOGIC OF GRACE

to be and was God who died in order to accomplish redemption.[52] Here we might wish for a needed qualifier—it was God the Son who died *qua homo*, in terms of his humanity, not in terms of his deity per se—but even so, Cassian again has his finger on a genuine problem, not just with 'Nestorius' but with the real Nestorius's thought. One of the driving forces behind Nestorius's entire Christology is the protection of divine impassibility by ascribing the death to the *homo assumptus*, not to the Logos in any sense whatsoever.[53] To Cassian, that is simply unacceptable.

Thus, we have seen that while Cassian's response to 'Nestorius' in *De incar. Dom.* is hardly a model of terminological precision or consistency, it is clear and consistent on one thing: our redemption depends on the downward movement of God's Son to both human birth and human death, and therefore on the personal continuity between the eternal Son and the Christ. Christ is not a man indwelt by God, nor is 'Christ' a word to refer corporately to both the Word and the man. Christ *is* the incarnate Son. If he were not, redemption would be impossible, according to Cassian. In a sense, then, this downward movement of the Word is the precondition for everything Cassian writes about salvation. Thus, human effort, even monastic striving, must be seen in the context of the gracious descent of God's Son to a human level. In general, this is very consistent with Augustine's and the post-correction Leporius's focus on the eternal Son as the person of Christ and thus on the downward movement of God's Son. Cassian's point in his picture of Christ is not to balance deity and humanity: it is to show that the divine Son underwent a human birth so that he could live a human life, suffer a human death, and rise from the dead. This is the Christology that Cassian sets in opposition to what he thinks was affirmed by the pre-correction Leporius, by 'Pelagius', and by 'Nestorius'.

While this Christology finds expression mainly in *De incar. Dom.*, the fact that Cassian was earlier involved in the correction of Leporius means that the key foci of this Christology had been well formed long before the summer of 430. In fact, this Christology stands in the background to his monastic writings as well and did not necessarily require any polemical context for its development. Codina has shown that the Christological references in Cassian's monastic writings are consistent with his extended treatment in *De incar. Dom.* Codina asserts that for Cassian, the goal of the monk's spirituality is the contemplation of the glorified Christ in his deity.[54] Moreover, Casiday suggests that Cassian's *De inst. coen.*, *Conlat.*, and *De*

---

[52] Cf. Casiday, *Tradition and Theology*, 240, who concludes: 'If we opt out of affirming with the Creed that it was Christ, 'very God of very God', who was born and died, we are left to suppose that Christ must have been more than one person. Regardless of how strenuously one claims that Christ was both of human and divine natures, if someone other than God died when Christ died, then Christ was two Persons—which is anathema.'

[53] On this, see John J. O'Keefe, 'Impassible Suffering? Divine Passion and Fifth-Century Christology', *TS* 58 (1997), 38–60.

[54] Viktor Codina, *El aspecto christológico en la espiritualidad de Juan Cassiano*, Orientalia Christiana Analecta 175 (Rome: Pontificum Institutum Orientalium Studiorum, 1966), 95. Cf. Stewart, *Cassian the Monk*, 95; Casiday, *Tradition and Theology*, 251.

incar. Dom. correspond to Evagrius's three spiritual steps—πρακτική, φυσική, and θεολογική. As a result, Casiday speculates that Cassian might have written a work on Christology even if no polemical need had arisen.[55] To take a striking example of the centrality of the glorified, divine Christ in Cassian's monastic works, we can look at the culmination of *Conlat.* 9–10 on prayer. In 10.7, Cassian famously asserts that in pure prayer everything about the monk's life will 'be God'. But this is no contentless mysticism: Cassian bases his thought here on Jesus's high priestly prayer in Jn. 17 and focuses on our sharing in the love and unity between the Father and the Son. The goal of the monk's prayer is to deepen his participation in the communion that the Father and Son have eternally shared, and as a result, monastic contemplation inevitably focuses on Christ as God, Christ in his glorified deity.[56] This kind of focus evinces a Christology in which the personal continuity between the eternal Son before the Incarnation and Christ after the Incarnation is explicit. Jesus *is* the eternal, yet incarnate, Son.

Accordingly, we may confidently assume that in *Conlat.*, Cassian was working with a Christology comparable to that of *De incar. Dom.*, and we may ask whether and how that Christology affected the way he wrote about grace, especially in the controversial *Conlat.* 13. I now turn to that slightly earlier work.

Cassian's *Conlat.* 13 in Context

Of course, Cassian's *Conlat.* 13 belongs first and foremost to a monastic context. In addition, however, this conference is widely believed to occupy a polemical context as well. Scholars have generally agreed that Cassian is arguing against someone's understanding of grace in this conference, but they do not agree on whether the anonymous opponent is Augustine, Pelagius, or someone else. Closely related to this issue is the question of whether *Conlat.* 13 was written before or after Augustine's *De corrept. grat.* reached Gaul in 427. Thus, in this section I shall address the disputed polemical context before summarizing the monastic context.

The Date of *Conlat.* 13 and its Polemical Context

In the preface to *De inst. coen.*, Cassian indicates that 'Pope Castor' has commissioned him to write the work.[57] Castor was bishop of Apta Julia from 419 through 426, so *De inst. coen.* was written during that period and is the first of Cassian's three

---

[55] Casiday, *Tradition and Theology*, 252–8. Notice that Cassian hints at this in the preface to *De incar. Dom.* (CSEL 17.236) [*NPNF²* 11.549], when he writes that his two previous works brought us into the holy place, but now, in writing about the Incarnation, we are penetrating into the holy of holies.
[56] *Conlat.* 10.7 (CSEL 13.293) [ACW 57.377–8].
[57] *De inst. coen.*, praef. 2 (CSEL 17.3) [ACW 68.11].

84 CHRISTOLOGY AND THE LOGIC OF GRACE

extant works. His preface to the first part of *Conlat.* (Conferences 1–10) indicates that Castor has died, so Cassian dedicates these conferences to 'Pope Leontius and holy brother Helladius'.[58] Thus, this first part of *Conlat.* was likely completed in 426, not long after Castor's death. The tricky part of the chronology has to do with the date of part two of *Conlat.* (Conferences 11–17). Cassian dedicates this part to 'holy brothers Honoratus and Eucherius',[59] thus indicating that Honoratus was still a monk. According to the traditional chronology, Honoratus became bishop of Arles in 426, which suggests that Cassian completed part two of *Conlat.* earlier that year, and thus before *De corrept. grat.* reached Gaul in 427. In the preface to part three of *Conlat.* (Conferences 18–24), Cassian mentions having dedicated the second part to 'the blessed Bishop Honoratus',[60] thus indicating that Honoratus is now a bishop. Since the traditional chronology places Honoratus's death in January 429, part three of *Conlat.* must have been completed by or in 428.[61]

A major challenge to this traditional chronology came in 1945 from the pen of Owen Chadwick,[62] who points out that Prosper, in his letter to Augustine sparking the Gallic discussion, named Hilary as the bishop of Arles, and thus the controversy could not have begun until early 429. Chadwick argues, however, that *Conlat.* 13 'is a controversial piece of writing containing Cassian's famous opposition to Augustine upon the predestinarian controversy', and thus, *Conlat.* 13 must have been written later than traditionally assumed. Chadwick gives several arguments against the possibility that *Conlat.* 13 was not a direct response to Augustine, most significantly, that Prosper would have mentioned that conference in his letter to Augustine if it had already been written.[63] (One might also speculate that Prosper would have even sent a copy to Augustine.) In the light of this problem, Chadwick suggests a new chronology for the bishops of Arles in the late 420s. One manuscript of Prosper's letter to Augustine names not Hilary but Euladius as the bishop of Arles, and a ninth-century list of bishops includes Euladius between Patroclus and Honoratus. On the basis of this evidence, Chadwick adopts the following chronology: In 426 Patroclus died and Euladius was elevated to the episcopacy of Arles. In 427 *De corrept. grat.* arrived in Gaul. In response, Cassian wrote *Conlat.* 13 and dedicated its group (Conferences 11–17) to Honoratus, who was still abbot of the monastery in Lerins. In 428, Euladius died, and Honoratus was bishop from 428 through January 430. During that time, Cassian published *Conlat.* 18–24, mentioning that Honoratus was now bishop.[64]

---

[58] *Conlat.* 1 praef. 2 (CSEL 13.3) [ACW 67.29].

[59] *Conlat.* 2 praef. 1 (CSEL 13.311) [ACW 67.399].

[60] *Conlat.* 3 praef. 1 (CSEL 13.503) [ACW 67.625].

[61] For a concise explanation of the traditional chronology, see Edgar C. S. Gibson, Prolegomena to 'The Works of John Cassian', in *NPNF²* 11.189-90. See also Jaros, 'The Relationship of the So-Called Semi-Pelagians', 160-1.

[62] Owen Chadwick, 'Euladius of Arles', *JTS* 46 (1945), 200-5.

[63] Ibid., 200-2.

[64] Ibid., 203-5.

Writing in 1990, Robert Markus revisited the issue by questioning the contention that Cassian wrote *Conlat*. 13 explicitly against Augustine. He writes: 'It seems more natural to interpret the *Conference* in the context of the Pelagian views apparently held in Gaul ... as an attack not on Augustine's, but on Pelagian, views, albeit from a point of view more in line with a pre-Augustinian theological tradition than with Augustine's anti-Pelagian theology', and he suggests that *Conlat*. 13 was drawn into the controversy only later.[65] Writing in 1996, Rebecca Harden Weaver returned to the important question of why Prosper did not mention *Conlat*. 13 in his letter to Augustine in 427, if in fact it had already been written. She contends that Prosper's silence about the conference in his letter to Augustine can be explained by saying that he was more concerned about Hilary's reaction to Augustine than about Cassian's, since Hilary was a bishop. Only later, when Aug's *De corrept. grat.* was so widely criticized in Gaul, did Prosper turn his attention directly to Cassian's *Conlat*. 13. With this reasoning, she argues in agreement with Markus that *Conlat*. 13 was composed in 426.[66]

Then in 2003 Donato Ogliari reaffirmed Chadwick's chronology and strongly opposed Markus's contention that the main target of *Conlat* 13 was 'Pelagianism'.[67] He concludes emphatically, 'Supported by the opinion of many scholars we believe, in fact *saluo meliori iudicio*, that Cassian's *Conlatio* 13 was written under the direct stimulus of Augustine's *De correptione et gratia*.'[68] An equally strong voice on the other side is that of Casiday, who argued in 2007 against the entire rubric of placing the Gallic writers on a continuum between Pelagius and Augustine and specifically criticized the contention of both Prosper and modern scholars that Augustine was the target of *Conlat*. 13.[69] Casiday insists that 'the major authors of Christian Gaul were full of admiration for Augustine, albeit not the sort of uncritical admiration that we have found in Prosper'.[70]

More recently, scholars have taken somewhat mediating positions on the issue of Cassian's opponents, while no longer seeking to support Chadwick's and Ogliari's revised chronology. Writing in 2011, Alexander Hwang asserts, '*Conlatio* 13 may not have specifically targeted Augustine's *De correptione et gratia*, but that it attacked Augustine's teaching on grace is clear'.[71] In 2014, Boniface Ramsey argued

---

[65] Robert A. Markus, *The End of Ancient Christianity* (Cambridge: Cambridge University Press, 1990), 178.

[66] Rebecca Harden Weaver, *Divine Grace and Human Agency: A Study of the Semi-Pelagian Controversy*, PMS 15 (Macon, Georgia: Mercer University Press, 1996), 96–7.

[67] Donato Ogliari, *Gratia et Certamen: The Relationship Between Grace and Free Will in the Discussion of Augustine with the So-Called Semipelagians* (Leuven: Leuven University Press, 2003), 93–7, 133–4.

[68] Ibid., 133.

[69] Casiday, *Tradition and Theology*, 17–28.

[70] Ibid., 29.

[71] Alexander Y. Hwang, 'Prosper, Cassian, and Vincent: The Rule of Faith in the Augustinian Controversy', in *Tradition and the Rule of Faith in the Early Church: Essays in Honor of Joseph T. Lienhard, S.J.*, ed. Ronnie J. Rombs and Alexander Y. Hwang (Washington, DC: Catholic University of America Press, 2011), 71.

86   CHRISTOLOGY AND THE LOGIC OF GRACE

that Cassian's primary concern is balance, in this case between grace and free will. He sees his unnamed opponents, whether Augustine or the 'Pelagians', as having lost their balance, and in particular Augustine's theology of grace required a robust defence of human free will in response.[72] In 2017 Rossana Pinheiro-Jones argued that Cassian should be viewed in the light of the Eastern monastic tradition, not in terms of debates between Augustine and Pelagius at all.[73] In 2020, Jaros affirmed that to view *Conlat*. 13 as an attack on Augustine is 'to see only out of one eye', because Cassian clearly has Pelagian ideas in view as well.[74] And in 2021, Peter Smith likewise pointed out that Cassian is equally opposed to 'Pelagians' and Augustinians (or at least unnamed predestinarians) in his understanding of grace and free will.[75]

This survey shows that there is no clear-cut scholarly consensus on the possibility that in *Conlat*. 13, Cassian is directly opposing *De corrept. grat.*, or even that he is directly opposing Augustine's teaching at all. This is especially the case since an argument for a direct opposition to *De corrept. grat.* depends on an alternate chronology hinging on a variant reading in one manuscript, along with a bit of speculation. It is certainly likely that Cassian has both Augustinian ideas and 'Pelagian' ideas in mind as he writes (whether or not those ideas come directly from Augustine or Pelagius), but it is hard to be more specific than this.[76] Accordingly, we should perhaps do well to focus less on the alleged polemical context of *Conlat*. 13 and more on its overt and well-known monastic context.

The Monastic Context of *Conlat*. 13

Cassian's *Conlat*. 13 falls in the middle of a massive writing aimed at monks and purporting to represent twenty-four conversations between two monastic enquirers (Cassian himself and his friend Germanus) and fifteen 'abbas' who are anchorites from the Egyptian desert.[77] This means that nothing in the long work is

---

[72] Boniface Ramsey, 'John Cassian and Augustine', in *Grace for Grace*, 124–30.

[73] Rossana Pinheiro-Jones, 'Em torno do conceito de heresia: o caso de João Cassiano (Provença, Século V),' *Antíteses* 10 (2017), 1058–9.

[74] Jaros, 'The Relationship of the So-Called Semi-Pelagians', 161. Jaros points out correctly that Cassian is certainly referring to Pelagianism when he writes of those who attribute everything to free will and argue that God gives his grace in response to human merit. See Cassian, *Conlat*. 13.16 (CSEL 13.391) [ACW 57.487].

[75] Smith, 'John Cassian's Royal Road', 147–9.

[76] My statement here concurs with the judgement of Jaros, 'The Relationship of the So-Called Semi-Pelagians', 163–4.

[77] There is universal agreement that however many actual conversations lie behind the writing, we may take the words of the abbas as reflecting Cassian himself. See Jean-Claude Guy, 'Jean Cassien, historien du monachisme égyptien?' *StPatr* 8 (1966), 363–72; Boniface Ramsey, Introduction to *John Cassian: The Conferences*, ACW 57 (New York: Paulist Press, 1997), 9–11. In fact, even Prosper himself raised this question at the beginning of his critique of *Conlat*. 13 and concluded that he need deal only with Cassian, not with Abba Chaeremon who speaks in *Conlat*. 13. See *Con. Collat*. 2.1 (PL 51.218) [ACW 32.72–3].

directed at non-Christians, catechumens, or even new Christians: the entire work is written to men who are among the most committed of all Christians. Whenever we discuss Cassian's view of the *initium bonae uoluntatis* or claim that he believes a person can make the first move towards God, we need to remember this easily-forgotten larger context. Quite simply, he never writes about the first move towards God, because he is writing to people who already belong to God. Raúl Villegas Marín has corroborated this point in two recent works. Writing in 2013, he notes that in *Conlat.* 21.7, Cassian distinguishes those who are under the law from those who live by grace, and he includes only those who have taken monastic vows and are seeking perfection in the latter category. What he writes about grace in *Conlat.* applies only to ascetics, because *Conlat.* and *De inst. coen.* are addressed only to a monastic audience. Marín concludes that Cassian's thought cannot be reduced to the categories of 'Pelagianism' or regarded as a *uia media* between Pelagius and Augustine. Instead, Cassian's conception is more elitist than Augustine's in that he confines grace to the elite, the ascetics pursuing perfection.[78] And in another work from 2017, Marín concludes similarly, 'The debates between Augustine and the "Pelagians" revolved around the justification of what we might call either "secular Christians" or "inner-worldly ascetics". Cassian, on the contrary, has little to say to these "secular Christians".[79]

In addition to recognizing the audience for Cassian's monastic writings, it is important to pay attention to the structure of *Conlat.* Cassian returns to the same subject on numerous occasions, gradually building the full picture of his teaching. In fact, he organizes the work into both pairs (e.g. Conferences 1–2 introduce all the main themes of the work, 3–4 revisit the same themes, 5–6 touch the same themes again in a different way, and several other pairs match up as well: 14–15, 16–17, 18–19) and trilogies (1–3, 11–13, and 21–3). The trilogies are especially significant for our purposes, because they all deal with the relation between grace and the monastic task. The first trilogy (1–2 by Abba Moses and conference 3 by Abba Paphnutius) introduces the subject of grace by emphasizing that divine grace is necessary at every point in the monastic task. The second trilogy (11–13, all by Abba Chaeremon) revisits the subject of grace and locates the spheres of the monk's own responsibility within it, thus going beyond the initial trilogy. The third trilogy (21–3, all by Abba Theonas) brings the theme of monastic striving and grace to a conclusion by addressing perfection, perfect chastity, and significantly, the impossibility of complete sinlessness. As a result, the three trilogies on grace are microcosms of the three parts of the work as a whole. The first trilogy on grace (1–3), and the first part (1–10) all deal with the lofty goals of the monastic life; the

[78] Raúl Villegas Marín, 'Fieles *sub Lege*, fieles *sub gratia*: eclesiología y teología de la gracia en Juan Casiano', *Augustinianum* 53 (2013), 139–93. See especially 152–3, 168–70, 185.
[79] Raúl Villegas Marín, 'Asceticism and Exegetical Authority in John Cassian's *Conference* 23', *ETL* 93/4 (2017), 683.

88 CHRISTOLOGY AND THE LOGIC OF GRACE

second trilogy (11–13) and the second part as a whole (11–17) deal with the personal struggles involved in that life; and the third trilogy (21–3) and the third part as a whole (18–24) provide a needed realism about how obtainable the goals are.[80]

Within this structure, any reading of *Conlat.* 13 needs to bear in mind that the final word on its subject (grace and human action in the task of pursuing chastity) comes in *Conlat.* 23, which is in many ways the climax of the entire work. At the beginning of that conference, Theonas addresses the question of whether the struggles with sin described in Rom. 7:14–25 refer to Paul himself or to non-Christians. Germanus has argued in *Conlat.* 22.15–16 that these verses cannot refer to Paul, because he had obtained perfection. Theonas rejects that idea, insists that no one but Christ has ever been sinless, and then begins a discussion of why Paul cannot achieve perfect contemplation of God. I have discussed this conversation in some detail elsewhere,[81] and the highlights are as follows: First, what distracts Paul from perfect contemplation of God is not simply his own sinfulness, and is not necessarily bad. Paul's very ministry distracts him and leads him in Phil. 1:22 not to know whether he longs to die (so as to be with Christ and have uninterrupted contemplation of God) or to continue living (so as to see more people become Christians through his missionary work). Paul's choice is between two good options, not between a good one and a sinful one. Second, Paul in Rom. 9:3 would be willing to be cut off from Christ himself and suffer eternal punishment if it meant that all people were able to enjoy communion with Christ (*Christi consortio*). Communion with Christ is available not only to monks, but to all through the preaching of the gospel. Third, the monastic goal of uninterrupted communion with Christ is not the only valuable way of serving God, let alone the only way to salvation, because if it were, there would be no inner conflict in Paul's mind between good options. Instead, the monastic task is to anticipate in this world the perfect communion with God that all the saints will enjoy in eternity. The pattern in this climactic conference is that communion with God is first given, and then monastic service is one response (again, not the only acceptable one) to that gift. That no monk achieves perfect contemplation in this world is not the point, because the point is to anticipate—to the degree possible amidst both sins and other non-sinful distractions—the perfect *consortio Christi* that will characterize the coming age.[82]

Here we need to remember that Cassian would later describe his task in writing *De incar. Dom.* as penetrating into the holy of holies. What is held before the monk throughout *Conlat.* is not the task of actually gaining salvation through one's monastic striving, but the privilege of deepening one's contemplation of the glorified,

---

[80] See de Adalbert Vogüé, 'Pour comprendre Cassien: Un survol des *Conférences*', *CCist* 39 (1977), 250–72. [E.T. by John-Baptist Hasbrouck, 'Understanding Cassian: A Survey of the Conferences', *CistS* 19 (1984), 101–21.] See also Ramsey, Introduction to *John Cassian: The Conferences*, 12–13; Stewart, *Cassian the Monk*, 32–5.

[81] Fairbairn, *Grace and Christology*, 151–4.

[82] *Conlat.* 23.5 (CSEL 13.646–8) [ACW 57.894–6].

divine Christ, the one who has become human and lived a human life for our salvation, who has died and been raised as man, so that we might all share in contemplation of him. The monk, then, is to provide the foretaste for the whole church of the perfect contemplation of God that will characterize the age to come. And Christ the Son of God, who offered himself to the world in grace through his Incarnation, life, death, and resurrection, also offers grace to the monk in his special privilege and task. This, fundamentally, is the Christology that informs the charitology of *Conlat.* It is a Christology concerned very little with the terminological issues that dominate our Christological formulations, but it is Christology nonetheless, and in fact, it is a Christology of divine descent like that of Augustine and the post-correction Leporius, in which God the Son, the Word, is the personal subject of the incarnate Christ. This is the context in which we need to examine the emphasis on the monk's free will in *Conlat.* 13. The striking similarity of Cassian's Christology of divine descent to Augustine's serves to accentuate how differently the Gallic monk moves from Christology to charitology compared to the way the North African bishop does.

Conlat. 13: A Charitology of Emphasis?

It almost goes without saying that in *Conlat.* 13, Cassian attributes salvific actions to human effort in some places and to divine grace in other places. Indeed, one of the most striking aspects of the conference is the mass of biblical passages Cassian assembles to show that both human action and God's grace are operative. To take merely one example, in *Conlat.* 13.9 alone, he quotes seven groups of passages (sometimes pairs, sometimes triplets or even four passages in a group),[83] and in every case the first passage indicates the need for human action, and the other passage or passages show the insufficiency of that action and the need for grace.[84] As a result, the obvious question is how to interpret this emphasis on both grace and free will. Prosper of Aquitaine was the first to raise this issue, when he argued in *Con. Collat.* (c.432)[85] that Cassian began well by attributing the beginning of good works and good thoughts to grace in *Conlat.* 13.3, but that he then turned aside from his own first principle in arguing that sometimes God produces the beginning of a good will in a person, but at other times God finds such a good will and augments it. Prosper reads Cassian as distinguishing two classes of people: those

---

[83] These are Is. 1:19 and Rom. 9:16; Rom. 2:6 and Phil. 2:13, Eph. 2:8–9; James 4:8, and Jn. 6:44; Prov. 4:26, and Ps. 5:9, 16[17]:5; Ezek. 28:31 and Ezek. 1:19–20; Jer. 14:9 and Ps. 50[51]:9, 12; Hos. 10:12 and Ps. 12[13]:4, 93[94]:10, 145[146]:8.

[84] *Conlat.*13.9 (CSEL 13.372–4) [ACW 57.474–5].

[85] Gennadius, *De uir. illust.* 84 (85) (PL 58.1108) [*NPNF*[2] 3.399], calls this 'an anonymous book against certain works of Cassian, which the church of God finds salutary, but which he brands as injurious'.

90   CHRISTOLOGY AND THE LOGIC OF GRACE

who need God to change their will so that they can move towards him, and those who make the first move towards God on their own. For the first class, Prosper asserts, Cassian has properly made Christ a saviour, but for the second group, he has made Christ merely a helper and refuge.[86] While Prosper's interpretation is surely hyperbolic, it has set the stage for modern scholars' varied attempts to account for Cassian's seemingly equal emphasis on both human action and grace.

Conlat. 13 in Modern Scholarship

Most modern scholars have regarded Cassian as simply affirming that both divine grace and human action are necessary for salvation. A few recent examples should suffice. Writing in 1996, Weaver argues that in *Conlat.* 13, Cassian seems to go beyond his normal concept that human action works in the context of divine grace, by arguing that in some cases a person may initiate the first move towards God. At the same time, he stresses the variegated ways grace acts, and his portrayal is thus more subtle than both the Pelagians' (in which grace is purely external) and Augustine's (in which all people were in the same situation and needed a drastic remedy).[87] In 2001, Thomas Smith pointed out that a dominant metaphor in Cassian's monastic writings is military combat, in contrast to Augustine's depiction of a radically passive posture in Christian life. He concludes that for Cassian, 'the theological affirmation of the gratuity of grace need not entail a potential lapse into idleness, just as growth in virtue need not lead to hubristic illusions of perfectability'.[88] Writing in 2004, Philip Turner asserts: 'Grace in all its forms is an aid to human will and residual goodness that may be weakened and distorted but never destroyed. Cassian's soteriology, in contradistinction to that of St. Augustine, is without question a form of synergism.'[89] Writing in 2007, Casiday proposes five major themes in Cassian's charitology: 1) God may in fact will the salvation of all, but not all are saved. 2) Grace initiates, sustains, and perfects human salvation. 3) Grace is capable of converting the unwilling. 4) In a life lived under grace, people initiate good

---

[86] See Prosper of Aquitaine, *Con. Collat.* 2.2–4, 18.2 (PL 51.218–20, 263) [ACW 32.73–5, 124]. I should note here that Richard J. Goodrich, *Contextualizing Cassian: Aristocrats, Asceticism, and Reformation in Fifth-Century Gaul,* OECS (Oxford: Oxford University Press, 2007), 231–2, disputes whether Cassian is actually the target of Prosper's *Con. Collat.* Goodrich's argument is not persuasive, because Prosper's extended discussion of whether one should take the abbas' words as indicative of the 'collator's' thought (*Con. Collat.* 2.1 [PL 51.218] [ACW 32.72–3]) can scarcely refer to any other work than Cassian's *Conlat.*, and Prosper even calls the work he opposes *De protectione Dei*, which is the title of *Conlat.* 13.

[87] Weaver, *Divine Grace and Human Agency*, 111–14.

[88] Thomas A. Smith, 'Agonism and Antagonism: Metaphor and the Gallic Resistance to Augustine', *StPatr* 38 (2001), 288.

[89] Philip Turner, 'John Cassian and the Desert Fathers: Sources for Christian Spirituality?' *ProEccl* 13 (2004), 477.

actions on their own, and God deems them meritorious. 5) Judging the precise flourishing of salvation in individual cases demands discernment.[90]

Some scholars, in addition to recognizing that Cassian obviously emphasizes both grace and human action, have suggested that he has a nuanced view of the relation between them. In 1998, Stewart asserted not only that for Cassian there is a mysterious interplay between divine and human action, but more importantly, that Cassian is writing in the midst of the monastic striving after perfect chastity. He concludes, 'Cassian is describing the trajectory observable in monastic life, which begins with an experience of divine call and radical renunciation. He is writing in medias res: for the monks, grace has already prevened.'[91] Similarly, Ogliari, writing in 2003, argued for a sequential understanding of divine and human action:

> Yet, even though divine action is believed to be present at the beginning and end of man's good will, Cassian reiterates that there is a very short interval belonging to man's initiative. This interval is located between the *initium uoluntatis bonae*, inspired by God, and the *perfectio uirtutum*, which is also the work of God in various ways. Man's capability in enthusiastically accepting or ignoring the invitation of grace is contained in this short interval or time span.[92]

In contrast, in 2010 Hwang proposed a different scheme by arguing that Cassian works from two conflicting models of the relation between grace and human action. One is a cooperative model, in which God initiates salvific action throughout Christian life, but the human will is able either to conform to or resist God's grace. The other is what Hwang calls an alternative model, in which either human or divine will can initiate the process: the initial good will can be produced either by God or by the monk himself. Hwang argues that the cooperative model is addressed to the monks and that the alternative model is designed to oppose Pelagius and Augustine. He also insists that the two models are contradictory because the cooperative model requires that grace be resistible, but the alternative model implies that in the cases where God institutes the beginning of a good will, grace must be irresistible.[93]

---

[90] Casiday, *Tradition and Theology*, 67. Cf. Ramsey's insistence that *Conlat.* 13 is primarily about balance between grace and free will, in Ramsey, 'John Cassian and Augustine', in *Grace for Grace*, 124–30, cited above.

[91] Stewart, *Cassian the Monk*, 78–9.

[92] Ogliari, *Gratia et Certamen*, 133.

[93] Alexander Y. Hwang, 'Manifold Grace in John Cassian and Prosper of Aquitaine', *SJT* 63 (2010), 97–100. Cf. the same argument in Alexander Y. Hwang, *Intrepid Lover of Perfect Grace: The Life and Thought of Prosper of Aquitaine* (Washington, DC: The Catholic University of America Press, 2009), 147–51. Cf. the approving restatement of Hwang's proposal in Jérémy Delmulle, *Prosper d'Aquitaine contre Jean Cassien: Le* Contra Collatorem, *L'Appel à Rome du parti Augustinien dans la querelle postpélagienne*, Textes et Études du Moyen Âge 91 (Rome: Fédération Internationale des Instituts d'Études Médiévales, 2018), 252–7.

We should notice here that Hwang's cooperative model is akin to what Stewart and Ogliari suggest and is consistent with, although more specific than, what the majority of scholars propose—grace initiates and concludes salvation, as well as working in the middle. On the other hand, Hwang's alternative model has marked similarities to what Prosper claimed Cassian was affirming—some people can initiate salvation on their own, but in the case of others, God must and does begin the work. Indeed, Jérémy Delmulle, writing in 2018, points out that Prosper has ignored Cassian's cooperative model and has interacted only with the alternative model.[94] Still more recently, Jaros, writing in 2020, explicitly rejects the contention that Hwang's two models are mutually exclusive and argues instead that Cassian is following his teacher Chrysostom in holding to a concurrence model in which there is no tension between grace and human action,[95] and asserts that a concurrence model 'would alleviate any tension that exists for the problem passages found in *Conlatio* 13 and elsewhere'.[96] This understanding does not assign grace-focused and human-action-focused passages to different periods in the Christian's salvation (as do Stewart's and Ogliari's proposals, as well as Hwang's first model), nor does it assign such diverse passages to different people (as in Prosper's understanding of Cassian, echoed in Hwang's alternative model), but instead applies them both to the concurrent working of grace and human action at the same time.

As I step into this discussion, I suggest that we need to view *Conlat.* 13 with its monastic context firmly fixed in our minds, and that doing so enables us to navigate the differences between the sequential view of Ogliari/Hwang and the alternate view of Prosper/Hwang. As I stated above, nothing Cassian writes in *Conlat.* is meant to apply directly to non-Christians or even to Christians outside the monastery. Everything he writes is meant for monks, men who have already been adopted into God's family and granted communion with the Lord, and who strive for perfect contemplation of their glorified Lord. What this means is obvious but still must be grasped—Cassian is never writing about the very beginning of salvation, in *Conlat.* 13 or anywhere else in his monastic corpus. As Stewart has helpfully put it, everything he writes is *in medias res*, written by a pilgrim to fellow pilgrims who are already well on the way. In the light of this context, the passages that seem to suggest some people can begin the work of salvation on their own need to be reinterpreted. They are not about the very beginning of salvation, but about situations in a monk's life when he takes the initiative and is supported in his intentions by grace, as opposed to other situations in the same monk's life when God needs to take the initiative to rescue the monk's recalcitrant will from itself. With this in mind, let us turn to *Conlat.* 13 to see whether all of Cassian's assertions can be seen to make sense in this framework.

---

[94] Delmulle, *Prosper d'Aquitaine contre Jean Cassien*, 256.
[95] Jaros, 'The Relationship of the So-Called Semi-Pelagians', 172–8.
[96] Ibid., 178.

Conlat. 13 as an Exploration of Grace in a Monk's Life

The subject of *Conlat.* 13 (as also of *Conlat.* 23, the culmination of Cassian's treatment of grace) is perfect chastity, and the discussion is set up by Germanus's perplexity in 13.2 over Abba Chaeremon's claim in 12.15 that chastity is the result of the Lord's mercy, not the monk's own efforts. Germanus likens the situation to a farmer who should be able to attribute a good crop to his own labour.[97] Here, both the subject (chastity) and the analogy (a farmer's crop) indicate that this is not a discussion about salvation in the broadest sense. Germanus is asking about monastic perfection in chastity, and Chaeremon accepts the question on those terms when he takes up the analogy and insists that God provides both the rain needed for the crop to grow and the farmer's strength and initative to work hard. Following this discussion of the farmer, Chaeremon summarizes:

> From this it is clear that the origin not only of good acts but even of good thoughts (*non solum actuum, uerum etiam cogitationum bonarum*) is in God. He both inspires in us the beginnings of a holy will (*initia sanctae uoluntatis inspirat*) and grants the ability and the opportunity (*uirtutem atque oportunitatem ... tribuit*) to bring to fulfillment the things that we rightly desire.... But it is up to us to conform humbly to the grace of God that daily draws us on (*ut cotitidie adtrahentem nos gratiam dei humiliter subsequamur*).[98]

It may well be the case that as he writes this, Cassian has 'Pelagian' ideas in mind and wants to distance his thought from those ideas. But be that as it may, the main point of this important passage is to reiterate, in response to Germanus's objection, the point he has made at the end of *Conlat.* 12. Whatever degree of chastity a monk achieves is ultimately the result of God's grace, but this fact does not obviate human responsibility to cooperate with grace. Notice that salvation in the broadest sense is not in view in this passage. The word *salus* does not occur, and the starting point is the assertion that whatever the monk does that is good has its origins in God. The fact that the monk's good desires and actions are themselves not the very beginning of salvation does not need to be spoken, because the Incarnation, redemption, and the glorified Christ stand behind everything Cassian writes in *Conlat.* Although this passage meets with Prosper's approval, the fact that Prosper takes it as a reference to salvation in the broadest sense means that he already misunderstands Cassian to some degree, and he sets himself up for a significant misassessment of what Cassian writes later in *Conlat.* 13.

This narrow focus is even more apparent shortly afterwards. Germanus objects that what Chaeremon asserts would destroy free will and would also fly in the face

---

[97] See *Conlat.* 12.15 (CSEL 13.358) [ACW 57.453], 13.2 (CSEL 13.363) [ACW 57.467].
[98] *Conlat.* 13.3 (CSEL 13.364) [ACW 57.468–9].

94 CHRISTOLOGY AND THE LOGIC OF GRACE

of experience, since even pagan philosophers successfully achieve chastity without the help of God.[99] Chaeremon responds that such philosophers have merely external chastity, not the true chastity of heart and mind that the monks seek,[100] thus demonstrating again that this conference is about its stated subject, not about salvation in general. Chaeremon then reiterates:

> Consequently, although it can be shown that in many things, indeed in all things, human beings need God's help (*auxilio dei*), and that without the help of God (*sine adiutorio dei*), human frailty by itself alone can accomplish (*perficere*) nothing which pertains to salvation (*ad salute pertinet*), this is still nowhere more evident than in acquiring and maintaining chastity (*adquisitione atque custodia castitatis*). For since the discussion on the difficulty concerning its integrity has been put off for so long, now let us briefly discuss its means (*instrumentis*).[101]

Again, we should remember that Germanus has objected to such a robust role for grace in monastic striving, and again we see that Chaeremon responds by stressing the monk's absolute dependence on grace. Notice in this passage that the word *salus* does occur (unlike earlier in the discussion), but it is tied to the accomplishment of chastity. Indeed, the word rendered 'accomplish' is *perficere*, which indicates that the aspect of salvation Cassian has in view here is the monastic goal of perfect chastity. As earlier, so also here, salvation in the broadest sense is not in view. And as earlier, so also here, even in the narrower salvific task of achieving chastity, the need for God's grace is abundantly clear.

In the light of this discussion, I suggest that Prosper, along with later interpreters who see *Conlat*. 13 as a work about salvation in general, is making the mistake of transposing a spiritual discussion on a narrow topic into a theological treatise on soteriology in general. But if I am right about the significance of the monastic context to *Conlat*. 13 and thus about its narrow application, what gives interpreters the impression that it is meant more broadly? The answer to that question is ready to hand, because in the following chapter, Cassian discusses the universal salvific will of God, and that chapter must indeed be understood in reference to salvation in the broadest sense. Cassian's logic in this chapter starts from the explicit insistence that God wills the salvation of all, coupled with the assumption that not all are saved. Therefore, he insists, those who perish do so against his will. Taking 1 Tim. 2:4 to refer to something other than all people without exception (that is, taking it to mean 'all kinds of people' or 'all whom he has chosen for salvation') would fly in the face of the Lord's appeal in Mt. 11:28 for all who are burdened and heavy

---

[99] *Conlat*. 13.4 (CSEL 13.365) [ACW 57.469].
[100] *Conlat*. 13.5 (CSEL 13.365–7) [ACW 57.469–70].
[101] *Conlat*. 13.6 (CSEL 13.367) [ACW 57.470, translation modified]. Ramsey's translation in ACW 57 here is slightly incoherent at the beginning and seems to be the result of a redaction mistake. Gibson's rendering (*NPNF*[2] 11.424) reflects the Latin more accurately.

laden to come to him. He even asserts that understanding God's salvific will in a restrictive sense would imply a denial that all have sinned.[102]

We have seen that Hwang has insisted this must mean God's grace is resistible.[103] This is certainly true, but Cassian's purpose is not to turn from the implication of resistible grace to a general discussion of soteriology, grace, and human action in the broadest sense. Instead, his purpose is to discuss grace and human effort in the life of a monk. In fact, his general discussion of God's salvific will in 13.7 remains anchored in his more specific focus, as shown by the fact that at the beginning of the discussion, just after claiming that God wills the salvation of all, he adds: 'When his kindness sees shining in us the slightest glimmer of good will (*bonae uoluntatis ... quantulamque scintillam*), which he himself has in fact sparked (*quam ipse ... excuderit*) from the hard flint of our heart, he fosters it, stirs it up, and strengthens it with his inspiration.'[104] Interpreters who have taken *Conlat.* 13 to mean that a human being can make the first move towards God have, I believe, misunderstood this passage in two ways. First, they have failed to grasp the fact that the glimmer of good will God sees in us is also that which he himself has sparked.[105] The relation between the human will and divine grace is far more subtle than what would be implied by the assertion that in some people God stirs up a good will, and other people produce such a will themselves. And secondly, interpreters misunderstand that, as I have emphasized all along, the beginning of a good will is not the beginning of salvation. It is itself a response to the grace of the Son's Incarnation, passion, resurrection, and his adoption of a person into his family.

If, therefore, this chapter is not a change of subject from the pursuit of chastity to soteriology more broadly, why does Cassian bring up the subject of God's universal salvific will? Surely part of the reason is the fact that restrictive interpretations of 1 Tim. 2:4—whether from Augustine or from Masilians of a predestinarian bent— are in the spiritual air of Gaul, and thus, scholars who see *Conlat.* 13 as a rejection of such views are not wrong, just as scholars who see the conference as a rejection of 'Pelagian' views are not wrong either. But in the broad context of *Conlat.*, and especially in the specific context of *Conlat.* 13, I do not believe this answer alone is sufficient. Rather, this general discussion of the Lord's salvific will needs to be seen in the light of Cassian's purpose to foster the pursuit of chastity. I suggest, then, that the general discussion serves to encourage monks in their pursuit of chastity and to spur them on in that pursuit. The God who does not desire anyone to perish,

---

[102] *Conlat.* 13.7 (CSEL 13.368–70) [ACW 57.471–2].

[103] Hwang, 'Manifold Grace in John Cassian and Prosper of Aquitaine', 100. This is what Hwang calls the 'cooperative' model of grace and human action.

[104] *Conlat.* 13.7 (CSEL 13.369) [ACW 57.472].

[105] This is also the pattern in the rest of the conference. See the following passages affirming that what God finds/sees in us is that which he himself has produced/engendered: 13.8 (CSEL 13.371–2) [ACW 57.474], in which Chaeremon says that the good will making an appearance in us was planted by God; 13.9 (CSEL 13.374) [ACW 57.475], in which Chaeremon affirms that the beginnings of a good will come from the good nature that God has implanted.

96   CHRISTOLOGY AND THE LOGIC OF GRACE

who wills all to be saved, surely also wants the monk who is already an adopted son
to succeed in his pursuit of monastic perfection. Such a God will make his grace
readily available to the monk; he will stir the monk up to holy desires; he will pour
grace upon the holy desires he sees the monk exhibit (desires the Lord himself has
inflamed); he will crown the monk's efforts with a degree of success and ultimately
bring him to perfection/glorification/salvation. The universal salvific will of God
means that the monk is never working at cross-purposes with the Lord, that God is
always pulling for him to succeed, not to fail. And *that* should be far more encour-
aging and incentivizing to a monk than any incentive that might come from his
getting credit himself for his own successes.

In the light of this context, we should not understand the varied aspects of grace
Cassian discusses in the remainder of *Conlat.* 13 as references to salvation in general that apply strictly and without overlap to different people, as Prosper does
when he claims Cassian means that Christ is not the saviour but only the helper
for certain people who can turn to God on their own. Instead, we should see these
varied aspects as illustrations of different situations in the life of a given monk, situations in which the Lord works graciously and differently in connection with the
needs and struggles of the monk at that time. Sometimes he strengthens the monk's
will to carry through that which he wills.[106] Sometimes he crowns the monk's
meagre efforts with greater reward than those efforts warrant.[107] Sometimes he allows the monk to fail without apparently aiding him, so as to hone and sharpen the
monk's recognition that his victories are the result of the Lord's grace.[108] Cassian's
repeated references to 'sometimes' and 'other times' (*nunc . . . nunc*) blunt the force
of his references to some people and others, so his statements that in the case of
some, God assists their wills, but in the case of others, he moves them against their
wills,[109] should not be taken as mutually exclusive. Rather, any given monk will
surely need different kinds of grace in different situations, even as some monks are
more likely to need one kind than another.[110]

This analysis suggests that Hwang's 'alternative model'[111] is not in fact inconsistent with his cooperative model, because Cassian is not writing about how salvation in general comes to different people, nor is he implying that some people do
not need the Lord to act first in salvation and that in the case of those who do need
God to act first, grace is irresistible. Those are simply not questions that he considers. In fact, at one point in the discussion, Chaeremon asserts that human free

---

[106]   *Conlat.* 13.11 (CSEL 13.377-8) [ACW 57.478].

[107]   *Conlat.* 13.3 (CSEL 13.382-3) [ACW 57.481].

[108]   *Conlat.* 13.14 (CSEL 13.387-8) [ACW 57.485].

[109]   See, e.g., *Conlat.* 13.17 (CSEL 13.392-3) [ACW 57.488]; 13.18 (CSEL 13.396) [ACW 57.490].

[110]   Although Jaros does not point out the significance of the fact that nothing in *Conlat.* 13 is referring to the beginning of salvation, his discussion of the varied action of grace in Cassian's thought
is consistent with the point I am making here. See Jaros, 'The Relationship of the So-Called Semi-
Pelagians', 184–7.

[111]   Hwang, 'Manifold Grace in John Cassian and Prosper of Aquitaine', 100.

will and divine grace 'are mixed together and fused so indistinguishably that which is dependent on which is a great question as far as many people are concerned (*inter multos magna quaestione uoluatur*)—that is, whether God has mercy on us because we manifest the beginnings of a good will, or we acquire the beginnings of a good will because God is merciful'.[112] We should note the touch of irony in these words: this may be a great question to 'many', but not to Cassian. He is content to affirm both divine grace and human free will in the Christian life of the monk, because he has established the priority of grace in human salvation through his teaching on the Incarnation and on adoption.[113]

Conclusions on Cassian

Scholarly dissatisfaction with Cassian seems to derive from asking from him something other than what he seeks to deliver. Some scholars want consistent Christological terminology and a fair assessment of Nestorius's complex notion of πρόσωπον of union, but Cassian gives us outrage at the implication (or at least potential implication) of 'Nestorius's thought: that Christ is not the incarnate Son, but instead a man who received the Son. Some scholars want a theological disputation on the role of grace and free will in salvation considered in its broadest sense, but Cassian gives us a detailed psychological reflection on the varied ways God's grace acts in the monastic pursuit of chastity. Calling him a poor Christologist fails to get at the importance of his shock at 'Nestorius': Cassian believes salvation hinges around the personal continuity between the eternal Son and the incarnate Christ. The Son *himself* was sent to live, die, and be raised for our redemption, that we might contemplate him in his glorified divinity. Likewise, calling Cassian an inconsistent thinker on charitology, or even claiming that he lies mid-way on a spectrum between Pelagius and Augustine, misses the significance of his positive statement when it is considered on its own terms: Cassian believes that divine grace holds priority at all points in salvation, that the Lord who has made the monk his adopted son is also at work by grace at every point in the monk's life—initiating and responding, engendering holy desires and cultivating them, and ultimately crowning monastic efforts with success.

This means that Cassian's relation to Augustinian thought is considerably more nuanced than the idea of a spectrum suggests. It is not simply the case that he is a synergist who tries to balance divine and human, whereas Augustine is a monergist who emphasizes only the divine. Rather, Cassian and Augustine share a remarkably

---

[112] *Conlat.* 13.11 (CSEL 13.375–6) [ACW 57.476].

[113] Augustine Casiday, 'Grace and the Humanity of Christ according to St. Vincent of Lérins', *VigChr* 59 (2005), 30, concurs with my interpretation when he writes, 'The gradual re-fashioning of the Christian will is therefore understood by Cassian as the unfolding of the grace that is first poured forth in the mystery of the Incarnation.'

consistent Christology, thus enabling both of them to play a role in the correction of Leporius. For Cassian, Augustine, and the post-correction Leporius, the crucial Christological truth is not whether the Christological union is described 'adequately', but whether one clearly affirms that the baby born from Mary, the man who lived, died, and was raised for our redemption, is indeed the eternal Son of God. All three answer that question 'yes', and Nestorius, or at least 'Nestorius' as Cassian perceives him, answers the question 'no'.

Furthermore, Augustine and Cassian show the same concern to root salvation in the priority of gracious divine action, in contrast to a 'Pelagian' or 'Nestorian' view in which human action takes the primary place and divine grace is auxiliary. This is another reason not to think of Cassian as emphasizing divine action any less than Augustine does, as the moniker 'Semi-Pelagian' might lead one to do. But in spite of these commonalities, Augustine and Cassian make very different logical moves when discussing grace. Augustine finds in Scripture a strong parallelism between the humanity of Christ, which was taken into the person of the Word through no merits of its own, and the salvation of human beings, who are predestined through no merits of our own to be united to the incarnate Christ. Because he establishes the priority of the divine in salvation through the doctrine of predestination, there is little room for free human action in this logical movement. The priority of the divine demands both the predestination of Christ's humanity and the predestination of men and women, so the effects of the Incarnation apply largely or only to the predestined. On the other hand, Cassian establishes the priority of divine action through his treatment of the Incarnation and the adoption of Christians as God's children, not through a doctrine of predestination, and thus he allows a more cooperative understanding of the way divine and human action interact in the process of Christian life. There is a different logical link between Christology and grace in Cassian than in Augustine, even though they are to some degree responding to similar mistakes—those they find in the 'Pelagians', and the similar mistakes they find in the 'proto-Nestorian' Leporius and (in Cassian's case) in the actual 'Nestorian', Nestorius himself.

Augustine's Christology functions in the service of his doctrine of predestination, as we saw in chapter 1. But Cassian's similar Christology functions differently; it is the very basis for the establishment of divine priority in Christian life, such that a way is open to affirm genuine human free action under the umbrella of divine grace. For Augustine, predestination is the hinge around which soteriology turns, but for Cassian, the Incarnation itself is the hinge. In fact, Cassian never mentions predestination at all; his discussions of the particularity of grace have to do with varying situations in the life of a monk, not with any attempt to peer into God's discrimination between an elect person and a non-elect one. One could reasonably surmise that for Cassian, predestination depends on God's foreknowledge of how human beings will use their freedom to cooperate with grace, but this would simply be a guess. When one establishes the priority of the divine in salvation through the universal effects of the Incarnation on the human race, the relation between predestination and foreknowledge becomes a less urgent question than if predestination itself is the basis for establishing divine priority.

Thus, while Augustine and Cassian hold essentially the same Christology, the fact that they use different concepts to establish the priority of the divine in salvation and thus place the Incarnation in different places in the logic of grace leads to quite different depictions of the way grace operates in Christian life. With this in mind, I now turn to Vincent of Lérins, who has long been regarded as an opponent of Augustine but whose explicit references to the doctor of grace are always favourable and who, like Cassian, reserves most of his invective for 'Nestorius'.

4

Vincent of Lérins

'Nestorius', Christian Orthodoxy, and Grace

In the previous chapter, we saw that Cassian's 'Semi-Pelagianism' recedes substantially when one considers his writings in the light of his stated opposition to 'Nestorius'. Cassian's disagreements with Augustine—as significant as they are—are not about degrees of emphasis on divine and human action, such that one might rank him on a spectrum between Pelagius and Augustine. Instead, Cassian and Augustine both prioritize divine action, but they do so in different ways, through a different logic of grace. When we turn our attention to Vincent of Lérins, we find another fifth-century Gallic writer who was long considered 'Semi-Pelagian' but who looks rather different upon closer study. In Vincent's case, the primary reasons for regarding him as anti-Augustine (not just non-Augustinian) and thus 'Semi-Pelagian' were that he was believed to be the author of the *Obiect. Vincent.* (a writing that we possess only through its refutation in Prosper's *Resp. obiect. Vincent.*), that the *Obiect. Vincent.* was written against Augustine's charitology, and that Vincent's *Excerp.* (in which he quotes extensively from Augustine in order to combat Arianism, Photinianism, and Nestorianism) was unknown to us until 1940. By considering Vincent's well-known *Comm.* in connection with the *Excerp.* and without *Obiect. Vincent.*, we find him to be less opposed to Augustine than he was reputed to be, but perhaps more significantly, we find him to be much more concerned about 'Nestorianism' than any other heresy. While Cassian was the first Western writer to respond at length to 'Nestorius', Vincent was surely also concerned to respond to him as well, Indeed, the response to 'Nestorius' looms large in Vincent's understanding of a dynamic and developing tradition of Christian orthodoxy, the very understanding for which he is best known.[1] Vincent's anti-'Nestorian' Christology and his charitology will be the subjects of this chapter.

---

[1] The famous Vincentian canon, *quod ubique, quod semper, quod ab omnibus creditum est*, is found in *Comm.* 2.5 (CCSL 64.149) [FC 7.270].

Christology and the Logic of Grace in Fifth-Century Gaul. Donald Fairbairn, Oxford University Press.
© Donald Fairbairn 2025. DOI: 10.1093/9780198936220.003.0005

Questions of Authorship in Connection with
Vincent's Alleged 'Semi-Pelagianism'

The belief of earlier scholars that Vincent was strongly opposed to Augustine and thus deserved to be called 'Semi-Pelagian'[2] is certainly understandable in the light of the *Obiect. Vincent*. If Prosper's presentation is to be trusted, that work consists of sixteen theses summarizing the thought of some unnamed predestinarians about God's restricted salvific will. Although Prosper describes opponents, plural, most scholars assume the author is referring to Augustine. The author claims that the unnamed opponents believe God does not will all people to be saved but created most for condemnation and that Christ did not die for all. The author casts this thought in a very dim light indeed, by stating that it implies God is the author of even the worst sins and that in his predestination he withholds the possibility of repentance and salvation from most people.[3] One could scarcely be faulted for concluding that the author of such a work was an ardent opponent of Augustine. Actually, though, even prior to 1940, scholars recognized the complexity of Vincent's relation to Augustine. For example, in 1897, Harnack, while claiming that Vincent's *Comm.* was an anti-Augustinian work, also contended (surely correctly) that Vincent had taken his rules for the understanding of tradition from Augustine himself.[4] And just a few years later, when Brunetière and de Labiolle published their French translation of *Comm.*, they wrote separately to preview the work. In the preface, Brunetière stated directly that he did not believe *Comm.* was directed against Augustine. In the introduction, de Labriolle called it an exaggeration to say that Vincent was writing against Augustine, although it was not impossible that the work was intended to serve the interests of Semi-Pelagianism. He suggests that Vincent, without wanting to attack Augustine by name or even to use his own name (he called himself *peregrinus*[5]), nevertheless may have wanted to

---

[2] Thomas G. Guarino, *Vincent of Lérins and the Development of Christian Doctrine*, Foundations of Theological Exegesis and Christian Spirituality (Grand Rapids, MI.: Baker Academic, 2013), xxiv, traces the idea that the *Comm.* is an anti-Augustinian tract back to Voss and Noris in the seventeenth century. He cites Harnack, Madoz, and Pelikan as twentieth-century scholars who have claimed that the *Comm.* is an anti-Augustinian work. Madoz is particularly significant because he would later be the one who discovered the *Excerp.*, as we shall see.

[3] See Prosper, *Resp. obiect. Vincent* (PL 51.177–86) [ACW 32.163–77].

[4] Adolf von Harnack, *History of Dogma*. Vol. 3, trans. from vol. 2 of the 3d German edition by J. Millar (London: Williams & Norgate, 1898. Reprint, New York: Russell & Russell, 1958) [German 1st edition, *Lehrbuch der Dogmengeschichte*, vol. 2, 1889. German 3d edition, vol. 2, 1897], 230n1. Notice the similarity between, e.g., Vincent's claim that we should 'prefer the decrees of a previous ecumenical council (if there was one) to the temerity and ignorance of a small group' in *Comm.* 3 (CCSL 64.149–50) [FC 7.271] and Augustine's insistence that the authority of a local council is not as great as that of an ecumenical council in *De bapt.* 2.14 (PL 43.134–5) [WSA I/21.433–4].

[5] The actual title of *Comm.* is *Tractatus peregrini pro Catholicae fidei antiquitate et uniuersitates aduersus profanas omnium haereticorum nouitates*. See CCSL 64.147.

102 CHRISTOLOGY AND THE LOGIC OF GRACE

show that Augustine's teaching on grace and predestination was a private opinion, not to be placed on a par with the ancient unanimity of the church.[6]

The Discovery of the *Excerp.*

In the late 1930s in Spain, José Madoz noticed that the catalogue of Ripoll codices (in Catalonia) mentioned a work attributed to Vincent of Lérins consisting of passages from Augustine supporting *ecclesiae antiquam et uniuersalem fidem*, a phrase consistent with the language and main theme of the *Comm.*[7] The manuscript so described[8] is a tract on the Trinity and the Incarnation consisting of excerpts from Augustine's writings organized into two parts of five sections each, with only a prologue, an epilogue, and a few lines of transition between some excerpts provided by the author/editor. This brought to Madoz's mind the fact that an anonymous ninth-century writing describes 'a book of Vincent, presbyter on the island of Lérins, that he composed from the books of the blessed Augustine and sent to the holy Pope Sixtus, a book that is useful to be read on this matter [that is, on the catholic faith]'.[9] Of course, Madoz also remembered that in *Comm.* 16 Vincent announces his intention to write a more detailed refutation of Photinus, Apollinaris, and Nestorius.[10] Putting all of this together, Madoz believed he had found the lost work in which Vincent kept the promise he made in *Comm.* 16.[11]

Madoz's ground-breaking 1940 article gives a thorough summary of the contents of the *Excerp.* and a convincing demonstration that Vincent is the author/ editor. Madoz places side by side the descriptions from the *Comm.* and the *Excerp.* about Nestorius's teaching, the fundamentals of the faith, the nature of heresy as 'profane novelty', and the final anathemas in order to show the striking verbal consistency between the two works.[12] He notes that the two works use similar language to describe both Nestorius's teaching and the orthodox faith.[13] Madoz concludes that Vincent was the compiler of the *Excerp.* and that since it was written after the *Comm.* (in fulfilment of a promise given in that work to write such a tract) and

---

[6] Ferdinand Brunetière and Pierre de Labriolle, *Saint Vincent de Lérins*, La Pensée Chrétienne: Textes et Études, (Paris: Librarie Bloud, 1906), xiii, lxxxii–lxxxv. It is also worth noting that on xciv, de Labriolle claims the view that Vincent wrote the *Obiect. Vincent.* suffers from difficulties and is problematic.

[7] José Madoz y Moleres, 'Un tratado desconocido de San Vicente de Lerins', *Gregorianum* 21 (1940), 75–6.

[8] Codex *Ripoll* n. 151. See Madoz, 'Un tratado desconocido', 76.

[9] Madoz, 'Un tratado desconocido', 77. See also Roland Demeulenaere, Preface to 'Vincentii Lerinensis, *Commonitorium; Excerpta*', CCSL 64.132.

[10] *Comm.* 16.9 (CCSL 64.169) [FC 7.298].

[11] Madoz, 'Un tratado desconocido', 78.

[12] Ibid., 82–5.

[13] Ibid., 85–7. Madoz devotes the latter part of the article (88–90) to a demonstration of the similarities between the *Excerp.* and the *Quicunque Vult.*

dedicated to Sixtus III (pope from 432 to 440), it must have been written between 434 and 440.[14]

Since the re-discovery and publication of the *Excerp.*, scholars quickly and unanimously joined Madoz in affirming its Vincentian authorship.[15] Not surprisingly, though, this milestone did not immediately lead scholars to reject the idea that Vincent was an anti-Augustinian. Madoz himself suggested in the light of the *Excerp.* that Vincent saw a sharp distinction between Augustine's teaching on the Trinity and the Incarnation on the one hand, and his teaching on predestination and grace on the other.[16] And as late as 1971, Jaroslav Pelikan still affirmed the older categorization of Vincent as a Semi-Pelagian.[17] But some two decades after Madoz's discovery, another blow was dealt to the assumption that Vincent was a Semi-Pelagian writing directly against Augustine.

The Possible Spuriousness of the *Obiect. Vincent.*

Writing in 1963, William O'Connor subjected the longstanding view that the *Comm.* was a polemic against Augustine to a sustained critique. Two substantial planks in his argument were his contention that the discovery of the *Excerp.* should have forced a rejection of that view (although it did not do so immediately), and that Vincent did not write the *Obiect. Vincent.* I shall summarize the latter of these contentions now.

O'Connor begins by reciting various stylistic similarities between the *Obiect. Vincent.* and Vincent's *Comm.* that had been used to argue for common authorship, and he asserts—certainly correctly—that those similarities are largely coincidental and not very significant. He also rejects the claim that identical doctrines are presented in the two works by pointing out that the theological ideas are presented in response to different heresies and simply happen to include some of the same ideas.[18] Then O'Connor states his positive case that the author of the *Obiect. Vincent.* is not Vincent of Lérins: 'The doctrine expounded in the Objections is so *evidently* foreign to the mind of Augustine, as expressed in his works, that no intelligent man who studied these same works, could ever have, in good faith and

---

[14] Ibid., 91–2.

[15] See, e.g., William O'Connor, 'Saint Vincent of Lérins and Saint Augustine: Was the *Commonitorium* of Saint Vincent of Lérins Intended as a Polemic against Saint Augustine and his Doctrine on Predestination?' *Doctor Communis* 16 (1963), 131–5; Demeulenaere, Preface to 'Vincentii Lerinensis, *Commonitorium; Excerpta*', CCSL 64.132–3. Scholars after the time of Demeulenaere have assumed Vincentian authorship.

[16] Madoz, 'Un tratado desconocido', 94.

[17] Jaroslav Pelikan, *The Christian Tradition: A History of the Development of Doctrine, Vol. 1: The Emergence of the Catholic Tradition (100–600)* (Chicago: University of Chicago Press, 1971), 333.

[18] O'Connor, 'Saint Vincent of Lérins and Saint Augustine', 146–55. Here O'Connor is responding primarily to Hugo Koch, 'Vincenz von Lerin und Gennadius: Ein Beitrage zur Literaturegeschichte des Semipelagianismus', TU 31.2 (1907), 43–7.

without malice, attributed it to him.'[19] O'Connor further argues on the basis of the *Excerp.* that Vincent had read Augustine's works carefully, and if he had written the *Obiect. Vincent.*, he could not have caricatured Augustine so badly by accident. He must have done so through deliberate malice, which is unthinkable. O'Connor concludes that the Vincent of the *Obiect. Vincent.* could not have been Vincent of Lérins.[20]

O'Connor's argument that this Vincent was not the author of the *Obiect. Vincent.* has gained general scholarly acceptance. Writing in 1985 in the introduction to his critical edition of the *Comm.* and the *Excerp.*, Demeulenaere concluded that after the study by O'Connor, it was not possible any longer to attribute the *Obiect. Vincent.* to Vincent.[21] Nevertheless, it is important to note that some scholars continue to believe Vincent was the author, but that his target in the *Obiect. Vincent.* was not Augustine himself, but some Augustinians in Gaul—either Prosper or others.[22] Thus, it is likely that Vincent of Lérins was not the author of the *Obiect. Vincent.*, or if he was, he was not opposing Augustine per se but was rejecting the thought of certain Augustinians in Gaul. Given these possibilities, and especially given the fact that we do not possess the *Obiect. Vincent.* directly, I shall not use that work in my reconstruction of Vincent's thought in this chapter.

Recent Scholarly Views on Vincent as 'Semi-Pelagian'

Despite the significance of Madoz's and O'Connor's work, however, the older interpretative assumption of a clash between 'Semi-Pelagians' in Gaul and Augustinian thought remained in force. In fact, O'Connor himself seems never to have questioned this basic dichotomy. He asserts that Vincent lived in an environment where both his own abbot (Faustus, who had not yet become the bishop of Riez) and the most celebrated abbot in the area (Cassian) were Semi-Pelagian opponents of Augustine. Therefore, O'Connor argues, Vincent would have had no reason to conceal any Semi-Pelagian leanings and every reason to conceal any agreement with Augustine. O'Connor even speculates that the reason we are missing the bulk of the second Commonitory is that in that work, Vincent may have praised Augustine, and his Semi-Pelagian superiors may then have believed the praises needed to be muted.[23] (In support of this conjecture is the fact that Gennadius claims the

---

[19] O'Connor, 'Saint Vincent of Lérins and Saint Augustine', 156–72.

[20] Ibid., 173.

[21] Demeulenaere, Preface to 'Vincentii Lerinensis, *Commonitorium; Excerpta*', CCSL 64.133. Cf. Guarino, *Vincent of Lérins and the Development of Christian Doctrine*, xviii.

[22] See Augustine Casiday, *Tradition and Theology in St John Cassian*, OECS (Oxford: Oxford University Press 2007), 33–4; T. Kurt Jaros, 'The Relationship of the So-Called Semi-Pelagians and Eastern Greek Theology on the Doctrine of Original Sin: An Historical-Systematic Analysis and its Relevance for 21st Century Protestantism', Ph.D. Dissertation, University of Aberdeen, 2020, 233.

[23] O'Connor, 'Saint Vincent of Lérins and Saint Augustine', 179–80.

VINCENT OF LÉRINS   105

second Commonitory was stolen [*a quibusdam furatam perdidit*].[24]) Furthermore, another major plank in O'Connor's argument is Vincent's insistence in *Comm*. 28 that for the sake of orthodoxy, one should not quote from unorthodox writers.[25] To O'Connor, this must mean that if Vincent were a Semi-Pelagian, he would have regarded Augustine as unorthodox/heretical, and therefore he could not—in view of his own principles—have quoted Augustine at all.[26] Clearly, O'Connor sees the discussion in terms of the traditional dichotomy between Semi-Pelagians and Augustinians; he simply insists that Vincent belongs on the Augustinian side rather than the Semi-Pelagian side.

As late as 2011, Alexander Hwang accepted the same basic dichotomy. He contends that Vincent's argument in *Comm*. parallels that of Prosper's *Con. Collat.* too closely to be a coincidence and that Vincent's purpose in the work must have been to refute Prosper (and thus, Augustine).[27] He asserts, 'Vincent labels teachings that do not meet the test of catholicity as novelties, namely, the teaching of Augustine, caricatured in chapter 26. Although not mentioned by name, it becomes clear that Augustine's doctrine of predestination is the novelty Vincent was concerned with refuting.'[28]

Even as some scholars continued to preserve the Semi-Pelagian/Augustinian dichotomy, other interpreters of Vincent have begun to move away from it. Writing in 1989, Robert Markus asserted that Vincent (and, for that matter, Pope Celestine) seemed to make a distinction between what was true and what was orthodox. Some questions, such as predestination, could be matters of genuine disagreement without requiring one to pronounce a different opinion to be a heresy.[29] We should note that Markus's contention in effect undermines O'Connor's argument about Vincent's affinity for Augustine. It *was* true that for Vincent, one should not quote heretical authors, but Markus suggests plausibly that Vincent was also able to distinguish between a simple error and an error grave enough to be called a heresy. If Vincent thought Augustine was wrong on predestination, that does not necessarily

---

[24] Gennadius, *De uir. illust.* 64 (65) (PL 58.1097) [*NPNF*[2] 3.396].

[25] Vincent, *Comm*. 28.6–8 (CCSL 64.187) [FC 7.321–2].

[26] O'Connor, 'Saint Vincent of Lérins and Saint Augustine', 254.

[27] Alexander Y. Hwang, 'Prosper, Cassian, and Vincent: The Rule of Faith in the Augustinian Controversy', in *Tradition and the Rule of Faith in the Early Church: Essays in Honor of Joseph T. Lienhard, S.J.*, eds, Ronnie J. Rombs and Alexander Y. Hwang (Washington, DC: Catholic University of America Press, 2011), 76–7. Cf. the same claim in Hwang, *Intrepid Lover of Perfect Grace: The Life and Thought of Prosper of Aquitaine* (Washington, DC: The Catholic University of America Press, 2009), 168.

[28] Ibid., 77. Cf. Guarino, *Vincent of Lérins and the Development of Christian Doctrine*, xx–xxviii, who adroitly surveys various scholarly views on these questions. While Guarino is non-committal on the question of whether Vincent was Semi-Pelagian, his comment (xxvii) that if Vincent was, we should not judge him too harshly, suggests that Guarino may ultimately count Vincent as Semi-Pelagian.

[29] Robert A. Markus, 'The Legacy of Pelagius: Orthodoxy, Heresy and Conciliation', in *The Making of Orthodoxy: Essays in Honour of Henry Chadwick*, ed. Rowan Williams (Cambridge: Cambridge University Press, 1989), 220.

106   CHRISTOLOGY AND THE LOGIC OF GRACE

mean he would regard Augustine as heretical and therefore, un-quotable in the defence of orthodoxy more generally.

Writing in 2006, Raúl Villegas Marín provided a nuanced argument akin to that of Markus. But instead of arguing that Vincent distinguishes a mistake from a heresy, Marín claims persuasively that he distinguishes between a saintly man who makes a doctrinal mistake and the heretics who propagate that mistake. Marín notes that in *Comm.* 7.3, Vincent cites the account of Noah's sons turning away from their father's nakedness and covering him [Gen. 9:20–7] and uses this passage to explain the difference between Cyprian and the Donatists, both of whom affirmed rebaptism of repentant *lapsi*. Cyprian, Vincent claims, was a saintly man who was wrong on this point. The Donatists were the heretics who spread the practice of rebaptism even after the church had rejected that practice. Marín claims that because of the saintliness of Augustine the man, Vincent passes over his erroneous teaching on predestination in silence but refers to his supporters in Gaul, who are diffusing the false teaching, as the new heretics. In this understanding, the fact that Vincent accepts Augustine's authority on Trinitarian and Christological issues does not mean (contrary to O'Connor's judgement) that Vincent is Augustinian. At the same time, he is not anti-Augustine because he reveres the man himself even though he disagrees with him on a crucial point, predestination. Instead, he is anti-Augustinian because his true opponents are Augustine's supporters in southern Gaul.[30] Marín concludes that Vincent's criticism of Augustine is veiled because of his respect for the saintly man. The criticism centres not around Augustine's magisterial exposition of Christology, but solely around his teaching on predestination. In *Comm.* we see equally Vincent's desire to safeguard the prestige and respect for the figure of Augustine and the desire to critique the mistakes of Augustinianism about predestination.[31]

Augustine Casiday has struck a similarly nuanced chord through various writings from 2005 to 2014. In 2005, Casiday pointed out that in *Excerp.* 2.8, Vincent frames his understanding of Christology using the language of grace and even quotes Augustine's last writing, *De praed. sanct.* He concludes that study by stating, 'This analysis of *Exc.* 8 gives us added reason for rejecting the facile claim that Vincent was part of a covert resistance of Augustine's theology of grace that was spearheaded by the monastic leadership of Gaul.'[32] Casiday returns to *Excerp.* 2.8 in another piece written in 2010, which I shall address later in this chapter. Then in 2014, Casiday points out that both O'Connor and Madoz work from the assumption that Pelagianism and Augustinianism are polar opposites, between which one must locate the Gallic writers.[33] He concludes that such scholarship 'presumes that

---

[30] Raúl Villegas Marín, '*Auersi texerunt eum*: la crítica a Agustín y a los agustinianos sudgálicos en el *Commonitorium* de Vicente de Lérins', *Augustinianum* 46 (2006), 483–508.

[31] Ibid., 527.

[32] Augustine Casiday, 'Grace and the Humanity of Christ according to St. Vincent of Lérins', *VigChr* 59 (2005), 314.

[33] Casiday, 'Vincent of Lérins's *Commonitorium, Objectiones,* and *Excerpta*', 137–8.

Augustine's late theological interventions against Pelagianism provide the criteria for the modern study of the reception of Augustine's writings by near contemporaries like Vincent'.[34] Casiday argues further that 'taking grace and predestination as the point of departure produces huge difficulties in accounting for the response to Augustine's Christology that we find in Vincent's *Excerpta*',[35] and he even asserts that Vincent 'accepts predestination, but with special attention to its Christological elements'.[36]

In these assertions over the course of a decade, Casiday has contended that Vincent's work is not a mere response to Augustine, whether in disagreement, as most argue, or in agreement, as O'Connor contends. Like Markus and Marín, he sees Vincent as a nuanced thinker who distinguishes clearly where he agrees and disagrees with Augustine and the Augustinians. But Casiday goes beyond the two of them in claiming that Vincent's engagement with Augustine begins with Christology before moving to grace. I believe this is the most fruitful vantage point from which to consider Vincent's thought, since it should be clear to any reader that 'Nestorianism'—at least as much as Augustinianism—provides the starting point for Vincent's reflections. It is now time for us to turn directly to Vincent's *Comm.* and *Excerp.* as I seek to develop Casiday's thoughts about the relation between Christology and grace in Vincent of Lérins.

Vincent's Christology

In the *Comm.*, Vincent mentions various heretics by name. In *Comm.* 2., he names Novatian, Sabellius, Donatus, Arius, Eunomius, Macedonius, Photinus, Apollinaris, Priscillian, Jovinian, Pelagius, Caelestius, and Nestorius,[37] and he deals in some detail with Donatism in *Comm.* 4–9. In *Comm.* 10 he adds the name of Valentinus while repeating those of Donatus, Photinus, and Apollinaris.[38] Then in *Comm.* 11 he turns his attention to 'this unfortunate man, Nestorius, [who] suddenly changed from a sheep into a wolf'.[39] Vincent certainly casts a wide net by referring to men associated with heresies of an ecclesiastical character (Novatian and Donatus), of a dualistic/Gnostic sort (Valentinus and Priscillian), of a Trinitarian nature (Sabellius, Arius, Eunomius, and Macedonius), of a charitological sort (Pelagius, Caelestius, and in a quite different way, Jovinian), and of a Christological character (Photinus, Apollinaris, and Nestorius). This wide variety of heterodox

---

[34] Ibid., 139.
[35] Ibid., 140.
[36] Ibid., 140–1.
[37] *Comm.* 2.3 (CCSL 64.149) [FC 7.269–70].
[38] *Comm.* 10.4 (CCSL 64.159) [FC 7.284].
[39] *Comm.* 11.2 (CCSL 64.160) [FC 7.285].

108 CHRISTOLOGY AND THE LOGIC OF GRACE

beliefs is fitting in a work whose primary purpose is to provide guidance in adjudicating between orthodoxy and heresy in general.

At the same time, though, it is abundantly clear that in the *Comm.*, Christological heresy is the primary issue on Vincent's mind. He describes the teaching of Photinus and Apollinaris from *Comm.* 11.1–12.8, and then Nestorius occupies his attention from *Comm.* 12.9–16.7. In these chapters, Trinitarian terminology receives just enough attention to set the stage for Vincent's Christological pronouncements about the one *persona* and two *substantiae* of Christ, but Christology dominates his treatment. Moreover, he concludes the discussion of heresies by announcing in *Comm.* 16.8–9 his intention to produce a treatise to explain the Trinity and the person of Christ further, an intention that he fulfils by compiling the *Excerp.* As he returns to his main theme of how to recognize orthodoxy and heresy, Vincent adds a few new names of heretics (Origen and Tertullian),[40] circles back to several previously mentioned names (Pelagius, Caelestius, Arius, Sabellius, Novatian, and Priscillian),[41] and adds the standard claim that Simon Magus was the fount from which the entire stream of heresy flowed.[42] As Vincent's rambling discussion winds on, another Pelagian, Julian of Eclanum, gets a mention,[43] before Vincent brings the first Commonitory to a close and dedicates the second book—lost or suppressed, but summarized in the current *Comm.* 29–33—to Nestorius and the Council of Ephesus.[44]

In the midst of all this shotgun-blast name-calling, several things should be apparent. First, Vincent's overwhelming concern is Christology, and specifically 'Nestorianism'. Second, of course, Augustine is never named directly. Third, inasmuch as grace-related issues are on Vincent's mind, his opponents are Pelagius, Caelestius, and Julian, who are mentioned in three different places in the treatise. To treat the work as a covert attack on Augustine seems to me to require more subterfuge on Vincent's part than is warranted, although it is certainly true that Vincent disagrees with some Augustinian ideas, and we should remember Marín's

---

[40] *Comm.* 17–18 (CCSL 64.169–73) [FC 7.298–303].

[41] *Comm.* 24.8–10 (CCSL 64.181) [FC 7.314].

[42] *Comm.* 24.10 (CCSL 64.181) [FC 7.314].

[43] *Comm.* 28.15 (CCSL 64.189) [FC 7.323].

[44] There is some discussion about how accurately Vincent presents the proceedings at Ephesus. Thomas Graumann, 'Towards the Reception of the Council of Ephesus (431): Public Sentiment and Early Theological Responses', *StPatr* 45 (2010), 157, suggests that the lost second Commonitory was perhaps devoted almost entirely to Ephesus, given how clear the extant summary of it is and how prominently it figures in his understanding of the way tradition is applied to new situations. He concludes (160), 'Vincent proves a very attentive, and creative, reader of the acts. His approach is thematic, giving preference to those passages that he finds conducive to his task of conceptualizing tradition. However this interest does not go against the intentions of the council, or its documentary record, but captures a main tendency very well.' Mark S. Smith, *The Idea of Nicaea in the Early Church Councils, AD 431-451*, OECS (Oxford: Oxford University Press, 2018), 111–13, offers a concurring opinion when he asserts that Vincent has accepted Cyril's presentation of the council and his own role in it without addressing the underlying tensions, and that he uses the council as an example of dynamic re-appropriation of a tradition that is not static but ever growing and ripening.

compelling argument that Vincent is passing over the name of the saintly but erring man in silence. At the time Vincent writes in 434, the Christological scene back East is unsettled, the Formula of Reunion is scarcely a year old, and Nestorius has not yet been exiled to Upper Egypt. Nestorius is certainly not yet firmly ensconced in the pantheon of arch-heretics, but Vincent not only names him as such but directs most of his attention towards him. If he had actually thought Augustine needed to be attacked with equal fervour, he might still have refrained from naming him, but would he have withheld the names of 'the Augustinians'? It seems unlikely, and I suggest instead that an alleged anti-Augustine or anti-Augustinian undercurrent to the *Comm.* could be a *product of* scholars' belief that there was a Semi-Pelagian/ Augustinian dichotomy, rather than a *source for* such a dichotomy. In contrast to the bog to which such a slippery notion leads us, we should be on firmer ground to assume that Vincent's treatise is directed against the people he states it is directed against, even though he certainly does not fully agree with Augustine and the Augustinians. Indeed, I think this is likely even before we consider the *Excerp.* as a witness to Vincent's thought.

In the *Excerp.*, the focus on Christology is even more pronounced than in the *Comm.* Vincent names Arius, Apollinaris, and Nestorius as the three heretics he is opposing,[45] but of the ten *tituli* into which Vincent organizes his excerpts from Augustine's writings, the first is Trinitarian and nine are directly related to Christology.[46] Moreover, Arius's and Apollinaris's mistakes are never spelled out, whereas those of 'Nestorius' are enumerated in some detail.[47] Even more striking is that the Christological mistakes of Apollinaris are not even directly countered; virtually all of the work deals with the unity of Christ and thus with the use of Augustine to counter 'Nestorius'. Here, as in the *Comm.*, Vincent's attention is dominated by Christology, and for the most part, anti-'Nestorian' Christology. What, then, does Vincent consider 'Nestorianism' to entail?

'Nestorius' as Vincent Sees Him

In *Comm.* 12, Vincent gives a fairly lengthy appraisal of Nestorius, which is worth our careful attention. He begins:

> Nestorius, who suffered from a disease quite contrary to that of Apollinaris, suddenly introduces two persons (*duas introducit repente personas*) while pretending to distinguish two substances in Christ (*dum sese duas in Christo substantias*

---

[45] *Excerp.* Prologus (CCSL 64.199).
[46] *Excerp.* Prologus (CCSL 64.200–1).
[47] *Excerp.* Prologus (CCSL 64.199). I should point out that late in the work, Vincent names Photinus on the grounds that both he and Nestorius reject the true sense of the title *Theotokos*. See *Excerp.* 10 (CCSL 64.231).

110 CHRISTOLOGY AND THE LOGIC OF GRACE

distingere simulat). In his unheard-of wickedness he assumes that there are two sons of God, two Christs—the one God, the other man (*unum Deum alterum hominem*): one begotten of the Father, the other, of the mother (*unum qui ex patre, alterum qui sit generatus ex matre*). Thus, he asserts that Holy Mary is not to be called 'Theotokos' (Mother of God), but 'Christotokos' (Mother of Christ), since the one born from her was not that Christ who is God (*ille Christus qui Deus*) but the one who was man (*ille qui erat homo*).[48]

At first glance, this looks like a fairly standard, and seemingly unjustified, criticism of Nestorius—two sons, two Christs, two persons. But what is striking in this passage is the juxtaposition of *introducit* with *distingere simulat*. Vincent is not claiming that Nestorius *says* he is affirming two separate persons: that would indeed be a blatant caricature. Instead, Vincent claims that what Nestorius means by the two *substantiae* of Christ—the entities he intends (or less charitably, 'pretends') to distinguish—amounts to two *personae*. As we have seen, one of the genuine problems with Nestorius's thought was that he used πρόσωπον to refer both to the Logos and the *homo assumptus* (considered individually), and to the united appearance between them (the πρόσωπον of union), and it seems here that Vincent has his finger on exactly this problem. If the πρόσωπον/*persona* of Christ is merely the united appearance (the πρόσωπον of union), then for all practical purposes the φύσεις/*substantiae* amount to two distinct persons. The masculine pronouns *unum* and *alterum* drive that point home: although Nestorius calls each of those two entities a substance or nature (that is, an 'it'), each is actually a 'he' (a person). By referencing Nestorius's qualms about the title *Theotokos* at this juncture, Vincent furthers the point that for Nestorius, even if he claims there is one Christ, the one who is God is a different *ille*, a different person, from the one who is man. This is a brief but fairly sophisticated assessment of the main problem with Nestorius's thought and should not be called a caricature. This is not merely 'Nestorianism' but actually Nestorianism.

Vincent continues by stating directly what he has just implied: 'But, if one believes that he speaks in his writings of *one* Christ and that he teaches *one* Person of Christ, let him be careful not to give too easy credence to such an interpretation.'[49] Then Vincent suggests two possibilities regarding Nestorius's thought:

Well, either he deceitfully (*fraudulentiae causa*) overemphasizes in certain passages of his writings that he believes in *one* Christ and *one* Person of Christ (*unum Christum, et unam Christi personam credere se iactitat*), or he pretends that, only after the birth from the Virgin, both Persons were united in *one* Christ (*in unum Christum duas perhibet conuenisse personas*).[50]

[48] *Comm.* 12.9–10 (CCSL 64.163) [FC 7.289, translation modified].
[49] *Comm.* 12.11 (CCSL 64.163) [FC 7.289].
[50] *Comm.* 12.12 (CCSL 64.163) [FC 7.290].

Of course, accusing a heretic of deliberate deceit is the oldest trope in the book, and we should surely insist that Nestorius never meant to deceive people. But the first possibility is still a poignant one. The frequent insistence in Nestorius's writings that there is one Christ, one πρόσωπον/*persona*, does actually obscure the fact that Nestorius is treating the deity and humanity as persons in their own right, even though Nestorius could not have meant to deceive. For Nestorius, the one 'person' is not a real person: it is a kind of collective united appearance. The real persons, the real subjects of actions and experiences, are the Logos and the *homo assumptus*. This first possibility grows directly out of the analysis Vincent has already perceptively laid out.

But Vincent also sets forth a second possibility, that Nestorius means the union of the two persons to make one Christ took place after the conception/birth. This is the possibility Vincent seems to adopt, for he continues:

> But this statement is made in such a way that it means that at the time of the Virgin's conception or bearing, and even for some time after, two Christs existed. Thus, though Christ, as merely man, was born the first (*Christus homo communis primum et solitarius natus sit*), and unique, and not joined in Unity of Person to the Word of God (*necdum Dei uerbo personae unitate sociatus*), afterwards the Person of the Word descended into Him, assuming Him (*postea in eum adsumentis uerbi persona descenderit*). Although now, having been assumed (by the Word), He abides in the glory of God, yet it would seem that for a time there was no difference between Him and other men (*aliquandiu tamen nihil inter illum et ceteros homines interfuisse uideatur*).[51]

Here Vincent's presentation clearly departs from the real Nestorius; it is absolutely not true that Nestorius believed a mere man was born, whom the Word assumed only later. As we have seen, Cassian has made the same inaccurate accusation four years earlier.[52] But as with Cassian, so also with Vincent, there is a larger point here. If Christ were merely a man assumed by God—regardless of when that happened—then his 'deity' was the result of his ascent, not an aspect of who he has always been. In that case, salvation would be an upward movement, a trail blazed first by Christ and then followed by Christians. Missing in such a scheme is the downward movement of God through the Incarnation and death of Christ. Even if Christ is now abiding in the glory of God, if he has not always (that is, from eternity past) so abided, then he cannot save us. So, Christ has to be the eternal Son of God, not merely a man who has been assumed by that Son. By suggesting that Nestorius believed the union took place later than the conception of Christ, Vincent is passing from a plausible depiction of Nestorius to a caricature, to 'Nestorius'. But

---

[51] *Comm.* 12.13 (CCSL 64.163) [FC 7.290].
[52] Cassian, *De incar. Dom.* 5.1 (CSEL 17.302) [*NPNF*² 11.581].

112   CHRISTOLOGY AND THE LOGIC OF GRACE

for purposes of this book, how the Gallic writers perceived Nestorius is our main concern, and Vincent's perceptive insight into the problems with affirming one 'he' and another in Christ shows that as with Cassian, so also here, 'Nestorius' is not altogether removed from Nestorius.

In the *Comm.*, there is no indication that Vincent links Nestorius's thought to that of Leporius, as Cassian has done. But if we turn our attention to the *Excerp.*, we find such a connection.[53] He begins his description of Nestorius in that work as follows:

> Nestorius, the champion of a profane novelty, has attempted, by a wicked and impious dissension, to divide our one God and Saviour (*unum Deum et Saluatorem*) Jesus Christ into two christs (*in duos christos*). And now this is as if he has, in necessary consequence, denied the faith in the Trinity and introduced to us the worship of a quaternity. For he asserts two sons of God, two christs: one God, the other man (*alterum Deum alterum hominem*). And that he says Saint Mary gave birth in a fashion not to God the Word but to Christ a mere man like other men (*hominem solitarium communi hominum*), and therefore she is to be named not 'Theotokos' but 'Christotokos'.[54]

Here we see several of the same elements that we saw in Vincent's *Comm.*, and we should remember that the similarities in the descriptions of Nestorius were part of Madoz's reason for concluding that Vincent wrote the *Excerp.* Both works see his mistake as dividing the one Christ into two christs. Note especially the use of the masculine adjective form *alterum*: Vincent believes 'Nestorius' teaches that there is one 'he' and another 'he' in Christ; the first 'he' is God, and the second 'he' is man. Here Vincent also writes that 'Nestorius's' thought effectively implies that Christ is not our God and Saviour, which evidently means that the primary 'he' in Christ is the man. This concurs with Vincent's insinuation in the *Comm.* that 'Nestorius's' thought implies salvation is not a downward movement of God the Son himself to the human sphere. Both works reference Nestorius's (earlier) refusal to call Mary *Theotokos* and argue that the refusal means he thinks Mary gave birth to a mere man. And just after the portion of the *Excerp.* that I quote here, Vincent accuses Nestorius of stating his beliefs not openly but in a hidden way and fraudulently (*occulte et fraudulenter*),[55] as he has charged in the *Comm.*

In addition to those commonalities, there is an important new element in the *Excerp.* Vincent states that the division of Christ into two christs implies the worship of a quaternity. We have seen that about the year 415 Augustine began to insist

---

[53] Thomas L. Humphries, *Ascetic Pneumatology from John Cassian to Gregory the Great*, OECS (Oxford: Oxford University Press, 2013), 102–3, points out that Vincent uses Cassian's understanding of 'Nestorianism' to frame the way he presents Augustine's Trinitarian theology in the *Excerp.*

[54] *Excerp.*, Prologus (CCSL 64.199). All translations from the *Excerp.* are my own.

[55] *Excerp.*, Prologus (CCSL 64.199).

that no quaternity was formed through the Incarnation[56] and that this was a significant issue in his correction of Leporius.[57] Vincent's mention of this as an aspect of 'Nestorius's' thought may imply that Vincent's perception of 'Nestorius', like Cassian's, represents a conflation of Nestorian and Leporian ideas. Of course, this is not a particularly significant conflation; the much more important one is that Cassian conflates 'Nestorianism' with the grace-related ideas of the pre-correction Leporius. We shall need to pay attention to whether Vincent also exhibits Christological/charitological connections similar to those of Cassian.

Vincent's Positive Christology in the *Comm.*

Against the backdrop of this common Gallic understanding of 'Nestorius', Vincent expounds his positive Christology beginning in *Comm.* 13. He starts by linking the terminology used to describe the Trinity with that used of Christ:

> For it [the church] adores one Divinity in the plenitude of the Trinity and the equality of the Trinity in one and the same Majesty; and confesses one Jesus Christ, not two, the same Jesus Christ being at once God and man. The Church believes that there are in Him one Person (*Vnam quidem in eo personam*), but two substances (*sed duas substantias*); two substances, but one Person. Two substances because the Word of God is immutable, so that he could not be converted into flesh (*quia mutabile non est uerbum Dei, ut ipsum uerteretur in carnem*); one Person, lest by acknowledging two Sons (*duos profitendo*) it seem to adore a quaternity instead of a trinity.[58]

Here we see a reference to the idea that affirming or implying two sons would amount to the worship of a quaternity, a not-so-subtle reminder that 'Nestorius' as he is perceived in Gaul is the main heretic in Vincent's sights. He also uses standard Latin terminology: *persona* for ὑπόστασις/πρόσωπον and *substantia*, rather than the synonym *natura*, for φύσις.

Vincent then elaborates on the relation between substance/nature and person as one speaks of both the Trinity and Christ, and in the process, he adds another method for making his point clear. He follows a time-honoured technique of using masculine and neuter forms of *alius*—masculine to correspond to *persona* and neuter to correspond to *substantia*. Since published translations normally handle such constructions a different way in the interest of creating elegant English,[59] in

---

[56] See Augustine, *Ep.* 169.8 (CSEL 44.617) [WSA II/3.110]; Augustine, *De praed. sanct.* 2.67 [= *De don. pers.* 67] (CSEL 105.270) [WSA I/26.236].

[57] See Augustine, *Ep.* 219.1 (CSEL 57.428–9) [WSA II/4.69].

[58] *Comm.* 13.3–4 (CCSL 64.163–4) [FC 7.290–1, translation slightly modified].

[59] For example, in the following passage, the FC translator. Rudolph Morris, renders 'one "he" and another "he"' as 'diversity of persons', and 'one "it" and another "it"' as 'diversity of substances'.

114   CHRISTOLOGY AND THE LOGIC OF GRACE

the following several quotations I shall modify the translations to something much more literal (albeit admittedly quite clumsy), so as to make clear exactly what Vincent is doing in Latin:

> In God there is one substance, but three Persons (*una substantia sed tres personae*); in Christ, two substances, but one Person (*duae substantiae sed una persona*). In the Trinity there is one 'he' and another 'he' (*alius atque alius*), but not one 'it' and another 'it' (*non aliud atque aliud*). In our Saviour there is one 'it' and another 'it' (*aliud atque aliud*), but not one 'he' and another 'he' (*non alius atque alius*).[60]

Juxtaposing the use of masculine and neuter pronouns with the use of terms is especially important in Latin, because in that language *persona* and *substantia* are both feminine, and the grammatically prescribed gender of any pronouns or adjectives one used would obscure the fundamental point about person and nature.

In fact, Vincent seems to sense this grammatical problem, because only after he uses the masculine and neuter pronouns in the statement just quoted does he go on to use feminine forms of *alius* in grammatical agreement with *persona* and *substantia/natura*:

> How is it that in the Trinity there is one 'he' and another 'he' (*alius atque alius*) but not one 'it' and another 'it' (*aliud atque aliud*)? Because the Father is one Person (*alia est persona Patris*), the Son, another (*alia Filii*), the Holy Spirit, a third (*alia Spiritus Sancti*). Yet, Father, Son, and Holy Spirit are not one nature and another, but one and the same (*sed tamen Patris et Filii et Spiritus sancti non alia et alia, sed una eademque natura*).[61]

Here we should note the movement from the masculine and neuter forms of *alius* to the grammatically mandated feminine forms. Vincent is carefully walking the reader through the levels of unity and plurality within the Godhead—plurality at the level of the 'he', the person, and yet unity at the level of the 'it', the substance. Notice that in this passage he also uses the word *natura* to supplement *substantia* in describing the divine nature.

With these matters clarified through references to Trinitarian theology, now Vincent is ready to apply the same terminological distinctions to Christ:

> Why in our Saviour is there one 'it' and another 'it' (*aliud atque aliud*), not one 'he' and another 'he' (*non alius atque alius*)? Because there is one substance of divinity (*altera substantia diuinitatis*) and another of humanity (*altera humanitatis*).

---

[60] *Comm.* 13.5 (CCSL 64.164) [FC 7.291, translation modified].
[61] *Comm.* 13.6 (CCSL 64.164) [FC 7.291, translation modified].

Yet, His Godhead and His humanity are not one 'he' and another 'he' (*sed tamen deitas et humanitas non alter et alter*), but one and the same Christ (*unus idemque Christus*), one and the same Son of God (*unus idemque Filius Dei*), and one and the same Person of one and the same Christ and Son of God (*unius eiusdemque Christi et Filii Dei una eademque persona*).[62]

Here again we see Vincent using masculine and neuter forms to make his meaning clear before he switches to the terms that require feminine adjectives. This terminological precision is a significant improvement over Cassian's muddled language, and we may assume that unlike Cassian (whose primary strategy in refuting Nestorianism was to insist on the deity of Christ, not to devise consistent terminology), Vincent's approach to the 'two sons' taught by 'Nestorius' is to state precisely where one may and may not speak of any two-ness in Christ. Duality has to come at the level of 'it', of substance or nature, not at the level of son or person. As a result of Vincent's terminological exactness, scholars who are primarily interested in technical Christology rate him considerably higher than they rate Cassian.[63] But at the same time, this terminology serves the same purpose as Cassian's more vituperative rhetoric: to contrast the true Christ with the Christ of 'Nestorius', a Christ in which the Son and the man are *alius atque alius*, one 'he' and another 'he'.

Later in the same chapter, Vincent continues to drive home the point that one may not say—as he claims 'Nestorius' does—that the Word and the man are different persons. He writes:

Hence, there are also two substances (*duae substantiae*) in one and the same Christ (*in uno eodemque Christo*), the one is divine, the other human (*una diuina altera humana*); one is from God the Father, the other from the Virgin Mother (*una ex patre Deo altera ex matre uirgine*); one co-eternal and co-equal with the Father, the other temporal and less than the Father; one consubstantial with the Father, the other consubstantial with the Mother. Therefore, there is not one Christ-God and another Christ-man (*Non ergo alter Christus Deus alter homo*); not one uncreated and another created (*non alter increatus alter creatus*); not one impassible, the other passible (*non alter inpassibilis, alter passibilis*); not one equal to the Father and the other less than the Father (*non alter aequalis Patri alter minor Patre*); not one from the Father and the other from the Mother (*non alter ex Patre alter ex matre*).[64]

---

[62] *Comm.* 13.7 (CCSL 64.164) [FC 7.291, translation modified].

[63] See, e.g., Torsten Krannich, *Von Leporius bis zu Leo dem Großen: Studien zur lateinischsprachigen Christologie im Fünften Jahrhundert nach Christus*, Studien und Texte zu Antike und Christentum 32 (Tübingen: Mohr Siebeck, 2005), 155.

[64] *Comm.* 13.9–10 (CCSL 64.164–5) [FC 7.291–2].

116   CHRISTOLOGY AND THE LOGIC OF GRACE

Here again, one must seek duality in Christ at the level of the substances, but one may not understand these diverse substances as if they were different persons. There is not, for example, an uncreated 'he' and a created 'he' in the Saviour. Most striking here are the closely parallel phrases *una ex patre Deo altera ex matre uirgine* and *non alter ex Patre alter ex matre*. What may be ascribed to different origins—from the Father or from the mother—are different substances (denoted by the feminine adjectives *una* and *altera*, since *substantia* is feminine), but not different persons (denoted by the masculine adjective *alter*).

Having established this point, in *Comm.* 14, Vincent probes in some detail what the word *persona* must and must not mean when used in reference to Christ:

> The Catholic faith affirms that the Word of God was made man in such a way that He assumed the things that are ours (*quae nostra sunt*), not fallaciously and un-really, but in truth and reality (*non fallaciter et adumbrate, sed uere expresseque*); that He did not imitate human nature as being something different, but rather as His very own (*quae erant humana, non quasi alienae imitaretur, sed potius ut sua prereret*); furthermore, that He was that which He acted and whom he acted—precisely like ourselves, who, in so far as we speak, think, live, and exist, do not imitate, but actually are, human beings.[65]

Two things are noteworthy about this passage. First, Vincent describes the Incarnation as the Word's assuming *quae nostra sunt*. That is to say, everything that pertains to being human was assumed by the Word. This assertion contrasts sharply with Nestorius's treatment of the *homo assumptus* as a human person in his own right. For Vincent, Christ's humanity cannot be even quasi-independent, because it is a set of qualities and components that the Word takes into himself so that *he himself* can be human as well as divine. The second noteworthy aspect of the passage is that Vincent insists the Word made his humanity 'his very own (*sua*)'. He sets this assertion in contrast to the idea that the Word might have merely imitated human nature, which suggests that in Vincent's mind, the Word's assumption of a quasi-independent man would have meant that the Word was not truly human but merely appearing to be human. By making these assertions, Vincent is implying—although he does not yet say so directly—that the 'person' of Christ must be the Word himself, not merely a grammatical or additive subject envisioned when one considers the Word and the *homo assumptus* together.

What he has implied in the passage just quoted, Vincent affirms directly later in the chapter:

---

[65]   *Comm.* 14.5 (CCSL 64.166) [FC 7.293–4, translation modified].

VINCENT OF LÉRINS   117

We must, therefore, completely reject any notion of 'Person' that is built on fiction or imitation, on a permanent difference between being and pretending, and on the assumption that the acting 'he' never is that 'he' whom he enacts (*ille qui agit, numquam is est quem agit*). Let us get rid of the idea that God the Word assumed the person of a man (*personam hominis suscepisse*) in such a fallacious way (*hoc fallaci modo*).[66]

Here, what Vincent rejects is described with the puzzling expression *ille qui agit, numquam is est quem agit*. The context demands that *agit* not have the exact sense in its second occurrence as it does in the first instance, or there would be no contrast to justify the use of the word *numquam*. In my modification of the published translation above, I have tried to convey the contrast through 'acts' and 'enacts'. Rudolph Morris, the Fathers of the Church translator, is surely correct when he renders the entire clause 'the acting individual never is the individual whom he represents'.[67] In spite of the puzzling uses of *agit*, it is clear that Vincent is rejecting any notion that one can divide Christ into *ille* (that man Jesus whom we see acting in his earthly ministry) and *is* (the Word on behalf of whom he acts or whom he represents). Here Vincent seems to be arguing against Nestorius's idea of prosopic union, by which both the Logos and the *homo assumptus* are πρόσωπα in their own right, but there is another kind of πρόσωπον that is formed when one considers them collectively, as being united. Then at the end of the passage, Vincent directly rejects the idea that the Word assumed *personam hominis*. Again, if the humanity of Christ is a person in his own right, then the Word is assuming a quasi-independent person, and if one then uses the word *persona* to refer to the result of that assumption, this is a fallacious way of speaking. Vincent does not accept any concept of *persona* that might allow for such a collective understanding.

Turning to an affirmative understanding of *persona*, Vincent continues in the same sentence:

Let us rather realize that, His substance remaining immutable (*incommutabili sua manente substantia*), He Himself existed as flesh, as man, as a human person (*ipse caro, ipse homo, ipse persona hominis exsisteret*), when He assumed to Himself the nature of a perfect man (*in se perfecti hominis suscipiendo naturam*); that He existed so, not by simulation, but really, not by imitation, but substantially; and finally, that His existence did not cease with His acting, but remained permanently in its substance.[68]

---

[66] *Comm.* 14.9–10 (CCSL 64.167) [FC 7.294, translation modified].
[67] FC 7.294.
[68] *Comm.* 14.10 (CCSL 64.167) [FC 7.294–5, translation modified].

118   CHRISTOLOGY AND THE LOGIC OF GRACE

The referent for 'he himself' is God the Word from the earlier part of the sentence, which I quoted and discussed above. Thus, Vincent here forcefully insists that the Word himself (*ipse…ipse…ipse*) lived as a bodily being (*caro*), as a man (*homo*), as the person of a man (*persona hominis*). The Word did not unite *personam hominis* to himself to make a new kind of composite *persona*. Instead, he united *naturam perfecti hominis* to himself so as to be a *persona hominis* himself.

Vincent concludes his positive treatment of the Incarnation in the *Comm.* by defending the use of the title *Theotokos* for Mary. Unlike Cassian, who was writing before Nestorius reluctantly agreed to the use of that title, Vincent knew, or at least could have known, that Nestorius had consented to it prior to Ephesus. Nevertheless, the way Vincent defends the title is significant:

> Furthermore, since the body of the Lord was made and created (*inde etiam ut carne Domini facta, carne Domina creata*), it is said that the 'Word' of God Himself 'was made' (*ipsum uerbum Dei factum*), His wisdom filled up, His knowledge created. … Through this Unity of Person it also becomes perfectly clear—by reason of a similar mystery—that it is most truly Catholic (*catholicissime*) to believe (and most impious to deny) that the Word of God Himself was born from the Virgin (*ipse Deus uerbum natus ex uirgine*), even as the flesh of the Word was born from an Immaculate Mother (*carne uerbi ex integra matre nascente*).[69]

Strictly speaking, of course, human, bodily birth is something that pertains to bodily human beings, not to the Word considered in himself. Thus, Vincent believes one can speak with technical correctness in saying that the flesh/body of the Lord is what is made/created. But because—as Vincent has already made abundantly clear—the body/flesh belongs to the Word as his very own, it is still appropriate and even necessary to say that the Word *himself* has been made as a man; the Word *himself* has been born of the Virgin when his flesh was born of her. Notice in particular that the nominative forms *ipse* and *natus* at the end of the passage are unambiguously masculine (the accusative form *ipsum* earlier in the passage could be masculine or neuter), even though *uerbum* is neuter. Vincent is allowing the masculine word *Deus* rather than the neuter *uerbum* to control his gender usage, and in the process he is emphasizing even more that the Word as a 'he' was truly born in a human way through Mary.

Thus, in spite of Vincent's earlier, mistaken claim that 'Nestorius' believes the Christological union took place later than the conception of Christ,[70] the timing of the union is by no means the heart of his disagreement with Nestorius. Rather, the most significant issue for Vincent, as for Cassian, is whether the person who is

---

[69] *Comm.* 15.4–6 (CCSL 64.167–8) [FC 7.295–6].
[70] *Comm.* 12.13 (CCSL 64.163) [FC 7.290], discussed above. See also the gratuitous reiteration of and rejection of that possibility in *Comm.* 15.1–3 (CCSL 64.167–8) [FC 7.295].

man is the Word himself. Vincent's consistent terminology, clear statement of what he means by *persona*, and explanation of why the title *Theotokos* is important, all mark a noteworthy improvement over Cassian, but the two Gallic writers clearly agree on the fundamental truth to be defended. As we have seen with Cassian, this question of who the person of Christ is dovetails with the insistence that salvation requires the initiative of God's downward action through the Incarnation, and we shall have occasion to look for this idea in Vincent's writings. First, though, we need to consider his further development of his Christology in the *Excerp.*

Vincent's Positive Christology in the *Excerp.*, Part One

In the prologue to the *Excerp.*, Vincent lists ten *tituli* under which he will organize his excerpts from Augustine and his relatively rare comments on those passages. Of these ten headings, only the first is Trinitarian. The other nine pertain to Christology, a fact that once again illustrates Vincent's overriding concern for Christology in the light of the threat posed by 'Nestorius'. Vincent discusses these nine titles in two parts, with numbers 2–5 sharing a common theme—the need to see duality in Christ at the level of substance, not person—and numbers 6–10 also dealing with a common theme—the depiction of the incarnate Christ according to what one might call verbal symmetry following the pattern 'the God who is man and the man who is God'. I shall look in some detail at these two parts, and as I do so, I shall combine Vincent's initial statements of the headings in the prologue with his more extended treatments of the headings in the body of the *Excerp.*

In the *Excerp.* just as in the *Comm.*, Vincent establishes Trinitarian terminology in order to set up the terms for his discussion of Christ. His statement of his first heading in the prologue uses both *substantia* and *natura* to describe the undivided divine substance, by virtue of which the Trinitarian persons are one God.[71] His expansion on this heading in part one of the *Excerp.* includes three quotations from Augustine, with essentially no comment of his own.[72] In the passages quoted, Augustine emphasizes the unity of substance and operation within the Trinity as well as the distinction of the persons,[73] underlines the fact that Father, Son, and Spirit share the same eternity, unity, and equality,[74] and adduces a host of biblical passages on the equality of the persons.[75]

---

[71] *Excerp.*, Prologus (CCSL 64.200). Humphries, *Ascetic Pneumatology from Cassian to Gregory the Great*, 103–5, points out that Vincent's excerpts from *De trin.* come only from books 1–4, and that as a result, he does not use *essentia* alongside *substantia*, since Augustine begins to use *essentia* as a term only in book 5. Thus, it seems that the Gallic monks' only knowledge of Augustine's *De trin.* came from books 1–4, and thus perhaps only through Vincent's *Excerp.*

[72] *Excerp.* 1.1 (CCSL 64.202–5).

[73] Augustine, *De trin.* 1.7 (CCSL 50.34–6) [WSA I/5.69–70].

[74] Augustine, *De doc. christ.* 1.5 (CCSL 32.9) [WSA I/11.108].

[75] Augustine, *Con. Max.* 2.26.14 (PL 42.814) [WSA I/18.328–9].

120 CHRISTOLOGY AND THE LOGIC OF GRACE

Then, in the prologue, Vincent immediately proceeds to his second (Christological) heading by stating: 'There are not two christs or two sons of God, but Jesus Christ is one (*unus*), the Son of God, our Lord and Savior (*Filius Dei, Dominus et Saluator noster*). He is neither God alone nor man alone, but equally God and man; and just as he is perfect God, so also is he perfect man, subsisting of a rational soul and human flesh (*ex anima rationali et humana carne*).'[76] Here the masculine word *unus* locates the unity of Christ at the level of person, and his assertion that this one person is *Filius Dei* implies that the person is the Word himself, not a composite. This one person, the Son of God, is both perfect God and perfect man, and Vincent adds the explanation—obligatory in the post-Apollinarian thought world—that his humanity includes not only *caro* but also *anima rationalis*. It is important to note that Vincent's analysis begins with the one person, even though his brief discussion of the Trinity in the first heading has dealt with substance and has not even used the word *persona* or named the Father, Son, and Spirit individually. What he writes about Christ in the following discussion is controlled by his initial statement that the one person of Christ is the Son of God. This statement is strengthened by the fact that in Vincent's expansion in part one of the *Excerp.*,[77] he quotes a long passage from Augustine's *De trin.* in which Augustine claims that the biblical texts asserting the Father's superiority to the Son are based on the difference between viewing the Son as God and as man, in the form of God and in the form of a servant, by nature and in his incarnate condition.[78] The Son is less than the Father as man, not as God, in the form of the servant, not in the form of God, and in his incarnate condition, not in his own nature per se.

Back in the prologue, Vincent then pushes into a discussion of the two substances of Christ in heading three:

> There are two substances in one and the same Christ (*in uno eodemque Christo duae substantiae sunt*): one (*una*) co-eternal and consubstantial and equal to God the Father, the other (*altera*) by which (*qua*) the Father is greater, and which (*quae*) is consubstantial to the mother, in order that it may be most catholically and truly (*catholicissime uerissimeque*) said that according to one 'it' and another 'it' (*secundum aliud atque aliud*), there is one and the same Christ (*unus idemque*), both not made and made (*non factus et factus*), both uncreated and created (*increatus et creatus*), both *homoousios* with God the Father and *homoousios* with the mother, both equal to the Father and less than the Father (*aequalis Patri et minor Patre*).[79]

---

[76] Vincent, *Excerp.*, Prologus (CCSL 64.200).
[77] *Excerp.* 1.1 (end)–3 (beginning) (CCSL 64.205–7).
[78] Augustine, *De trin.* 1.14 (CCSL 50.44-6) [WSA I/5.74-5].
[79] *Excerp.*, Prologus (CCSL 64.200).

Here, as in the *Comm.*, Vincent uses both the word *substantia* and the grammatically required feminine adjectives and pronouns to indicate the two natures/substances of Christ, and he uses masculine adjectives and pronouns to indicate the person of the Son whom he has introduced in the previous heading. Notice that the very absence of the word *persona* forces the reader to focus not on some concept of *persona* by which Word and *homo assumptus* could count as one *persona*, but instead on the person of the Son himself. His point is not simply that the two natures are different in that one is created and the other uncreated, etc. Rather, the point is that by virtue of the two *substantiae*, the Son himself must be said to be both *non factus* and *factus*, both *increatus* and *creatus*, both *aequalis Patri* and *minor Patre*. To speak with these arresting paradoxes is to speak *catholicissime* and *uerissime*.

Vincent's expansion of this idea in part one is particularly revealing. He quotes a passage from Augustine's *De trin.* (immediately following the long passages he has just quoted) in which Augustine deliberates over the fact that when all things are subjected to the Son, he himself will remain subject to the Father [1 Cor. 15:28].[80] Augustine actually discusses two possible interpretations,[81] but Vincent quotes only the one that Augustine thinks is more likely, namely, that even after the resurrection Christ's human condition will remain (and thus, in terms of that condition, he will remain subject to the Father). One may not suppose that Christ, considered as man, will be turned into the divine condition. Vincent adds a comment of his own at this point: 'Hence indeed the holy evangelists are very careful to distinguish divinity from humanity in one and the same Christ, that is, in the one person of Christ.'[82] In order to make sure the reader understands that the superiority of the Father to the Son applies only when one considers the Son as man, Vincent then quotes from Augustine's *De consens. euang.*,[83] in which Augustine cites biblical passages indicating the equality of the Son to the Father.[84]

Headings four and five, as Vincent introduces them in the prologue, provide important qualifiers to avoid any misunderstanding of the striking language at the end of heading three. In heading four as Vincent introduces it in the prologue, he insists that speaking paradoxically of the incarnate Son does not mean that the divinity has changed (*conuertit*) into flesh, but rather that it has assumed (*adsumpsit*) flesh taken from the Virgin's flesh.[85] In part one Vincent bolsters this point with more passages from Augustine's *De trin.* in which he belabours the distinction between the form of God and the form of a servant.[86] Especially significant is the final

---

[80] *Excerp.* 1.3 (CCSL 64.207).
[81] Augustine, *De trin.* 1.15 (CCSL 50.46–7) [WSA I/5.75].
[82] *Excerp.* 1.3 (CCSL 64.207).
[83] *Excerpt.* 1.3 (CCSL 64.207–8).
[84] Augustine, *De consens. euang.* 1.7 (CCSL 43.6–7) [WSA I/15 & I/16.141–2].
[85] *Excerp.*, Prologus (CCSL 64.200–1). Here Vincent also takes another unneeded swipe at the idea that the Christological union took place later than Christ's conception by insisting that it occurred *a primo statim momento maternae conceptionis*.
[86] The passages are from Augustine, *De trin.* 1.22–3, 28 (CCSL 50.60–1, 69) [WSA I/5.82, 86]. Vincent quotes them in *Excerp.* 1.4 (CCSL 64.208–10).

122 CHRISTOLOGY AND THE LOGIC OF GRACE

passage, in which Augustine insists that if it were not the case that one and the same 'he' is Son of God and Son of man, then it would not have been true that the Jews crucified the Lord of glory [1 Cor. 2:8].[87] In Vincent's hands, these quotations serve to emphasize that the Son remained in the form of God even after assuming the form of a servant, which means that deity was not converted into humanity.

Likewise, in heading five as Vincent introduces it in the prologue, he stresses that the *substantia* of the Word remains *immutabilis* and *impassibilis*, and 'the divinity did not confuse (*confudit*) the assumed humanity (*adsumptam humanitatem*) with itself, but united it (*uniuit*).[88] Here one might have preferred that Vincent write that the Word himself (rather than the divine nature) assumed flesh, but the previous headings make clear that Vincent is writing here of an action of the Word in the incarnation. It is especially significant that Vincent uses the phrase *adsumpta humanitas* in the fifth heading, because this phrase—coupled with the constant use of neuter pronouns and adjectives to speak of the Son's humanity as an 'it'—preempts any tendency the reader might have to misunderstand the forthcoming frequent use of *homo* to mean that Vincent intends a quasi-independent *homo assumptus*.

On this point, Vincent quotes especially generously from Augustine in part one of the *Excerp*, with no fewer than eight quotations from *De trin*. First, he continues quoting Augustine's application of seemingly contradictory biblical passages to either the Word considered in the form of God or the same Word considered in the form of a servant.[89] This time Vincent adds Augustine's explanatory proviso that because of God's inseparable operations, a given action may be ascribed to one person when it properly belongs to all three.[90] Then Vincent quotes three passages in which Augustine asserts that seemingly contradictory claims of Christ need to be understood of him according to one 'it' and another 'it' within him.[91] In the midst of these quotations, he offers another comment of his own: 'By this rubric of "according to one 'it' and another 'it'" are easily solved the objections the heretics raise when they say, "Greater is the one who sends than the one who is sent. Hence, greater is the Father than the Son, because the Son himself regularly reminds us that he is sent by the Father."'[92] Here again, Vincent—like Augustine whom he is quoting—uses masculine and neuter pronouns and adjectives to distinguish clearly the levels of unity and duality within Christ, and even more important, to stress that at the level of person, Christ is the Word. Rather than speaking of one

---

[87] Augustine, *De trin*. 1.28 (CCSL 50.69) [WSA I/5.86], quoted in *Excerp*. 1.4 (CCSL 64.210).

[88] *Excerp*., Prologus (CCSL 64.201).

[89] Augustine, *De trin*. 1.24 (CCSL 50.62–3) [WSA I/5.83–4], quoted in *Excerp*. 1.5 (CCSL 64.210–11).

[90] Augustine, *De trin*. 1.25 (CCSL 50.64–5) [WSA I/5.84], quoted in *Excerp*. 1.5 (CCSL 64.211).

[91] Augustine, *De trin*. 1.27, 2.7, 2.8 (CCSL 50.67–8, 87, 89) [WSA I/5.85–6, 101, 102], quoted in *Excerp*. 1.5 (CCSL 64.212–13).

[92] *Excerp*. 1.5 (CCSL 64.213).

'he' and another we need to speak of a single 'he' in whom we may distinguish two 'its'.

Following these passages, Vincent quotes a passage in which Augustine uses the word *homo* to describe that which was united to the Word. Augustine writes, 'So a man (*homo*) was coupled (*copulatus*) and even in a certain sense compounded (*unitus*), with the Word of God as one person (*ad unitatem etenim personae*), when the Son of God was *sent into this world at the fullness of time, made of woman* [Gal. 4:4], in order to be also the Son of man.'[93] Here, Augustine's words on their own might imply that a quasi-independent man was united with the Word to make a unity of person, but Vincent himself immediately adds, 'that is, the same "he" (*ipse*) who from eternity was the Son of God.'[94] This shows the way Vincent understands Augustine's use of *homo*. If the one who is Son of Man is the same 'he' (*ipse*) as the one who has always been the Son of God, then *homo* cannot mean a separate person, a quasi-independent man, and thus *ad unitatem personae* cannot mean the creation of a single person from two existing ones. Instead, *homo* is a reference to the humanity of Christ as that which the Word assumed into his own person. In chapter 1 we saw that Augustine himself intends *homo* either in the sense of *humanitas* or in the sense of 'the Word understood as man', and Vincent's gloss corroborates that understanding even though he quotes a passage from Augustine that is itself ambiguous. This Vincentian passage is crucially important, because in part two of the *Excerp.* Vincent will repeatedly quote Augustine using *homo* to describe the Incarnation, and the reader must be prepared to understand those forthcoming passages correctly.

Vincent continues with two more quotes from Augustine, one from *De trin.* and the other from *De pecc. mer. rem.*, both of which indicate that whatever is said of the incarnate Christ must be said of the Word; one may not predicate some actions and experiences of the Son of God and others of the Son of man.[95] Between these two quotes, Vincent offers a fairly extended and important comment of his own:

> For he assumed (*Assumpsit*) flesh; he did not convert himself (*non se conuertit*) into flesh. Thus, by virtue of that which was made (*Qua facta*), the Word of God is said to have been made (*dicitur factum*), and in the same way, by that which was crucified (*crucifixum*), the Lord of majesty is said to have been crucified (*dicitur crucifixus*), and in the same way as well, by that which was created (*creata*) or needed to be created (*creanda*), the very Wisdom himself, co-eternal (*coaeterna*) with the Father, is regarded as having been created (*creata*) and to exist from himself. Indeed, therefore, all things are referred to the Word of God (*ad Dei*

---

[93] Augustine, *De trin.* 4.30 (CCSL 50.201) [WSA I/5.175], quoted in *Excerp.* 1.5 (CCSL 64.213).

[94] *Excerp.* 5 (CCSL 64.213).

[95] Augustine, *De trin.* 4.31 (CCSL 50.203) [WSA I/5.176] and Augustine, *De pecc mer. rem.* 1.60 (CSEL 60.60) [WSA I/23.69]; both quoted in *Excerp.* 1.5 (CCSL 64.214).

124   CHRISTOLOGY AND THE LOGIC OF GRACE

Verbum referuntur), so that a single person of God's Son (*una Filii Dei persona*) is implied.[96]

Here Vincent starts not with his customary masculine and neuter adjectives, but instead with the grammatically prescribed words: *Qua facta* is feminine because *caro* is feminine. But then he switches from feminine to neuter (*factum*—modifying *Verbum*) and masculine (*crucifixus*—modifying *Dominus*), thus showing unambiguously that the events that happened to the flesh/humanity are said to have happened to the Word/Lord. In the second half of the quotation, *sapientia* is also feminine, so the gerund and adjectives (all feminine) are ambiguous in a strictly grammatical sense; they could technically refer either to the Wisdom/Word/Lord or merely to the flesh. But by this point in the comment, Vincent's overall point is crystal clear, and in context this must mean that the prior use of *creata* refers to the flesh but the later one refers to the Wisdom. The person who is born, made (as man), and crucified, is the Word/Lord/Wisdom himself. Even with a potentially ambiguous quote from Augustine, Vincent's own comments leave nothing unclarified.

Finally, Vincent concludes his discussion of the fifth heading, and of part one as a whole, with yet another quotation from *De trin.*, in which Augustine argues that the flesh of Christ was not without a rational soul.[97] This entire discussion of headings four and five is significant because, as we saw in chapter 2, part of the reason the pre-correction Leporius was reluctant to speak of the Son being born or crucified was that he thought doing so would confuse the natures or imply that the Word was changed into a man. Vincent denies that such change in the Word took place while still insisting very strenuously that it was the Word himself who was born and suffered. While the concern of Leporius (and Nestorius) is genuine, Vincent will not allow that concern to lead away from treating the Word as the person of Christ, the subject of his incarnate experiences and actions.

Vincent's Positive Christology in the *Excerp.*, Part Two

Part two of the *Excerp.* deals with what I have been calling verbal symmetry, following the pattern 'the God who is man and the man who is God'. Because the headings in this part overlap almost completely rather than being logically sequential, I think it best to quote all of the headings together, from the prologue, before looking at Vincent's expansion by means of quotations from Augustine. Headings six through ten, as Vincent states them in the prologue, read as follows:

---

[96] *Excerp.* 1.5 (CCSL 64.214).
[97] Augustine, *De trin.* 4.31 (CCSL 50.203–4) [WSA I/5.176], quoted in *Excerp.* 1.5 (CCSL 64.214).

VI. That in one and the same Christ, according to the unity of person (*propter personae unitatem*), the things that are proper to God (*quae Dei propria sunt*) are attributed to the man (*tribuuntur homini*), and the things that are proper to the man (*quae hominis propria*) are attributed to God (*tribuuntur Deo*).

VII. That in one and the same Christ, according to the unity of person, the man is true God in man (*Deus uerus in homine homo est*), and God is true man in God (*homo uerus in Deo Deus*).

VIII. That in one and the same Christ, just as through the propriety of substance (*per substantiae proprietatem*) God has brought forth (*genuit*) God and man has brought forth man, so through the unity of person (*per unitatem personae*) God has brought forth man and man God (*Deus hominem et homo Deum*).

IX. That Saint Mary, the blessed mother of one and the same Christ, must be believed to have given birth (*peperisse*) not only to God or only to man, but equally to God and man in the unity of person (*Deum pariter et hominem in unitate personae*); and for this reason she is said Christianly and catholically to be not only the bearer of Christ (*christotocos*), but even the bearer of God (*theotocos*).

X. That one and the same Christ, since the property and reality of each substance (*utriusque substantiae proprietate et ueritate*) remains in him, is present everywhere as God (*secundum Deum*), but is [now] in heaven as man (*secundum hominem*).[98]

All of these headings use the words *homo* and *Deus*, and numbers six through nine might very well give the impression that Vincent means the Word and the man are separate subjects. But three things militate against that impression. First is the fact that Vincent has made it abundantly clear through his discussion of the first five headings that the person of Christ is the Word. The prior discussion controls the way the ambiguous word *homo* should be understood in these headings. Second is the fact that heading ten clearly indicates that the two substances both subsist in the one person, by which he is spoken of *secundum Deum* and *secundum hominem*, not that *Deus* and *homo* may be spoken of separately. Third, in Vincent's expansion of these headings in part two of the *Excerp.*, he relies on even more extensive quotation from Augustine than he has in part one, and in the quotes he marshals from Augustine's writings, ambiguity caused by the use of *homo* is resolved by clear statements that the Word is the person of Christ. Let us now look at the passages Vincent quotes.

Under heading seven, Vincent offers three more passages from *De pecc. mer. rem.*[99] (He has already quoted from this work once in 1.5.) In these passages, Augustine emphasizes that the one born from Mary was the Word, the Son of God.

---

[98] *Excerp.*, Prologus (CCSL 64.201).
[99] These three are from Augustine, *De pecc. mer. rem.* 1.60 and two passages from 2.38 (CSEL 60.60–1, 110–11) [WSA I/23.69–70, 105–6]. They are quoted in *Excerp.* 2.7 (CCSL 64.219–20).

126 CHRISTOLOGY AND THE LOGIC OF GRACE

Especially noteworthy is the passage in 2.38 in which Augustine asserts that the one who was naturally born of God deigned to be born of flesh (*ille qui de Deo naturaliter natus est, nasci etiam misericorditer de carne dignatus est*).[100] Similarly, under heading eight, Vincent quotes another passage from *De consens. euang.* (which he has cited in 1.3),[101] in which Augustine asserts that the Word/Son was the one who lived, died, and was raised in his humanity. Likewise, under headings seven and eight, Vincent quotes three more times from *Con. Max.* (from which he has also quoted previously in 1.2).[102] These passages propose the verbal symmetry of saying that the Son of God descended and the Son of man was crucified, along with saying that the Son of man descended and the Son of God was crucified. But the quotations further explain that it was the Word/Son who was born twice (from God before eternity and from Mary in time). By juxtaposing passages such as these, Vincent indicates that the ambiguous verbal symmetry needs to be understood in terms of the controlling idea that it was the Word himself who experienced the human events of Christ's life.

In part two, Vincent also quotes from a number of Augustinian works he has not cited previously. Under headings six and seven, he quotes nine different passages from Augustine's *Ep.* 137 to Volusian.[103] The thrust of these quotations is to emphasize the omnipresence, infinity, and immutability of the Word as he assumes *homo*, and in the process, it is clear that Augustine is using *homo* either to refer to the human nature the Word assumes or to refer to mankind as a whole on whose behalf the Word assumed human nature.[104] Furthermore, Vincent's discussion of headings seven, eight, and ten includes five quotations from Augustine's *Ep.* 187 to Dardanus,[105] the very letter that has been the source of scholarly controversy about whether Augustine's Christology is Antiochene/Theodorean or Chalcedonian/Cyrillian. In my discussion of this letter in chapter 1, I have considered the two passages from the letter that Vincent quotes at greatest length in the *Excerp.*[106] On the basis of these passages, I have argued that Augustine is using *homo* in the sense of 'assumed human nature' and that he writes of the Incarnation as grace not in the Theodorean sense that the Word unites a man to himself because of the man's

---

[100] Augustine, *De pecc. mer. rem.* 2.38 (CSEL 60.110) [WSA I/23.105], quoted in *Excerp.* 2.7 (CCSL 64.220).

[101] Augustine, *De consens. euang.* 1.53 (CSEL 43.58–9) [WSA I/15 & I/16.167], quoted in *Excerp.* 2.8 (CCSL 64.221).

[102] These three passages are from Augustine, *Con. Max.* 1.7, 1.19, 2.20.3 (PL 42.749–50, 757–8, 789–90) [WSA I/18.252–3, 261, 301–2]. They are quoted in *Excerp.* 2.7, 2.8 (CCSL 64.219–22).

[103] These nine passages are from Augustine, *Ep.* 137.2, 4, 6–7, 8, 9, 10, 11, and two passages from 12 (CSEL 44.98–113) [WSA II/2.213–19]. These are quoted in *Excerp.* 2.6 and 2.7 (CCSL 64.214–18).

[104] See my discussion of Augustine's *Ep.* 137.8, 12 (CSEL 44.107, 111) [WSA II/2.217, 219] in chapter 1.

[105] These five passages are from Augustine, *Ep.* 187.3–4, 8–9, 10, 38–9, and 40 (CSEL 57.82–4, 87–8, 89, 116–18) [WSA II/3.232–5, 248–9]. They are quoted in *Excerp.* 2.7, 2.8, and 2.10 (CCSL 64.218–19, 223, 223–4, 229, 230).

[106] Augustine, *Ep.* 187.9, 40 (CSEL 57.88–9, 116–17) [WSA II/3.235, 249].

(foreseen) worthiness, but in the sense that the not-previously existent human nature of Christ had no preceding merits by which to deserve such union. Moreover, under heading nine, Vincent quotes three times from *Ep.* 205 to Consentius.[107] All of these passages deal with the differences between Christ's physical body and ours, differences Augustine attributes to divine power while still insisting that it is a real physical body even though it does not decay. This focus on the differences between Christ and us shores up the idea that as a person, he is not a quasi-independent man but the Word incarnate possessing a physical body (and a real human mind, but that is not the point in these passages). Vincent's expansion of heading nine also includes five quotations from Augustine's *Enchir.*[108] In these quotations (one of which I have discussed in chapter 1), Augustine emphasizes the completeness of Christ's humanity while at the same time using *secundum deum* and *secundum homo* language to indicate that the incarnate Son is both equal to the Father and less than him. This language shows that here, Augustine is thinking of *homo* as 'the incarnate Son considered as a man', rather than as a quasi-independent man. Therefore, all of these quotations serve to clarify that the ambiguous use of *homo* and the verbal symmetry between God and man within the person of Christ do not imply an independent man.[109]

In the midst of these many quotations from Augustine's writings, Vincent makes a number of comments of his own. Two of Vincent's interpolations under headings seven and eight, if taken in isolation, could certainly be understood as implying that the *homo* is a quasi-independent man,[110] but as we have seen, when one takes all of his comments and Augustine's discussions together, such an interpretation is ruled out. Instead, the *deus/homo* language must be understood as referring to the Word considered as God or as man, or the word *homo* must refer to the humanity that the Word assumed into his own person. Others of Vincent's comments in part two are aimed at 'Nestorius' and other heretics directly. Under headings eight and nine, he again rejects the idea—which of course Nestorius never affirmed—that the Christological union took place later than at Christ's conception.[111] Under heading ten, in a kind of postscript after his last quotation from Augustine, Vincent asserts the need to call Mary both *Theotokos* and *anthropotokos*, anathematizes

---

[107] These three passages are *Ep.* 205.2–3, 4, 9, and 10 (CSEL 57.324, 326–7, 330–2) [WSA II/3.378–9, 381–2]. They are quoted in *Excerp.* 2.9 (CCSL 64.227–9).

[108] These five passages are from Augustine, *Enchir.* 34, two quotations from 35, 37, and 49 (CCSL 46.68, 69, 70, 76) [WSA I/8.295–7, 303]. They are quoted in *Excerp.* 2.9 (CCSL 64.226–7). See my discussion of the longest of the quoted passages, Augustine's *Enchir.* 35 (CCSL 46.69) [WSA I/8.295–6], in chapter 1.

[109] Vincent also quotes three times from Augustine's *De praed. sanct.* 1.30 and 2.67 [= *De don. pers.* 67], both in his discussion of heading eight. I shall consider these passages in the final section of this chapter.

[110] See *Excerp.* 2.7 (CCSL 64.219), in which he argues that Augustine's discussion in *Ep.* 187 gives us a rule that 'the things proper to God are attributed to the man, and the things proper to man are ascribed to God'. See also *Excerp.* 2.8 (CCSL 64.222), in which he confesses 'that the man in God is the Son of God and that God in the man is the son of the Virgin'.

[111] *Excerp.* 2.8 (CCSL 64.224), 2.9 (CCSL 64.227).

128   CHRISTOLOGY AND THE LOGIC OF GRACE

Nestorius and Photius for using one or the other term but not both, insists that the unity does not involve conversion of deity into flesh, affirms the presence of both flesh and soul in Christ, and finally, confesses that his excerpts from the books of Augustine serve to show true doctrine on the basis of the Holy Scriptures.[112]

As Vincent expresses this Christology, he makes several revealing comments in which he links Christology to grace, especially in the *Excerp.* but also in the *Comm.* I shall consider these comments in the final section of this chapter.

Christology and Grace in *Vincent's Writings*

For someone who is reputed to be a 'Semi-Pelagian', Vincent has astonishingly little to say about grace and human effort, and we are reminded again that only if one both considers him the author of the *Obiect. Vincent.* and believes those articles were written against Augustine does he appear to fall on a spectrum between Pelagius and Augustine. Nevertheless, there are several passages in the *Comm.* and the *Excerp.* in which Vincent discusses charitological issues, including one in particular that explicitly links grace to Christology. This rather limited evidence will be our concern now.

After Vincent's long treatment of Christology in the *Comm.*, he turns his attention to Origen and Tertullian, and then to the development of doctrine more generally. Then in *Comm.* 24, he addresses 'Pelagianism' by writing:

> Who, before the profane Pelagius, ever dared to attribute such power to free will (*uirtutem liberi . . . arbitrii*) as not to believe in the indispensable help of God's grace (*adiuuandum necesariam Dei gratiam*) for our good deeds in every act? Who, before his monstrous disciple, Caelestius, denied that the entire human race was bound by the guilt of Adam's transgression (*reatu praeuaricationis Adae*)?[113]

Later in the same chapter, Vincent mentions Priscillian, bishop of Gallaecia, who held to a fatalistic Manichaean/Gnostic sort of belief. Vincent writes:

> He actually makes the statement that God with His own hand created such a nature in man (*talem hominum . . . creare naturam*) that he, by his own initiative and by his entirely determined will (*necessariae cuiusdam uoluntatis impulsu*), neither can do nor want to do anything but sin (*nihil aliud uelit nisi peccare*), because he is driven and inflamed by the furies of all the vices and dragged down by unquenchable lust into the abyss of depravity.[114]

---

[112]   *Excerp.* 2.10 (CCSL 64.230–1).
[113]   *Comm.* 24.8 (CCSL 64.181) [FC 7.314, translation slightly modified].
[114]   *Comm.* 24.11 (CCSL 64.181-2) [FC 7.314-15].

Taken on its own, the second of these passages would be easy to misinterpret. It might give the impression that Vincent is opposing the idea that the human race is enslaved to sin. But considering that he has just criticized Caelestius for denying that the whole human race is bound by Adam's transgression, that cannot be what Vincent means. Rather, he is criticizing a fatalistic belief that lays the blame for human sin at God's door. It is not true, according to Vincent, that the will of a fallen human being is entirely determined towards evil. If we put these two passages together, we see a measured affirmation that Adam's sin did indeed affect the whole race, but that effect should not be understood as producing a complete incapacity to will the good. Nevertheless, no good action can come to fruition without the help of grace.

After these fairly inconsequential comments, Vincent returns to charitological issues again in *Comm.* 26.

> Here are the promises by which the heretics usually mislead those who are wanting in foresight. They dare to promise in their teaching that in *their* church— that is, in their own small circle, is to be found a great and special and entirely personal form of divine grace; that it is divinely administered, without any pain, zeal, or effort on their part (*sine ullo labore, sine ullo studio, sine ulla industria*), to all persons belonging to their group, even if they do not ask or seek or knock.[115]

Of course, here we must ask who the heretics in question are. We have seen that Hwang regards this passage as a blatant caricature of Augustine's thought and as the primary reason for thinking that the *Comm.* as a whole is directed against Augustine.[116] Guarino goes further, arguing that this passage denies what Augustine explicitly affirms in *De praed. sanct.* 2.64: that grace comes to us without our seeking, knocking, or asking.[117] Thus, Guarino suggests that this is directed at Augustine but is not actually a caricature. However, we must recognize that in the passage from *De praed. sanct.*, Augustine is not denying that we should ask, seek, and knock (after all, the Lord himself commands us to do so in Mt. 7:7–8), but rather he is denying that the ability to ask, seek, and knock comes from ourselves. Rather, Augustine argues, not only the ability but the very act is itself produced by grace. I find it hard to believe that Vincent could misread or misrepresent Augustine this badly. On the other hand, we have seen that Casiday regards Vincent's opponents as Gallic predestinarians, not as Augustine himself, and in fact, Casiday states directly that *Comm.* 26.8–9, in which Augustine is not named, should not trump the *Excerp.* (in which, obviously, he is named and honoured) as

---

[115] *Comm.* 26.8–9 (CCSL 64.185) [FC 7.319].

[116] Hwang, 'Prosper, Cassian, and Vincent', 77.

[117] Guarino, *Vincent of Lérins and the Development of Christian Doctrine*, xxv. See Augustine, *De praed. sanct.* 2.64 [= *De don. pers.* 64] (CSEL 105.268) [WSA I/26.235].

130 CHRISTOLOGY AND THE LOGIC OF GRACE

the source for a reconstruction of Vincent's attitude towards Augustine. I am inclined to agree with Casiday here; the heresy in Vincent's rifle sights seems more like a form of Gnosticism (notice the insistence on '*their* church'), and perhaps the target is still Priscillian at this point.

But however one resolves that thorny question, we should look at this passage for what it says positively about Vincent's own charitology. Vincent is arguing against a view of grace that denies its general effects altogether, and in the process, that denies the need for a human response to general grace. Thus, he is arguing for a general component to grace and the need for human response, whether or not he also wishes to see a personal element, and whether or not he would agree with Augustine that the human responses—the seeking, asking, and knocking—are themselves products of grace. Again, this is not particularly consequential, but Vincent does rule out a 'Pelagian' understanding in which grace is purely external and a Gnostic/Manichaean fatalism with no room for human action at all. There is no overt, or even discernible, connection between grace and Christology here.

In the *Excerp.*, however, Vincent does tie grace directly to his understanding of the Incarnation. Under heading eight, after his very long quotation from Augustine's *Ep.* 187.40 about the difference between Christ and Christians (a passage I have discussed both in chapter 1 and briefly in the previous section of this chapter), Vincent writes:

> Therefore, to overcome and remove the mortal tumour, this medicine came from heaven: God who is humble descended through his mercy to man (*hominem*) who was puffed up with pride, entrusting a unique and extraordinary grace (*singularem praecipuamque commendans*) to that man (*in illo homine*) whom he received with such love on account of those who participated with him (*participibus suis*). And it is not the case that he was conjoined (*coniunctus*) to the very Word of God due to the preceding merits of his will (*praecedentibus suae uonluntatis meritis*) so that he became one Son of God and again one Son of man (*unus Filius Dei et idem ipse unus filius hominis*) by the conjoining. Of course, it is appropriate that he be one. But if this could come about, not through a unique gift from God (*per singulare Dei donum*), but through the free will shared by all men (*per commune hominum liberum arbitrium*), there would be two or three or more.[118]

This is an extremely complex passage that requires careful unpacking. First, we need to sort out how Vincent is using *homo*. The first instance, of course, refers to the human race in its entirety, and I suggest that the second (the phrase *in illo homine*) is being used in two ways, one of which Vincent affirms and the other of

---

[118] *Excerp.* 2.8 (CCSL 64.224).

which he rejects. He denies the possibility that *ille homo* could have been a quasi-independent man united to the very Word of God due to the preceding merits of his will. Notice that in that possibility, even though Christ would somehow be 'one', there would still be one (*unus*—masculine) Son of God and one (likewise *unus*—masculine) Son of man, effectively two persons in the sense of two acting subjects, even if one finds some way to describe them as a unity. Thus, the possibility Vincent rejects is Nestorianism, or better (in the light of the use of the word *meritum*), a Leporianized 'Nestorianism'. The grounds on which Vincent rejects this 'Nestorian' picture of Christ is that if that were the case—if that kind of union of a man with the Word by the man's merits were possible, we would see it happen not once but multiple times. Instead, the Christological union must have been *per singulare Dei donum*.

Since that is the case, the question becomes what picture of the Incarnation Vincent is accepting. It is theoretically possible that he means by *ille homo* an independent man, as long as that man was united to the Word by a free and unique gift of God rather than by merit. But of course, that would fly in the face of the picture of Christ Vincent has argued for throughout the *Excerp*. Instead, I think that Vincent is rejecting the idea of *ille homo* as an independent man, not just the idea of the union being the result of merit. Thus, we need to understand *ille homo* in this passage—in the sense Vincent affirms, not the 'Nestorian' sense he rejects—to mean 'the humanity of the incarnate Word'. If this is correct, then the connections between Christ and Christians begin to come into focus. Vincent states that God, who came to the human race in mercy, received *ille homo* with love on account of his *participes*, and he insists that this was a singular act of grace. We need to read this to mean that the act of grace consisted of the Word's descent to the human condition, so as to share divine love with his own humanity, so that other humans who participate with him in humanity may receive that love as well. Only with this understanding do Vincent's comments about the uniqueness of the grace and his use of the word *participes* to refer to other human beings make sense. This way of thinking about salvation being wrought through the interplay between the incarnate Word and his own humanity is a strikingly Cyrillian idea and lies close to the heart of the way Cyril himself responded to Nestorius.[119] Vincent seems to be using the same idea to reject 'Nestorius' as he understands him.

While discussing this passage in 2010, Casiday affirms: 'Vincent presents salvation as the merciful descent of a humble God in order to cure "man swollen with *pride*". Interestingly, Vincent is keen to make a principled distinction between the relationship of God and '"that man"' which obtains in Christ on the one hand, and God's relationships to other people on the other'.[120] While Casiday does not

---

[119] On the importance of this idea in Cyril's thought, see Donald Fairbairn, *Grace and Christology in the Early Church*, OECS (Oxford: Oxford University Press, 2003), 99–103.

[120] Augustine Casiday, 'Prosper the Controversialist', *StPatr* 49 (2010), 377, emphasis his.

132 CHRISTOLOGY AND THE LOGIC OF GRACE

go into more detail, his point concurs with the way I have understood the same passage. We should remember from previous chapters that the Gallic writers see 'Nestorius' as emphasizing only the similarity between the *homo assumptus* and Christians, whereas Cassian believes we need to stress the difference as well. Here, Vincent brings that difference into sharp focus: the *homo* in Christ is the Son's own humanity, with a unique relationship with God. Indeed, the very same relationship that the Son himself has to God, because he is the Son considered as a man. (The use of *homo* in the sense of Christ's human nature and the use of the same word in the sense of 'the Son considered as a man' come together here.) It is only because of the uniqueness of that relationship—offered as the Word descends to human life so as to live as a man and to give divine love to his own humanity—that we who become *participes* with the Lord in his humanity can become sharers in divine love and life.

There is yet one more thing we need to note. It is probably significant that in *Excerp.* 2.8 Vincent quotes three times from *De praed. sanct.* 1.30–1[121] and once from 2.67,[122] passages in which Augustine compares the predestination of Christ's humanity to the predestination of Christians (passages discussed at length in chapter 1 of this book). But Vincent quotes only the portions of the passages dealing with the predestination of Christ's humanity, not the portions describing the predestination of Christians. In fact, his quotes from *De praed. sanct.* 1.30–1 surround the section where Augustine discusses the predestination of Christians yet skip that section itself, and his quote from 2.67 ends with the sentence immediately prior to the one in which Augustine transitions from discussing Christ to discussing Christians. The omissions are so striking that one can hardly consider them to be accidental; Vincent seems to have intentionally left out Augustine's parallel between the predestination of Christ and that of believers. In fact, in an important discussion that I mentioned briefly in the Introduction to this book, Jaros devotes extensive attention to Vincent's significant omissions in these quotations from Augustine. Jaros uses the theological categories of *historia salutis* (the events in time, culminating in the life, death, and resurrection of Christ, through which God works to effect the salvation of people) and *ordo salutis* (the steps of God's work in the salvation of a particular human being) to explain them. Jaros argues that Augustine sees a strict parallel between God's action in the Incarnation for salvation generally and God's gracious action to save each person, but that Vincent does not.[123] While we must remember, as I argued in chapter 1, that Augustine does not treat the predestination of Christ and that of Christians in *exactly* the same way, he overwhelmingly focuses on the parallel between them. Jaros concludes

---

[121] These three are from Augustine, *De praed. sanct.* 1.30 and 1.31 (CSEL 105.206–7) [WSA I/26.173–4], quoted in *Excerp.* 2.8 (CCSL 64.224–5).
[122] This is from Augustine, *De praed. sanct.* 2.67 [= *De don. pers.* 67] (CSEL 105.270) [WSA I/26.236], quoted in *Excerp.* 2.8 (CCSL 64.225).
[123] Jaros, 'The Relationship of the So-Called Semi-Pelagians', 240–9.

succinctly: 'Vincent simply does not go as far as stating that God's predestination of Christ's humanity in *historia salutis* constitutes as evidence of God's predestination of the Saints in *ordo salutis*.'[124]

To switch from Jaros's terms to the ones I am using in this book, Augustine links Christology and grace in a parallel way because his concept of predestination controls the way both Christology and grace function. In contrast, Vincent connects Christology to grace differently, in such a way that the predestination of the humanity of Christ does not imply an Augustinian-style predestination of each Christian. Whether Vincent is directly arguing against Augustine or not, he *is* fully affirming Augustine's Christology, but he is *not* affirming Augustine's view of the (almost) strict parallel between the predestination of Christ's humanity and the predestination of Christians.

Conclusions on Vincent

The Christology of the *Excerp.* matches that of the *Comm.* in presenting Christ as the Son of God himself who has taken humanity into his own person so as to live, die, and be raised as a man. It is a Christology that is at once precise—with careful use of *substantia* and *persona* to distinguish the levels of duality and unity within the person of Christ—and ambiguous—with a fondness for verbal symmetry and a use of the word *homo* that could be misconstrued as implying that the man Jesus is a distinct, quasi-independent person from the Word. As we have seen, ambiguity about the word *homo* was hardly unique to Vincent. It pervaded Western Christology, and because verbal symmetry between *deus* and *homo* would soon be enshrined in the *Quicunque Vult*, it would be common for centuries to come in the West.[125] But the lengthy explanations from Augustine and the shorter comments from Vincent show clearly that this language needs to be understood as referring to the Word/Son himself, whom we are to consider both as God and as man. Vincent's Christology is perfectly consistent with, and even very similar to Augustine's, and it is also consistent with Cassian's although expressed with much more precise terminology for substance/nature and person. Furthermore, it is crystal clear that this Christology is expressed in explicit opposition to 'Nestorius', who of all heretics dominates Vincent's thought, just as he dominates Cassian's attention.

At the same time, Vincent does not seem to connect Christology and grace with the same logic Augustine uses. For Vincent, as for Augustine, the predestination

---

[124] Ibid., 249.
[125] Indeed, this verbal symmetry is a marked similarity between Vincent's writings and the *Quicunque*, and some have suspected that Vincent was the author of that summary of the faith. Other suggestions have been Hilary of Arles and Caesarius of Arles. See John N. D. Kelly, *The Athanasian Creed* (New York: Harper & Row, 1964), 123, who concludes that the document was composed by someone in the Lérinian school in the late fifth or very early sixth century.

of Christ's humanity is an act of unique grace, but Vincent at least fails to mention, and more likely deliberately excludes, Augustine's logical move by which the bishop of Hippo sets the predestination of Christians for salvation parallel to the predestination of Christ's humanity. For Vincent, as for Augustine, the relationship between the humanity of Christ and believers is crucial, but Vincent, unlike Augustine, does not wish to draw the parallel between Christ and Christians using the concept of predestination. As with Cassian, so also with Vincent, we can only guess how he would have interpreted predestination—whether as a consequence of foreknowledge or in some other way. But it is clear that he ascribes no centrality to the concept.

Of course, Vincent does not explore the interaction of grace and human agency in the life of a Christian to any degree at all, let alone to the degree that Cassian—one of history's great spiritual masters—does. But there are enough hints in Vincent's writings for us to be confident that Vincent connects Christology to grace like Cassian and differently from Augustine, even though both see Christ in very much the same way Augustine does. Vincent and Cassian both seem to reason logically from the Fall to the Incarnation, not from the Fall to predestination to the Incarnation as Augustine does. Both Vincent and Cassian are thus in more of a position to emphasize the general and universal aspects of grace than Augustine is. For them, the universal effects of the Incarnation open up a new sphere of genuinely human and genuinely salvific agency under the general umbrella of grace.

Indeed, when we place the two Gallicans side by side, we begin to see what might be called a genuinely Gallic conception of Christology and grace, a conception whose view of Christ is expressed better and more completely by Vincent and whose charitology finds richer expression in Cassian, but is nevertheless a consistent and coherent Gallic conception. By 'Gallic conception', I mean simply an understanding common to those in Gaul. I do not mean that such a conception was unique to Gaul and thus merely a regional conception that had no wider currency in the church. This conception should not be called 'Semi-Pelagian' because it is not concerned with balancing divine and human action between the extremes of 'Pelagian' and Augustinian thought. Instead, it is just as concerned as Augustine's thought with establishing the priority of divine action and divine grace in salvation, and it is also just as concerned as Augustine's thought with stressing, in opposition to 'Nestorius', the downward movement of the Word to the human sphere so as to accomplish that salvation. In this Gallic conception, however, it is the Incarnation itself—rather than the concept of predestination—that establishes the priority of divine grace and divine action in salvation. As a result, this Gallic conception is free to explore the genuine sphere of human salvific action in response to that divine descent, without ascribing to predestination a central role. With this emerging conception in mind, I now turn to Prosper of Aquitaine.

5

Prosper of Aquitaine

Grace, 'Nestorianism', and God's Salvific Will

Thus far in this book, I have argued that Cassian and Vincent should not be seen as 'Semi-Pelagians', because neither of them thought of grace in terms of balancing emphases on divine and human action, and thus neither can be placed on a spectrum of emphases between Pelagius and Augustine. While Cassian and Vincent disagreed with portions of Augustine's teaching, they expressed those disagreements not primarily by emphasizing a need to balance divine and human action in salvation, but by connecting Christology and grace differently than the way Augustine did.

Now we come to Prosper of Aquitaine, who is in some ways the most puzzling writer in the 'Semi-Pelagian Controversy'. On the one hand, he was Augustine's most vocal defender in fifth-century Gaul and arguably the one who created the notion of 'Semi-Pelagianism', although that exact term would not see the light of day until 1,100 years after his time. But on the other hand, Prosper's thought underwent a significant change between the 420s and the 450s. By the time he wrote *De uoc.*, he had put some distance between Augustine and himself by arguing for God's universal salvific will. In this chapter I shall survey the development of Prosper's charitological thought and the reasons scholars have suggested for his change of mind. I shall then raise the question of whether Christology had a role to play in Prosper's evolution and shall seek to answer that question by examining his general Christological outlook in the early work *De prouid. Dei* of which he was likely the author,[1] as well as what he writes about 'Nestorianism' and other Christological issues in *Epitaph*, *Auctor.*, and *Chron.*

The Development of Prosper's View of Grace

It is widely recognized that Prosper's thinking on grace underwent substantial development during his literary career. As far back as 1929, Cappuyns argued for

---

[1] On the Prosperian authorship of *De prouid. Dei*, see Miroslav Marcovich, Preface to *Prosper of Aquitaine: De prouidentia Dei: Text, Translation and Commentary*, SVigChr 10 (Leiden: Brill, 1989), ix–xi. See also Alexander Y. Hwang, *Intrepid Lover of Perfect Grace: The Life and Thought of Prosper of Aquitaine* (Washington, DC: The Catholic University of America Press, 2009), 17–19.

Christology and the Logic of Grace in Fifth-Century Gaul. Donald Fairbairn, Oxford University Press.
© Donald Fairbairn 2025. DOI: 10.1093/9780198936220.003.0006

136 CHRISTOLOGY AND THE LOGIC OF GRACE

three distinct periods in Prosper's thinking: up to the year 432 (which Cappuyns labels 'the period of intransigence'), the years 433–435 ('the period of first concessions'), and the years after 435 ('the period of great concessions'),[2] and Cappuyns's lines of demarcation have been followed in the middle of the twentieth century by De Letter[3] and at the beginning of the twenty-first by Teske.[4] In 2009, Alexander Hwang pronounced Cappuyns's three periods to be the scholarly standard, although he himself has adopted a framework with four periods, 417–425, 426–430, 430–440, and 440–455.[5] For purposes of this book, it will be sufficient simply to observe the differences between Prosper's writings from the early years of the grace-related discussions in the 420s and early 430s, and his later writings from the 450s.

Prosper's Charitology in the 420s and Early 430s

As early as his *Ep. ad Ruf.* from *c*.428, Prosper already takes aim at those who, he claims, are deliberately bringing charges against Augustine by 'saying that he completely sets aside free will and under cover of grace upholds fatalism. He wants us to believe, they add, that there are in the human race two different masses (*duas illum humani generis massas*) and natures (*duas . . . naturas*).'[6] Prosper continues shortly thereafter by characterizing these alleged opponents of Augustine as follows: 'Desirous of taking pride in their own justice (*in sua justitia*), rather than glorying in God's grace (*in Dei gratia gloriari*), they are displeased when we oppose the assertions they make in many a conference (*inter multas collationes*) against a man of the highest authority.'[7] The reference to *multas collationes* is an obvious allusion to Cassian's *Conlat.* and shows clearly that at this point—four years before he wrote *Con. Collat.*—Prosper is already convinced that Cassian's thought on grace is not only different from Augustine's but directed specifically against him.

Later in 428, in his *Ep. ad Aug.* Prosper describes Augustine's Gallic opponents as affirming that Christ died for all people and that God predestined to salvation those whom he knew would accept the faith and persevere in it.[8] In the case of baptized infants who die in childhood, Prosper claims Augustine's opponents believe that they are saved or condemned on the basis of God's foreknowing what they would have done if they had lived. He indignantly complains: 'But so

---

[2] M. Cappuyns, 'Le premier représentant de l'augustinisme médiéval, Prosper d'Aquitaine', *RTAM* 1 (1929), 310.

[3] P. De Letter, Introduction to *St. Prosper of Aquitaine: The Call of All Nations*, ACW 14 (New York: Newman Press, 1954), 10–11.

[4] Roland Teske, 'The Augustinianism of Prosper of Aquitaine Revisited', *StPatr* 43 (2003), 500.

[5] Hwang, *Intrepid Lover of Perfect Grace*, 31–2.

[6] *Ep. ad Ruf.* 4 (PL 51.79) [ACW 32.23, translation slightly modified].

[7] *Ep. ad Ruf.* 5 (PL 51.79–80) [ACW 32.24].

[8] *Ep. ad Aug.* 3, 6 (CSEL 57.457, 463) [ACW 32.39, 43–4].

much do they subordinate the divine election to some sort of invented merits (*quibuscumque commenticiis meritis*) that, for want of past merits, they imagine future ones that will never exist (*quia praeterita non extant, futura, quae non sint futura, confingant*). By this novel kind of absurdity of theirs it follows that God would have foreknown what will never happen and that what He has foreknown would never take place.'[9] Later in this letter, Prosper famously claims that there are only a few 'intrepid lovers of perfect grace' (*perfectae gratiae intrepidos amatores*), who are unafraid to contradict their monastic superiors.[10] He labels those superiors 'remainders of the Pelagian heresy' (*Pelagianae reliquiis prauitatis*), and he describes their error as giving the human will precedence over divine grace by claiming that human beings are helped by grace because they first desired the good on their own.[11]

With these two letters, Prosper effectively creates the notion of what would later be called 'Semi-Pelagianism'. He holds Augustine's thought as the standard by which others are to be judged[12] to such a degree that he regards the belief that Christ died for all as being problematic. He rejects out of hand the idea that God might foreknow what someone would have done if he or she had lived longer. And most important of all, he insists that people who never actually write derogatorily of Augustine by name are deliberately opposing him, and he calls them *Pelagianae reliquiae prauitatis* as if their thought amounted to 'Pelagianism' despite their consistent disavowal of that heresy. In all these ways, Prosper sets the stage for the way much of modern scholarship would later interpret the grace-related discussions of the fifth century. In fact, Casiday has recently complained that in *Ep. ad Ruf.*, 'Prosper lays down a set of principles from which he never diverts and which become fixed points for scholarship for the next millennium and a half. The first is his assertion that his enemies are surreptitiously attacking Augustine. Even in his later writings, he repeatedly avers to whispering campaigns against Augustine. With Prosper's claims, these whispers pass over into documented history.'[13]

Furthermore, Hwang has recognized that part of what was driving Prosper at this point in his life was his conviction that there could not be varied views on

[9] *Ep. ad Aug.* 5 (CSEL 57.462) [ACW 32.42–3, translation slightly modified].
[10] *Ep. ad Aug.* 7 (CSEL 57.465) [ACW 32.45]. Hwang identifies nine such Augustinians in Gaul: Prosper himself, Hilary, Hilary's parents and his brother and sister-in-law, the deacon Leontius, and the unknown authors of *Hypomnesticon* and the *Capitula sancti Augustini*. See Alexander Y. Hwang, "*Pauci Perfectae Gratiae Intrepidi Amatores*: The Augustinians in Marseilles", in *Grace for Grace: The Debates after Augustine and Pelagius*, ed. Alexander Hwang et al. (Washington, DC: The Catholic University of America Press, 2014), 50.
[11] *Ep. ad Aug.* 7 (CSEL 57.465) [ACW 32.45].
[12] Hwang, *Intrepid Lover of Perfect Grace*, 92, summarizes: 'Prosper was so utterly convinced by Augustine that he assumed Augustine was synonymous with authority and orthodoxy—that Augustine's doctrines were the expressions of the catholic Church. In defending Augustine, Prosper believed he was defending the Church. Prosper naively thought the Church's endorsement of Augustine's anti-Pelagianism extended equally to Augustine's alternative doctrine to Pelagianism.'
[13] Augustine Casiday, 'Rehabilitating John Cassian: An Evaluation of Prosper of Aquitaine's Polemic against the "Semipelagians"', *SJT* 58 (2005), 275.

138 CHRISTOLOGY AND THE LOGIC OF GRACE

grace. Any viewpoint that did not line up with Augustine's *in toto* was suspicious in his eyes and demanded a refutation. As Hwang aptly summarizes, 'Prosper had a vested interest in portraying the situation as gravely as possible to Augustine. Prosper's purpose was to provoke a response from Augustine by describing the situation in terms that he hoped would rouse the old bishop to action. . . . Prosper appealed to Augustine's fears: a possible new Pelagian movement within the Church.'[14]

In response to the *Pelagianae reliquiae prauitatis*, in *Ep. ad Ruf.* Prosper emphasizes that the Lord's invitation to come to him in Mt. 11:28 applies not to everyone, but to those whom God's grace arouses to do so.[15] He argues that grace initially makes a dead person alive and a bad person good, not a good person better, although it will also do that later.[16] Prosper claims boldly that it is just as much an offence against the truth to deny that God has predestined a fixed number of the elect as it is to deny grace altogether,[17] and he insists on the priority of predestination, not foreknowledge of merit, in the salvific purposes of God.[18] Finally, he defends Augustine against the alleged charge of affirming two masses of humanity by insisting that all human beings have been created from a single mass, that of Adam, and that through the sin of the first man, this single nature failed miserably and can be restored only through the grace of Christ.[19]

Not long after Augustine's death in August 430, two priests from Genoa (Camille and Theodore) write to Prosper with questions about several points Augustine has made in his last treatise, *De praed. sanct.* Above all else, their perplexity has to do with the seeming arbitrariness of God's decision to save some and not save others. As Prosper responds, he is at pains not to base that divine salvific decision on God's foreknowledge alone but to ascribe it entirely to grace (and predestination).[20] Several examples of this pattern should suffice.

Excerpt 4 comes from *De praed. sanct.* 1.8,[21] in which Augustine insists that the Lord prepares in the elect the will to believe. Prosper agrees with the Genoese priests that no one denies the saved wish to believe and the unsaved do not wish to believe. But he continues:

---

[14] Hwang, *Intrepid Lover of Perfect Grace*, 116.

[15] *Ep. ad Ruf.* 6 (PL 51.81) [ACW 32.25–6].

[16] *Ep. ad Ruf.* 8–10 (PL 51.82–3) [ACW 32.27–9].

[17] *Ep. ad Ruf.* 12 (PL 51.83) [ACW 32.29–30].

[18] *Ep. ad Ruf.* 14 (PL 51.85) [ACW 32.31].

[19] *Ep. ad Ruf.* 19 (PL 51.88) [ACW 32.36].

[20] Hwang, *Intrepid Lover of Perfect Grace*, 139, describes this writing thus: 'Prosper responded with little tact and much condescension. It was an unwarranted and unprovoked attack—these priests had the courtesy to ask for clarification rather than simply draw their own conclusions. They were not attacking Augustine's doctrine per se, but Prosper took their curiosity as nothing less than an attack on a person who was so clearly catholic in Prosper's estimation.'

[21] Augustine, *De praed. sanct.* 1.10 (CSEL 105.189) [WSA I/26.158].

There you have both God's mercy and His justice (*misericordia et judicium*): mercy for the elect who obtained the true justice of God, His just judgment of the others who were blinded. Yet, it is certain, the first believed because they wished to believe, the second failed to believe because they did not wish to believe. Accordingly, both God's mercy and His justice are operative in the very wills of men (*in ipsis voluntatibus facta sunt*).[22]

Here Prosper places election logically prior to the human will to believe. The cause of faith, ultimately, is not merely the believing human being, but God's election of that person so that by his grace he will change the person's desire not to believe into a desire to believe.

Excerpt 6 comes from *De praed. sanct.* 1.16,[23] in which Augustine insists that God would have been perfectly just to save no one at all, and the reasons for his decisions to save some and not others are unsearchable. Here again, the priests are troubled by the apparent arbitrariness of God's decrees, and Prosper responds not by allaying their fears but by confirming them:

Just as we have no right to complain because in past ages God left all nations to walk in their own ways, so also we would have no reason for complaint if God even now withholding His grace allowed us to perish together with those whose condition is the same as ours (*cum eis, cum quibus nobis fuit causa communis*). But as in those times grace saved a few the world over, so in our day it saves us in countless numbers from all parts of mankind....[24]

Here again, Prosper's answer provides no inkling of any fairness on God's part in choosing some but not others. God is just or merciful, yes, but is he fair? This seems to be an important question to the Genoese, but not to Prosper.

Excerpt 8 comes from *De praed. sanct.* 2.35,[25] in which Augustine asserts that if God foreknew whom he would grant to believe, he also foreknew by what gifts he would work out that belief and salvation. Prosper's long reiteration of Augustine's assertion amounts to a rejection of foreknowledge as a means of discriminating between the elect and the non-elect. Instead, God's grace causes both faith and perseverance, and one is again left with no answer other than election to explain why some believe and others do not.[26] Prosper concludes: 'But the reason why He does not save all or saves some in preference to others, there is no need for us to inquire, nor is it possible for us to find out. Without considering the reason of that discrimination, it should be enough for us to know that mercy does not do away

---

[22] *Resp. excerpt. Gen.* 4 (PL 51.192) [ACW 32.54].
[23] Augustine, *De praed. sanct.* 1.16 (CSEL 105.194) [WSA I/26.163].
[24] *Resp. excerpt. Gen.* 6 (PL 51.194) [ACW 32.59].
[25] Augustine, *De praed. sanct.* 2.35 [= *De don. pers.* 35] (CSEL 105.244) [WSA I/26.213].
[26] *Resp. excerpt. Gen.* 8 (PL 51.196–7) [ACW 32.62–3].

140 CHRISTOLOGY AND THE LOGIC OF GRACE

with justice, nor justice with mercy, in Him who condemns no one except in justice and saves no one except through mercy.'[27] While 'don't ask' seems to satisfy Prosper as it has Augustine, we may guess that it does not satisfy the Genoese, just as it has not satisfied many other Christians before and since.

Of course, Prosper's most extensive work from the early phases of the Gallic grace-related discussion is his *Con. Collat.* from *c.*432. Writing in 2018, Jérémy Delmulle argues exhaustively and persuasively that Prosper intended this work primarily for the newly crowned Pope Sixtus III and meant it not merely as a doctrinal rebuttal, but as an accusation, a juridical demonstration of Cassian's heterodoxy.[28] In *Con. Collat.*, Prosper takes Cassian's *Conlat.* 13 to be referring to the beginning of salvation (which I have argued in chapter 3 is a mistaken interpretation of it) and (mis)reads Cassian as distinguishing two classes of people: those who need God to change their will so that they can move towards him, and those who make the first move towards God on their own. For the first class, Prosper asserts, Cassian has properly made Christ a saviour, but for the second group, he has made Christ merely a helper and refuge.[29] Throughout the work, Prosper belabours the distinction Cassian has allegedly made between two classes of people, and he concludes poignantly:

> Thus, according to this distinction of yours, there will be, you say, a new discrimination within the one Church: our Lord Jesus Christ . . . is not the Saviour (*salvator*) of all Christians but of some only, and of others He is only the refuge (*susceptor*). He saves those only whom God compels to accept grace against their own desire and will (*quos ad suscipiendam gratiam Deus aversos reluctantesque compulerit*), but He is the refuge of those who anticipated the divine call by the fervor of their free action (*qui vocationem spontanei cursus fervore praevenerint*). To the former He grants a gratuitous gift, to the latter He renders a just reward.[30]

In the process of making his extended argument against what he believes Cassian is asserting, Prosper insists that the proper starting point for understanding grace is the Fall. Adam was created in a happy condition and had the capacity through free will to remain in that condition and to reach a state where he would never leave that condition. But he sinned, and as he perished, we all perished in him. If

---

[27] *Resp. excerpt. Gen.* 8 (PL 51.197–8) [ACW 32.64].

[28] Jérémy Delmulle, *Prosper d'Aquitaine contre Jean Cassien: Le* Contra Collatorem, *L'Appel à Rome du parti Augustinien dans la querelle postpélagienne*, Textes et Études du Moyen Âge 91 (Rome: Fédération Internationale des Instituts d'Études Médiévales, 2018). Delmulle further suggests that Prosper had written much of the work prior to his trip to Rome in 431 but refrained from presenting it to Pope Celestine, who might have been loath to consider a critique of Cassian, whom he had asked to help him with the case of Nestorius. Thus, Prosper waited until the accession of Pope Sixtus III to publish the work. See esp. 53–65, 153–8, 289–90.

[29] *Con. Collat.* 2.2–4 (PL 51.218–20) [ACW 32.73–5].

[30] *Con. Collat.* 18.2 (PL 51.263) [ACW 32.124].

we could have practised the virtues Adam had before the Fall, then we would not have needed grace.[31] Prosper continues: 'But now that no one can escape from eternal death without the sacrament of regeneration, does not the uniqueness of the remedy (*ex ipsius remedii singularitate*) show clearly the very depth of evil in which the nature of all mankind has sunk (*in quam profundum malum totius humani generis natura demersa sit*) because of the sin of the one in whom all have sinned and lost all that he lost?'[32] This focus on the Fall ties directly to Prosper's earlier stress on the single *massa damnata* of humanity and the corresponding priority of predestination in the understanding of grace. If one's starting point for deliberation is the fact that all are dead in sin, it is ruthlessly logical to say that only those whom God rouses from spiritual death by choosing them and causing them to will to believe come to Christ.

A couple of years later, in *c.*434, Prosper pens replies to two sets of objections to his Augustinian teaching. The first set comes from some people in Gaul who have drawn up an antagonistic summary of Augustine's teaching as they understand it, and the second set is the *Obiect. Vincent.* that I have discussed in chapter 4. As Prosper replies to these two sets of objections, he touches again on several themes similar to the ones that have dominated his writings in these early years, but now he begins to offer a bit more nuance than we have seen from him previously. When the Gallic objectors point out that Augustine's teaching implies not all people are called to grace, Prosper agrees and even uses the fact that there are nations where the gospel is not known as evidence that we should not believe God calls all people to grace.[33] When the Gallicans object that Augustine's teaching implies God does not want all people to be saved, Prosper again agrees and reiterates as Augustine often does that God's judgements are unsearchable. We should not seek to understand why he chooses to save some and not others.[34] But in response to other Gallic objections, he stresses that God does not actively will anyone to do evil or be condemned. Instead, he affirms that God calls some to faith, but he does not call anyone to unbelief.[35] And when Vincent (who may not be Vincent of Lérins) raises the same objection, Prosper is a bit coy, insisting that we must profess that God wills all to be saved while still acknowledging that we cannot fathom God's reasons for discriminating between whom he will and will not save.[36]

Of particular importance in these two responses are Prosper's comments on the atonement, which again show more nuance than we have seen before. Remember that in 428 in *Ep. ad Aug.*, he has objected to the Gallic monks' assertion that Christ

---

[31] *Con. Collat.* 9.3 (PL 51.237) [ACW 32.92–3].

[32] *Con. Collat.* 9.3 (PL 51.237) [ACW 32.93].

[33] *Resp. obiect. Gall.* 1.4 (PL 51.159–60) [ACW 32.143]. Cf. the same point in 1.10 (PL 51.166) [ACW 32.151–2].

[34] *Resp. obiect. Gall.* 1.8 (PL 51.162–4) [ACW 32.146–9].

[35] See *Resp. obiect. Gall.* 1.5 (PL 51.160) [ACW 32.143–4]. He continues to insist that God does not predestine any to evil in *Resp. obiect. Gall.* 1.11, 1.13, 1.14 (PL 51.166–70) [ACW 32.152–6].

[36] *Resp. obiect. Vincent.* 2 (PL 51.179) [ACW 32.165].

142   CHRISTOLOGY AND THE LOGIC OF GRACE

died for all people. Now he explains to the Gallic objectors that salvation requires not only the birth and death of Christ but our being reborn in him and dying with him. He continues: 'Accordingly, though it is right to say that the Saviour was crucified for the redemption of the entire world (*pro totius mundi redemptione*), because He truly took our human nature and because all men were lost in the first man, yet it may also be said that He was crucified only for those who were to profit by His death (*potest tamen dici pro his tantum crucifixus quibus mors ipsius profuit*).'[37] In part two of the work (in which he qualifies the points he has made in part one), he elaborates on this apparent equivocation as follows: 'For it is certain that the blood of our Lord Jesus Christ is the price for the entire world (*pretium totius mundi sit*). But they are excluded from this price (*a quo pretio extranei sunt*) who either cherishing their captivity refused to be liberated (*qui aut delectati captivitate redimi noluerunt*) or having been liberated returned to their captivity (*aut post redemptionem ad eandem sunt servitutem reversi*).'[38] Similarly, he tells Vincent that 'one must say that the blood of Christ is the redemption of the entire world. But they who pass through this world without coming to the faith and without having been reborn in baptism, remain untouched by the redemption.'[39] Notice here than Prosper is affirming one thing out loud ('one *must* say') and another thing more quietly, just as he has claimed that we must say God wills to save all people, even though quietly we understand that God discriminates for reasons we cannot grasp.[40]

In these writings from early in the grace-related discussions, we should notice that Prosper, like the later Augustine, makes the severity of the Fall the starting point for understanding salvation and treats election/predestination as the beginning point for all discussions of grace. All people are dead in sin, part of a *massa damnata*, and God chooses—for reasons we cannot fathom—whom he will rescue from this condemned lump of humanity. At first Prosper attaches no significance to general grace given to all people and instead emphasizes the particularity of God's grace given only to the elect. This particularity shows up in his initial surprise that the Gallic monks believe Christ died for all, as well as his insistence that grace transforms what a person wills only if that person is elect. At this point in his life, Prosper is being faithful to Augustine's later thought on the points most objectionable to many people in Gaul. But as time goes on, Prosper begins to feel the force of the objections he has been fending off, and his rigid logic from the starting point of predestination starts to yield to an acknowledgment of some sort of universal

---

[37] *Resp. obiect. Gall.* 1.9 (PL 51.165) [ACW 32.150].

[38] *Resp. obiect. Gall.* 2.9 (PL 51.172) [ACW 32.159, translation slightly modified].

[39] *Resp. obiect. Vincent.* 1 (PL 51.177–9) [ACW 32.164].

[40] Delmulle sees during this time period a movement on Prosper's part from strictly affirming the most extreme of Augustine's later statements to trying to construct an Augustinianism that is in some ways more Augustinian than Augustine himself. He takes the absence of the word *praedestinatio* in *Con. Collat.* to indicate that that work as well shows hints of such a movement on Prosper's part. See Delmulle, *Prosper d'Aquitaine contre Jean Cassien*, 280–8.

PROSPER OF AQUITAINE   143

salvific will and some universal aspects of the atonement. We should remember that Cappuyns considers the years 433–435 a transitional stage in Prosper's development, compared to the years up to 433.

Prosper's View in the 450s

Of course, the key writing for describing the later development in Prosper's view of grace is *De uoc.*, written *c.*450. In fact, so pronounced is the difference between this work and Prosper's writings two decades earlier that a number of modern scholars, such as Quesnel in the seventeenth century, believed Prosper could not have been the author.[41] But in 1927, Cappuyns affirmed Prosperian authorship,[42] and he was followed (albeit with some hesitation) by De Letter in 1954.[43] More recently, in 2003 Teske gave a thorough defence of Prosper's authorship of the work by pointing out that the manuscripts attribute the work to Prosper, Ambrose, or Augustine. Since Ambrose died before the Pelagian Controversy began, and since the later Augustine could not have argued for God's universal salvific will (as *De uoc.* does), those two attributions are both impossible, leaving us with Prosper as the only viable option.[44] Teske also provides satisfactory responses to the earlier reasons for denying Prosperian authorship and notes that the vocabulary and style of the work, as well as the historical situation, support the claim that Prosper was the author.[45] In 2009, Teske and Weber give even more detail on these arguments,[46] and they conclude that 'there is strong external and internal evidence for the present consensus of scholars that the author of VocGen is Prosper of Aquitaine.'[47] We may now regard the Prosperian authorship of *De uoc.* to be firmly established.

Recent scholars, working with the conviction that Prosper was in fact the author of *De uoc.*, have generally agreed on the work's major emphases and thus on the contours of the shift in Prosper's thought. In 1954, De Letter described Prosper's task in the work as follows: 'Against Semi-Pelagianism he had to assert the absolute gratuitousness of grace, but in such wise as to safeguard a real universal salvific will. On the other hand, in spite of St Augustine's teaching, he had to maintain the universalism of God's will to save men, without, however, impairing the gratuitousness of grace.... To effect this synthesis, one way alone was open, namely,

---

[41] See Roland J. Teske and Dorothea Weber, Introduction to *Prosper: De uocatione omnium gentium*, CSEL 97 (Berlin: De Gruyter, 2009), 29.

[42] M. Cappuyns, 'L'auteur du "De vocatione omnium gentium"', *Revue Benedictine* 39 (1927), 198–226.

[43] De Letter, *St. Prosper of Aquitaine: The Call of All Nations*, 164–5n52. De Letter argues that whether Prosper wrote it or not, the important thing is that the treatise belongs to the milieu in Gaul in which Catholic doctrine on grace began to be separated from Augustine's theories.

[44] Teske, 'The Augustinianism of Prosper of Aquitaine Revisited,' 494–5.

[45] Ibid., 495–6.

[46] Teske and Weber, Introduction to *Prosper: De uocatione omnium gentium*, 23–33.

[47] Ibid., 33.

144 CHRISTOLOGY AND THE LOGIC OF GRACE

to disconnect the gratuitous character of grace from the Augustinian doctrine on predestination.'[48] He continues, 'The originality of St. Prosper's *De uocatione* in solving the problem of the salvation of all mankind lies in this idea of a general grace given to all men. He has been the first to state this in explicit terms.'[49] In 2003, Teske asserted that during this latest period, Prosper envisions a general grace given to all human beings, a grace that is sufficient but not necessarily efficacious.[50] In 2009, Teske and Weber asserted that three main propositions govern the work: 'that God wills the salvation of all men, that no one is saved except by the grace of Christ, and that the judgments of God in distributing that grace are at present inscrutable to human minds'.[51] The first of these ideas, they point out, departs from Augustine's later writings and Prosper's own earlier ones.[52] Later they continue: 'Despite Prosper's movement away from the later Augustine, he still maintains the Augustinian position that no one is saved except by the grace of God and that every step on the path to salvation from the beginning of faith to final perseverance is a gift of divine grace.'[53]

Hwang has done the most detailed recent work on Prosper's life and development, and in his theological biography of the Aquitainian published in 2009, he summarized *De uoc.* as arguing for four different senses of God's will: 'one for general humanity (2.25, 31); one for those who have heard or will hear the gospel (2.15–18); one for a segment of humanity given special grace, but without election (2.26, 29); and one for a segment of humanity given special grace and election (2.33–37)'.[54] Of the third, Hwang summarizes: 'God's special grace prepares, exhorts, moves, inspires, rouses, and illumines the human will to cooperate with God's work. Nonetheless, this help can be refused, even by those who will persevere, because God did not take away the human will's *mutabilitas*. It is possible for the beginners and the advanced in faith to refuse God's help and thus leave the faith. If they fall, it is due their own *mutabilitas*, if they succeed to salvation, it is due to the help of grace.'[55] Conversely, of the fourth, Hwang summarizes: 'However, if the good works of human free will are preordained and caused by election, such a view of free will does not entail the same freedom of the will enjoyed by those with only special grace, who are free to refuse or accept God's help. Apparently, for those elected their wills are not prone to *mutabilitas*.'[56]

---

[48] De Letter, Introduction to *St. Prosper of Aquitaine: The Call of All Nations*, 12.

[49] Ibid., 15.

[50] Teske, 'The Augustinianism of Prosper of Aquitaine Revisited', 503.

[51] Teske and Weber, Introduction to *Prosper: De uocatione omnium gentium*, 11.

[52] Ibid., 11–12.

[53] Ibid., 17.

[54] Hwang, *Intrepid Lover of Perfect Grace*, 212. Cf. the same point in Alexander Y. Hwang, 'Manifold Grace in John Cassian and Prosper of Aquitaine', *SJT* 63 (2010), 102–3.

[55] Ibid., 213–14.

[56] Ibid., 214–15.

As we look at these scholarly summaries, we should remember that in Prosper's earlier works, his starting point for discussing grace was predestination and that he virtually ignored any general aspects of grace in preference to its particular action in the elect. As these scholars recognize, moving from particular to general and away from predestination (at least away from election as the starting point) constituted quite a shift indeed, so much so that in 1996 Weaver characterized it as 'an unsuccessful attempt to introduce the Semi-Pelagian emphasis on distinct human agency into an Augustinian logic that necessarily undercut such an emphasis'.[57] That may or may not be so, and it is not my purpose to assess the systematic consistency of the later Prosper's thought. Instead, I should like simply to give a few examples from *De uoc.* of the new Prosperian perspective on grace. My interest will then be on the question of what precipitated the shift in his thinking.

At the beginning of *De uoc.*, Prosper states the issue that has been plaguing Gaul for two decades:

> A great and difficult problem has long been debated among the defenders of free will and the advocates of the grace of God. The point at issue is whether God wills all men to be saved (*utrum velit deus omnes homines salvos fieri*); and since this cannot be denied (*negari hoc non potest*), the question arises, why the will of the Almighty is not realized (*cur voluntas omnipotentis non impleatur*). When this is said to happen because of the will of men, grace seems to be ruled out; and if grace is a reward for merit, it is clearly not a gift but something due to men. But then the question again arises: why is this gift, without which no one can attain salvation, not conferred on all, by Him who wills all to be saved?[58]

Here we should notice that Prosper declares that it cannot be denied (*negari hoc non potest*) that God wills all people to be saved. Of course, not only *can* it be denied, but Prosper himself *has* denied it for most of his career. Now, however, he treats such an assertion as indubitable, so the question becomes how to explain that not all are saved when God wills all to be saved. This is a very different starting point from what we have seen at earlier phases in Prosper's life, and doubtless this point of reference is much more congenial to almost everyone in Gallic monastic circles.

Later in book one, Prosper reiterates his lifelong emphasis on the inability of fallen humanity to accomplish anything related to salvation: 'Mortal man, born according to the flesh from a source that was cursed in Adam, cannot come to the spiritual dignity of the new birth except through the guidance of the Holy Spirit

---

[57] Rebecca Harden Weaver, *Divine Grace and Human Agency: A Study of the Semi-Pelagian Controversy*, PMS 15 (Macon, Georgia: Mercer University Press, 1996), 152. She reiterates this claim that Prosper is inconsistent in Rebecca Harden Weaver, 'Prosper's Theological Legacy and its Limits', *StPatr* 49 (2010), 383–4.

[58] *De uoc.* 1.1 (CSEL 97.79) [ACW 14.26].

146   CHRISTOLOGY AND THE LOGIC OF GRACE

(*nisi spiritu sancto regente non pervenit*). Indeed, he cannot even foster any desire for it as long as he has not received from God the ardour of his desire. . . .'[59] In this passage, notice that the mental move is not from the extent of the Fall to predestination, but from the extent of the Fall to the need for the Holy Spirit's action.[60] In the same paragraph, Prosper again affirms that everything salvific derives from God's grace: 'It is in our own best interest, therefore, to hold that all good things, especially those conducive to eternal life, are obtained through God's favour (*dei munere haberi*), increased through God's favour (*dei munere augeri*), and preserved through God's favour (*dei munere custodiri*).'[61]

Also in book one, Prosper returns to his longstanding concern about why God does not save all people:

> For, this we do know beyond any doubt: all beginning and all increase of merit is for every man a gift of God (*omne principium et omne profectum boni meriti unicuique homini ex dei donatione conferri*). Moreover, it is impossible that He who wills all men to be saved (*qui omnes vult salvari*) would, for no reasons whatever, not save the greater part of them (*nullis causis existentibus plerosque non salvet*). But we are not able to know these reasons (*has causas nostrae scientiae non patere*), which would not have remained secret had it been necessary for us to know them.[62]

This focus on the inscrutability of God's judgements is not new, but it now has a new urgency about it in the light of Prosper's affirmation of God's universal salvific will. Whereas the troubling question was previously why God would not want to save everyone, it is now why God would somehow not save certain people whom he wills to save.

While this question is somewhat altered, Prosper makes no more attempt to answer it now than he has earlier in his life. He admits, 'We indeed see it happen that the grace of the Saviour passes by some men (*aliquos . . . praeterierit*) and that the prayers of the Church in their favour are not heard (*recepta non fuerit*). This must be ascribed to the secret judgments of divine justice (*occulta divinae iustitiae iudicia referendum est*). We must acknowledge that we cannot understand this profound mystery in this life.'[63] Ultimately, Prosper retreats to God's inscrutable will: 'God's will, therefore, is the sole reason why grace is bestowed on any man (*causa percipiendae gratiae voluntatis est*), whatever be his nation or race, his

---

[59]   *De uoc.* 1.11 (CSEL 97.88) [ACW 14.36].
[60]   Thomas J. Humphries, Jr., 'Prosper's Pneumatology: The Development of an Augustinian', in *Grace for Grace: The Debates after Augustine and Pelagius*, ed. Alexander Hwang et al. (Washington, DC: The Catholic University of America Press, 2014), 112–13, points out this shift. I shall return to his work as I discuss the reasons for Prosper's development below.
[61]   *De uoc.* 1.15 (CSEL 97.92) [ACW 14.40].
[62]   *De uoc.* 1.15 (CSEL 97.92) [ACW 14.41].
[63]   *De uoc.* 1.27 (CSEL 97.105) [ACW 14.53].

state or age. In that will does the motive of his election lie hidden (*ratio electionis abscondita est*). Merit begins with grace (*gratia incipientibus meritis*), which was itself received unmerited (*quam accepere sine meritis*).[64] In these passages Prosper still sounds very much like Augustine, although he has substantially altered the question. But that very alteration of the question—with a new focus on why the salvific will of God is not always brought to fruition—provides the opportunity for productive reflection on the interaction between grace and human action in book two of *De uoc.*

Prosper begins the second book by laying out the points he has already established in book one:

> First, we must confess that God wills all men to be saved (*deum velle omnes homines salvos fieri*) and to come to the knowledge of the truth (*et in agnitionem Veritatis venire*). Secondly, there can be no doubt that all who actually come to the knowledge of the truth and to salvation, do so in virtue not of their own merits (*non suis quemquam meritis*) but of the efficacious help of divine grace (*sed ope atque opera divinae gratiae*). Thirdly, we must admit that human understanding is unable to fathom the depths of God's judgments (*altitudinem iudiciorum dei humanae intelligentiae penetrabilem esse non posse*), and we ought not to inquire (*non oportere disquiri*) why He who wishes all men to be saved does not in fact save all (*cur non omnes salvet qui omnes vult salvos fieri*).[65]

This articulation of the first point matches the Latin text of 1 Tim. 2:4 almost verbatim. The biblical passage long perplexed Augustine, and Prosper after him, but now the latter is willing to take it at face value. On the second point Prosper has never wavered and does not waver now. It is the third point that now vexes him, and although he states that we may not inquire into the reasons for the fact that not all whom God wills to save are saved, he nevertheless seeks to illustrate from Scripture that this is in fact the case.

Accordingly, much of book two is an exploration of the general and specific aspects of God's grace in the Old Testament. God shows gracious concern for all, but special attention to both Jews and those Gentiles who turn to him in response to his general grace.[66] Prosper concludes: 'We meet with many more frequent and more numerous cases of men to whom the heavenly bounty grows as its gifts are granted little by little (*cui particulatim quiquid superna largitas donat accrescit*), so that the reasons for granting further gifts arise from those already bestowed (*ut conferendorum munerum causae de his quae sunt collata pariantur*).'[67] Here

---

64 *De uoc.* 1.36 (CSEL 97.114) [ACW 14.63].
65 *De uoc.* 2.1 (CSEL 97.141) [ACW 14.89, translation slightly modified].
66 *De uoc.* 2.15–17 (CSEL 97.154–7) [ACW 14.104–6].
67 *De uoc.* 2.18 (CSEL 97.157) [ACW 14.106–7, translation modified].

148 CHRISTOLOGY AND THE LOGIC OF GRACE

the full extent of Prosper's developmental shift is on display. Rather than focusing only on particular gifts of grace given to the elect, he now has room in his understanding for general gifts of grace given to everyone. Even more striking is that at least to some degree, further special gifts are added in the case of those who use general gifts of grace well.

As a result of this new openness to a human role in responding to grace, Prosper also moderates his view of what makes grace efficacious. Later in book two, he writes that God's grace is the more prominent factor in everyone's justification. But even so,

> Man's will is also associated with grace as a secondary factor (*sed etiam voluntas hominis subiungitur ei atque coniungitur*). For it is roused by the above-mentioned aids in order that it may co-operate with God's work which is being accomplished in man (*ut divino in se cooperetur operi*), and that it may begin to practise and gain merit (*incipiat exercere ad meritum*) from that for which the divine seed inspires the effective desire (*quod de superno semine concepit*). Thus its eventual failure is due to its own fickleness; but its success is due to the help of grace (*gratiae opitulatione*).[68]

The ascription of a role (albeit a secondary one) to human action is striking coming from the pen of Prosper, and the fact that he does so enables him to attribute any failure to human action while still affirming a genuinely co-operative role for the human will.

Near the end of the work, Prosper turns his attention to 1 Tim. 4:10 (Christ is the saviour of all men, especially of believers), and he writes:

> For by saying, *who is the Saviour of all men*, the Apostle affirmed that God's goodness is general and takes care of all men. But by adding, *especially of the faithful*, he showed that there is a section of humankind (*partem generis humani*) whom God, thanks to their faith which He himself inspired (*merito fidei divinitus inspiratae*), leads on with special helps to the supreme and eternal salvation (*ad summam atque aeternam salutem specialibus beneficiis provehatur*). In doing this, God, who is supremely just and merciful, is above all injustice, and we have not to discuss His judgment about these rulings—that would be arrogance—but rather to praise it in awe and trembling.[69]

This passage aptly summarizes Prosper's new understanding. There are both general and particular elements to God's gracious action with humanity. The general elements come first and are given to all people. The particular elements follow in

---

[68] *De uoc.* 2.43 (CSEL 97.183) [ACW 14.135].
[69] *De uoc.* 2.51 (CSEL 97.191–2) [ACW 14.144].

the case of that *pars generis humani* that believes, with a faith that is both human and itself produced by God's inspiration.

Reasons for Prosper's Development

Ever since the consensus emerged that Prosper was the author of *De uoc.*, scholars have given attention to the question of what caused his charitological development, and they have identified several complementary reasons for the shift. The most widely noted, and surely the most significant, is that Prosper's involvement with the Roman see[70] led him to recognize that the Christian tradition was broader than Augustine's teaching. In 1929, Cappuyns wrote that Rome judged theological disputes rather than taking part in them, and that the papal see had no interest in wading into the controversy in Gaul. He argued likewise that it was 'by no means improbable' that Leo's personal influence brought about Prosper's change of heart.[71] Likewise, Weaver asserted in 1996 that part of the reason for Prosper's moderation may have been that by the middle of the 430s he was in Rome in the service of Archdeacon Leo (who became Pope in 440), and Leo's respect for Cassian may have led Prosper to modify his views.[72] In the same vein, Teske and Weber argued in 2009: 'By the time of VocGen Prosper's concern is not mainly the defense of Augustine's teaching, but of the faith of the Roman Church. . . . After the aggressive discussion about inherited sin and free will which is found in Augustine's late writings, had cooled down, Prosper as papal secretary must have been more interested in presenting a compromise than stirring up the controversy.'[73]

The most comprehensive treatment of Prosper's shift in allegiance from Augustine to Rome came from Hwang in 2009. Hwang asserts of his study:

> The main thesis is that Prosper's theological development is marked by his evolving understanding of the Church. There are four stages in this development. Prosper initially had a very limited and general understanding of the Church. Then came a period of study and encounter with south Gallic monasticism, Augustine, and the Church. Based on these initial encounters, Prosper naively assumed Augustine represented the catholic Church's view and defended him accordingly. Prosper's understanding of the catholic Church then became

---

[70] Prosper and Hilary travelled to Rome in 431–432 in an unsuccessful attempt to persuade Pope Celestine (whose archdeacon was Leo) to rule against the Gallic monks and in favour of Augustine on grace. Some scholars also believe he spent the 440s and 450s in Rome as at least a friend of (now Pope) Leo and perhaps also his adviser or secretary. See the discussion below in connection with the question of whether Leo's Christological writings are relevant for our purposes.

[71] Cappuyns, 'Le premier représentant de l'augustinisme médiéval, 326–7. Cf. Hwang, *Intrepid Lover of Perfect Grace*, 31.

[72] Weaver, *Divine Grace and Human Agency*, 138.

[73] Teske and Weber, Introduction to *Prosper: De uocatione omnium gentium*, 16.

150 CHRISTOLOGY AND THE LOGIC OF GRACE

increasingly connected with the Roman Church and Prosper attempted to synthesize Augustine's doctrine to conform to his emerging appreciation of the Roman Church. The final stage in his development was Prosper's full conviction that the Roman Church was the center of the catholic Church.[74]

Hwang's thorough and comprehensive biographical study of Prosper's life amply demonstrates the truth of his initial assertion,[75] and we may be very confident that Leo played the main role in Prosper's growing awareness of the breadth of the Christian theological tradition and thus on the increasing nuance and moderation in his teaching on grace.

Another factor in Prosper's development was an increasing appreciation for the work of the Holy Spirit. Thomas Humphries argues in 2014 that beginning with *Con. Collat.* in *c.*432, Prosper begins to include the Spirit in his arguments. At first he works with a model of competing agencies. Although we will, it is the Holy Spirit who acts, and where there are two agents, 'one must be the "real" actor, while the other sits aside'.[76] By the time of *De uoc.*, however, Prosper focuses less on whether grace precedes or follows the human will, and more on the role of the Holy Spirit in reforming the human will.[77] This increased focus on the Holy Spirit brought a more personal dimension to a charitology that had previously been dominated by the stark category of predestination, and it also enabled the later Prosper to write with more nuance about general and particular aspects of grace.[78]

What scholars have not mentioned in connection with the shift in Prosper's charitology is any potential influence that Christology might have had on his changing views. This absence of attention is certainly understandable. Unlike Cassian and Vincent, who wrote (or at least collated, in Vincent's case) extensively on Christology, Prosper's oeuvre has very little on the subject. He mentions Nestorius (and Eutyches) only intermittently in *Chron.*, and his only undisputed work that could be said to be devoted to Christology is the short, enigmatic poem *Epitaph.*, written in *c.*432 in the aftermath of the Council of Ephesus. (Prosper may also have been the author of three broadly Christological inscriptions in Rome dating from

---

[74] Hwang, *Intrepid Lover of Perfect Grace*, 1–2.

[75] Delmulle also emphasizes the importance of the papal see in Prosper's thought in connection with his argument that Pope Sixtus III was the primary audience for *Con. Collat.* See Jérémy Delmulle, *Prosper d'Aquitaine contre Jean Cassien*, 289.

[76] Humphries, 'Prosper's Pneumatology: The Development of an Augustinian', 107–8.

[77] Ibid., 112–13.

[78] See, e.g., *De uoc.* 2.19 (CSEL 97.158) [ACW 14.107]. In this passage, Prosper emphasizes the role of the Holy Spirit in impelling a Christian towards charity: 'Indeed, since the sum total of all God's bounty and the soul of all virtues is given with this ineffable gift (*enarrabili dono*) [that is, the gift of the Holy Spirit], all other gifts are granted us to enable the yearning of the faithful soul to strive effectively after perfect charity. As this is not only from God (*non solum ex deo*) but is God Himself (*sed etiam deus est*), it makes steadfast, persevering, and unconquerable (*stabiles et perseverantes atque insuperabiles*) all those whom it floods with its delight.'

the papacy of Sixtus I,[79] but these inscriptions add nothing of Christological consequence to what we may learn from the *Epitaph.*, and I shall not discuss them.) In spite of this paucity of source material, I should like to suggest that Christology did play a role in Prosper's charitological transformation, and I now turn to his relatively few statements on that subject.

Prosper's Christology

One initial question to be considered on the subject of Prosper's Christology is whether we should also include Leo's Christological sermons and letters—most notably the famous *Tomus ad Flauianum* (*Ep.* 28). At the end of the fifth century, Gennadius reported that certain of Pope Leo's writings against Eutyches were believed to have been spoken (*dictatae creduntur*), that is, perhaps dictated, by Prosper.[80] Many scholars have interpreted Gennadius's cryptic statement to mean that Prosper became Leo's secretary, and Gaidioz, working from this assumption in 1949, subjected the material of the *Tomus* to a minute investigation. He concluded that while there were many traces of Prosper's language and style in the document, his only significant theological contribution to the *Tomus* was the substitution of *natura* for *substantia* in describing Christ's humanity.[81] A generation later, Norman James conducted similar stylistic studies on other writings of Leo and claimed that Prosper's influence on the famous pope was more extensive than Gaidioz had allowed. Writing in 1993, James argued that Leo used Prosper to write not only the anti-Eutychian letters but also some anti-'Pelagian' epistles and Leo's paschal letters for the years 453–455.[82] James suggests that in important theological matters, Prosper at least provided advice and perhaps rough drafts which the pope would then vet and make his own.[83]

---

[79] The first of these is the dedication for the Lateran Baptistery (later part of the Basilica of St. John Lateran), a sixteen-line inscription that describes the offering of Christ's life and the redemption secured through his wounds on the cross to those who are baptized. The second is the dedication for the Basilica of St. Mary Major, an inscription of eight lines that celebrates Mary's role as *Theotokos*. The third is the dedication for the Basilica of St. Peter in Chains, a ten-line inscription that celebrates Philip (one of the Roman delegates at Ephesus in 431) and describes Ephesus as a victory for Christ. See Jérémy Delmulle, 'Prosper d'Aquitaine, poète de l'antinestorianisme triomphant? À propos de trois poèmes épigraphiques romains', in Nihil veritas erubescit: *Mélanges offerts à Paul Mattei par ses élèves, collègues et amis*, ed. Clémentine Bernard-Valette et al., 539–56, Instrumenta Patristica et Mediaevalia (Turnhout: Brepols, 2017). See, especially, Delmulle's arguments for Prosperian (rather than Leonine) authorship, 547–9, 553–4. He concludes on 555 that Prosperian authorship of the first inscription is probable, and that it is at least worth raising the possibility that Prosper may have written the other two as well.
[80] Gennadius, *De uir. illust.* 84 (85) (PL 58.1108) [*NPNF*[2] 3.399].
[81] J. Gaidioz, 'S. Prosper d'Aquitaine et le Tome à Flavien', *RevSR* 23 (1949), 284, 300.
[82] Norman W. James, 'Leo the Great and Prosper of Aquitaine: A Fifth Century Pope and His Adviser', *JTS*, n.s., 44 (1993), 567.
[83] Ibid., 567–8.

152   CHRISTOLOGY AND THE LOGIC OF GRACE

In contrast to the line of reasoning espoused by Gaidioz earlier and James later, Robert Markus, writing in 1986, expressed doubt about the whole idea that Prosper was Leo's secretary. Of the similarities between Prosper's *Chron.* and Leo's letters, Markus writes: 'For these similarities it is very easy to account without turning Prosper into a papal secretary, simply by observing that Prosper had already been given access to Roman archives in 431–2 . . . and that he continued to have such access later on, at a time when he was probably living in Rome, perhaps as the pope's friend.'[84] Markus argues that the influence ran the other way, not from Prosper to Leo but from Leo to Prosper.[85] Then in 2008, Bernard Green argued similarly to Markus, directly countering James's claim that Prosper was involved in the writing of Leo's theological treatises and sermons.[86] The next year, in his biographical study, Hwang surveyed the evidence anew and admitted that Markus's argument cast doubt on efforts to find Prosper's hand in Leo's letters based on stylistic similarities. Nevertheless, he remains convinced that Prosper was Leo's secretary and had some role in the writing of the theological letters.[87] In 2013 James entered the discussion again, prompted largely by Green's critique of his own earlier arguments, and argued anew for his earlier contention that Prosper was Leo I's theological adviser.[88] Still more recently, Michelle Renee Salzman, writing in 2015, questioned anew the notion that Prosper was Leo's secretary or even that he ever lived in Rome. She argues instead that he was an independent aristocrat, deeply influenced by Leo but coming to his own conclusions, not a mere notary for the pope.[89]

In the light of the uncertainties regarding Prosper's possible role in drafting (or editing) Leo's theological writings, and especially in the light of Gaidioz's argument that even in the event of such dependence of Leo on Prosper, the latter had little *theological* impact on the content of the *Tomus ad Flauianum*, I believe it is best to assess Prosper's Christology simply on the basis of his own writings. At the same time, it is important to remember that a large part of the reason for Prosper's development was Leo's influence on him, as we have already seen. Whether or not Prosper was Leo's secretary, Markus and Salzman are surely right that Leo influenced Prosper (James himself admits as much),[90] and that influence

---

[84] Robert A. Markus, 'Chronicle and Theology: Prosper of Aquitaine', in *The Inheritance of Historiography 350–900*, ed. Christopher Holdsworthy and T. P. Wisemen (Exeter: Exeter University Press, 1986), 35.

[85] Ibid., 36.

[86] Bernard Green, *The Soteriology of Leo the Great*, OTM (Oxford: Oxford University Press, 2008), 193–201.

[87] Hwang, *Intrepid Lover of Perfect Grace*, 198.

[88] Norman W. James, 'Prosper of Aquitaine Revisited: Gallic Friend of Leo I or Resident Papal Adviser?' *StPatr* 69 (2013), 267–75.

[89] Michelle Renee Salzman, 'Reconsidering a Relationship: Pope Leo of Rome and Prosper of Aquitaine', in *The Bishop of Rome in Late Antiquity*, ed. G. D. Dunn (Farnham, UK: Ashgate, 2015), 109–25.

[90] Ibid., 273.

may have extended to Christology as well as to grace. Accordingly, in considering Prosper's Christology I shall not use Leo's sermons and letters but shall confine myself to Prosper's poems *De prouid. Dei* and *Epitaph.*, and his brief references to Christology in the *Auctor.* and *Chron.* As we examine these latter two writings, we need to remember that by the time they were written, 'Nestorianism' had been replaced by Eutychianism as the latest Christological heresy of note.

Christology in *De prouid. Dei*

De prouid. Dei is an exercise in theodicy. Gaul had been devastated by a flood, both the Vandals and Visigoths had overrun it from 406 to 415, and King Ataulf had left the region for Spain in 415. Writing in the near aftermath of these calamities, the author (probably Prosper) responds to the complaints about why God has allowed innocent people to suffer with a long poetic description (972 lines) of God's providential care for the universe. Much of the poem highlights the elements of God's care exhibited by the events of Scripture, and the descriptions of Christ provide indications of Prosper's early Christology.

While discussing the early chapters of Genesis, Prosper comments on the fallenness of human nature:

> Many rewards awaited such men because of the merit of their way of life,
> And yet their tainted nature (*vitiate ... natura*) dragged them to death.
> For that nature could not be freed from the bonds of our first parent
> until Christ, being born in this nature without impairment to His majesty
>   (*quam maiestate incolumi generatus in ipsa*),
> destroyed the causes and seeds of death (*destrueret leti causas et semina*).[91]

Here we should notice that 'Christ' is clearly the Son or Word, not a quasi-separate man, because he possesses divine majesty. The Son is born in human nature without detriment to the majesty he already possessed. This comment early in the poem sets up Prosper's later depictions of Christ as God's Son who has become human, not as God and man who might be considered separately.

Prosper's direct discussion of Christ is prompted by an assertion that no people or nation is bereft of God's care. Instead, all nations reflect the same light, that of Christ. He then describes Christ as follows:

> He, with God the Father, is always God (*Qui cum Patre Deo semper Deus*), and while remaining (*manens*)

---

[91] *De prouid. Dei* 5, ll. 298–302 (SVigChr 10.22–3).

154   CHRISTOLOGY AND THE LOGIC OF GRACE

in the majesty of His Father, He takes part (*miscetur*)
in the human condition: and the Word becomes flesh, and the Creator of
the world
undergoes birth, and the Author of eternity submits to the course of the years.[92]

In these lines we see a strong insistence that the acting subject in the Incarnation is the Son or Word. The actor is God, and he remains God. Nevertheless, he shares in the human condition—the Creator is born as a created being; the Author of eternity enters time and lives within it.

As the description of Christ continues, there is one point where Prosper writes of a roadway on which one must stay, without falling off one side of the pathway by thinking of Christ as merely man, or on the other side by considering him to be merely God.[93] This passage, taken in isolation, might suggest that Prosper's Christological concern is merely with adequately balancing divinity and humanity within Christ. But this statement comes only after others that clearly affirm the divine Son as the acting subject in Christ, and in fact, Prosper's insistence on this point extends even to his discussion of Christ's death. He writes:

The Judge was condemned, the Word remained silent, the Light was spat upon.
He was Himself the instrument of His own punishment: He drank gall and
vinegar
as if they were sweeter than honey. He, a holy one (*sanctus*), became an ac-
cursed man
condemned to the cross, and Christ died while Barabbas lived.
Unholy race, daring such a great sin, did you feel your madness
when the whole universe was condemning it? Why, the sun fled from its orbit,
and the midday turned into night. The earth shook and quaked,
and when God submitted to death (*mortemque Deo subeunte*), the bodies of
the saints
were brought out of their tombs and came to life.[94]

This passage insists that the crucifixion was not merely a matter of a holy man being condemned unjustly. That would be scandalous enough, but the outrage of the cross is far greater than this. It was the Judge, the Word, the Light who was condemned. Even more strikingly, it was God who submitted to death (*mortemque Deo subeunte*).

As Prosper describes the resurrection and glorification of Christ, there is a potentially puzzling passage that calls for some attention. He writes:

---

[92] *De prouid. Dei* 6, ll. 463–6 (SVigChr 10.32–3).
[93] *De prouid. Dei* 7, ll. 473–9 (SVigChr 10.32–5).
[94] *De prouid. Dei* 7, ll. 522–30 (SVigChr 10.36–7, translation slightly modified).

Thus far, Jesus, we have known you as one of ours;
henceforth, all that is ours becomes yours; so that the two are no longer separate
but one, for life is in Life, and light in Light—
as a growth, not as an end, of man. But after your glorification (*Quo glorificato*)
you are as Man and as God (*sic homo, sic Deus es*), not one and another (*ut non
alter et alter*).[95]

If one were to read the final two lines in isolation, one might interpret Prosper as asserting that Jesus was a mere man who became divine after his glorification. But that cannot be the correct reading, for two reasons. First, it would fly in the face of the earlier assertions that the Son who was already divine became human while remaining what he was. Second, the topic of this passage is the way we perceive Jesus. While he was on earth, we knew him as a man, but now, after his resurrection and glorification, we see him as he really is—*sic homo, sic Deus*. Significantly, Prosper indicates that we now recognize he is not *alter et alter*. While Jesus was on earth, one could perhaps have thought of him as one person and the Son/Word as another, but that is not possible after the resurrection. The glorification of Christ enables us to see that the divine Son is the same person as Jesus who was crucified, died, raised, and glorified.

As a result, we see that long before the rise of the Nestorian Controversy, the young Prosper saw Christ in what could be called a broadly Cyrillian way. The subject of the human events of Christ's life, including the birth, death, and resurrection, is the divine Son who has taken into himself our nature precisely so that he could undergo such human events. With this early work in mind, we now need to turn to the way Prosper perceives Nestorianism.

'Nestorianism' as Prosper Sees It

Like Cassian and Vincent, Prosper sees 'Nestorianism' in connection with 'Pelagianism', as a comparison of what he writes in *Chron.* about the two heresies will show. In the entry for the year 413, Prosper writes:

At that time the Briton Pelagius set forth the doctrine bearing his name against the grace of Christ; Caelestius and Julian [of Eclanum] were his assistants. He attracted many people to his erroneous views. He proclaimed that each person is guided to righteousness by his own will (*ad iustitiam uoluntate propria regi*) and receives as much grace as he deserves (*tantumque accipere gratiae quantum meruerit*), since Adam's sin injured (*laeserit*) only himself and did not also bind

---

[95] *De prouid. Dei* 7, ll. 542–9 (SVigChr 10.38–9, translation modified).

156   CHRISTOLOGY AND THE LOGIC OF GRACE

(*obstrinxerit*) his descendants. For this reason it would be possible for those so wishing (*volentibus*) to be completely without sin and for all little children to be born as innocent as was the first man before transgression; nor are children to be baptized so they can be divested of sin (*ut peccato exuantur*) but so they can be honored with the sacrament of adoption (*ut sacramentum adoptionis honorentur*).[96]

While this passage does not directly mention Christology, we should notice the similarity of what Prosper writes here with the pre-correction Leporius: we find the same focus on merit, the same idea that Adam's sin affected only himself, the same belief that a human being who so wills can live without sin, and the idea that human beings are guided to righteousness. Whether this is fair to Pelagius and whether Pelagius directly influenced Leporius are both immaterial for our purposes. What is relevant is that there seems to have been a shared Gallic understanding of 'Pelagianism', into which it was believed Leporius himself had fallen. In spite of Prosper's checquered relationship with the Gallic monastic scene, he appears to have imbibed this common Gallic understanding.

It is against this common understanding of 'Pelagius'/Leporius that we should view Prosper's description of 'Nestorius', in the entry for the year 428:

Nestorius, bishop of Constantinople, tried to introduce a new error into the churches. He proclaimed that Christ was born of Mary as a man only, not also as God (*Christum ex Maria hominem tantum, non etiam deum natum*), and divinity was conferred upon him because of his merits (*divinitatem conlatam esse pro merito*). The diligence of Bishop Cyril of Alexandria in particular and the authority of Pope Celestine opposed this impiety.[97]

We should immediately notice that this is similar to the way Cassian and Vincent (and later Gennadius) describe 'Nestorius', with the exception that there is no direct mention that the conferral of divinity came later. As I discussed both Cassian and Vincent in previous chapters, I argued that the main point of the criticism was not the timing of the union but the basis. The Gallic monks may have been 'Leporianizing' Nestorius by introducing the Latin concept of 'merits', but the idea that the *homo assumptus* is united to the Word because of God's good pleasure at his virtue was central to the thought of Theodore and Nestorius. Here Prosper seems to have absorbed the same idea of a Leporianized 'Nestorius' as a man united to God by virtue of his 'merits', yet without the obviously incorrect claim that the

---

[96] *Chron.* 1251 (MGH:AA 9.467) [Murray, 65].
[97] *Chron.* 1297 (MGH:AA 9.472) [Murray, 68, translation slightly modified].

union came after Christ's conception. It is also noteworthy in this passage that Prosper credits Pope Celestine as well as Cyril with opposing Nestorius's impiety.[98]

There is also a reference to 'Nestorius' in the entry for 431: 'A synod of more than two hundred bishops gathered at Ephesus. Nestorius was condemned along with the heresy bearing his name and many Pelagians who supported it because the doctrine was related to their own (*eum multis Pelagianis, qui cognatum sibi iuvabant dogma*).'[99] This brief statement adds very little, but it is nevertheless significant that the condemnation of Pelagianism at Ephesus is regarded not as a separate matter from the affair of Nestorius, but as a closely-related one. Prosper asserts that the 'Pelagians' found in 'Nestorianism' a teaching recognizably similar to their own (*cognatum sibi*) and thus supported it.

These brief comments from *Chron.* give almost no specifics at all, especially when viewed in comparison to the much longer treatments in Cassian's *De incar. Dom.* and Vincent's *Comm.* and *Excerp.* But there is just enough here to suggest that Prosper was working from a common Gallic understanding of 'Nestorius', linked to 'Pelagianism', with the connection perhaps coming through the thought of the pre-conversion Leporius. Prosper's 'Nestorius' is recognizably similar to the conception of the heretic that Cassian and Vincent hold. Nevertheless, this is not quite all that Prosper writes about 'Nestorianism'. From his pen we also possess a short poem of twenty-four lines, the *Epitaph.*, which uses striking imagery to link 'Nestorianism' and 'Pelagianism'. This poem alludes to the Council of Ephesus, seemingly as a recent event, and thus was probably written *c.*432. It has received little scholarly treatment,[100] with the noteworthy exception that David Maxwell, writing in 2003, translates a few lines of it and concludes that the poem shows Prosper understood Christology and grace to be connected.[101] It is worth granting the poem some attention for purposes of this book. The poem is printed in PL 51 without line numbers, but in my quotations below I shall insert such numbering for ease of reference. I shall also divide the poem into six stanzas of four lines each and treat each stanza in turn.

The first stanza of the poem establishes that the speaker—the heretical mother, in the poem's imagery—is 'Nestorianism'.

---

[98] Prosper likewise credits Celestine with aiding Cyril in the extirpation of Nestorianism in *Con. Collat.* 21.2 (PL 51.271) ACW 32.134].

[99] *Chron.* 1306 (MGH:AA 9.473) [Murray, 68].

[100] Hwang, *Intrepid Lover of Perfect Grace*, 16, notes that the poem links the Pelagian and Nestorian heresies and calls it 'Prosper's thinly veiled attack on Prosper's Gallic opponents'. Later (Ibid., 171–2), Hwang notes that the poem does not mention Augustine and teases the idea that the lack of such mention in a work attacking the Gallic monks 'anticipates more pronounced and explicit expressions of Prosper's changing estimation of Augustine'. But this treatment begs the question of whether the poem's actual purpose is to criticize the Gallic monks, and regardless of how one answers that question, Hwang does not address the significance of the essential feature of the poem—its link between Pelagianism and Nestorianism.

[101] David R. Maxwell, 'Christology and Grace in the Sixth-Century Latin West: The Theopaschite Controversy' (Ph.D. Dissertation, University of Notre Dame, 2003), 56–8.

1. I, the Nestorian scourge, have followed the Pelagian (*Nestoriana lues successi Pelagianae*),
2. Which yet sprang forth beforehand from my womb (*Quae tamen est utero praegenerata meo*).
3. I am the unhappy mother of the wretched child and the daughter of the babe (*Infelix miserae genitrix et filia natae*),
4. I have sprung up from the same shoot to which I gave birth (*Prodivi ex ipso germine quod peperi*).[102]

These initial lines establish a mother–daughter relationship between 'Nestorianism' and 'Pelagianism', even as Prosper acknowledges that chronologically, 'Pelagianism' came first.[103] 'Nestorianism' *followed* (*successi*) 'Pelagianism', and yet 'Pelagianism' sprang up earlier (*praegenerata*) from the womb of 'Nestorianism'. Thus, 'Nestorianism' is both the mother (*genitrix*) of the child and the daughter (*filia*) of the baby. Paradoxically, then, 'Nestorianism' sprang from the shoot to which it gave birth.

Biologically, of course, this makes utterly no sense. But the obvious contradiction of these lines may show why Prosper chooses to communicate this idea in a poem. He wants to convey something about 'Nestorianism' and 'Pelagianism' that needs to be communicated poetically, precisely because it is biologically impossible. I suggest that his point here is that the relationship between the two heresies is very specific—not just a connection, but a *causal* connection. One heresy produced the other, gave birth to the other, *caused* the other to spring forth. That generative heresy was 'Nestorianism'. But of course, 'Nestorianism' did not come first, so how can Prosper argue that it was the cause? He does so poetically, through the striking imagery of a chronologically later movement causing an earlier one.

For our purposes, this striking beginning is vitally important, because it indicates not merely a connection between the ideas of the two heresies, but a link in which one needs to start with the Christological problem—'Nestorianism'—and then move to the anthropological one—'Pelagianism'. As we have seen, during Prosper's strongly Augustinian phase, his first logical step was to move from fallen humanity's incapacity to predestination, but the later (more 'Catholic') Prosper moved first from fallen humanity's incapacity to the universal salvific will of God. I have already asked whether Christology had anything to do with this shift, and I propose that the stunning imagery of this poem suggests it did. More specifically, I contend that at this point—still early in his career but after the Council of

---

[102] *Epitaph.* (PL 51.153). Translations from the poem are my own, with thanks to Gillian Clark who caught a few problems with my initial renderings.

[103] Green notes that in this poem Prosper sees Nestorianism as both the mother and daughter of Pelagianism. He regards this imagery as evidence that Prosper and Cassian, probably under Augustine's influence, were already exploring alleged links between Pelagianism and Nestorianism. See Bernard Green, *The Soteriology of Leo the Great*, OTM (Oxford: Oxford University Press, 2008), 34–5.

Ephesus—Prosper is already beginning to grasp the priority of the Incarnation in shaping soteriology. Placing 'Nestorianism' prior to 'Pelagianism' implies—or could be said to imply—that one should think of the Incarnation first, then of the complex of events related to grace, election, the human will, and salvation in the light of the Incarnation. I do not pretend that in 432 Prosper would have been able to express the incipient shift in his thinking this precisely, but nevertheless, such a shift seems to be beginning. He appears to sense at this point that the Incarnation needs greater weight in his thinking, because otherwise there would be no felt need to advance the idea that a later heresy is the mother of an earlier one.

The second stanza of the poem describes 'Nestorianism's' goal of fighting against the truth by means of her daughter 'Pelagianism':

5. For having earlier arisen from the arrogant, I willed to establish a stronghold for merits (*Nam fundare arcem meritis prior orsa superbis*),
6. To lead the work from the Head to the body (*De capite ad corpus ducere opus volui*).
7. But while my offspring is fitted with the armour from the lowest point to the highest (*Sed mea dum proles in summa armatur ab imis*),
8. I have had no suitable occasions to wage war (*Congrua bellandi tempora non habui*).[104]

Keeping in mind that the speaker is 'Nestorianism', the *arcem meritis* is 'Pelagianism', with its focus on the merits of Christians. In l. 6, the work of these two heresies is to focus attention away from the Head (Christ) to the body (the Church). The effect of both 'Pelagianism' and 'Nestorianism' is to concentrate the attention of soteriology on the Christians, the body, the believers, rather than on Christ the Saviour, the Head of the body. In ll. 7–8, the theological conflict between a focus on Christ and a focus on believers is poetically described with military imagery, and 'Nestorianism' seems to lament the fact that unlike her offspring 'Pelagianism', she has no opportunity to fight. This is a surprising comment, perhaps, but it may reflect the fact that in Prosper's milieu, the theological concepts and categories lend themselves more readily to discussions of anthropology (thus, 'Pelagianism') than of Christology (hence, 'Nestorianism').

The third stanza continues the military motif and describes the outcome of the conflict Prosper has introduced in the previous stanza:

9. And after the sad wounds of kindred treachery (*Et consanguineae post tristia vulnera fraudis*),

---

[104] *Epitaph.* (PL 51.153).

160   CHRISTOLOGY AND THE LOGIC OF GRACE

10. The harsh battles of my fellow slave whose end is the same (*Aspera conserui praelia fine pari*).
11. Yet a single decree has conquered me, sentenced me to death (*Me tamen una dedit victam sententia letho*):
12. She who wished to rise again has fallen twice (*Illa volens iterum surgere bis cecidit*).[105]

Here 'Nestorianism'—kindred to 'Pelagianism'—has suffered the same fate as her kindred heresy. The *una sententia* in l. 11 is a reference to the Council of Ephesus: Prosper avers not only that the council has conquered 'Nestorianism' (again, remember that she is the poem's speaker), but it has also caused her to fall twice. That is, she fell in the council's condemnation of 'Nestorianism' as its main action, but again in the council's condemnation of 'Pelagianism'. At this point in the poem, the kindred relationship between the two heresies is so tightly drawn that 'Nestorianism' herself can be said to have fallen in the condemnation of 'Pelagianism'. We should note that Prosper affirms the same thing in the nearly contemporaneous *Con. Collat.*, in which he writes: 'Celestine, again, cleansed the Eastern Churches of a twofold scourge (*gemina peste*): to Cyril, Bishop of Alexandria and the most renowned defender of the Catholic faith, he lent the help of the apostolic sword to extirpate the Nestorian impiety, and so the Pelagians also, kin and comrades of the Nestorians in error, received a new blow.'[106]

The fourth stanza describes the death and burial of the two heresies condemned at Ephesus:

13. With me she rises, with me she dies, with me she enters the tomb (*Mecum oritur, mecum moritur, mecumque sepulcrum*)
14. And is placed in the bottommost depths of infernal prison (*Intrat, et inferni carceris ima subit*).
15. Our frenzied arrogance has cast us headlong into this prison (*Quo nos praecipites insana superbia mersit*),
16. Are we deprived of gifts and puffed up with merits (*Exutas donis, et tumidas meritis*)?[107]

Here we should notice the word *superbia* in l. 15, which Prosper regards as the source of the two heresies, since it was what led to their being cast into prison. Remember that in l. 5 Prosper has associated *superbia* with 'Nestorianism' and *meritum* with 'Pelagianism'. There, and again here, he indicates that arrogance is the ultimate source. It is the arrogance of reliance on oneself for salvation, rather

---

[105] *Epitaph.* (PL 51.153).
[106] *Con. Collat.* 21.2 (PL 51.271) ACW 32.134, translation slightly modified].
[107] *Epitaph.* (PL 51.154).

than focusing on Christ himself, that leads one to fancy he or she has merit to be saved. This connection enables us to understand l. 16. The merits with which 'Nestorianism' and 'Pelagianism' are puffed up are imagined merits, confidence in their own righteousness for salvation. Being puffed up with such imagined merits deprives one of the divine gifts that alone provide actual salvation.

The fifth stanza provides an even more explicit link between the two heresies:

17. For we who consider Christ to be God through works of piety and as a re-ward (*Nam Christum pietate operum et mercede volentes*)
18. Have not stood in covenant with the Head (*Esse Deum, in capitis foedere non stetimus*);
19. And we who hope for a crown for the soul through freedom (*Sperantesque animi de libertate coronam*),
20. Have lost that righteousness that grace gives (*Perdidimus quam dat gratia justitiam*).[108]

Here we see that people are not in fellowship with the Head, Christ, if they regard him to be God only by virtue of his works, not by virtue of his eternal existence. This again is the 'Nestorian' idea that Christ is a man who was elevated to deity by virtue of his merits. To Prosper, if he is a man elevated to divine status (no matter when that elevation happened), then he is not the very Head, the Lord himself. Similarly, in ll. 19–20, those who hope to obtain reward through their free actions forfeit the righteousness that the Head gives through grace. A reliance on oneself, on one's own works or righteousness, is unavailing for salvation. This, of course, is a classic emphasis of the early Prosper, but what is new here is that he connects this idea directly to Christology by writing that righteousness by grace is given by the Head, Christ, on the basis of our connection to him. The question of whether Christ really is the Head or merely a man united to the Head lies at the root of the Pelagian/Nestorian question, as Prosper now sees it.

In the final stanza, for the first time the speaker, 'Nestorianism', addresses Christians more generally:

21. And therefore, if any of you feels compassion for the ruins of a double down-fall (*Quique igitur geminae miseraris busta ruinae*),
22. Beware lest you share in our ruin (*Ne nostro exitio consociare cave*).
23. For if you believe that the gifts we confess too late to be given by the Lord (*Nam si quae Domini data munera sero fatemur*),
24. Are given as a debt to man, you will be ours (*Haec homini credis debita, noster eris*).[109]

---

[108] *Epitaph.* (PL 51.154).
[109] *Epitaph.* (PL 51.154).

162   CHRISTOLOGY AND THE LOGIC OF GRACE

Nestorianism and Pelagianism have undergone downfall and ruin; the question is whether believers will share in that ruin. The narrator concludes with the ominous warning that anyone who believes divine gifts are given as a reward belongs to them, that is, to 'Nestorianism' and 'Pelagianism'.

Neither in this poem nor in any other of his extant writings does Prosper go into detail about 'Nestorianism'. There is no wrestling with Nestorius's nuance in using the word 'Christ' to refer both to the *homo assumptus* or with Nestorius's πρόσωπον of union comprised of both Logos and man. Nor is there any discussion of Christological terminology, of the levels at which unity and duality exist in the one Christ. But from this short poem, it emerges that Prosper is beginning to connect the gratuity of God's grace with the identity of Christ as the eternal Son of God and the Head of the body. Moreover, he is starting to give a logical priority to the identity of the Saviour in his consideration of grace. It appears that anti-'Nestorian' Christology does have some role to play in Prosper's charitological development.

The Emergence of 'Eutychianism'

Unlike Cassian, who died in the 430s not long after the Council of Ephesus, and Vincent, who may have lived until *c.*450 but had no apparent knowledge of the events immediately prior to Chalcedon, Prosper was acquainted not only with 'Nestorianism', but also with 'Eutychianism'. In his entry in *Chron.* for the year 448, he writes:

> At this time the Eutychian heresy arose. It was created by Eutyches a certain priest who presided over a renowned monastery in Constantinople. He proclaimed that Jesus Christ, our Lord and son of the blessed Virgin Mary, had no maternal substance (*nihil maternae habuisse substantiae*), but only the nature of God's word was in him in the likeness of a human (*sed sub specie hominis solam in eo verbi dei fuisse naturam*). On account of this impiety he was condemned by Flavian, bishop of the same city, for he would not be corrected. But relying on royal friendship and the favor of courtiers, he asked to be heard by a universal synod. Theodosius gave his consent and ordered all the bishops to assemble at Ephesus in order to withdraw this condemnation. In this council, Eutyches was absolved and Dioscurus, bishop of Alexandria, claiming primacy for himself, proposed a sentence of condemnation against Flavian, bishop of Constantinople.[110]

Two things about this passage are noteworthy. First, if a Gallic writer were going to describe Christology in terms of balancing emphasis on the deity and humanity

---

[110]   *Chron.* 1358 (MGH:AA 9.480) [Murray, 72–3].

of Christ, the church's correction of Eutyches would have provided the perfect occasion for doing so. One could easily think of 'Nestorianism' as an excessive emphasis on the humanity and 'Eutychianism' as an excessive emphasis on the deity, and then treat Christological orthodoxy as the proper balance between those extremes. But Prosper does not put 'Eutychianism' on the opposite end of a spectrum from 'Nestorianism', and furthermore, he describes 'Eutychianism' in a way almost unrelated to the way he has depicted 'Nestorianism'. The earlier mistake, in Prosper's estimation, treats Christ as a man united to the Word by virtue of his merits, and he never mentions technical Christological terminology in describing it. In the case of this latter error, however, Prosper uses the term *substantia*, and claims that Eutyches denied a *materna substantia* in Christ. This charge could mean either that Christ had no humanity, or that his humanity did not come from Mary. But it is clear from the following clause (*sed sub specie hominis solam in eo verbi dei fuisse naturam*) that Prosper means the first. Eutyches in fact denied the double consubstantiality of Christ and refused to speak of two natures after the union. Nevertheless, it is likely that he actually did not shortchange Christ's humanity but simply preferred not to use the word οὐσία to describe that humanity,[111] but that issue is not germane to our study. Prosper, probably wrongly, took Eutyches to mean that Christ was not truly human. Eutyches's own thought, and 'Eutychianism' as Prosper perceived it, are not the same thing.

The second noteworthy aspect of this passage is the way it summarizes the chaotic proceedings of the years 448 and 449. The trial of Eutyches came at a Home Synod (σύνοδος ἐνδημοῦσα) in Constantinople in 448, headed by Patriarch Flavian.[112] Prosper attributes this to Flavian alone, without mention of a synod. The council headed by Alexandrian Patriarch Dioscorus that reinstated Eutyches was the Ephesine Synod of 449 (not the Ecumenical Council at Ephesus in 431),[113] and Prosper goes on to describe the objection of the papal legates to Dioscorus's proceedings and Flavian's attempts to acquaint Pope Leo with the proceedings before Flavian's death.[114] But Prosper does not mention that Leo famously dubbed

---

[111] Richard Price comments that Eutyches rejected the double consubstantiality of Christ 'not because he doubted the reality of Christ's human nature but because he feared that the expression undermined Christ's uniqueness as the Son of God'. He adds that Eutyches's rejection of the expression 'two natures after the union' meant 'not that he doubted the presence in Christ of two sets of attributes, one divine and one human, but that he refused to call them "two natures," which, in the language of the time, implied that they were two distinct entities'. See Richard Price, Commentary on the First Session, in *The Acts of the Council of Chalcedon: Volume 1*, TTH 45 (Liverpool: Liverpool University Press, 2005), 115.

[112] The Acts of the Home Synod of 448 dealing with Eutyches are extant only as part of the Acts of the First Session of the Council of Chalcedon. For an introduction to the Home Synod and a guide to the location within the Chalcedonian Acts of the relevant Acts of the Home Synod, see Michael Gaddis, General Introduction to *The Acts of the Council of Chalcedon: Volume 1*, TTH 45 (Liverpool: Liverpool University Press, 2005), 25–30.

[113] The Acts of the Ephesine Synod of 449 are also extant only as part of the Acts of the First Session of the Council of Chalcedon. For a summary of the proceedings and a guide to the location within the Chalcedonian Acts of the relevant Acts of the Ephesine Synod, see Michael Gaddis, General Introduction to *The Acts of the Council of Chalcedon: Volume 1*, 30–7.

[114] *Chron.* 1358 (MGH:AA 9.480) [Murray, 73].

164   CHRISTOLOGY AND THE LOGIC OF GRACE

the synod the *latrocinium* or 'Robbers' Synod'.[115] Given that Prosper is usually regarded as having been Leo's adviser/secretary and that his overarching purpose in writing *Chron.* is to demonstrate the centrality of the papal see,[116] why would he not mention the pope's angry reaction to the Synod of Ephesus in 449? We should perhaps regard this lacuna as evidence that Prosper may not have been as close to the pope as scholars sometimes assume. But it may also be that this constitutes indirect evidence that 'Eutychianism' was not as important to Prosper as 'Nestorianism' was. What Prosper accuses Eutyches of is certainly a grave mistake, but it may not have been as likely to be taken up and affirmed by others as the mistake of 'Nestorianism', amalgamated as it was with 'Pelagianism' that by this time had held a long and pernicious hold on the Western Christian world.

Prosper mentions the Council of Chalcedon twice in *Chron.* His entry for the year 450 describes the accession of Emperor Marcian after Theodosius II's death and continues: 'By his [Marcian's] edicts, which complied with the authority of the apostolic see (*apostolicae sedis auctoritatem secutis*), the synod of Ephesus was condemned, and it was decided that an episcopal council should be held at Chalcedon, so that forgiveness might heal the reformed and the intransigent might be driven out with their heresy'.[117] And his entry for 453 includes the following: 'The Synod of Chalcedon ended. Eutyches and Dioscorus were condemned. All who disassociated themselves from them were received into communion. Universally confirmed was the faith that was proclaimed by holy Pope Leo (*fide, quae . . . per sanctum papam Leonem praedicabatur*) with respect to the incarnation of the Word, according to the evangelic and apostolic doctrine'.[118] These two passages predictably emphasize the role of the papal see in both the organizing of the Council of Chalcedon and its Christological proclamation, but they provide no further specificity about Christological heresy.

Prosper's Positive Christology

In the previous section, we have seen that in contrast to the abundant material from the pens of Cassian and Vincent about Christology, we have very little to go on when we examine Prosper. The only positive expressions of his Christology come in the early work *De prouid. Dei*, and our only material from the main parts of his career is brief summaries of heresies and one short poem, also focused on heresies. As a result, we may make only relatively general observations about Prosper's positive Christology.

---

[115] In his letter to the Empress Pulcheria in 451. See Leo, *Ep.* 95.2 (PL 54.943) [*NPNF*[2] 12.71].
[116] Remember the central role he has ascribed to Pope Celestine in the condemnation of Nestorius at Ephesus in 431. As we shall see shortly, he would also ascribe a crucial role to Leo at Chalcedon.
[117] *Chron.* 1362 (MGH:AA 9.481) [Murray, 73].
[118] *Chron.* 1369 (MGH:AA 9.482) [Murray, 74].

First, it is clear that he was in favour of using *substantia* to describe Christ's humanity, and thus of speaking of two *substantiae* or *naturae* in Christ. We may assume that Prosper learned his Christological terminology from Leo (although again, his omission of Leo's scathing rebuke of the Ephesine Synod of 449 might give us pause), and we can guess that perhaps Vincent's *Excerp.* played a formative role in his understanding as well. Second, and for our purposes more important, Prosper connected the 'Nestorian' heresy with 'Pelagianism' and saw it as a mistake about the identity of the Saviour. Christ is not a man who somehow merited union with God the Word, as the amalgamation of Nestorius with both Pelagius and Leporius into 'Nestorianism' was said to affirm. Instead, he himself is the Head of the body, the Word who is also human. Third, from the *Epitaph.* it seems plausible that 'Nestorianism' impelled Prosper to give the Incarnation and this understanding of the Saviour's identity priority in the way he reasoned about grace and salvation. Rather than moving logically from the Fall to predestination, as Augustine has done in his latest treatises and as Prosper has done earlier in his life, he may have begun to reason from the Fall to the Incarnation, with a corresponding shift in his understanding of the salvific will of God.

On this third point, it is worth asking whether we may say more than just 'may have begun to reason. . . .' Is there any concrete evidence from Prosper's writings that he actually changed the way he connected grace and Christology and began to move from Christology to grace the way the other Gallicans did? I suggest that there is a bit of such evidence, to which I now turn.

From Christology to Grace

I have found four passages in Prosper's *Auctor.* and *De uoc.*, both from *c.*450, that suggest he is now reasoning from the Fall to the Incarnation to grace, rather than from the Fall to predestination to grace. Two of these come in *Auctor.*, in which Prosper marshals evidence from the Pelagian Controversy (quotes from Popes Innocent and Zosimus and from the Council of Carthage in 418) and from the liturgy to demonstrate the church's teaching on grace. It is noteworthy that at this point in his life, he does not mention predestination at all, nor does he name Augustine.[119]

In article 2 of *Auctor.*, Prosper begins: 'No one has any goodness of himself unless he be given a share in the goodness of Him (*nisi participationem sui ille donet*) who alone is good (*qui solus est bonus*).'[120] He supports this assertion with a quote

---

[119] See Weaver, *Divine Grace and Human Agency*, 139–41. She comments on 141 that in leaving these things out, Prosper shows that the official, binding teaching of the Church on grace includes the broad framework of Augustinianism but does not necessarily include the extremes of Augustine's position,
[120] *Auctor.* 2 (PL 51.206) [ACW 32.179].

166   CHRISTOLOGY AND THE LOGIC OF GRACE

from Pope Innocent I (pope from 401 to 417) in which he criticizes those who think their goodness comes from themselves and neglect the grace God gives them to attain it.[121] Innocent's comments are actually very general and impersonal; they have to do with whether a Christian's goodness can be ascribed to himself or herself, or only to God's grace. Prosper's use of Innocent's pronouncement, on the other hand, specifically ties a Christian's goodness to the goodness of the Saviour. We do not merely become good by grace (rather than our own actions); we become good as we share in Christ's goodness. The incarnate Christ stands as the grace by which Christians are made good, and the fact that Prosper affirms this in a commentary on a papal proclamation that itself does not do so is evidence of the centrality the incarnate Christ as a person holds in Prosper's new understanding of grace.

In *Auctor.* article 4, Prosper again cites Pope Innocent I, this time in order to show that no one uses free will well unless Christ helps him. He quotes Innocent as affirming that 'freedom itself so deceived the first man [Adam] that, using its power of control too freely, he allowed himself to be thrown down into sin by pride. And he could not have been raised up from this fall, had not the coming of Christ the Lord restored the state of his original freedom by providing regeneration (*nisi ei providentia regenerationis statum pristinae libertatis Christi Domini reformasset adventus)*.'[122] In this passage we see a direct logical move by Prosper (and by Innocent, whom he is quoting) from the Fall to the Incarnation. Regeneration restores the original state of freedom that was Adam's before the Fall, and it is the coming of Christ that accomplishes this restoration. Both of these passages suggest that Prosper is reasoning from the Fall to the Incarnation (rather than merely or directly to predestination). In one case he reasons this way even though his authority, Innocent, does not. In the other case he reasons this way because Innocent, his authority has himself done so. We see evidence here of the influence of the papal see on Prosper, but more important, we see evidence of a shift in the way he thinks about grace, a shift in which Christology comes logically prior to and shapes his understanding of divine grace.

In book two of *De uoc.*, Prosper discusses God's grace and mercy in the Old Testament through his service of created things, the doctrine of the Law, the oracles of the Prophets, the language of miracles, and the help of angels. He then affirms:

> But He has shown His mercy for all men (*misericordiam suam universis hominibus*) in a far more extraordinary manner (*multo magis aliter*) when the Son of God became the Son of man (*quando filius dei factus est filius hominis*),

---

[121] Innocent I, *Ep.* 29.3 (PL 20.584).
[122] *Auctor.* 4 (PL 51.207) [ACW 32.180, translation slightly modified]. Prosper is quoting Pope Innocent I, *Ep.* 30.3 (PL 20.591).

so that He could be found by those who did not seek Him and seen by those who did not call upon Him. Since then the glory of the race of Israel shines not in one people only. To Abraham a numerous posterity is born among all nations under the heavens. The promised heritage falls no longer to the sons of the flesh, but to the sons of the promise.[123]

This passage is crucial for several reasons. First, it shows that in Prosper's mind the Incarnation of the Son is an act of mercy or grace, indeed the supreme act of grace, towards all human beings. Second, the phrase *filius dei factus est filius hominis* shows that the person of Christ is the Son himself. Prosper, we have seen, has shown no inclination towards technical Christological terminology, but he has demonstrated a concern with the identity of the Saviour. He must be and is the Son himself, not a man connected to the Son (by his merits), and Prosper reiterates that assertion here. Third, this passage indicates that the downward movement of the Son through the Incarnation is key to the universal salvific will of God which is the main subject of *De uoc*. The reason we know God desires all to be saved is that the Son became human to save all—not just Jews, and not just those who call upon him or make a hypothetical first move towards him.

Later in *De uoc*. book two, Prosper affirms that Abraham was justified by faith before he received the commandment of circumcision. Then, once already justified through faith, he received the sign of circumcision in the part of the body through which the seed would advance until 'without the seed of the flesh, the Son of God, God *the Word, was made flesh* [Jn. 1:14] and was born of Abraham's daughter, the Virgin Mary. He assumed and made participants in this birth all those (*assumptis omnibus in huius nativitatis consortium*) who, having been reborn in Christ, would believe what Abraham believed (*qui in Christo regenerati quod Abraham credidit credidissent*).'[124] Here again, as in the passage just discussed above, we see Prosper's thinking about grace (and thus about God's salvific will) linked directly to the Word who was made flesh. His human birth opens up to us the possibility of re-birth because we participate in that birth and are thus reborn in Christ. Again, we know that God's will for human salvation is universal because of the human birth of the incarnate Word.

Thus, while we have limited evidence, we can see that among the various factors leading Prosper towards the affirmation of God's universal salvific will, one is his recognition of the centrality of the Saviour's identity for the way we construe grace. Christology plays a role in Prosper's evolution, because it leads him to change the logical steps of his thinking. Where (logically) does he go after a consideration of the Fall? Not directly to predestination, as he once did, but instead to the

---

[123] *De uoc*. 2.14 (CSEL 97.153–4) [ACW 14.103].
[124] *De uoc*. 2.25 (CSEL 97.163) [ACW 14.113, translation modified].

Incarnation, which is for *all people* and which correspondingly re-shapes the way he writes about grace and God's will.

Conclusions on Prosper

It is of course ironic to speak of Prosper of Aquitaine in the same breath with the Gallic monks Cassian and Vincent. For much of his adult life he was their ardent opponent as he sought to defend Augustine's teaching on grace and predestination against objections coming from the Gallic monastic world. But there is no question that Prosper's thought on grace evolved substantially over the last two decades of his life, and his later affirmation of the universal salvific will of God is the fruit of that development. It is certainly true that Prosper's growing recognition of the breadth of the Christian tradition beyond Augustine's own teaching and his increasing appreciation for the doctrine of the papal see played a major role in his shifting thought on grace. But I have suggested in this chapter that his increasing appreciation for the identity of the Saviour also played a role in re-directing his thought. Rather than moving logically from the Fall to predestination, and only then to the Incarnation and atonement, Prosper begins to reason from the Fall to the Incarnation, and only *then* to grace, with a less central focus on predestination. Prosper makes this shift while holding—so far as we can tell—to a Christology consistent with that of Augustine, the post-correction Leporius, Cassian, and Vincent—an anti-'Nestorian' Christology in which the eternal Son is the subject of the actions and experiences of Christ. Admittedly, the evidence for Prosper's positive view of Christ is scant, but we know he sees 'Nestorius' the same way that Cassian and Vincent do, and responds just as negatively as they do, so we are on reasonably safe ground in assuming that his positive Christology would be consistent with theirs.

Stepping back to view our findings as a whole, then, we see that the teaching of the later Prosper seems to be consistent with the emerging 'Gallic' conception of Christology and grace that we have found in Cassian and Vincent. These three writers have different emphases that overlap only to a limited degree. Cassian is concerned with the identity of the Saviour, the eternal Word, and with the varied ways the grace of Christ operates in the life of a monk. Vincent is concerned with the identity of the Saviour and with the articulation of traditional Christian orthodoxy more generally, and he exhibits far more focus on technical Christological terminology than Cassian does. Vincent's attention to grace is relatively general in comparison to Cassian's, but largely consistent. With Prosper we find for the first time a Gallic writer intensely concerned with grace in connection with the very beginning of salvation, with the question of whether God's saving will is universal or restricted, and also with questions related to predestination. But if we admit the general consistency of their perspectives and put their ideas together, we find our emerging 'Gallic' view of grace to be enhanced and furthered. Previously we have seen in Cassian and Vincent that a view of Christ focusing on the downward movement of the Son leads to an emphasis on genuinely free human cooperation with divine grace. Now with Prosper, we see that such a view of Christ allows for a view of God's saving will that is universal, as well as a complex view of predestination that leaves room for a general offer of grace to all and for predestination to be related (in some way) to God's foreknowledge of what people will do with general grace. All three writers prioritize grace, and they do so by linking the divine initiative to the Incarnation and as a result, to God's saving will. And yet all three writers see room for, and the need for, human cooperation with God's initiative, in faith, Christian life, and perseverance. For all three writers, and especially clearly in Prosper's case, the logic of grace moves from a consideration of the Fall to a recognition of the universal significance of the Incarnation.

Obviously, this is not the way the later Augustine reasons from the Fall to grace. In spite of the similarity between his Christology and that of Cassian, Vincent, and (presumably) Prosper, he moves logically from the Fall to predestination, and only then to the Incarnation. By doing this, the later Augustine sets himself up to see the Incarnation only in terms of its particular effects on the elect, not in terms of its general purposes for all human beings. Cassian and Vincent never agree with him on this logic. Prosper agrees with him at first, but then later changes his mind. As a result, we are now in a position to recognize that even with corresponding Christologies, different Christian writers construe grace very differently depending on the logical sequence of their thinking about grace—from predestination to Christ to grace in the life of a Christian, or from Christ to grace for humanity as a whole to grace in the life of a Christian. The fact that the Gallic writers agree with Augustine on Christology but disagree significantly on grace does not mean that Christology and charitology are unrelated. Instead, I suggest, it means that they relate Christology and grace differently, and more precisely that they reason from the one to the other in different logical sequences. To say this another way, Vincent, Cassian, and Prosper all agree with Augustine on the priority of divine grace and divine action in salvation, and thus none should be called 'Semi-Pelagian'. But the three of them (considering the later Prosper) do not use predestination as the controlling theme for asserting that divine priority; instead they allow the iIncarnation itself to hold that function. Thus, for them Christology functions in a universal way to effect change and offer grace to the entire human race, rather than merely in a particular way to effect the salvation of the predestined.

With this Gallic conception of Christology and grace emerging into full view, and with due allowance for the surprising irony that it is *Prosper* who brings it into the light of day, we now have one more major fifth-century Gallic charitological thinker to consider, Faustus of Riez.

6

Faustus of Riez

'Nestorianism' and *Prima Gratia*

If the early Prosper arguably created the concept of a coherent group of Augustinian detractors who would later be called 'Semi-Pelagians' when he branded his opponents as *Pelagianae reliquiae prauitatis*, it was Faustus who arguably gave posterity the rubric for understanding this group. He is famous for championing the 'royal way' (*uia regia*) that affirms both human obedience and divine grace without falling off the path on one side ('Pelagianism') or the other (extreme predestinarianism). To later thinkers working from Augustinian/Pelagian categories, it could and did seem as if Faustus advocated the balancing of emphases that became the traditional hallmark of 'Semi-Pelagianism'. But was Faustus actually trying simply to balance seemingly contradictory emphases, merely to steer a middle course between opposing heresies? And did the Christological opposition to 'Nestorius' that animated Cassian, Vincent, and even Prosper contribute to Faustus's thinking about grace as well? These are the questions I shall address in this chapter. First, I shall consider Faustus's descriptions of the royal way and the views of various scholars about his efforts to balance emphases on grace and human action. Then I shall describe scholarly opinions on whether his attempts at balance mark him as a 'Semi-Pelagian'. Next, I shall explore Faustus's understanding of 'Nestorianism' and his elaboration of his own positive Christology in his *Ep. ad Graec.* Finally, I shall consider the question of whether Christology had a significant influence on Faustus's charitology in *De grat.*, and particularly on his most distinctive charitological emphasis in that work, the concept of *prima gratia*.

The Royal Way and Faustus's Balancing of Emphases

The *uia regia* or royal way—an ancient public road wide enough that a group of travellers could stay on it without turning off to the right or left, and thus could pass legally and safely through otherwise private land—was a common theme in late antique literature. It is mentioned in Num. 21:22, when Sihon, king of the Amorites, refuses to allow the wandering Hebrews to use the royal road to traverse his land. This biblical use of the phrase, along with the command in Prov. 4:27 not to turn to the right or the left, provided the jumping-off point for Christian writers to use the

---

Christology and the Logic of Grace in Fifth-Century Gaul. Donald Fairbairn, Oxford University Press.
© Donald Fairbairn 2025. DOI: 10.1093/9780198936220.003.0007

idea of a royal road with respect to spiritual life.[1] Most notably for our purposes, Cassian uses the image to discuss moderation in ascetic practice, avoiding opposite extremes.[2] Throughout Faustus's life, the concept of the *uia regia* was important to his portrayal of doctrine, and he employed this image in writing about both Christology and grace. In his *Ep. ad Graec.* (written while he was abbot of Lérins from 433 to 457), he addresses Graecus's mistakes in understanding the person of Christ, and I shall give this letter significant attention later in this chapter. For now, it is important to note that early in the letter, Faustus chides Graecus by writing: 'In your consultation on such an important issue, regarding which you have deviated greatly from the royal road (*longe uiam regiam reliquisti*), you ought to question other men of expert wisdom, elders in erudition and age, whom you might be able to believe more easily....'[3]

After he becomes bishop of Riez, in *c*.471 Faustus writes to Lucidus,[4] who was accused of holding to a form of predestinarianism that appeared to encourage inactivity on the part of Christians. Early in this letter, Faustus insists: 'Therefore, speaking about the grace of God and the obedience of man, we must see to this in every way, that we walk along the royal road (*regia magis gradiamur uia*) neither leaning toward the left nor inclined toward the right (*ut neque proni in sinistram neque inportuni in dexteram*).'[5] Shortly afterwards, he explains the errors on the right and the left as follows:

> I therefore will discuss briefly, to the extent that I can speak with one who is absent, what you ought to believe along with the catholic church, that is, that you always must link the actions of a baptized servant with the grace of the Lord (*ut cum gratia domini operationem baptizati famuli semper adiungas*), and that, along with the teaching of Pelagius, you must detest the one who asserted predestination, to the exclusion of the labor of man (*eum, qui praedestinationem excluso labore hominis adserit, cum Pelagii dogmate detesteris*).[6]

---

[1] See Marianne Djuth. 'The Royal Way: Augustine's Freedom of the Will and the Monastic Tradition', in *Augustine: Biblical Exegete*, ed. Frederick Van Fleteren and Joseph C. Schnaubelt (New York: Peter Lang, 2001), 130–2.

[2] Cassian, *De inst.* 11.4 (CSEL 17.196) [ACW 58.241–2]. See the discussion in Peter J. Smith, 'John Cassian's Royal Road: Discretion, Balance, and the Tradition of the Fathers', *DR* 139 (2021), 145–7.

[3] *Ep. ad Graec.* (CSEL 21.200, ll. 18–20) [TTH 30.247]. Since this letter does not include numbered paragraphs, I include the line numbers from CSEL 21 along with the page numbers.

[4] For the history of this interaction with Lucidus and the background to Faustus's *De grat.*, see Gustave Weigel, *Faustus of Riez: An Historical Introduction* (Philadelphia: Dolphin Press, 1938), 93–103; Rossana Barcellona, *Fausto di Riez interprete del suo tempo: un vescovo tardoantico dentro la crisi dell'impero* (Soveria Mannelli, Italy: Rubbettino, 2006), 39–49.

[5] *Ep. ad Luc.* (CSEL 21.161, ll. 10–13) [TTH 30.249].

[6] *Ep. ad Luc.* (CSEL 21.162) [TTH 30.250, translation slightly modified].

172 CHRISTOLOGY AND THE LOGIC OF GRACE

This letter clearly shows that for Faustus, the royal way involves emphasizing both grace and human action, in contrast to either a Pelagian reliance on human effort alone or the assertion of predestination in such a way that human effort is excluded.

Lucidus was condemned at councils in Arles (473) and Lyons (474), but some in the area seem to have believed that those who condemned Lucidus's predestinarianism had themselves lapsed back into 'Pelagianism', and Faustus was commissioned to write a longer work refuting both errors. He begins *De grat.*, written *c*.474, with a more extensive discussion of the royal way. In the letter to bishop Leontius of Arles that serves as the work's prologue, Faustus describes the danger of an overreaction to 'Pelagian' thought by writing, 'Then, having left the royal way by falling to the right (*omissa uia regia in dexteram cadens*), he might believe that we are falling to the left (*in sinistram declinare nos crederet*), and by speaking of labor as the servant of grace we may seem to place a stumbling block before the feet of the blind.'[7] Then at the beginning of book one, Faustus uses a classic nautical image to impress on his readers the importance of following the middle/royal way. He describes Pelagians and the predestinarians as follows:

> But this is just as if they were reckless sailors who begin to sail through an uncharted sea without a pilot, not knowing how to govern the ship's motion, and even unfamiliar with the use of the rudder. On one hand, some will surely be tragically carried off to the peril of Scylla on the right, and the others will wind up dashed against Charybdis on the left. And what must they do between these extremes, if you were to ask? They must entrust the ship foundering on the waves to the navigator who has been provided, and they must hold a middle course [*medium teneant cursum*] and both be led correctly through the storm to the harbor.[8]

Faustus continues immediately: 'Let us see to which impiety we may liken or compare this double error. They [the 'Pelagians' and the predestinarians] run aground against the rock of stumbling in the same way as those who, having abandoned the light of discretion, have dared to assert that Christ the Lord is merely God (*Christum dominum solum deum*) or those who have asserted that he is merely man (*solum hominem*).'[9]

These passages from both the middle and the end of Faustus's career all feature prominently in significant doctrinal letters/treatises. It is clearly important to Faustus to steer a middle course between divergent doctrinal errors, to follow

---

[7] *De grat.*, Prologus (CSEL 21.4) [Smith, 68]. *De grat.* has not been translated into English *in toto*, but significant portions of it have been translated by Smith and Gumerlock. I shall cite their translations on passages for which they exist. When no translation is indicated in the footnote, the translation in the text is my own.

[8] *De grat.* 1.1 (CSEL 21.7–8).

[9] *De grat.* 1.1 (CSEL 21.8).

the *uia regia*. Moreover, it is apparent that Faustus believes we need to steer such a course on both grace—avoiding the extremes of the 'Pelagians' and of the predestinarians—and Christology—avoiding the mistake of treating Christ as *solus deus* and that of viewing him as *solus homo*. Virtually all scholars of Faustus have recognized this emphasis.[10] For our purposes, we should note that this is the first time in this study of the Gallic writers that we have seen an explicit focus on avoiding extremes on doctrinal questions, although of course Cassian has emphasized the need to follow the *uia regia* in ascetic matters. It is not too much of an exaggeration to say that Faustus is the first of the 'Semi-Pelagians' who sounds 'Semi-Pelagian'. But is he actually so? On this question there has been a significant shift in scholarly opinion, and it will be worth our while to trace that shift and notice its implications.

Scholarly Opinion on Faustus as a 'Semi-Pelagian'

Early in the twentieth century, it was common to regard Faustus's focus on balancing emphases as tantamount to 'Semi-Pelagianism'. Typical is P. Godet's summary from 1913. He argued that both Cassian and Faustus were engulfed in the errors of 'Semi-Pelagianism', Faustus even more than Cassian.[11] Godet concludes: 'Without completely excluding grace from the work of salvation, Faustus attributes the principal role therein to the will, and in doing so he transforms the character of salvation into something entirely natural. Overall, his Semi-Pelagianism is equal to, and even surpasses here and there, that of Cassian.'[12] Similarly, Gustave Weigel, in his 1938 biographical study of Faustus, asserted that what we now call 'Semi-Pelagianism' arose in fifth-century Gallic monastic circles, that it influenced Faustus through his time in Lérins, and that his depiction of grace in contrast to Pelagius and the predestinarians in *De grat.* provided the culminating voice of the 'Semi-Pelagian' outlook.[13]

---

[10] See, e.g., P. Godet, 'Fauste de Riez', in *DTC* 5/1 (1913), 2013; Weigel, *Faustus of Riez*, 104; Ralph W. Mathisen, *Ecclesiastical Factionalism and Religious Controversy in Fifth-Century Gaul* (Washington, DC: The Catholic University of America Press, 1989), 263; Thomas A. Smith, *De Gratia: Faustus of Riez's Treatise on Grace and Its Place in the History of Theology* (Notre Dame, IN.: University of Notre Dame Press, 1990), 47; Marianne Djuth, 'Faustus of Riez and the Royal Way' *AugSt* 22 (1991), 208–9; Thomas A. Smith, 'Agonism and Antagonism: Metaphor and the Gallic Resistance to Augustine', *StPatr* 38 (2001), 288–9; Paul Mattei, 'Le Fantôme Semi-Pélagien: Lecture du Traité *De Gratia* de Fauste de Riez', *Augustiniana* 60 (2010), 92–3; Matthew Pereira, 'Augustine, Pelagius, and the Southern Gallic Tradition', in *Grace for Grace: The Debates after Augustine and Pelagius*, ed. Alexander Hwang et al. (Washington, DC: The Catholic University of America Press, 2014), 187; T. Kurt Jaros, 'The Relationship of the So-Called Semi-Pelagians and Eastern Greek Theology on the Doctrine of Original Sin: An Historical-Systematic Analysis and its Relevance for 21st Century Protestantism', Ph.D. Dissertation, University of Aberdeen, 2020, 277.

[11] Godet, 'Fauste de Riez', 2103.

[12] Ibid., 2104, my translation.

[13] Weigel, *Faustus of Riez*, 49, 104–6.

174 CHRISTOLOGY AND THE LOGIC OF GRACE

By the late twentieth century, however, scholars began to look with more favour on Faustus's *uia regia* and his desire to avoid extremes, and they have rejected the 'Semi-Pelagian' label. Writing in 1989, Mathisen pointed out that the southern Gallic bishops were more muted than the northern Gallicans in their criticisms of 'Pelagianism'. As a result, a condemnation of predestinarianism in southern Gaul could easily be read in the north as an affirmation of 'Pelagianism', and the southern Gallicans thus needed their spokesman, Faustus, to argue against 'Pelagianism' as well as predestinarianism.[14] In 1990, Thomas Smith actually argued for the largely Augustinian concerns expressed in Faustus's *De grat.*, in spite of the significant disagreements between the two men.[15] In 1991, Marianne Djuth cautioned against the use of the 'Semi-Pelagian' moniker by writing: 'Neither wholeheartedly Pelagian nor wholeheartedly Augustinian, Faustus prefers to define his position in the middle. And since that middle position cannot be defined without bias if it is characterized as either Semipelagian or Semiaugustinian, it is perhaps best delineated, in Faustus' own terms, as the royal way.'[16]

In the twenty-first century, Augustine Casiday insisted in 2007 that Faustus, like the other monastic leaders in Gaul, had no patience for 'Pelagianism'. The resistance to Pelagius was broad and, in Gaul, expressed in other ways than those of Augustine. Thus, departures from Augustine's thought should not be taken *ipso facto* as expressions of sympathy with 'Pelagianism', and the label 'Semi-Pelagianism' is not appropriate.[17] Likewise, Paul Mattei, writing in 2010, concluded an important study by asserting that Faustus is not a 'Semi-Pelagian', although he does use 'imprudent expressions and imprecisions in both terminology and conceptualization' that sometimes obscure what he is saying. Mattei is particularly concerned that Faustus's insistence on the continuation of the original grace after the Fall 'fails to bring into plain view the centrality of Jesus Christ (the incarnate Word and Saviour through his death and resurrection)'.[18]

These more recent scholars are certainly correct to point out that trying to steer between two different heresies is not in and of itself a problem, and they confirm the impression that we have seen throughout this book that the phrase 'Semi-Pelagian' is not helpful in understanding the Gallic writers. At the same time, Mattei's comment in the previous paragraph is important for our purposes,

---

[14] Mathisen, *Ecclesiastical Factionalism and Religious Controversy in Fifth-Century Gaul*, 261–5.

[15] Smith, De Gratia, 184–216. See his conclusion on 227: 'That he [Faustus] should attempt to align himself with Augustine in more than a purely cosmetic manner deserves our attention.... the *De gratia* should probably be seen as at least representing the attempt to receive a palatable interpretation of Augustine's doctrine of grace into the theological mainstream of fifth-century Gaul.'

[16] Djuth, 'Faustus of Riez and the Royal Way', 216. Djuth later argues in more detail that Faustus seeks to maintain a delicate balance between a variety of competing ideas, those of Augustine, Pelagius, Cassian, and numerous others. See Marianne Djuth, 'Defending Augustine: How Augustinian is Faustus of Riez' De Gratia?' *StPatr* 128 (2021), 413–24, esp. 423–4.

[17] Augustine Casiday, *Tradition and Theology in St John Cassian*, OECS (Oxford: University Press, 2007), 41–2.

[18] Mattei, 'Le Fantôme Semi-Pélagien', 114, my translations.

because it points to a potential problem with Faustus even as Mattei exonerates him of a heresy charge, and also because that potential problem has to do with the intersection between Christology and grace. In Faustus's *De grat.*, he argues that the original grace given to Adam (*prima gratia*) remains significantly unimpaired in fallen humanity, and this *prima gratia* figures prominently in his rejection of an Augustinian notion of predestination. Mattei raises the possibility that such a focus on *prima gratia* undercuts the significance of the Incarnation and the grace offered to the human race through that event. This possibility warrants a careful investigation, which I shall undertake first by examining Faustus's Christology in *Ep. ad Graec.* and then by asking whether and how his Christology affects his understanding of *prima gratia* in *De. grat.*

Faustus's Christology in *Ep. ad Graec.*

Ep. ad Graec. is Faustus's only surviving letter from nearly a quarter-century as abbot at Lérins.[19] He describes Graecus as a deacon[20] and mentions a 'little composition (*scripturula*)'[21] that Graecus has sent him, to which the letter is a response. There are noteworthy ambiguities about both the date and the situation of the letter.

The Situation and Date of the Letter

Graecus's composition evidently contained significant Christological mistakes, because as we have seen early in this chapter, Faustus states baldly that Graecus has 'deviated greatly from the royal road (*longe uiam regiam reliquisti*)'.[22] To make matters worse, Graecus appears to claim that he received his Christological ideas from some sort of direct divine illumination.[23] Furthermore, Graecus's errors evidently have something to do with Augustine, because Faustus feels compelled to defend the African bishop's Christology, even as he expresses reservations about other aspects of his thought.[24] Finally, Faustus's letter describes Graecus's mistake as claiming there is a single nature of God and man.[25]

---

[19] See Weigel, *Faustus of Riez*, 61.

[20] *Ep. ad Graec.* (CSEL 21.200. ll. 5–6) [TTH 30.246]. Mathisen's translation omits the most intensely doctrinal sections of this letter, including its discussions of 'Nestorianism' and of Graecus's errors. I cite Mathisen's translations in TTH 30 for all passages on which such translations exist. In cases where there are no citations from Mathisen, the translations are my own.

[21] *Ep. ad Graec.* (CSEL 21.201, l. 5) [TTH 30.247].

[22] *Ep. ad Graec.* (CSEL 21.200, ll.18–19) [TTH 30.247].

[23] See *Ep. ad Graec.* (CSEL 21.201, ll. 18–19), where Faustus cites Graecus's claim that his Christological ideas came by a prophetic stirring (*more prophetico*).

[24] *Ep. ad Graec.* (CSEL 21.201, ll. 12–17) [TTH 30.247].

[25] *Ep. ad Graec.* (CSEL 21.202, l. 14) [TTH 30.247].

176 CHRISTOLOGY AND THE LOGIC OF GRACE

Pulling together these strands of information from Faustus's letter, Weigel has come up with a possible reconstruction of the situation:

> Graecus, it appears, was a hermit who led a life of strict retirement away from the world of men. In his solitude he indulged in theological speculation unchecked either by sound counsel or by the hermit's own better sense. He had evolved a theory on the personality of Christ, which he believed to be the result of divine inspiration but which actually was sheer monophysitism. He then read some writings of Augustine which did not harmonize with the theory he had elaborated and his immediate conclusion was that Augustine must be heretical. Still, he was vexed with doubts and in his doubts he appealed to Faustus.[26]

While this reconstruction generally accounts for the internal evidence from the letter itself, it stands in tension with what Gennadius wrote about Graecus at the end of the fifth century. In Gennadius's entry on Faustus in *De uir. illust.*, he claims that Graecus had left the Catholic faith and gone over to the Nestorian impiety. According to Gennadius, Faustus admonishes Graecus 'to believe that the holy Virgin Mary did not bring forth a mere human being, who afterwards should receive divinity, but true God in true man'.[27] Of course, Gennadius could be wrong if, for example, his knowledge of the letter is second hand. But Gennadius mentions other works by Faustus and declines to comment on them because he has not read them, a statement that strongly implies he has read this one. Is it possible, therefore, to account for both Faustus's statement that Graecus affirms only one nature in Christ and Gennadius's claim that he was a Nestorian?

A clue to help us here is that Faustus describes Graecus's mistake as a 'double error (*duplicem errorem*)'[28] and a 'two-part error (*alterutrae partis errorem*)',[29] and he explains the two-fold error as the denial of either the divinity or the humanity of Christ.[30] From these statements, it seems that Graecus affirmed simply that there was one nature in Christ, without specifying whether that nature was divine or human. Thus, he was at least potentially vulnerable to either 'Nestorianism' (if he meant that the one nature was the assumed man, and Christ was divine not by nature at all, but only by some sort of conjunction) or 'Eutychianism' (if he meant that the one nature was the Word, and Christ's humanity faded from view). It is revealing that an ancient reader, Gennadius, interpreted this (potentially) dual problem in one way—as 'Nestorianism'—but a modern reader, Weigel, interpreted it in another way—as 'Monophysitism'. But aside from what those interpretations say about the differing concerns of the ancient and modern interpreters, this does

---

[26] Weigel, *Faustus of Riez*, 61–2.
[27] Gennadius, *De uir. illust.* 85 (86) (PL 58.1110) [*NPNF*² 3.400].
[28] *Ep. ad Graec.* (CSEL 21.201, l. 21).
[29] *Ep. ad Graec.* (CSEL 21.203, ll.15–16).
[30] *Ep. ad Graec.* (CSEL 21.202, ll. 20–2). I shall consider this passage in more detail shortly.

seem to resolve the problem of what Graecus actually said. If we work from the assumption that he asserted a single nature in Christ, without further specificity, we can do justice both to what Faustus writes in reply and to what Gennadius tells us about Faustus's letter.

If this is the situation, then when did Faustus write the letter? The crucial bit of evidence on this question is the fact that Faustus never mentions 'Eutychianism' by name, even though he does name 'Nestorianism'. If Graecus's thought put him in danger of two heresies, and if names were ready to hand for both of them, it seems quite unlikely that Faustus would name one but not the other. Thus, we may reasonably guess that the letter pre-dated the arrival in Gaul of news about Eutyches. In 1891 Augustus Engelbrecht argued in the prolegomena to his critical edition of Faustus's works (CSEL 21) that the Council of Chalcedon would have made the news of Eutyches widely known, and thus that the letter must have been written before 451.[31] Weigel, writing in 1938, concurred but also noted the fact that Faustus tells Graecus he should have consulted 'elders in erudition and age' about the matter.[32] In Weigel's opinion, this comment implies that Faustus himself was not particularly old at the time he wrote, and he suggests a date of about 440 for the letter.[33] I think Faustus's comment could refer simply to men older than Graecus, not necessarily older than Faustus himself, so I do not think a date as early as 440 is necessary. Barcellona, writing in 2006, places the letter between 440 and 451, and I think this is probably as precise as we can be.[34] Graecus then emerges as either a potential 'Nestorian' or a proto-'Eutychian', depending on how one takes his apparently ambiguous expressions. With this background in mind, it is time to examine the letter in some detail.

Faustus's Understanding of 'Nestorianism' and of Graecus's own Errors

Faustus begins his discussion of Graecus's doctrinal errors with a commendation of Augustine's Christology, since Graecus had evidently commented that he found Augustine's view of Christ objectionable. Faustus writes:

> Even if the most learned men think something in the writings of the blessed bishop Augustine to be suspect, you should know that there is nothing

[31] Augustus Engelbrecht, Prolegomena to 'Fausti Reiensis praeter *Sermones* Pseudo-Eusebianos *Opera* accedunt Ruricii *Epistulae*', in CSEL 21 (Vienna: F. Tempsky, 1891), xxi–xxii.

[32] *Ep. ad Graec.* (CSEL 21.200, l. 21–201, l. 1) [TTH 30.247].

[33] Weigel, *Faustus of Riez*, 63–4.

[34] Barcellona, *Fausto di Riez*, 104–5. But note that some place it later: Ralph. W. Mathisen, Notes to *Ruricius of Limoges and Friends: A Collection of Letters from Visigothic Gaul*, trans. Ralph Mathisen, TTH 30 (Liverpool: Liverpool University Press, 1999), 246, dates the letter to c.450–5, without explanation. 'Faustus 1', in *PCBE* 4 (2013), 737, places the letter in the early years of Faustus's episcopacy, c.463.

178 CHRISTOLOGY AND THE LOGIC OF GRACE

reprehensible in those sections that you thought should be condemned, but know that, in particular, the sense of faith in the Catholic church regarding our Lord and Redeemer's two substances or natures—of God and of man (*de duabus substantiis uel naturis dei et hominis*)—is not only accepted by the authority of the fathers but is also confirmed by apostolic pronouncements.[35]

Given that Graecus himself affirms only one nature in Christ, and since Faustus answers by defending Augustine's and the church's affirmation of two *substantiae* or *naturae*, it is apparent that Graecus has taken objection to passages in Augustine's writings where he makes that affirmation. As I have mentioned in chapter 4, Thomas Humphries suggests that most of the Gallic world knew Augustine's *De trin.* through Vincent's *Excerp.*,[36] and it is thus possible that the *Excerp.* was Faustus's main source for Augustine's Christology, although it is also clear that he has some familiarity with Augustine's *Sermones de fide catholica*, which he quotes in the letter.[37] Here we see that Faustus has a respectful attitude towards Augustine and accepts his Christology as consistent with that of the whole church, while distancing himself from other unnamed aspects of the African bishop's thought—surely his teaching on predestination, which Faustus explicitly argues against some three decades later in *De grat.*

After this commendation of Augustine, Faustus sharply criticizes Graecus: although he claims to have learned his Christology from a prophetic stirring, it is not of the Holy Spirit and is worthy of condemnation by both God and human beings unless Graecus himself condemns it first. Faustus reacts viscerally to the idea that Mary might not be called 'Mother of God', which may mean that Graecus has floated an objection to that title. Faustus warns of the danger not just of saying, but even of imagining (*non dicam scribitur, sed cogitatur*) that one should not agree to call her 'Mother of God'.[38]

Naturally, this subject leads Faustus to a consideration of 'Nestorianism'. He reminds Graecus:

> For you know about the impiety into which the Nestorian heresy has sunk, that it does not shrink from the profane audacity (*profano ausu*) of claiming that the blessed Mary became merely the mother of a man, not also of God, and for this reason the heresy has been strongly condemned throughout the entire world of the Catholic Church. He says that we should not accept that a human being is the mother of God. But where is such an assertion in either the prophetic word

---

[35] *Ep. ad Graec.* (CSEL 21.201, l. 12–18) [TTH 30.247, translation modified].

[36] Thomas L. Humphries, *Ascetic Pneumatology from John Cassian to Gregory the Great*, OECS (Oxford: Oxford University Press, 2013), 103–5.

[37] Augustine, *Ser. II de fid.* 7 (PL 39.2179), quoted in *Ep. ad Graec.* (CSEL 21.202, ll. 11–13), a passage I shall discuss just below.

[38] *Ep. ad Graec.* (CSEL 21.201, ll.25–6).

or the word of the Gospel? *Behold, a Virgin shall conceive and shall bear a son, and you shall call his name Emmanuel, which interpreted means, 'God with us.'* [Is. 7:14], and it is the same in the Gospel: *What will be born from you is holy and shall be called the Son of God* [Lk. 1:35]. Furthermore, where is such an assertion [that we should not call a human being the mother of God], since the authority accepted throughout all islands and the churches of the fathers speaks against Nestorius? For it [that authority] says, "Cursed is the one who does not confess that the Son of God, true God, has been recently born from Mary for our salvation (*maledictus ... qui filium dei deum uerum de Maria nonne nuper natum pro nostra salute non confitetur*)".[39]

In this passage we should notice that the description of 'Nestorianism' as a 'profane audacity' is similar to Vincent's calling the heresy a 'profane novelty'.[40] Faustus has probably picked up his label for 'Nestorianism' from his mentor at Lérins.[41] Beyond the title *Theotokos* itself, however, the only indications from this passage regarding the way Faustus understands 'Nestorianism' come from the Augustinian quote at the end.[42] This malediction may be modelled after the anathemas at the end of the Creed of Nicaea, because it uses several phrases closely similar to those in the second article of the Creed. The *filius dei*, the one who is *uerus deus* (cf. Θεὸν ἀληθινὸν ἐκ Θεοῦ ἀληθινοῦ, 'true God from true God'), has indeed been born from Mary, and this birth has taken place *pro nostra salute* (cf. δι' ἡμᾶς τοὺς ἀνθρώπους, καὶ διὰ τὴν ἡμετέραν σωτηρίαν, 'for us human beings and for our salvation').[43] This malediction, like the title *Theotokos*, serves to underline the personal identity of the Saviour. Christ is not a man united to the Son/Word; he is the Son/Word who has come to earth and been born in time of Mary for our salvation.

Later in the letter, Faustus returns twice to the danger of 'Nestorianism'. In a paragraph contrasting it with Arianism, he affirms, 'the one who declines to believe that God has become Son of man [*qui deum filium hominis credendum denegat*] has been tainted with the impiety of Nestorius'.[44] This statement is akin to his earlier association of Nestorius with a denial of the title *Theotokos*. And in a longer discussion in which he does not name 'Nestorianism', he writes:

---

[39] *Ep. ad Graec.* (CSEL 21.201, l. 27–202, l. 13).

[40] Vincent, *Excerp.*, Prologus (CCSL 64.199). Vincent also calls Pelagius 'profane' in *Comm.* 24.8 (CCSL 64.181) [FC 7.314] and uses the word 'profane' to describe heresies in general in the title of *Comm.*

[41] Notice also the odd statement that the authority he quotes is accepted 'throughout all islands'. Of course, Lérins is an island, and Faustus, who still lives there when he writes this, betrays an islander's view of the world!

[42] Again, this is from Augustine, *Ser. II de fid.* 7 (PL 39.2179).

[43] For the text of the Creed of Nicaea, see, e.g., *Ges. Chalc.* 5.32 (*ACO* 2.1.2.127) [TTH 45.2.202].

[44] *Ep. ad Graec.* (CSEL 21.204, ll. 16–18).

180   CHRISTOLOGY AND THE LOGIC OF GRACE

If it is a great error to have believed that there is one simple substance (*unam et simplicem credidisse substantiam*) in our Lord and Saviour, how great an error is it to have asserted a double person (*duplicem adseruisse personam*)? Now if there were not two substances in the alliance with the assumed flesh (*in societate carnis adsumptae*), the form of a servant (*formam famuli*) with which God clothed himself, then God would not be in man (*in homine deus non fuit*), and the person of man would be separate from God (*separata a deo persona hominis fuit*), and thus in this understanding you will suddenly see a fourth person added from nowhere, and in consequence of this perversity, comprehension will be thrown down, so that it will no longer be necessary to confess the Trinity.[45]

This latter description fills out Faustus's earlier discussions a bit: turning the humanity into a quasi-person would separate the person of the man from God and would thus add a fourth person to the Trinity. We have seen this concern not to introduce a fourth person from the pens of Augustine,[46] Leporius,[47] and Vincent[48] as well.

The great surprise in these descriptions of 'Nestorianism' is that Faustus does not offer the standard Gallic (and more specifically, Lérinian) talking points. There is no mention of the idea that Christ is a man united to the Word (whether at conception or later) and thus no assertion that this union came about by the man's merits. Gennadius's summary of the letter includes these talking points (as we have seen, he claims Faustus exhorts Graecus 'to believe that the holy Virgin Mary did not bring forth a mere human being, who afterwards should receive divinity, but true God in true man'),[49] but the letter itself does not. One should be cautious about arguments from silence, but this silence may well be significant. For Cassian, Vincent, and Prosper, 'Nestorianism' did not merely, or even primarily, involve mistakes about terminological and technical Christological issues. At heart, they believed, 'Nestorius' was proposing a model of salvation akin to that of 'Pelagianism', in which (as they understood it), human beings could rise up to God by following the example of the man Christ who himself rose up to God and was united to the Word by his merits (foreseen merits if one granted that the Christological union took place in Mary's womb, or actual merits if one thought incorrectly that Nestorius believed the union came later). As we have seen in this book, it was this—far more than the simple mistake of separating deity and humanity too much within the one person—that shocked the Gallicans. We might legitimately have expected some hint that Faustus sees the problem of 'Nestorianism'

---

[45] *Ep. ad Graec.* (CSEL 21.205, ll. 9–16).
[46] Augustine, *Ep.* 169.8 (CSEL 44.617) [WSA II/3.110]; *Ep.* 219.1 (CSEL 57.428–9) [WSA II/4.69]; *De praed. sanct.* 2.67 [= *De don. pers.* 67] (CSEL 105.270) [WSA I/26.236].
[47] Leporius, *Lib. emend.* 3 (CCSL 64.113–14).
[48] Vincent, *Comm.* 13.3–4 (CCSL 64.163–4) [FC 7.290–1]; *Excerp.*, Prologus (CCSL 64.199).
[49] Gennadius, *De uir. illust.* 85 (86) (PL 58.1110) [*NPNF*² 3.400].

FAUSTUS OF RIEZ 181

the same way, that he reasons similarly about the *significance* of identifying the Word as the person of Christ, not merely that he affirms the *fact* of that identification. But such hints come only from Gennadius's summary, not from Faustus himself. If the concern that animated the other Gallicans was also important to Faustus, this would have been a place where we should have expected him to voice that concern.

Instead, after his initial, fairly minimalistic description of 'Nestorianism' and corresponding defence of calling Mary *Theotokos*, Faustus immediately turns to Graecus's own error, which he explains as follows:

> It follows that you say there is a single nature of God and man (*dei et hominis unam esse naturam*); in this manner God has a single substance (*unam dei esse substantiam*). You would have spoken rightly if you had spoken about the Trinity alone, where the nature is one and the same (*una atque eadem est . . . natura*) in the distinctions of the three persons (*sub trium personarum distinctione*). But when it comes to the incarnation of assumed man (*cum ad hominis adsumpti incarnationem uenitur*), just as we confess that there is a single person of man and God (*sicut hominis et dei unam confitemur esse personam*), we likewise know that there is a double substance (*ita duplicem scimus esse substantiam*).[50]

Here Faustus's statement that Graecus would be right in saying there is one nature if he were talking about the Trinity seems to have two possible sources. It may echo the way Vincent has set up Christological terminology in the *Excerp.* by means of a refresher about Trinitarian terminology.[51] Or it may derive from something Graecus wrote in his own letter that has led Faustus to believe Graecus is moving incorrectly from Trinitarian terms to Christological ones. In either case, Faustus patiently explains to Graecus how the words *substantia/natura* and *persona* should function in Christological discourse. Notice that Faustus uses the ambiguous word *homo* to refer to Christ's humanity. In Mathisen's translation, he interprets *hominis adsumpti* as 'the assumption of human form', but for now I shall leave it as 'assumed man' (not necessarily *the* assumed man). As with Augustine, Cassian, and Vincent, so also with Faustus, we need to pay attention to how the writer uses the ambiguous *homo* when discussing the Incarnation.

At this point, Faustus addresses the double problem inherent in Graecus's simple affirmation of one *natura* in Christ: 'But whoever asserts the Lord, the Redeemer, to be of one nature (*unius naturae*) has denied either man in divinity (*hominem in diuinitate*) or God in a body (*deum . . . in corpore*), since our redemption has been accomplished not by one or the other, but by both (*non ex alterutro, sed ex utroque*).'[52] Here we see that Faustus not only uses *homo* of Christ's humanity,

---

[50] *Ep. ad Graec.* (CSEL 21.202, ll. 14–19) [TTH 30.247, translation modified].
[51] See Vincent, *Excerp.*, Prologus (CCSL 64.200), 1.1 (CCSL 64.202–5), discussed in chapter 4.
[52] *Ep. ad Graec.* (CSEL 21.202, ll. 20–2).

but also employs *deus* of his divinity, thus leaving one to wonder whether he is referring to divinity and humanity as natures, or to God and an assumed man considered as separate persons. The pronouns in the last phrase do nothing to resolve the ambiguity; they could be either masculine or neuter. Faustus could have written this clearly by using the feminine words *diuinitas* and *humanitas,* or the feminine phrases *diuina natura* and *humana natura*, followed by feminine pronouns. But we have seen that Vincent has also used this kind of verbal symmetry in part two of the *Excerp.* when more precise expressions were available, and indeed, most of the Western church shows the same carelessness about using *homo* and *deus* when it means *humanitas* and *diuinitas*. It is ironic that such sloppiness turns up even in passages like this one that give pride of place to terminological precision regarding the use of *natura, substantia*, and *persona*, but Western writers simply never feel compelled to be as precise with *homo/humanitas* as they are with *natura/substantia*. Nevertheless, we need to remember that just above, Faustus has clearly identified the Word/Son as the personal subject in Christ. As a result, we are on fairly safe ground in assuming that in this passage, Faustus is using *hominem in diuinitate* and *deum ... in corpore* for verbal and rhetorical symmetry: saying there is only one nature means that one will lose sight of either Christ's deity or his humanity. One should not push the use of *homo* rather than *humanitas* to the point of thinking that Faustus means Christ's humanity is a quasi-independent man. I shall return to the interpretation of Faustus's use of *homo* just below.

Be that as it may, what emerges from this portion of Faustus's letter is an understanding of 'Nestorianism' and of Graecus's error that is largely terminological, with no apparent connection to 'Pelagianism', as has been the case with Cassian, Vincent, and even Prosper. In the rest of the letter, Faustus describes and defends his positive Christology with reference to Graecus's error, 'Nestorianism', and also Arianism.

Faustus's Positive Christology

As one would expect in the light of Graecus's error, the bulk of Faustus's Christological treatment consists of affirming two natures or substances in the single person of Christ. As he repeatedly insists on this affirmation, Faustus accomplishes two things. First, he makes clear that his ambiguous use of *homo* is meant in the sense that the incarnate Son/Word does certain things as a man, not in the sense that an assumed man acts quasi-independently of the Son. Second, he gives several indications of why it is important to keep the 'as God/as man' distinction in mind as one considers the life and death of Christ. Let us look specifically at the way Faustus accomplishes these interwoven tasks.

Shortly after his initial treatment of both 'Nestorianism' and Graecus's error, Faustus turns his attention to Christ's crucifixion, death, and burial. He recoils against ascribing these to the substance of divine majesty,[53] and in contrast, he claims: 'God experienced all these things not in himself, but in the nature of assumed man (*in natura suscepti hominis*). For God feels nothing with the feeling of one who suffers, but he feels through his compassion for a fellow-sufferer (*sensit conpatientis affectu*). He feels nothing because of the diversity of substances (*pro diuersitate substantiae*), but he feels because of the unity of person (*pro unitate personae*).'[54] Here Faustus is concerned to safeguard against any idea that God the Son suffered in his own nature, a danger that Nestorius himself was very keen to avoid, and also a danger with the proto-'Eutychian' potential latent in Graecus's error. In the process of protecting against this mistake, Faustus sounds 'Nestorian', in that he writes of *susceptus homo*. Mathisen's translation renders *in natura suscepti hominis* as 'through the nature he had assumed as a man', but we have to ask whether this is too generous an interpretation, given that Faustus writes of the one who suffers on the cross as *conpatiens* with whom God has compassion. This passage is certainly vulnerable to an 'Antiochene' or 'Nestorian' interpretation in which the assumed man is a quasi-independent person, and the *unitas personae* is more superficial than real. So, we need to consider whether Faustus actually sees the *homo* in Christ as a quasi-independent man (notwithstanding his affirmation of *Theotokos*), or whether he means *homo* in the sense of human nature or 'the Son considered as a man' (in which case his treatment of the one who suffered on the cross as *conpatiens* is an incautious expression at odds with his overall thought). Faustus goes on to emphasize that we must confess one and the same (*unum eundemque*) as God and man, and he quotes in support of this the Ambrosian hymn *Veni, Redemptor Gentium*[55] that probably also lies behind Leporius's reference to Christ as 'a giant of two-fold substance'.[56] Here the masculine pronouns *unum* and *eundem* suggest that it is the Son himself who is one and the same, which in turn supports a reading of Faustus in which the person of the incarnate experiences of Christ is the Son, not a composite akin to Nestorius's πρόσωπον of union.

Faustus then continues by contrasting the 'he' who is one and the same with Graecus's description of him: 'Therefore, holy brother, flee from this two-part error. If you said that he had only the nature of God, you would impose on God the condition of passion and death (*inposuisti deo condicionem passionis et mortis*), and indeed, if you said that he had only the nature of man, you would remove from God the glory of redemption (*subtraxisti deo gloriam redemptionis*) and take away from the author the power of reparation (*subtraxisti auctori potentiam reparatoris*).'[57] In addition to reiterating the need to avoid imposing on God the passion and death, Faustus here adds a new idea—the need to avoid removing

---

[53] *Ep. ad Graec.* (CSEL 21.203, ll. 1–4).
[54] *Ep. ad Graec.* (CSEL 21.203, ll. 4–7) [TTH 30.248, translation modified].
[55] See Herman Adalbert Daniel, *Thesaurus Hymnologicus* (Leipzig: J.T. Loeschke, 1855), 1.12.
[56] *Ep. ad Graec.* (CSEL 21.203, ll. 7–14). Cf. Leporius, *Lib. emend.* 6 (CCSL 64.117).
[57] *Ep. ad Graec.* (CSEL 21.203, ll. 15–22).

184   CHRISTOLOGY AND THE LOGIC OF GRACE

from God the glory/power of redemption/reparation. A Christ who was merely human—united to God though he may be—would not be God himself accomplishing human redemption. As a result, it seems that Faustus does see the 'he' who is the subject of Christ's human actions and experiences as the Son himself. Faustus presses the point that this 'he' possesses both divine and human natures by juxtaposing three pairs of biblical passages and one pair of biblical events/ideas:

> Hear how the sacred words explain both natures in the one person. Concerning the divine nature he says, *I and the Father are one* [Jn. 10:30]; according to the human substance he confesses, *The Father is greater than I* [Jn. 14:28]. Concerning the celestial nature he pronounces, *All that the Father has is mine* [Jn. 16:15]; according to the infirmity of the terrestrial nature he says, *The Son of Man has nowhere to lay his head* [Mt. 8:20]. As man he says, *My soul is sorrowful to the point of death* [Mt. 26:38]; as God he insists, *I have the power to lay it [my soul] down and the power to take it up again* [Jn. 10:18]. According to the nature of the flesh he was hanged from the cross; according to the substance of divinity he granted paradise and the celestial kingdom [cf. Lk. 23].[58]

Again, it is not crystal clear that the 'he' so described is the Son (rather than some entity akin to Nestorius's πρόσωπον of union), but the accumulating effect of Faustus's proclamations strongly suggests that he intends the incarnate Son as the subject of these experiences and actions.

At this point in the letter, Faustus sets up a contrast between Arianism and 'Nestorianism', with much more attention to the former because he has already discussed 'Nestorianism' to some degree. As we saw in the previous section, he summarizes 'Nestorius' as denying that God has become Son of man. Of Arianism he writes:

> The Arians ... have referred back to God things that pertained to man (*ad deum, quae erant hominis, rettulerunt*) and have believed that divinity was spoken of as being less (*credentes, quod minor loqueretur diuinitas*), where merely the weakness of man was demonstrated (*ubi sola hominis demonstrabatur infirmitas*). Setting up no boundary between heavenly and earthly thoughts while they refuse to accept two natures in God and man (*dum naturas in deo et homine duas recipere nolunt*), they divide God's substance and, while they consider these to be merely the words of a man, they have lost sight in their minds of God, who is the fullness of glory. ... the one who does not believe there are two substances in the Redeemer (*qui duas substantias in redemptore non credit*) has been entangled in the snare of Arius.[59]

---

[58] *Ep. ad Graec.* (CSEL 21.203, l. 19–204, l. 8).
[59] *Ep. ad Graec.* (CSEL 21.204, ll. 9–19).

At first glance this might seem to be a rather strained attempt to make Arianism fit Faustus's schema in which heresies must deny either the two substances or the one person, but I suggest that there is more to the critique than meets the eye. If Faustus means by 'divinity' specifically the kind of divinity the Word possesses, he is right that Arianism speaks less of *this* divinity (in comparison to that of the Father), because it does not recognize that statements in the Gospels that seem to denigrate the Word's divinity actually refer to him as man, not as God. Thus, Faustus can say with some accuracy that the Arians divide God's substance—that is, they distinguish between the greater substance of the Father and the lesser substance of the Son/Word. Ironically, then, a division in the substance of God incorrectly takes the place of a distinction between the two substances of Christ, on the basis of which one may assign human-befitting predicates to him as man, and God-befitting predicates to the same person as God.[60]

In contrast to both Arianism and 'Nestorianism', then, Faustus insists: 'But my most beloved brother, we must believe by a perfect and inseparable distinction in Christ the Lord, so that we will recognize there is of God and man a single person (*dei et hominis simplicem personam*) and a double substance (*et duplicem ... esse substantiam*). As soul and body make a human being, so Christ is one, divinity and humanity (*diuinitas et humanitas unus est Christus*).'[61] Faustus then once again turns his attention directly to Graecus:

But you, having arrived at what [you think] must be stated by a double error, suppose that what has been agreed on concerning the two substances must not be accepted—that God is the Father of a man (*ut deus pater hominis sit*) and that a human being is the mother of God (*ut homo mater dei sint*). But we faithfully and salvifically affirm that in him is one person of God and man (*unam dei hominisque personam*), who *was in the beginning* [Jn. 1:1] and who in time was for our redemption *made in the likeness of sinful flesh* [Rom. 8:3], that is in the reality of man but the likeness of sinful flesh—we, I say, testify that God is the Father of the man in the unity of person, and that by the embrace of the same unity a human being is confessed as Mother of God, according to the authority of the Creed, to pass over others, by which we say, 'I believe in Jesus Christ, the Son of God, who was conceived by the Holy Spirit, born of Mary the Virgin.'[62]

---

[60] Faustus also deals with Arian errors in *Ep. I ad Rur.* Most of this letter addresses the image of God in humanity, but Faustus also explains that although the Father is the source (*auctor*) of the Son, the Son is nevertheless not after him (*ex illo est, set posterior illo non est*). See *Ep. I ad Rur.* (CCSL 64.406–7) [TTH 30.93–4].

[61] *Ep. ad Graec.* (CSEL 21.204, ll. 19–23).

[62] *Ep. ad Graec.* (CSEL 21.204, l. 24–205, l. 8). The wording from the Creed as Faustus quotes it here is closer to that of the Old Roman Creed in the third century than that of the post-400 evolution of the Apostles' Creed. See John N. D. Kelly, *Early Christian Creeds*, 3rd ed. (London: Longmans, 1972), 102; Liuwe H. Westra, *The Apostles' Creed: Origin, History, and Some Early Commentaries*, Instrumenta patristica et medievalia 43 (Turnhout: Brepols, 2002), 68.

186 CHRISTOLOGY AND THE LOGIC OF GRACE

Here of course we again see the insistence on two substances and one person, as we have seen throughout the letter. In this passage, the details strongly indicate that the 'he' who is both divine and human is the eternal Son himself. The prescription of the affirmation 'God is the Father of a man' along with the affirmation 'a human being is the mother of God' (that is, the affirmation of the title *Theotokos*) solidifies the crucial point that the man born of Mary is in fact the same person who has always been God's Son. Even more striking, it is the one person who is both with God in the beginning and made in the likeness of sinful flesh for our redemption. This passage provides the clarity needed in the face of the ambiguous use of *homo* throughout the letter.[63] For Faustus, the *homo* in Christ must be either Christ's human nature or the Son spoken of as a man. With that ambiguous word clarified, Faustus's earlier reference to God suffering by virtue of his compassion for the one who suffers on the cross[64] must be merely a careless use of words, not an indication that he sees the *homo* as a quasi-independent assumed man.

As a result, even though Faustus writes of the need to follow the *uia regia* between opposite mistakes, his Christology does much more than simply prescribe a balanced emphasis on the Saviour's deity and his humanity. Faustus's Christology as expressed in *Ep. ad Graec.* concurs with that of the post-correction Leporius, Cassian, Vincent, Prosper (as well as we may judge from limited information about his positive Christology), and for that matter, Augustine. It is a Christology that insists on the terminology of two natures/substances in one person, yet that clouds that terminological precision with terminological ambiguity in the use of the word *homo*. But despite this ambiguity, it is nevertheless clearly a Christology in which the incarnate Word/Son is the subject of Christ's human actions and experiences— a broadly Chalcedonian/Cyrillian Christology, not an 'Antiochene' or 'Nestorian' one.[65] Nevertheless, we should also remember that while Faustus is aware of the problems with 'Nestorianism', he does not link 'Nestorianism' to 'Pelagianism' as the other Gallic writers do. Nor does his *Ep. ad Graec.* show much of a link between charitology and his positive Christology. Most notably, we have seen that Faustus does not claim 'Nestorius' believed Christ was a man united to the Son by virtue

---

[63] Notice also that what follows this passage is a long series of 'as God/as man' statements showing the need to understand the one person, the Son, both as God and as man. See *Ep. ad Graec.* (CSEL 21.205, l. 17–206, l. 21).

[64] *Ep. ad Graec.* (CSEL 21.203, ll. 4–5), discussed above.

[65] See also *De Spir. Sanc.* 2.2 (CSEL 21.134), in which Faustus answers the objection that if the Holy Spirit indwells the body and soul of the Redeemer, that means that the Spirit himself has undergone incarnation. Faustus responds by stressing the sharp differences between the action of the Son and that of the Holy Spirit: the Spirit took part in the human conception of the Son, but the person of the Spirit was not received into the Virgin's womb. The Virgin's son is the Son of God who possesses soul and flesh personally and particularly, but in no way does the Holy Spirit have soul or flesh. Because of this, the Son of God, that is the God of glory, is said to be crucified, but this is in no way said of the Holy Spirit. Through these affirmations, Faustus shows his belief that the person who underwent the Incarnation and even the death for our redemption is the Son of God himself. He also indicates that indwelling is not the same thing as incarnation, which implies a rejection of Nestorius's notion of the incarnation as the indwelling of the Son in the *homo assumptus*.

of his merits, nor does he mention merit in his positive Christology. In fact, in 2003 David Maxwell seized on this omission to argue: 'Faustus's approach, however, is fundamentally different from all the other authors who have been examined, including Augustine. For the other authors, the central issue has been the role of merit in Christology and how that role plays out in the doctrine of grace. For Faustus, however, the central issue is that orthodoxy takes the middle position. He never brings up the role of merit in Christology.'[66] Given that Faustus's Christology is in line with that of the other Gallic writers and Augustine, we need to ask whether Maxwell is right that his approach to Christology and grace is fundamentally different from that of the other Gallic writers. We should do well to keep this question in mind as we turn to the 470s and Faustus's *De grat.*

Faustus's Understanding of Grace in the Light of his Christology

In the prologue of *De grat.*, Faustus asserts that 'Pelagius rudely exalts bare labour and foolishly believes that wild human infirmity is sufficient without grace; he has impiously proclaimed the task of building a tower of pride to heaven. . . .'[67] While such teaching is obviously wrong, Faustus argues that predestinarianism is an overreaction against it, and that when he seeks to correct the overreaction, it appears that he is falling back into 'Pelagianism'. This is the context for his first mention of the *uia regia* in that work. For our purposes, it is important to recognize that the starting point for his thinking about grace is an utter rejection of the idea that human beings can build a tower to heaven, can rise up to God. The general movement of salvation, for Faustus as for other Gallic writers, is a downward movement of God to humanity. While this idea gets little further treatment in the work, it is significant that he leads with it.

Moreover, just as the need for the downward movement of God in salvation is implied (not actually stated) at the beginning of *De grat.*, so also Christology itself makes a brief but important appearance early in the treatise. In 1.1 as Faustus describes the *uia regia*, he points out that it is just as important to avoid Scylla and Charybdis when considering grace and human action as it is to avoid those pitfalls when dealing with the deity and humanity of Christ. He concludes with a lengthy

---

[66] David R. Maxwell, 'Christology and Grace in the Sixth-Century Latin West: The Theopaschite Controversy', Ph.D. Dissertation, University of Notre Dame, 2003), 65. This pointed analysis contrasts sharply with the earlier, vaguer, and more favourable assessment of Weigel: 'The letter also gives us some knowledge of Faustus' mind, and of his ability as a theologian. He knew the decrees of Ephesus and the doctrines of Nestorius; and though the Council of Chalcedon had not yet been held, Faustus anticipates its decrees against Eutyches. In other words Faustus kept abreast of his times and knew how to evaluate new currents of theological thought even before they were matter of common discussion.' See Weigel, *Faustus of Riez*, 62.

[67] *De grat.*, Prologue (CSEL 21.4) [part of this is translated in Smith, 67].

188   CHRISTOLOGY AND THE LOGIC OF GRACE

statement, the beginning of which I have quoted earlier in this chapter. Let us now look at the entire passage:

> They [the Pelagians and the predestinarians] run aground against the rock of stumbling in the same way as those who, having abandoned the light of discretion, have dared to assert that Christ the Lord is merely God (*solum deum*) or those who have asserted that he is merely man (*solum hominem*). Either belief is almost too great by itself, for while it knows neither discretion nor distinction, it incurs equal guilt. Just as the one who has said Christ is merely man has denied the power of the Creator (*auctoris potentiam*), so also the one who has said Christ is merely God has lost the mercy of the Redeemer (*misericordiam redemptoris*). And just as those who acknowledge one substance (*substantiam*) in the Lord and Saviour will be constrained by the necessity either to imagine that mere man has come down from heaven (*solum hominem caelo lapsum*) or to say that mere God was crucified (*solum deum ... crucifixum*). But this is not so, for mere God would not have been able to experience (*sentire*) death, nor would mere man have been able to overcome (*superare*) it. And so on account of a two-fold substance (*pro geminae ratione substantiae*) man has undertaken [death] and God has conquered it. Therefore, restoring to both sides their own qualities (*proprietates suas*) and believing and asserting that Christ is God just as he is man, is just the same as (*perinde est ac si*) uniting grace with labour and not expelling human effort (*conatum*) from God's help (*adiutorio*).[68]

This passage echoes what Faustus has written earlier about Christology in *Ep. ad Graec.* and makes clear that for him, the fact that Christ is both divine and human corresponds exactly with the fact that salvation involves both divine help and human work/effort. Notice the poignant statement that without the deity of Christ, it would have been a mere man who came down from heaven. This is even more ironic than meets the eye, because not only could a merely human Jesus not have conquered death, a merely human Jesus could not have come down from heaven beforehand. He would have been earthly, of this world in his origins, not a divine Saviour who had come down by becoming man.

Taken together, these two statements from the prologue and the first chapter establish the downward movement of God through the Incarnation as the foundation of salvation and grace. From this point on, the long treatise *De grat.* includes no systematic discussion of Christology at all; Faustus spends two chapters arguing against the 'Pelagians', and the vast majority of the treatise (the remaining sixteen chapters of book one, and all twelve chapters of book two) disputing with the predestinarians. Nevertheless, it is significant that the descent of the Son to

---

[68] *De grat.* 1.1 (CSEL 21.8).

earth by becoming human as well as divine constitutes the jumping-off point for Faustus's discussion of grace. How then does Christology influence what Faustus actually writes about grace? To explore this question, in this section I shall discuss *prima gratia* in creation (which remains even after the Fall), and then grace in redemption. As I do so, we shall need to be attuned to any connections between the Incarnation and the topics under consideration, and more particularly, to any ways Faustus's broadly Chalcedonian/Cyrillian understanding of Christ influences the way he writes of grace.

Prima Gratia in Creation

In 1.1, Faustus emphasizes not only the need to stress both grace and human action and both the deity and humanity of Christ, but also the need to focus on God as both creator and redeemer. In fact, in the long quotation discussed in the previous subsection, he emphasizes both 'the power of the Creator' (*auctoris potentia*) and the mercy of the Redeemer (*misericordia redemptoris*). Later in the chapter, he criticizes Pelagius for claiming that humanity was created mortal, and in the process he quotes Rom. 5:12 and 6:23 to stress that 'mankind is God's work, sin is the devil's work, and death is the penalty of sin.'[69] He continues of Pelagius: 'When he says this, he blasphemes with a double impiety: he ascribes death to the Creator's envy (*ad auctoris inuidiam*), and by denying original sin (*uinculum*) he eliminates the Redeemer's grace.'[70] This focus on God's power displayed at creation, as well as the grace and mercy demonstrated in the life of the Redeemer, becomes a major mark of Faustus's teaching in *De grat.*, and the crux of the focus on creation is the concept of *prima gratia*.[71]

In *De grat.* Faustus uses the actual phrase *prima gratia* only once,[72] although he also writes of the first state (*prima aetas*) so as to emphasize that the initial human condition was one of grace.[73] Despite the scarcity of the actual phrase, however, virtually all scholars have noted the prominence of *prima gratia* in Faustus's thought. More than a century ago Adolf Harnack summarized: 'God wills the salvation of all; all need grace; but grace reckons on the will which remains, though weakened; *it always co-operates with the latter*; otherwise the effort of human obedience

---

[69] *De grat.* 1.1 (CSEL 21.10).

[70] *De grat.* 1.1 (CSEL 21.11). Weaver notes Faustus's delineation of two problems with Pelagius by writing: 'First, if death is an element of human nature as created, then God, as creator, must be held responsible for death. Second, if humankind is not held in the grip of original sin, then there is no need for a redeemer.' See Rebecca Harden Weaver, *Divine Grace and Human Agency: A Study of the Semi-Pelagian Controversy*, PMS 15 (Macon, GA: Mercer University Press, 1996), 165.

[71] See the assessment in Barcellona, *Fausto di Riez*, 83, that the concept of *prima gratia* is a key aspect of Faustus's ability to preserve human free will.

[72] *De grat.* 2.9 (CSEL 21.78).

[73] *De grat.* 1.8 (25) [Smith, 189].

190 CHRISTOLOGY AND THE LOGIC OF GRACE

would be in vain. . . . Our being saved is God's gift; it does not rest, however, on an absolute predestination, but God's predetermination depends on the use man makes of the liberty still left in him, and in virtue of which he can amend himself.'[74] In two articles from 1979 and 1981, Carlo Tibiletti pointed out that for Faustus, God created mankind positively equipped for and orientated towards the good, and that even after the Fall, the gifts given by grace at creation were not destroyed but weakened, and a capacity for the good remained. He argued further that this emphasis on grace given at creation came not from Pelagius but from the Eastern Christian tradition.[75] Writing in 1990, Thomas Smith argued that for Faustus, 'the entire complex of capacities and orientations that separate the human being from the broader creation may in a sense be designated as grace. . . . The will, with an innate or seminal potential for good, can also turn towards evil but cannot lose its essential freedom. Human righteousness, or at least access thereto, is granted to all, and so all have equal opportunity for salvation.'[76] More recently, in 2010 Mattei pointed out that Faustus sees the primitive nature of humanity as grace and that this primitive grace is retained even after the Fall. For Faustus, the *initium bonae uoluntatis* is a remnant of the *prima gratia* given at creation.[77]

The question that arises in relation to Faustus's emphasis on *prima gratia* is whether this focus amounts to a denigration of the special grace given in redemption, and thus in the process undercuts Faustus's high Christology stressing the downward movement of the Son to earth. On this question scholars have been somewhat ambivalent. Tibilleti acknowledges that Faustus could be considered 'Pelagian' on the grounds that the illumination leading to salvation does not derive from Christ, but he believes Faustus sees grace given at creation as also being Christ's grace.[78] Mattei, who (as we saw above) pointedly raises the question of whether Faustus's teaching undercuts the uniqueness of the grace of redemption, answers his own question by saying that Faustus and Cassian both use expressions that sound 'naturalist' and that were easy to caricature as advocating a natural capacity of mankind to move towards God. But Mattei also insists that these expressions could be interpreted in an acceptable way and that Fautus's *prima gratia* is the grace of Christ, because the Word is the one through whom mankind was made.[79] As I revisit this question in search of the relation between Faustus's Christology and his doctrine of *prima gratia*, it is important to consider carefully *De grat.* 2.9, the only chapter in which he uses the phrase and also his most extended treatment

---

[74] Adolf Harnack, *History of Dogma*. Vol. 5, trans. from vol. 3 of the 3d German edition by J. Millar (London: Williams & Norgate, 1898. Reprint, New York: Russell & Russell, 1958), 253, italics his.
[75] See Carlo Tibiletti, 'Libero arbitrio e grazia in Fausto di Riez', *Augustinianum* 19 (1979), 263–4; Carlo Tibiletti, 'Fausto di Riez nei giudizi della critica', *Augustinianum* 21 (1981), 569.
[76] Smith, De Gratia, 179.
[77] Mattei, 'Le Fantôme Semi-Pélagien', 105–7.
[78] Tibiletti, 'Fausto di Riez nei giudizi della critica', 574.
[79] Mattei, 'Le Fantôme Semi-Pélagien', 108–11.

of the relation between the image and likeness of God, as well as the relationship between Christians and Christ. To this chapter I now turn.

Faustus begins *De grat.* 2.9 by considering the idea that the one in whose image and likeness humanity was created was the future incarnate Christ himself. He rejects this idea on the grounds that 'it would debase (*humiliaret*) the glory of the first innocence (*primae innocentiae decus*) in mankind, if the one who was to be cured from the wounds of his future sin was initially formed immaculately after that exemplar. This would mean that at a time when no transgression yet existed, the form of the future intercessor (*futuri incessoris forma*) would nevertheless already display the guilt of transgression.'[80] Here the heart of Faustus's objection to the idea that Adam was formed in the image of the future incarnate Christ is that such a view would somehow make the Fall inherent in the initial creation, because the form/image of the incarnate Redeemer who would come to undo the results of the Fall was impressed upon pre-fallen mankind. Faustus is very keen to avoid any sense of fatalism about the Fall, and he apparently believes that any connection between the image of God in mankind and the *incarnate* Christ would imply such fatalism.

As a result, Faustus argues for a distinction between image and likeness, and he sees the image consisting of qualities related to the pre-incarnate Son, not qualities the Son in his incarnate state needed in order to rectify the wrong of the Fall:

> Thus, it was not fitting that he [Adam] be completed or perfected to the image of him through whom what was lost had to be repaired, lest under the name of the coming physician the ruin of the fall should be predicted in the very time of blessed origins. It is therefore more reasonable that in humankind, to whom the reality of grace (*gratiae res*), not of nature (*non naturae*), was handed on by God in the very likeness, *image* would rather designate something received from one who is prior and superior, and *likeness* is better seen as conferred from the truth that the Father rightly communicates to his Son by nature.[81]

Notice that in this passage, the distinction between image and likeness does not lead Faustus to argue that the likeness was bestowed later.[82] This fact is important, because a temporal distinction between image and likeness could set one up to see vocation/salvation in terms of an upward movement of mankind towards a higher condition (the achievement of the likeness), rather than the downward movement of God to fallen humanity to restore the original condition. Here again Faustus shows his overall focus on the downward movement of God in salvation.

---

[80] *De grat.* 2.9 (CSEL 21.77).

[81] *De grat.* 2.9 (CSEL 21.77) [Smith, 172].

[82] For the idea of the likeness as a separate, and later, bestowal, see, e.g., Irenaeus, *Adu. haer.* 4.38.2–3 (SC 100.948–56) [*ANF* 1.521–2]; Origen, *De princ.* 3.6.1 (Behr, 440–1).

192   CHRISTOLOGY AND THE LOGIC OF GRACE

His distinction between image and likeness instead accentuates two aspects of created gifts. The gifts of the image accentuate the fact that God is prior to and higher than humankind, so created capacities that he gives truly constitute grace. The gifts of the likeness are more relational and highlight the similarity between the natural Son and the created sons and daughters.

Immediately after this, Faustus continues:

> Hence, we must carefully direct our attention to the fact that our Lord Jesus Christ conferred from himself better things (*de suo meliora contulit*) in the first time period (*in primo tempore*), but in the second time period (*in secondo autem*) he assumed from us worse things (*de nostro deteriora suscepit*). And for this reason, when he prepared us from nothing, our maker appointed to us his own image (*imaginem suam factor adposuit*), and indeed once we were lost he repaired it (*quando uero nos perditos reparauit*), assuming as our Redeemer the form of a servant [cf. Phil. 2:7, which he then quotes].[83]

This passage further bolsters the argument that creation in the image was not simply an imitation of the future incarnate Christ. Instead, Christ gave from himself *meliora*, whereas he would later assume from us *deteriora*. Equally important is the fact that only if the person of the incarnate Christ is the Son himself may one say that the same Christ does both of these things.

Faustus argues further that the image must be that of the whole Trinity, not just of the to-be-incarnate Son, since the Father and the Holy Spirit do not become incarnate. He asserts that 'whatever the Trinity bestows in common upon man is derived from the likeness of the deity', emphasizes that the Trinity in unity speaks the creative command in Gen. 1:26, and concludes, 'When, therefore, this image is conferred by the Father, Son, and Holy Spirit, undoubtedly the one divinity of the three persons (*trium personarum una diuinitas*) grants the dignity of its image (*suae imaginis tribuit dignitatem*) to the first man.'[84] Then Faustus reiterates that these gifts constitute grace, and at this point uses the phrase *prima gratia* for the first and only time:

> You will hardly doubt that the freedom of his own will (*uoluntatis propriae libertatem*), albeit attenuated (*licet adtenuatam*), belongs to man, if you give attention to the first grace by which he was honored by God (*primam gratiam, qua a deo est honoratus*). Man therefore is called the image of God because truth kindly and graciously implanted justice in him; and reason, wisdom; and perpetuity, eternity. It is from the image of God that one understands, that one knows what is right, that one discriminates between evil and good by the scrutiny of

---

[83]   *De grat.* 2.9 (CSEL 21.77).
[84]   *De grat.* 2.9 (CSEL 21.78) [Smith, 162–3].

one's judgment. Since God is goodness, mercy, patience, and justice, the more one is found to be more just or patient, so much closer one is proved to be like God (*deo similis*), whose likeness (*similitudo*) is possessed not in appearances, but in virtues (*non in uultibus, sed in uirtutibus*).[85]

This important passage advances Faustus's argument in three ways. First, it reiterates the relation between image and likeness. Again, likeness is a more relational category by which human beings are like the God to whom we are related, and the etymological similarity of the words *similis* and *similitudo* is obvious when the two words are juxtaposed. Second, the passage again rejects, this time in a subtle way, the idea of creation in the image of the future incarnate Son: the similarity is not physical (*non in uultibus*) but moral (*in uirtutibus*). Here the wordplay on the superficially similar but contrasting words *uultus* and *uirtus* counters the similarity between the genuinely related words *similis* and *similitudo*. Third, and most important, the passage insists that the *prima gratia* given to humankind at creation continues after the Fall, and so the freedom that is part of that gift is attenuated but not eliminated. God has honoured the human race with liberty, and he will not revoke that honourable gift even though humanity has turned away from him.

Having established that the *prima gratia* remains after the Fall, Faustus drives home the point that this gift is *grace*; it is not somehow the human birthright by nature. He asserts:

Therefore it is said of God: subtle, simple, sincere. *Simple* certainly means that nothing extrinsic is added to him (*nihil illi extrinsecus adiectitium*), nothing has been granted from elsewhere (*nihil aliunde conlatum*), but in him are power, being, and substance (*in illo uirtus, essentia atque substantia*). And so, God is what he possesses (*deus quod habet est*). Man, unless he receives these gifts, does not possess them (*homo uero haec dona, nisi acceperit, non habet*). So, while God is both just and justice, merciful and mercy, holy and holiness, man can be just but not justice; merciful, but not mercy; holy, but not holiness ... what is grace in man is nature in God (*in homine gratia est, quod in deo natura est*).[86]

This assertion calls to Faustus's mind a mistaken view that argues from the permanence of human freedom to the conclusion that it is a natural part of human essence and thus does not depend on God. Thus, he claims:

They err, therefore, who regard justice and the other virtues as the substance of the soul (*animae ... substantiam*), without which it could subsist anyway by the vital power of its nature, without which even the devil is seen to remain in his

[85] *De grat.* 2.9 (CSEL 21.78-9) [Smith, 173–4].
[86] *De grat.* 2.9 (CSEL 21.79) [Smith, 162].

194   CHRISTOLOGY AND THE LOGIC OF GRACE

nature. These virtues are manifestly shown to have been added (*manifeste enim inueniuntur adposita*) when they are stripped away by the intervention of sins (*dum culpis interuenientibus exuuntur*). Only the power of choice and immortality (which is even implanted in evil people) are not removed, although the dignity and blessedness of immortality can be removed. Insofar as it pertains to freedom of choice and immortality, then, even evil people can possess the image of God, though tarnished by them and in them, but only the good can possess the likeness.[87]

With these assertions Faustus solidifies several points. First, everything good possessed by humanity is given by God's grace; nothing is inherently natural to the human condition as it is in the case of God. Second, certain gifts given to humanity can be substantially lost through the Fall, and the very fact that this is so demonstrates that these gifts were given by grace, not part of any natural constitution. Third, there are two things given to humanity by grace that are not lost through sin—freedom of choice and immortality. Immortal *blessedness* can be exchanged for immortal misery, but immortality itself cannot be lost through sin. In keeping with the idea that for Faustus, image is a constitutive gift and likeness a relational one, freedom of the will pertains to the image, but blessedness depends on relationship to God and is thus characteristic of the likeness.

Faustus then gives examples of Old Testament saints who chose good over evil: Abel, Enoch, and Noah.[88] The fact that they did so indicates that the freedom to choose the good was not obliterated by the Fall. He sums up this discussion by writing:

> No one's sin is so contrary to nature as to blot out the last vestiges of nature (*ut naturae deleat etiam extrema uestigia*). For it is because of this that even the ungodly think about eternal matters, and make praiseworthy laws even in the present world, and properly condemn many matters of human conduct. By what rules, in the end, do they judge these things if not by the natural rules, in which they see the way one should live, even if they themselves might not live this way?[89]

At this point, the idea that even sinful people know how to live, even when they do not do so, provides the occasion for an extended quotation of and reflection on Rom. 1:18–23, God's revelation by which the Gentiles know God but do not glorify him as God.

Faustus's long discussion of the image and likeness of God in connection with *prima gratia* is not directly tied to either 'Nestorianism' or his own

---

[87] *De grat.* 2.9 (CSEL 21.79) [Smith, 175–6].
[88] *De grat.* 2.9 (CSEL 21.80–1).
[89] *De grat.* 2.9 (CSEL 21.81) [Smith, 178].

positive Christology. Nevertheless, I suggest that there is an implicit connection that emerges in the several places in which Faustus emphasizes the downward motion of God for salvation, in contrast to an upward movement of mankind. We have seen that Faustus directly accuses 'Pelagius' of advocating such an upward movement (building a tower to heaven), and while he does not directly accuse 'Nestorius' of doing the same (nor does he accuse 'Nestorius' of seeing Christ as a man who rose up to union with God by his merits, as other Gallic writers do), one might certainly guess that this idea lies in the background to his thought. In contrast to such an ascending paradigm, Faustus argues for two important and related ideas. First, everything about mankind's 'natural' constitution is given by *prima gratia*. Qualitative gifts such as freedom and initial righteousness, and relational gifts such as likeness to God, are all given, not earned. Furthermore, when most of these gifts were lost through the Fall, salvation became a process that—while it involves human action using the freedom *not* lost in the Fall—depends primarily and utterly on the descent of the Son to earth to save the human race through the grace of redemption. What links *prima gratia* and *gratia redemptoris* is the idea that Faustus has earlier explained in *Ep. ad Graec.* and with which he has begun *De grat.*—that Jesus Christ is the same person as the eternal Son. He is not merely a man united to the Son by virtue of his own ascent (such a man could do no more than point us to the way of ascent), but he is the eternal Son made man. As the eternal Son, he is the source of both the initial gifts to mankind and the restoration offered through the Incarnation. The connection between initial grace and redemptive grace is precisely the person, the Son, who gives both kinds of grace. *Prima gratia* is therefore an aspect of Christology, not a separate act of God unrelated to it.

On the basis of *prima gratia*, in *De grat.* Faustus discusses grace largely in relation to redemption and Christian life, not creation. It now remains for us to look briefly at the tenor of these discussions.

Grace in Redemption

We have seen previously that two crucial questions for the Gallic writers were whether grace was given to everyone, and correspondingly, whether the atonement was intended for all. Not surprisingly, Faustus definitively sides with Cassian, Vincent, and the later Prosper on these issues. As he first turns his attention to the predestinarians in 1.3, Faustus insists that it would diminish grace to argue that it is not given to everyone:

> When they [the predestinarians] say 'everything is from God's grace,' who is not inclined with the affect of his whole heart toward so revered a term? Yet when we answer: 'Clearly everything is from grace, but the creator and redeemer offers

196   CHRISTOLOGY AND THE LOGIC OF GRACE

it to all (*omnibus eam offert*) and pours it out for the salvation of all (*ingerit ad salutem omnium*),' to this they retreat far from the path of piety and presume to answer: 'The savior did not grant it to all (*non eam saluator omnibus dedit*), for he did not die for all (*quia nec pro omnibus mortuus est*).' Behold: immediately in the second statement appears the impugner of grace (*gratiae impugnator*), who in the first was thought to be its champion (*assertor*).[90]

This passage provides an excellent summary of what I have been calling the logic of grace. For Faustus (as for the other Gallic writers), the same one is both creator and redeemer, and just as he offers grace to the whole human race at creation, so also he pours grace out for the salvation of all in redemption. The movement of thought is from human incapacity after the Fall to the universal dimensions of divine provision. Whereas other Gallic writers move from the Fall to the Incarnation (understood in terms of its universal import), Faustus's logic moves from the Fall back to *prima gratia* (whose gifts remain even in spite of the Fall) and then forwards to the Incarnation and redemption. In contrast, the predestinarians' logic moves from the Fall to predestination and the particularity of the atonement (*nec pro omnibus mortuus est*) and thus to the insistence that grace is not given to everyone.

Later in book 1 of *De grat.*, Faustus discusses Jn. 6:44 (in which Jesus affirms that no one comes to him unless the Father draws him) and argues that God's drawing is not violent or impetuous but is given freely and generally. Divine drawing does not usurp or override human powers previously given. In contrast to the predestinarians, who he claims see God's drawing as violent, Faustus insists of the servant who is so drawn:

He is not, is he, like stupid, senseless matter, one who must be moved about and pulled from place to place? Rather, the servant extends the hand of faith, by which he may be drawn (*manum fidei, qua adtrahatur*), to the Lord who assists and calls (*adsistenti et uocanti domino*), and he says, *I believe, Lord; help my unbelief* [Mk. 9:24]. So these two things are joined together: the power of the one who draws (*adtrahentis uirtus*) and the disposition of the one who obeys (*oboedientis affectus*), just as if some invalid tried to get up but his strength failed him, and therefore he must ask that a right hand be extended to him. The will cries out, because infirmity by itself, of its own resources, cannot be raised up. In this sense the Lord invites the willing (*ita dominus inuitat uolentem*), draws the desiring (*adtrahit desiderantem*), raises up the striving (*erigit adnitentem*).[91]

The thought of this passage might appear to be very similar to that of Cassian, in that both seem to affirm that the human will can make the first move (or at least

---

[90]   *De grat.* 1.3 (CSEL 21.15) [Smith, 73].
[91]   *De grat.* 1.16 (CSEL 21.52) [Smith, 207].

seek to make such a move) towards God in salvation. I have argued in chapter 3 that Cassian does not actually write about the very beginning of salvation, so his insistence that the monk sometimes takes the initiative in moving towards God is not analogous to a passage like this one from Faustus, who certainly has in view the beginning of a person's movement towards faith in Christ. Nevertheless, for Faustus as well, this is not the *very* beginning of salvation, because the ability even to be willing to believe is a result of *prima gratia*, not a natural faculty of the human will. Nevertheless, it is crystal clear that Faustus sees God's drawing in a universal sense, not a restrictive one.

Two chapters later, Faustus concludes book one by rejecting the predestinarians' idea that God wills anyone to perdition, and in the process, he makes clear his affirmation of the universal salvific will of God. Faustus marshals 2 Sam. 14:14, three passages from Ezekiel (18:32, 24:12, 33:11), Mic. 6:8, and 2 Pet. 3:9 to support his insistence that the Lord wills all to be saved, and he adduces Jer. 6:29, Mt. 23:37, and Lk. 19:41 to explain that any who are condemned perish through their own fault.[92] Most noteworthy is his discussion of Mt. 23:37, in which Jesus expresses his longing to gather Jerusalem as a hen gathers her chicks, and he laments the city's refusal to turn to him. Faustus comments:

> For, when he says, *How often I wanted and you refused*, there is expressed both the goodness of purpose in God (*in deo propositi bonitas*), and free will in humans (*in homine arbitrii*). But in saying, *Jerusalem, you who kill the prophets and stone those who have been sent to you*, he pronounces that he wanted to save them, although he obviously brought forth causes through which he would deny salvation to them. In this passage there is shown in a two-fold manner the iniquity of a cruel mind in the servant (*in seruo iniquitas cruentae mentis*), and the kindness of a most loving will in the Lord (*in domino indulgentia benignissimae uoluntatis*).[93]

In the light of this assertion of God's universal salvific will, Faustus insists early in book two that predestination is based on foreknowledge:

> One does not set about to do something because the authority of the foreknower might be about to compel him or her (*quia eum coactura sit praescientis auctoritas*). Rather, the freedom and the will of the one foreknown (*libertas praesciti hominis ac uoluntas*) impose a quality upon the foreknowing of God (*deo praesciendi ingerit qualitatem*). So the cause of sin is not imposed upon a person by a harshness of foresight; instead, the order of foreknowledge arises from the rewards deserved by people. So general foreknowledge, which lies before God and concerns the state of the whole world, arises from power. But as to

---

[92] *De grat.* 1.18 (CSEL 21.55–7) [Gumerlock, 152–5].
[93] *De grat.* 1.18 (CSEL 21.57) [Gumerlock, 154, translation slightly modified].

198 CHRISTOLOGY AND THE LOGIC OF GRACE

the state of human beings, the qualities and kinds of foreknowing depend on a consideration of human actions.[94]

Human freedom, which God chooses not to violate, therefore imposes a *qualitas* on his own foreknowledge. In fact, even when treating a passage such as Rom. 9:21 (in which Paul asserts that the potter may make from the clay a vessel for honour or dishonour), Faustus insists that one may move back and forth between being a vessel for honour and a vessel for dishonour, and that such movement depends on choice, not necessity. Unlike Augustine, who asserts that there are no preceding merits on the basis of which God chooses to make a person a vessel for honour, Faustus argues that there always are such preceding causes.[95]

We should not misinterpret this focus on foreknowledge and insistence of preceding causes to mean that Faustus sees grace and human action acting in a purely symmetric synergism. Instead, his concept of *prima gratia* enables him to accentuate both the primacy and the priority of grace, while locating human effort primarily in the living of Christian life, not in initial conversion to faith. This is clearest in his long discussions of two other Pauline passages, 1 Cor. 15:10 and Eph. 2:8–9. On the first of these passages, Faustus interprets *by God's grace I am what I am* to mean that the origin of Christian existence is by grace. He takes *I labored more than all of them* to imply that some credit goes to one's own labour. And finally, he regards *yet not I, but the grace of God within me* to mean that God's grace cooperates with one's labour.[96] He summarizes, 'As one piously subject, he [Paul] ascribes the beginnings to grace alone; as the teacher of obedience, he credits the middle parts to labor; and in the consummation, being restrained, he conjoins both grace and labor.'[97] On the second of these passages, Faustus writes of two *tempora gratiae*. The *tempus gratiae* in which we are redeemed has no regard for human works, but only for faith. But the *tempus gratiae* of consummation, required of those who have been converted and baptized, enjoins works as well.[98]

From these discussions we see that for Faustus, an adequate construal of grace must include universal elements. It begins at creation, and God's *prima gratia* remains, enabling all people to will to believe and to act, even if they are not able to carry out the desires of their will. The Incarnation, life, death, and resurrection of Christ were intended for the salvation of all people, not merely all kinds of people or all who were chosen. Those who are not saved perish through their own free choices; those who are saved are the ones who cooperate with the prior, higher, and persistent grace that is present at every point in their lives.

---

[94] *De grat.* 2.2 (CSEL 21.61) [Smith, 181].
[95] *De grat.* 1.11 (CSEL 21.36–7).
[96] *De grat.* 1.5 (CSEL 21.19–20).
[97] *De grat.* 1.5 (CSEL 21.20).
[98] *De grat.* 1.6 (CSEL 21.21–2).

Conclusions on Faustus

In this chapter we have seen that on both Christology and grace, Faustus is doing much more than simply balancing emphases on divine and human action. The *uia regia* and his admonitions to avoid Scylla and Charybdis do not mean that he is simply trying to place himself in the middle of a spectrum between 'Nestorianism' and proto-'Eutychianism,' between 'Pelagianism' and predestinarianism. Although Faustus's writing, unlike that of the other Gallic writers, has somewhat of a 'Semi-Pelagian' feel to it, even here we are not justified in using the pejorative label 'Semi-Pelagian' because he is just as concerned as the others to make divine grace and divine action the starting point of his soteriology. Instead, we find that while Faustus's Christology of divine descent lines up exactly with that of Augustine and the Gallic writers, his logic of grace is even more different from Augustine's than is the logic of the other Gallic writers.

Christologically, Faustus exhibits the same major emphases as the other writers we have considered. Unlike Cassian, but like Vincent, he writes very precisely of two *substantiae/naturae* and one *persona* in Christ. But in spite of this precision, he uses *homo* in ways that might lead one to believe he is affirming a *homo assumptus* quasi-independent of the eternal Son. Faustus shares this characteristically ambiguous use of *homo* with all writers I have considered in this study, and indeed with virtually the entire Western patristic church. Likewise, Faustus shares with Vincent and most of the Western church a fondness for verbal symmetry in describing, for example, 'the man who is God and the God who is man', and this verbal symmetry might also give the impression that his Christology is 'Antiochene' or 'Nestorian'. But upon closer inspection it becomes clear that like Vincent and others, Faustus means *homo* in the sense of either *humana natura* or 'the Son considered *qua homo*', and his verbal symmetry is merely verbal, not meant to be metaphysical or constitutive. Like Augustine, the post-correction Leporius, Cassian, Vincent, and Prosper, Faustus sees the Incarnation as the downward movement of the eternal Son to earth to accomplish human salvation, and so he insists on the personal continuity between the Word/Son and the one born of Mary. As a person, Christ is the eternal Son of God, not a quasi-independent man united to that Son.

Regarding grace, Faustus is certainly much more like Cassian, Vincent, and the later Prosper than he is like the later Augustine. He unambiguously affirms God's universal salvific will and even insists that limiting grace to the elect would diminish that grace. He sees substantial room for legitimate human action in Christian life as the Christian cooperates with God's grace. And unlike the earlier writers, he directly claims that predestination is based on foreknowledge. Notice that the later Prosper holds to a complex understanding of predestination that affirms God's universal salvific will and takes account of the way human beings use general gifts. Such a view indeed sounds like affirming that foreknowledge of how a person will use general gifts is the basis for that person's election or non-election, but Prosper does not write that explicitly. Faustus seems to be arguing the same thing—that one's use of general gifts determines whether one receives subsequent gifts and is saved—and it may be fair to say that when he claims foreknowledge is the basis for predestination, he is simply stating the logical conclusion of Prosper's later thought, a conclusion Prosper's remaining loyalty to Augustine prevents him from saying directly. But for all the Gallic writers, grace involves both general and particular gifts, and God interacts with people in the light of the way they use the general graces.

In this chapter, however, we have also found that Faustus's logic of grace is somewhat different from that of the other Gallic writers. They oppose Augustine by reasoning not from the Fall to predestination, but rather from the Fall to the Incarnation. Faustus opposes the same kind of reasoning on the part of the predestinarians (reasoning from the Fall to predestination) by a logic that moves from the Fall back to *prima gratia* and thus to human freedom that is not lost through sin. As a result, one could say that in spite of their differences, Augustine and the other Gallic writers share an understanding of grace that is primarily concerned with the restoration of fallen humanity. Faustus, on the other hand, expands the purview of grace by linking it much more explicitly to creation as well as to redemption/restoration.[99] As we have seen, this lessened distinction between creation and redemption makes Faustus vulnerable to the charge that his soteriology does not sufficiently centre around the Incarnation. What absolves Faustus of this charge, I suggest, is the fact that in his understanding, *prima gratia* is Christological, because it is given by the same person who gives redemptive grace. Only with a Christology in which the eternal Son—who, along with the Father and Spirit, gives *prima gratia*—is the very person who is born, lives, dies, and is raised for our salvation, can *prima gratia* and *gratia redemptoris* truly coinhere as gracious actions of the same divine person. With such a Christology, Faustus is able to express not only redemption but even creation as products of the same downward movement of God's Son to humanity. The Son who condescends to the human race in his action of gracing people with constitutive and relational gifts (the image and likeness of God) is the same one who condescends to the human race personally through the Incarnation to restore human beings to the marred image and lost likeness.

As a result, perhaps I should precise the way I have described the Gallic conception of the logic of grace. For them, the next logical step after the recognition of the inability of fallen human beings to save themselves is to turn to the Son, to consider his downward movement to humanity *both* through his giving of gifts at creation *and* through his Incarnation. Thus, the theological concept by which the Gallic writers preserve the priority of divine action and divine grace in salvation is not *just* the Incarnation, but *the eternal Son* who would become incarnate

---

[99] Smith, De Gratia, 216, makes this point.

but whose gracious condescension to the human race did not begin simply with the Incarnation. In this conception, all four writers have been clear about their Christology of divine descent, and each has provided his own important emphases. Cassian has given the most detail about the working of grace in the life of the monk. Vincent has provided the most terminological precision in Christology. Prosper has broadened the field of view to focus on God's universal salvific will. And now Faustus has widened the view even further to remind us that even the Incarnation is not the *very* beginning of salvation—that distinction belongs to *prima gratia*. Like Augustine, and unlike both 'Pelagius' and 'Nestorius', all of them stress the priority of divine grace in salvation. Unlike Augustine, they do not use the concept of predestination to do so, but instead focus on God's Son himself as the demonstration of the priority of grace, and so predestination becomes a much less central concept in their soteriology, as well as a concept they interpret differently from Augustine.

Conclusion

In this study, I have sought to build a coherent picture of fifth-century Gallic monastic teaching on Christology and grace. What I have called the 'Gallic conception' has emerged gradually, with Cassian providing important Christological underpinnings, to which Vincent added most of the Christological terminology. Likewise, Cassian provided the spiritual charitology for the monastic life, while Prosper added a broader view of grace and salvation in general. Faustus has inherited this Gallic conception and has added the important point that grace given at creation and retained by fallen humanity is Christological because it is given by the eternal Son himself. As I have considered each writer in turn, three general points have also emerged, and it is now time to bring them into focus: First, the Christology of the Gallic writers was not 'Antiochene' but specifically anti-'Nestorian' and broadly Chalcedonian/Cyrillian. Second, the charitology of the Gallic monks was not specifically anti-Augustine although it was certainly non-Augustinian on important points. Third, it was not so much the case that the Gallic monks lay at different points on a spectrum between Augustine and Pelagius, as it was that they reasoned between Christology and grace with a different logic than did Augustine. Let us briefly review these points.

Gallic Christology: 'Antiochene'?

In chapter 1 of this book, we saw that there is an ongoing scholarly disagreement about how to understand Augustine's Christology, and by extension, Western Christology more generally. At issue is the question of whether Augustinian/Latin Christology is more in tune with that of the 'Antiochenes' (Theodore and Nestorius) or that of the Cyrillian Chalcedonians. I have suggested that there are two major reasons one might consider Latin Christology to be broadly Antiochene: that it uses the word *homo* of Christ's humanity in a way that makes it seem as if that humanity is a quasi-independent man, and that it uses what I call verbal symmetry of the pattern 'the God who is man and the man who is God'. (In addition, Augustine's description of the Christological union as 'grace' has led some to connect his Christology directly to Theodore's.) Throughout this book, I have given attention to the way each writer uses the word *homo* in Christological passages and have noted the uses of verbal symmetry as well. I have argued that these passages do not actually imply that Christ's humanity is an independent or

---

Christology and the Logic of Grace in Fifth-Century Gaul. Donald Fairbairn, Oxford University Press.
© Donald Fairbairn 2025. DOI: 10.1093/9780198936220.003.0008

CONCLUSION   203

quasi-independent man, or even a man who can be considered separately from the Word. For Augustine, the post-correction Leporius, Cassian, Vincent, Prosper (as far as we can tell), and Faustus, the acting subject in Christ is the eternal Son who has taken humanity into his own person.

Of course, I have considered only a very small portion of Augustine's relevant writing, and my conclusions regarding him apply only to the way he expresses himself near the end of his life. But in the case of the other five writers of this study, we have seen everything they wrote on Christology. This, of course, is not very much material, and it is material that, in the case of Cassian, has not impressed scholars with its quality. Nevertheless, the material newly translated and/or surveyed in this book has shown that the Christology of these Gallic monks was anti-'Nestorian' and broadly Chalcedonian/Cyrillian, not 'Antiochene'. Thus, the little-studied writings of these monks support the contention that Latin Christology more generally should not be regarded as 'Antiochene' because of its use of *homo*. Indeed, the fact that these Gallic writers used the word *homo* so consistently even though they were arguing directly against 'Nestorius' suggests that they did not even think the use of that word was vulnerable to a 'Nestorian' interpretation. It is worth investigating whether this was the case with other Latin writers using the word *homo* in Christological contexts.

Gallic Charitology with Respect to Augustine's Thought

Throughout this book, we have also seen that scholars have long asked whether a given Gallic monastic writer was directly opposing Augustine in formulating his teaching on grace. Generally speaking, earlier scholars worked from the assumption that the monks perceived Augustine's teaching on grace and predestination as a threat to the striving that lay at the heart of their calling, that he was the unnamed target whenever they criticized any conception of grace that appeared to minimize such striving. In contrast, a significant body of more recent scholarship has increasingly called this assumption into question. I have raised this issue with respect to Cassian, Vincent, and Faustus, and I have agreed with scholars who find the evidence that Augustine is the direct target to be unpersuasive, or at least not conclusive. The Gallic monks certainly opposed the idea present in Gaul that predestination implied human passivity, and to the degree that the perpetrators of that idea called themselves 'Augustinians', the Gallic monks were 'anti-Augustinian'. But as Marín has pointed out and as we have seen, they treated the man himself with nothing but respect, even though they disagreed with both the priority Augustine gave to predestination (its place in the logic of grace) and the way he understood it (that is, in a way that appeared to minimize any general effects of Christ's work or of divine grace). These were issues of great importance, and they remain momentous today. But I suggest that they were not nearly as existential as has sometimes

204 CHRISTOLOGY AND THE LOGIC OF GRACE

been assumed. Augustine was surely not perceived in Gaul as a mortal threat to the monastic endeavour or to the Christian faith.

Furthermore, the Gallic understanding of grace did not develop in simple opposition to Augustine, and thus Augustinian thought on grace should not be the standard against which we evaluate the Gallicans. Instead, 'Pelagius' and 'Nestorius' stood at least as much in the background of the Gallic writings as Augustine did. No one I have considered in this study except perhaps Faustus saw grace-related issues in terms of a spectrum of emphases (such that one might rank a given person as 'semi-Pelagian' or 'semi-Augustinian'), and I have suggested that even he was doing something different from, and far more significant than, merely ranking positions in terms of degrees of emphasis. The Gallic monks, I argue, did not lie at various points on a line graph between 'Pelagius' and Augustine. Rather, they were teaching something qualitatively different than either. In addition, the spiritual influences on the Gallic monks' teaching extended far beyond even Augustine, 'Pelagius', and 'Nestorius'. The impress of Egyptian monasticism on Cassian, and through him on both Marseilles and Lérins, was arguably greater than any influence Augustine might have had on Gaul. Likewise, in Prosper's long doctrinal evolution, it was the papal see that came to play the decisive role in his thinking, in spite of his earlier reverential attachment to the bishop of Hippo. The fifth-century Gallic conversations about grace were not held simply in comparison to Augustine, were not argued simply using Augustine's categories, and should not be seen today simply in terms of Augustinian positions, their opposites, or a spectrum in between. I propose that it would be better for us to see Augustine neither as the Gallic monks' primary opponent, nor as the standard for understanding them, but instead as one of their interlocutors on charitology, and hardly the only interlocutor at that. They should not be called either 'semi-Pelagians' or even 'semi-Augustinians'.

The Logic of Grace in Fifth-Century Gaul

If, as I have argued, Augustine and the Gallic writers were working from the same broad Christology, in which the Son himself has personally descended to earth by taking humanity into his own person, and since they nevertheless arrived at very different understandings of grace, predestination, and God's salvific will, do these differences mean that Christology and grace are unconnected theological issues? In contrast to scholarship that has tended to see them as unrelated, I suggest that the very fact that the same Gallic monks who wrote so much on grace also wrote at least a bit—and in the case of Cassian and Vincent, a great deal—on Christology should lead us not to give up too easily in our search for a connection between the doctrines. And as the Gallic conception has emerged through this study, I have argued that it differs from Augustine's thought in the logic by which one reasons between the Fall, Christology, and grace/salvation.

As Augustine links Christology and grace at the end of his life, he does so in the context of discussions of predestination, and he writes of the election of the assumed humanity of Christ primarily in order to argue that there are no preceding merits on the basis of which God elects individual human beings for salvation. In other words, although his Christology is perfectly consistent with that of the Gallic monks, Christology is not the starting point for his soteriological reasoning or the means by which he asserts divine priority in salvation. In a sense, he is reasoning from the incapacity of fallen humanity to predestination, and only then to Christology. As a result, his concept of grace is governed by predestination, and he considers the grace of the Incarnation and subsequent grace in Christian life in terms of their particular effects on the elect, not in terms of any general effects on the human race as a whole.

In contrast, the Gallic writers reason from the same starting point, the incapacity of fallen humanity. But from this point they move not to predestination, but to the Son, to Christology. It is the Son who (along with the Father and Spirit) gave the gifts of *prima gratia* that the Fall did not eradicate, and it is the Son who personally came down to earth to live, die, and be raised as a man in order to offer salvation to the human race. A logic of grace that moves from the Fall to the Son sets the theologian up to consider the grace of Christ in a broad sense, as grace affecting all mankind. Thus, all four Gallic writers explicitly mention God's universal salvific will, and Faustus even argues that it would diminish grace to postulate that it is not offered to everyone. This point is particularly important, because Augustine and his followers believe it would diminish grace to postulate that it might be wasted on one who was not chosen for salvation. The difference is striking, and in the mind of the Gallic monks, the understanding of grace must begin with the general and universal grace given through the Son, with which individual human beings may cooperate or not, so as to participate in Christ or not, so as to be saved or not.

As striking as this difference is, however, we should not regard it as absolute. Both Augustine and the Gallicans stood in opposition to a 'Nestorian' or 'Pelagian' understanding of grace that would amount to little more than aid in a task that belongs to the human race itself. In such an understanding, it is not too great a caricature to say that people must follow the example of Christ who has risen up to God through the indwelling of the Word, and we follow with the grace offered through the corresponding indwelling of the Spirit in us. Both Augustinian and Gallic conceptions of grace reject this notion by tying grace to the downward movement of God's Son through the Incarnation, and thus seeing the grace given in the Incarnation as foundational, not just auxiliary. That agreement is more fundamental, I suggest, than the significant disagreements that divide Augustine and the Gallicans over the universal and particular aspects of grace.

If what I call the Gallic conception of Christology and grace is accurate and helpful in illumining the discussions long known as the 'Semi-Pelagian Controversy', there are two obvious areas that might be fruitfully studied further.

First is the settlement at the Second Council of Orange in 529. Was this event, orchestrated by Caesarius of Arles, actually a settlement or a compromise, incorporating an Augustinian view of how one comes to baptism and the beginning of faith and a non-Augustinian view of how one continues in faith? Or was it more fundamentally a simple re-statement of an existing Gallic conception? A second area for further study, of course, would be the relation between the Gallic conception and the Christology/charitology of other regions in the church. I have explicitly stated that by calling this conception 'Gallic', I am not implying that it is a merely regional conception, unique to Gaul. But I have also not offered any conjectures about how widespread it might have been beyond Gaul. My suspicion is that similar conceptions are surely there to be found elsewhere, and perhaps direct connections/influences from Eastern/Egyptian monasticism, from Rome, or from other regions may be established as well.

In some Christian circles, Augustine's thought has long been the standard for Christian teaching on grace. But on the point Augustine most emphasized at the end of his life—a particular conception of predestination and of its priority in soteriology—his teaching was certainly not the standard in Gaul, and maybe not in other regions of the church either. His logic of grace was not the only one that sought to do justice to divine priority in salvation, and other kinds of logic, like that of the fifth-century Gallic writers, might be fruitful for us to consider today as well.

Bibliography

Section 1: Texts and Translations of Patristic Writings
The bibliographical reference for each work includes:

- In parentheses, the abbreviated Latin title by which I cite the work in the book
- The full Latin title of the work, followed by the date of composition in brackets
- The edition of the text that I cite/quote in the book
- The English translation of the work (if any) that I cite/quote in the book

Ambrose of Milan:

Veni, Redemptor Gentium [*c*.397]; text in Herman Adalbert Daniel, *Thesaurus Hymnologicus* 1.12. Leipzig: J. T. Loeschke, 1855; E.T. in numerous places.

Augustine of Hippo:

(*Con. Iulian. opus imperf.*) *Contra Iulianum opus imperfectum* [*c*.428–30]; text in PL 45.1059–1608; E.T. in WSA I/25.55–721.

(*Con. Max.*) *Contra Maximinum haereticum Arianorum episcopum* [*c*.428]; text in PL 42.742–816; E.T. in WSA I/18.246–336.

(*De bapt.*) *De baptismo, contra Donatistas* [*c*.400]; text in PL 43.107–244; E.T. in WSA I/21.391–604.

(*De consens. euang.*) *De consensu euangelistarum* [*c*.404]; text in CCSL 43.1–418; E.T. in WSA I/15 & I/16.139–332.

(*De corrept. grat.*) *De correptione et gratia* [*c*.427]; text in CSEL 92.219–80; E.T. in WSA I/26.109–45.

(*De doc. christ.*) *De doctrina christiana* [begun *c*.396, completed *c*.426]; text in CCSL 32.1–167; E.T. in WSA I/11.101–244.

(*De grat. Christi*) *De gratia Christi et de peccato originali* [*c*.418]; text in CSEL 42.125–206; E.T. in WSA I/23.403–63.

(*De pecc. mer. rem.*) *De peccatorum meritis et remissione et de baptismo paruulorum ad Marcellinum* [*c*.412]; text in CSEL 60.3–151; E.T. in WSA I/23.34–137.

(*De praed. sanct.*) *De praedestinatione sanctorum* [*c*.428–9]; including book two that was later known separately as *De don. pers.*; text in CSEL 105.179–271; E.T. in WSA I/26.149–240.

(*De trin.*) *De trinitate* [*c*.400–420s]; text in CCSL 50.3–380, 50A.381–535; E.T. in WSA I/5.63–443.

(*Enchir.*) *Enchiridion ad Laurentium de fide et spe et caritate* [*c*.420]; text in CCSL 46.49–114; E.T. in WSA I/8.273–343.

(*Ep.*) *Epistulae* 137, 169, 187, 205, 219 [*c*.412–427]; texts in CSEL 44.96–125, 611–22; 57.81–119, 323–39, 428–31; E.T. in WSA II/2.212–24; II/3.106–13, 230–50, 377–85; II/4.69–71.

(*Ser. II de fid.*) *Sermo altera de fide catholica* (Sermones de diuersis 234); text in PL 39.2176–80.

Capreolus of Carthage:

(*Ep.* 1) *Epistula 1 ad Concilium Ephesinum* [431]; text in *ACO* 1.1.2.52–4; Lat.V. in *ACO* 1.2.64–5; E.T. in TTH 72.278–9.

(*Ep.* 2) *Epistula 2 ad Vitalem et Constantium* [*c*.431]; text in PL 53.849–58.

208 BIBLIOGRAPHY

Cassian, John:

(*Conlat.*) *Conlationes* [*c.*425–7]; text in CSEL 13.3–711; E.T. in ACW 57.35–860.

(*De incar. Dom.*) *De incarnatione Domini contra Nestorium* [430]; text in CSEL 17.235–391; E.T. in *NPNF*[2] 11.549–621.

(*De inst. coen.*) *De institutis coenobiorum* [*c.*424]; text in CSEL 17.3–231; E.T. in ACW 58.19–274.

Council of Chalcedon:

Virtually all documents related to the council in 451 are collected in *ACO* 2; E.T. of the most important documents in TTH 45.

Council of Ephesus:

Virtually all documents related to the twin councils held in Ephesus in 431 are collected in *ACO* 1; E.T. of the most important documents in TTH 72.

Faustus of Riez:

(*De grat.*) *De gratia Dei et libero arbitrio* [*c.*474]; text in CSEL 21.3–98; E.T. of significant excerpts in Thomas A. Smith, De gratia: *Faustus of Riez's Treatise on Grace and Its Place in the History of Theology, passim*. South Bend, IN: University of Notre Dame Press, 1990 [cited in the footnotes as 'Smith']; E.T. of 1.18 in Francis X. Gumerlock, *Fulgentius of Ruspe on the Saving Will of God: The Development of a Sixth-Century African Bishop's Interpretation of 1 Timothy 2:4 During the Semi-Pelagian Controversy*, 152–5. Lewiston, NY: Mellen, 2009 [cited in the footnotes as 'Gumerlock'].

(*De Spir. Sanc.*) *De Spiritu Sancto* [*c.*471]; text in CSEL 21.99–157.

(*Ep. ad Graec.*) *Epistula ad Graecum diaconum* [*c.*440–8]; text in CSEL 21.200–7; E.T. of portions in TTH 30.246–9.

(*Ep. ad Luc.*) *Epistula ad Lucidum* [*c.*472]; text in CSEL 21.161–5; E.T. of portions in TTH 30.249–50.

(*Ep. I ad Rur.*) *Epistula prima ad Ruricium* [*c.*477]; text in CCSL 64.406–8; E.T. in TTH 30.93–6.

Gennadius of Marseilles:

(*De uir. illust.*) *De uiris illustribus* [*c.*495]; text in PL 58.1059–1120; E.T. in *NPNF*[2] 3.385–402.

Innocent I:

(*Ep.*) *Epistulae* 29, 30 [417]; text in PL 20.583–93.

John of Antioch:

(*Ep. ad Nes.*) *Epistula ad Nestorium* [430]; text in *ACO* 1.1.1.93–6; E.T. in TTH 72.176–80.

Irenaeus of Lyons:

(*Adu. haer.*) *Aduersus haereses* [*c.*180]; Lat.V. in SC 100, 153, 211, 264, 294; E.T. in *ANF* 1.315–567.

Leo I:

(*Ep.*) *Epistula* 95 [451]; text in PL 54.942–4; E.T. in *NPNF*[2] 12.70–1.

Leporius:

(*Lib. emend.*) *Libellus emendationis* [*c.*418]; text in CCSL 64.111–23.

Nestorius:

(*Ep. I ad Cael.*) *Epistula prima ad Caelestinum papam* [428]; Lat.V. in *ACO* 1.2.12–14; E.T. in TTH 72.98–100.

(Ep. II ad Cyr.) Epistula altera ad Cyrillum Alexandrinum [430]; text in *ACO* 1.1.1.29–32; E.T. in TTH 72.122–7.

(Ep. ad Ioh.) Epistula ad Iohannem Antiochenum [430]; text in *ACO* 1.4.4–7; E.T. in TTH 72.180–4.

(Lib. Her.) Liber Heraclidis [*c.*450]; Fr.T. of Syr.V. in Nau, F., ed./trans. *Le Livre d'Héraclide de Damas*. Paris: Letouzey at Ané, 1910 [cited in the footnotes as 'Nau']; E.T. of Syr.V. in G. R. Driver and Leonard Hodgson, eds./trans. *The Bazaar of Heracleides*. Oxford: Clarendon Press, 1925 [cited in the footnotes as 'Driver/Hodgson'].

(Ser.) Sermones [428]; fragments of text and Lat.V. in Friedrich Loofs, ed. *Nestoriana: Die Fragmente des Nestorius*, 225–350. Halle: Max Niemeyer, 1905 [cited in the footnotes as 'Loofs'].

Origen:

(De princ.) De principiis [*c.*230]; fragments of text, Lat.V., and E.T. in John Behr, ed./trans. *Origen: On First Principles*. Two Volumes. OECT. Oxford: Oxford University Press, 2017 [cited in the footnotes as 'Behr'].

Prosper of Aquitaine:

(Auctor.) Praeteritorum episcoporum sedis apostolicae auctoritates de gratia Dei et libero uoluntatis arbitrio [probably after 450]; text in PL 51.205–12; E.T. in ACW 32.178–85.

(Chron.) Epitoma Chronicon [c. 455]; text in MGH:AA 9.385–485; E.T. of Prosper's continuation in Alexander Callander Murray, ed./trans. *From Roman to Merovingian Gaul: A Reader*, 62–76. Orchard Park, NY: Broadview Press, 2000 [cited in the footnotes as 'Murray'].

(Con. Collat.) De gratia Dei et libero arbitrio liber contra Collatorem [*c.*432]; text in PL 51.213–76; E.T. in ACW 32.70–138.

(De uoc.) De uocatione omnium gentium [*c.*450]; text in CSEL 97.79–199; E.T. in ACW 14.26–153.

(Ep. ad Aug.) Epistula ad Augustinum [*c.*428]; text in CSEL 57. 454–68; E.T. in ACW 32.38–48.

(Ep. ad Ruf.) Epistula ad Rufinum [*c.*428]; text in PL 51.77–90; E.T. in ACW 32.21–37.

(Epitaph.) Epitaphium Nestorianae et Pelagianae haereseon [*c.*432]; text in PL 51.153–4.

(De prouid. Dei) De prouidentia Dei [*c.*416]; text and E.T. in SVigChr 10.4–67.

(Resp. excerp. Gen.) Pro Augustino responsiones ad excerpta Genuensium [*c.*430]; text in PL 51.187–202; E.T. in ACW 32.49–69.

(Resp. obiect. Gall.) Pro Augustino responsiones ad capitula obiectionum Gallorum calumniantium [*c.*434]; text in PL 51.155–74; E.T. in ACW 32.139–62.

(Resp. obiect. Vincent.) Pro Augustino responsiones ad capitula obiectionum Vincentianarum [*c.*434]; text in PL 51.177–86; E.T. in ACW 32.163–77.

Tertullian:

(Adu. Prax.) Aduersus Praxean [*c.*200]; text in CSEL 47.227–89; E.T. in *ANF* 3.597–628.

Theodore of Mopsuestia:

(De incar.) De incarnatione [*c.*392]; fragments of text, Lat.V., and Syr.V. in H. B. Swete, ed. *Theodori Episcopi Mopsuesteni in epistolas b. Pauli Commentarii: The Latin Version with the Greek Fragments. Vol. 2: 1 Thessalonians — Philemon, Appendices, Indices*, 290–312. Cambridge: Cambridge University Press, 1882 [cited in the footnotes as 'Swete'].

(Hom. cat.) Homiliae Catecheticae [before 392]; Syr.V. and Fr.T. in Raymond Tonneau and Robert Devreesse., eds./trans. *Les homélies catéchétiques de Théodore de Mopsueste. Réproduction phototypique du ms. Mingana Syr. 561*. Vatican City: Biblioteca Apostolica Vaticana, 1949 [cited in the footnotes as 'Tonneau/Devreese']; E.T. of Syr.V. in *WS* 5, 6.

210   BIBLIOGRAPHY

Vidal and Tonancio:

(*Ep. Vit. Const.*) *Epistula seruorum dei Vitalis et Constantii Spanorum ad S. Capreolum episcopum catholicae Carthaginis* [*c*.431]; text in PL 53.847–9.

Vincent of Lérins:

(*Comm.*) *Tractatus peregrini fidei antiquitate et uniuersitate aduersus profanas omnium haereticorum nouitates* [434]; text in CCSL 64.147–95; E.T. in FC 7.267–332.

(*Excerp.*) *Excerpta Vincentii Lirinensis ex uniuerso beatae recordationis Augustini Episcopi in unum collecta* [*c*.434–40]; text in CCSL 64.199–231.

Another Vincent??

(*Obiect. Vincent.*) *Obiectiones Vincentianae* [*c*.434]; survives only in Prosper's *Resp. obiect. Vincent.*; text in PL 51.177–86; E.T. in ACW 32.163–77.

Section 2: Secondary Literature

Amann, Émile. 'L'affaire Nestorius vue de Rome', *RevSR* 23 (1949): 5–37, 207–44; 24 (1950): 28–52, 235–65.

Amann, Émile. 'Léporius', *DTC* 9/1 (1926): 434–40.

Amann, Émile. 'Nestorius et sa doctrine', *DTC* 11/1 (1931): 76–157.

Amann, Émile. 'Semi-Pélagiens', *DTC* 14/2 (1939): 1796–1850.

Azkoul, Michael. 'Peccatum originale: The Pelagian Controversy', *The Patristic and Byzantine Review* 3 (1984): 39–53.

Backus, Irena and Aza Goudriaan. '"Semipelagianism": The Origins of the Term and its Passage into the History of Heresy', *JEH* 65 (2014): 25–46.

Barcellona, Rossana. *Fausto di Riez interprete del suo tempo: un vescovo tardoantico dentro la crisi dell'impero.* Soveria Mannelli, Italy: Rubbettino, 2006.

Bartelink, Gerard. 'Die Invektiven gegen Nestorius und seine Häresie in Cassianus' *De Incarnatione*'. In *Heretics and Heresies in the Ancient Church and in Eastern Christianity: Studies in Honour of Adelbert Davids*, ed. Joseph Berheyden and Herman Teule, Eastern Christian Studies 10, 275–91. Leuven: Peeters, 2011.

Bevan, George A. 'Augustine and the Western Dimension of the Nestorian Controversy', *StPatr* 49 (2010): 347–52.

Bevan, George A. *The New Judas: The Case of Nestorius in Ecclesiastical Politics, 428–451 CE.* Leuven: Peeters, 2016.

Bonner, Gerald. 'A Last Apology for Pelagianism?' *StPatr* 49 (2010): 325–8.

Brand, Charles. 'Le *De Incarnatione Domini* de Jean Cassien: Contribution à l'étude de la christologie en Occident à la vielle du concile d'Éphèse', Ph.D. Dissertation, Université de Strasbourg, 1954.

Brunetière, Ferdinand, and Pierre de Labriolle, eds./trans. *Saint Vincent de Lérins.* La Pensée Chrétienne: Textes et Études. Paris: Librarie Bloud, 1906.

Cameron, Michael. 'Transfiguration: Christology and the Roots of Figurative Exegesis in St. Augustine', *StPatr* 30 (1996): 40–7.

Cappuyns, M. 'L'auteur du "De vocatione omnium gentium"', *Revue Benedictine* 39 (1927): 198–226.

Cappuyns, M. 'Le premier représentant de l'augustinisme médiéval, Prosper d'Aquitaine', *RTAM* 1 (1929): 309–37.

Casiday, Augustine. 'Cassian, Augustine, and *De Incarnatione*', *StPatr* 34 (2001): 41–7.

Casiday, Augustine. 'Grace and the Humanity of Christ according to St. Vincent of Lérins', *VigChr* 59 (2005): 298–314.

Casiday, Augustine. 'Prosper the Controversialist', *StPatr* 49 (2010): 369–80.

Casiday, Augustine. 'Rehabilitating John Cassian: An Evaluation of Prosper of Aquitaine's Polemic against the "Semipelagians"', *SJT* 58 (2005): 270–84.

BIBLIOGRAPHY 211

Casiday, Augustine. Review of Panagiotes Tzamalikos, *The Real Cassian Revisited: Monastic Life, Greek Paideia, and Origenism in the Sixth Century*. SVigChr 112. Leiden: Brill, 2012, *The Journal of Medieval Monastic Studies* 3 (2014): 119–25.

Casiday, Augustine. *Tradition and Theology in St John Cassian*. OECS. Oxford: Oxford University Press, 2007.

Casiday, Augustine. 'Vincent of Lérins's *Commonitorium, Objectiones,* and *Excerpta*: Responding to Augustine's Legacy in Fifth-Century Gaul'. In *Grace for Grace: The Debates after Augustine and Pelagius*, ed. Alexander Hwang et al., 131–54. Washington, DC: The Catholic University of America Press, 2014.

'Cassianus 1'. In *PCBE* 4 (2013): 430–7.

Chadwick, Owen. 'Cassianus, Johannes'. *Theologische Realenzyklopädie* 7 (1981): 650–7.

Chadwick, Owen. 'Euladius of Arles', *JTS* 46 (1945): 200–5.

Chadwick, Owen. *John Cassian: A Study in Primitive Monasticism*. Cambridge: Cambridge University Press, 1st ed. 1950; 2nd edition 1968.

Chéné, Jean. 'Les origines de la controverse semi-pélagienne', *L'année théologique augustinienne* 13 (1953): 56–109.

Chéné, Jean. 'Que signifiaient *initium fidei* et *affectus credulitatis* pour les Semipélagiens?' *RechSR* 35 (1948): 566–88.

Chéné, Jean. 'Le semipélagianisme du midi de la Gaule d'après les lettres de Prosper d'Aquitaine et d'Hilaire à saint Augustin', *RechSR* 43 (1955): 321–41.

Chitescu, N. 'Saint Jean Cassien a-t-il été semi-Pelagien?' In *Aksum—Thyateira: A Festschrift for Archbishop Methodios of Thyateira and Great Britain*, ed. G. D. Dragas, 579–89. London: Thyateira House, 1985.

Chitty, Derwas J. *The Desert a City: An Introduction to the Study of Egyptian and Palestinian Monasticism under the Christian Empire*. Oxford: Basil Blackwell & Mott, 1966.

Christophe, Paul. *Cassien et Césaire: Prédicateurs de la morale monastique*. Recherches et synthèses: Section de morale 2. Paris: Éditions J. Duculot, 1969.

Codina, Victor. *El aspecto christológico en la espiritualidad de Juan Cassiano*. Orientalia Christiana Analecta 175. Rome: Pontificum Institutum Orientalium Studiorum, 1966.

Collinge, William J. Introduction to *Saint Augustine: Four Anti-Pelagian Writings*, trans. John A. Mourant and William J. Collinge. FC 86.3–21, 93–110, 181–217. Washington, DC: The Catholic University of America Press, 1992.

Cristiani, Léon. *Jean Cassien: La spiritualité du désert*. 2 vols. Abbaye S. Wandrille: Éditions de Fontenelle, 1946.

Daley, Brian E. *God Visible: Patristic Christology Reconsidered*. Changing Paradigms in Historical and Systematic Theology. Oxford: Oxford University Press, 2018.

De Beer, Francis. 'Une tessère d'orthodoxie. Le "Libellus Emendationis" de Leporius (vers 418–421)', *REAug* 10 (1964): 145–85.

De Letter, P. Introduction to *Prosper of Aquitaine: Defense of St. Augustine*. ACW 32.3–20. New York: Newman Press, 1963.

De Letter, P. Introduction to *St. Prosper of Aquitaine: The Call of All Nations*. ACW 14.3–20. New York: Newman Press, 1954.

de Vogüé, Adalbert. 'Monachisme et Église dans la pensée de Cassien'. In *Théologie de la vie monastique: Études sur la Tradition patristique*, 213–40. Théologie 49. Aubier: Éditions Montaigne, 1961.

de Vogüé, Adalbert. 'Pour comprendre Cassien: Un survol des *Conférences*', *CCist* 39 (1977): 250–72. [E.T. by John-Baptist Hasbrouck, 'Understanding Cassian: A Survey of the Conferences'. *CistS* 19 (1984): 101–21.]

Delmulle, Jérémy. '*Gratia Adami, gratia Christi*: La nature, le Loi et la grâce dans le premier Augustinism', *Revue de l'histoire des religions* 229 (2012): 193–214.

Delmulle, Jérémy. *Prosper d'Aquitaine contre Jean Cassien: Le* Contra Collatorem, L'Appel à Rome du parti Augustinien dans la querelle postpélagienne. Textes et Études du Moyen Âge 91. Rome: Fédération Internationale des Instituts d'Études Médiévales, 2018.

212   BIBLIOGRAPHY

Delmulle, Jérémy. 'Prosper d'Aquitaine, poète de l'antinestorianisme triomphant? À propos de trois poèmes épigraphiques romains'. In Nihil veritas erubescit: Melanges offerts à Paul Mattei par ses élèves, collègues et amis, ed. Clémentine Bernard-Valette et al., 539–56, Instrumenta Patristica et Mediaevalia. Turnhout: Brepols, 2017.

Demeulenaere, Roland. Preface to 'Leporii, Libellus emendationis', CCSL 64.97–108. Turnhout: 1964.

Demeulenaere, Roland. Preface to 'Vincentii Lerinensis, Commonitorium; Excerpta', CCSL 64.127–44. Turnhout: 1964.

Devreese, Robert. Essai sur Théodore de Mopsueste. Vatican City: Biblioteca Apostolica Vaticana, 1948.

Dewart. See McWilliam.

Diepen, H. M. 'L'Assumptus Homo patristique', Revue Thomiste 63 (1963): 225–45, 363–88; 64 (1964): 33–52, 365–86.

Djuth, Marianne. 'Defending Augustine: How Augustinian is Faustus of Riez' De Gratia?' StPatr 128 (2021): 413–24.

Djuth, Marianne. 'Faustus of Riez: Initium bonae voluntatis', AugSt 21 (1990): 35–53.

Djuth, Marianne. 'Faustus of Riez and the Royal Way', AugSt 22 (1991): 207–16.

Djuth, Marianne. 'Ordering Images: The Rhetorical Imagination and Augustine's Anti-Pelagian Polemic after 418', StPatr 43 (2006): 81–8.

Djuth, Marianne. 'The Royal Way: Augustine's Freedom of the Will and the Monastic Tradition'. In Augustine: Biblical Exegete, ed. Frederick Van Fleteren and Joseph C. Schnaubelt, 129–43. New York: Peter Lang, 2001.

Dodaro, Robert. 'Sacramentum Christi: Augustine on the Christology of Pelagius', StPatr 27 (1993): 274–80.

Dorner, A. Augustinus, Sein theologisches System und seine religionsphilosophische Anschauung. Berlin: Verlag von Wilhelm Hertz, 1873.

Driver, Steven D. John Cassian and the Reading of Egyptian Monastic Culture. Studies in Medieval History and Culture. London: Routledge, 2002.

Engelbrecht, Augustus. Prolegomena to 'Fausti Reiensis praeter Sermones Pseudo-Eusebianos Opera accedunt Ruricii Epistulae'. In CSEL 21.v–lxxx. Vienna: F. Tempsky, 1891.

Fairbairn, Donald. 'Allies or Merely Friends? John of Antioch and Nestorius in the Christological Controversy', JEH 58 (2007): 383–99.

Fairbairn, Donald. Grace and Christology in the Early Church. OECS. Oxford: Oxford University Press, 2003.

Fairbairn, Donald. 'Interpreting Conciliar Christology: An Overview in the Service of Analytic Theology', Journal of Analytic Theology 10 (2022): 363–81.

'Faustus 1'. In PCBE 4 (2013): 734–44.

Ferreiro, Alberto. 'Simon Magus and Priscillian in the Commonitorium of Vincent of Lérins', VigChr 49 (1995): 180–8.

Fick, Rikus. 'Die Intensiteit van die Semi-Pelagiaanse stryd in die Galliese Kerk van die vyfde en sesde eeu', In die Skriflig/In Luce Verbi 41 (2007): 601–15.

Gaddis, Michael. General Introduction to The Acts of the Council of Chalcedon: Volume 1. In TTH 45, 1–56. Liverpool: Liverpool University Press, 2005.

Gaidioz, J. 'S. Prosper d'Aquitaine et le Tome à Flavien', RevSR 23 (1949): 270–301.

Gibson, Edgar C. S. Prolegomena to 'The Works of John Cassian'. In NPNF² 11.183–97, 1894.

Glorieux, Palémon. Prenestorianisme en Occident. Monumenta Christiana Selecta 6. Tournai: Desclée, 1959.

Godet, P. 'Cassien, Jean', DTC 2/1 (1910): 1823–29.

Godet, P. 'Fauste de Riez', DTC 5/1 (1913): 2101–05.

González, Justo L. A History of Christian Thought. Vol. 2: From Augustine to the Eve of the Reformation. Nashville: Abingdon, 1971.

Goodrich, Richard J. Contextualizing Cassian: Aristocrats, Asceticism, and Reformation in Fifth-Century Gaul. OECS. Oxford: Oxford University Press, 2007.

BIBLIOGRAPHY 213

Graumann, Thomas. 'Towards the Reception of the Council of Ephesus (431): Public Sentiment and Early Theological Responses', *StPatr* 45 (2010): 147–62.

Green, Bernard. 'Leo the Great and the Heresy of Nestorius', *StPatr* 43 (2006): 373–80.

Green, Bernard. *The Soteriology of Leo the Great*. OTM. Oxford: Oxford University Press, 2008.

Greer, Rowan A. 'The Analogy of Grace in Theodore of Mopsuestia's Christology', *Journal of Theological Studies*, n.s., 34 (1983): 82–98.

Greer, Rowan A. *Theodore of Mopsuestia: Exegete and Theologian*. Leighton Buzzard: Faith Press, 1961.

Grillmeier, Aloys. *Christ in Christian Tradition. Vol. 1: From the Apostolic Age to Chalcedon (451)*. Trans. John Bowden. London: A.W. Mowbray & Co, 1965. Rev. ed. 1975.

Guarino, Thomas G. 'Tradition and Doctrinal Development: Can Vincent of Lérins still Teach the Church?' *TS* 67 (2006): 34–72.

Guarino, Thomas G. *Vincent of Lérins and the Development of Christian Doctrine*. Foundations of Theological Exegesis and Christian Spirituality. Grand Rapids, MI: Baker Academic, 2013.

Guarino, Thomas G. 'Vincent of Lérins and the Hermeneutical Question: Historical and Theological Reflections', *Gregorianum* 75 (1994): 491–523.

Gumerlock, Francis X. *Fulgentius of Ruspe on the Saving Will of God: The Development of a Sixth-Century African Bishop's Interpretation of 1 Timothy 2:4 During the Semi-Pelagian Controversy*. Lewiston, NY: Mellen, 2009.

Guy, Jean-Claude. 'Jean Cassien, historien du monachisme égyptien?' *StPatr* 8 (1966): 363–72.

Guy, Jean-Claude. *Jean Cassien: Vie et doctrine spirituelle*. Théologie, pastorale et spiritualité: Recherches et syntheses 9. Paris: P. Lethielleux, 1961.

Harnack, Adolf von. *History of Dogma*. Vol. 5. Trans. from vol. 3 of the 3d German edition by J. Millar. London: Williams & Norgate, 1898. Reprint, New York: Russell & Russell, 1958. (German 1st edition, *Lehrbuch der Dogmengeschichte*, vol. 3, 1889. German 3d edition, vol. 3, 1897.)

Harper, James. 'John Cassian and Sulpicius Severus', *Church History* 34 (1965): 371–80.

Hay, Camillus. 'Antiochene Exegesis and Christology', *Australian Biblical Review* 12 (1964): 10–23.

Hoch, Alexander. *Lehre des Joannes Cassianus von Natur und Gnade: Ein Beitrag zur Geschichte des Gnadenstreits im 5. Jahrundert*. Freiburg: Herder'sche Verlagshandlung, 1895.

Holze, Heinrich. 'Die Bedeutung der *experientia* in der monastischen Theologie Johannes Cassians', *StPatr* 20 (1989): 256–63.

Holze, Heinrich. *Erfahrung und Theologie im frühen Mönchtum: Untersuchungen zu einer Theologie des monastischen Lebens bei den ägyptischen Mönchsvätern, Johannes Cassian, und Benedikt von Nursia*. Göttingen: Vandenhoeck & Ruprecht, 1992.

Humphries, Thomas L., Jr. *Ascetic Pneumatology from John Cassian to Gregory the Great*. OECS. Oxford: Oxford University Press, 2013.

Humphries, Thomas L., Jr. 'Prosper's Pneumatology: The Development of an Augustinian'. In *Grace for Grace: The Debates after Augustine and Pelagius*, ed. Alexander Hwang et al., 91–113. Washington, DC: The Catholic University of America Press, 2014.

Hwang, Alexander Y. *Intrepid Lover of Perfect Grace: The Life and Thought of Prosper of Aquitaine*. Washington, DC: The Catholic University of America Press, 2009.

Hwang, Alexander Y. 'Manifold Grace in John Cassian and Prosper of Aquitaine', *SJT* 63 (2010): 93–108.

Hwang, Alexander Y. '*Pauci Perfectae Gratiae Intrepidi Amatores*: The Augustinians in Marseilles'. In *Grace for Grace: The Debates after Augustine and Pelagius*, ed. Alexander Hwang et al., 35–50. Washington, DC: The Catholic University of America Press, 2014.

Hwang, Alexander Y. 'Prosper, Cassian, and Vincent: The Rule of Faith in the Augustinian Controversy'. In *Tradition and the Rule of Faith in the Early Church: Essays in Honor of Joseph T. Lienhard, S.J.*, eds. Ronnie J. Rombs and Alexander Y. Hwang, 68–85. Washington, DC: The Catholic University of America Press, 2011.

Jacquin, Mannes. 'À quelle date apparaît le term "semi-pélagien"?' *Revue des sciences philosophiques et théologiques* 1 (1907): 506–8.

214   BIBLIOGRAPHY

James, Norman W. 'Leo the Great and Prosper of Aquitaine: A Fifth Century Pope and His Adviser', *JTS*, n.s., 44 (1993): 554–84.

James, Norman W. 'Prosper of Aquitaine Revisited: Gallic Friend of Leo I or Resident Papal Adviser?' *StPatr* 69 (2013): 267–75.

Jaros, T. Kurt. 'The Relationship of the So-Called Semi-Pelagians and Eastern Greek Theology on the Doctrine of Original Sin: An Historical-Systematic Analysis and its Relevance for 21st Century Protestantism'. Ph.D. Dissertation, University of Aberdeen, 2020.

Jugie, Martin. *Nestorius et la controverse nestorienne*. Bibliothèque de théologie historique. Paris: Beauchesne, 1912.

Kavvadas, Nestor. 'An Eastern View: Theodore of Mopsuestia's *Against the Defenders of Original Sin*'. In *Grace for Grace: The Debates after Augustine and Pelagius*, ed. Alexander Hwang et al., 271–93. Washington, DC: The Catholic University of America Press, 2014.

Keech, Dominic. *The Anti-Pelagian Christology of Augustine of Hippo, 396-430*. OTM. Oxford: Oxford University Press, 2012.

Keech, Dominic. 'John Cassian and the Christology of Romans 8,3', *VigChr* 64 (2010): 280–99.

Kelly, John N. D. *Early Christian Creeds*. 3rd ed. London: Longmans, 1972.

Kelly, John N. D. *The Athanasian Creed*. New York: Harper & Row, 1964.

Kemmer, Alfons. *Charisma maximum: Untersuchungen zu Cassians Vollkommenheitslehre und seiner Stellung zum Messalianismus*. Louvain: Druckerie Fr. Ceuterick, 1938.

Koch, Hugo. 'Vincenz von Lerin und Gennadius: Ein Beitrage zur Lteraturegeschichte des Semipelagianismus', TU 31.2 (1907): 37–58.

Krannich, Torsten. *Von Leporius bis zu Leo dem Großen: Studien zur lateinischsprachigen Christologie im Fünften Jahrhundert nach Christus*. Studien und Texte zu Antike und Christentum 32. Tübingen: Mohr Siebeck, 2005.

Kuhlmann, Karl-Heinz. 'Eine Dogmengeschichtliche Neubewertung von Johannes Cassianus *De incarnatione Domini contra Nestorium libri 7*'. Th.D. Dissertation, University of South Africa, 1983.

Lam, Joseph Cong Quy. 'Revelation, Christology and Grace in Augustine's Anti-Manichean and Anti-Pelagian Controversies', *Phronema* 28 (2013): 131–49.

Lamberigts, Mathijs. 'Competing Christologies: Julian and Augustine on Jesus Christ', *AugSt* 36 (2005): 159–94.

Laporte, Jean. 'La grâce chez Augustin et dans l'Augustinisme', *Laval Théologique et Philosophique* 55 (1999): 425–44.

Laugier, Joseph. *Saint Jean Cassien et sa doctrine sur la grâce*. Lyons: Imprimerie Emmanuel Vitte, 1908.

'Leporius.' In *PCBE* 4 (2013): 1150-1.

Loofs, Friedrich. *Nestorius and His Place in the History of Christian Doctrine*. Cambridge: University Press, 1914. (Reprint, New York: Burt Franklin Reprints, 1975.)

Louth, Andrew. 'Messalianism and Pelagianism', *StPat* 17 (1982): 127–35.

McGuckin, John A. 'Did Augustine's Christology Depend on Theodore of Mopsuestia?' *The Heythrop Journal* 31 (1990): 39–52.

McWilliam (Dewart), Joanne. 'The Christology of the Pelagian Controversy', *StPatr* 17 (1982): 1221–44.

McWilliam (Dewart), Joanne. 'The Influence of Theodore of Mopsuestia on Augustine's *Letter 187*', *AugSt* 10 (1979): 113–32.

McWilliam (Dewart), Joanne. 'The Notion of "Person" Underlying the Christology of Theodore of Mopsuestia', *StPatr* 12 (1975): 199–207.

McWilliam (Dewart), Joanne. 'The Study of Augustine's Christology in the Twentieth Century'. In *Augustine: from Rhetor to Theologian*, ed. Joanne McWilliam, 183–205. Waterloo, ON: Wilfrid Laurier University Press, 1992.

McGuckin, John A. 'Did Augustine's Christology Depend on Theodore of Mopsuestia?' *The Heythrop Journal* 31 (1990): 39–52.

McWilliam (Dewart), Joanne. 'The Christology of the Pelagian Controversy', *StPatr* 17 (1982): 1221–44.

BIBLIOGRAPHY 215

McWilliam (Dewart), Joanne. 'The Influence of Theodore of Mopsuestia on Augustine's *Letter 187*, *AugSt* 10 (1979): 113–32.

McWilliam (Dewart), Joanne. 'The Notion of "Person" Underlying the Christology of Theodore of Mopsuestia', *StPatr* 12 (1975): 199–207.

McWilliam (Dewart), Joanne. 'The Study of Augustine's Christology in the Twentieth Century'. In *Augustine: from Rhetor to Theologian*, ed. Joanne McWilliam, 183–205. Waterloo, ON: Wilfrid Laurier University Press, 1992.

Madoz y Moleres, José. 'Un tratado desconocido de San Vicente de Lerins', *Gregorianum* 21 (1940): 75–94.

Maier, Jean-Louis. 'La Date de la rétractation de Leporius et Celle du "Sermon 396" de Saint Augustin', *REAug* 11 (1965): 39–42.

Malavasi, Giulio. 'The Involvement of Theodore of Mopsuestia in the Pelagian Controversy: A Study of Theodore's Treatise *Against Those who Say that Men Sin by Nature and not by Will*', *Augustiniana* 64 (2014): 227–60.

Markus, Robert A. 'Chronicle and Theology: Prosper of Aquitaine'. In *The Inheritance of Historiography 350-900*, ed. Christopher Holdsworthy and T. P. Wisemen, 31–43. Exeter: Exeter University Press, 1986.

Markus, Robert A. *The End of Ancient Christianity*. Cambridge: Cambridge University Press, 1990.

Markus, Robert A. 'The Legacy of Pelagius: Orthodoxy, Heresy and Conciliation'. In *The Making of Orthodoxy: Essays in Honour of Henry Chadwick*, ed. Rowan Williams, 214–34. Cambridge: Cambridge University Press, 1989.

Marín, Raúl Villegas. 'Asceticism and Exegetical Authority in John Cassian's *Conference 23*', *ETL* 93/4 (2017): 671–84.

Marín, Raúl Villegas. '*Auersi texerunt eum*: la crítica a Agustín y a los agustinianos sudgálicos en el *Commonitorium* de Vicente de Lérins', *Augustinianum* 46 (2006): 481–528.

Marín, Raúl Villegas. 'Fausto de Riez y la soteriología "misericordiosa": Otodoxia, gracia sacramental y responsabilidad ética del Cristiano en tiempos de la campana antinicena de Eurico (*c.*470)', *Sacris Eruditi* 53 (2014): 171–208.

Marín, Raúl Villegas. 'Fieles *sub Lege*, fieles *sub gratia*: eclesiología y teología de la gracia en Juan Casiano', *Augustinianum* 53 (2013), 139–93.

Marín, Raúl Villegas. 'Lucidus on Predestination: The Damnation of Augustine's Predestinationism in the Synods of Arles (473) and Lyons (474)', *StPatr* 45 (2010): 163–7.

Marín, Raúl Villegas. 'Prosper's 'Crypto-Pelagians': *De ingratis* and the *Carmen de prouidentia Dei*', trans. Gerardo Rodríquez-Galarza. In *Grace for Grace: The Debates after Augustine and Pelagius*, ed. Alexander Hwang et al., 51–71. Washington, DC: The Catholic University of America Press, 2014.

Marrou, Henri Irénée. 'Jean Cassien à Marseille', *Revue du moyen âge latin* 1 (1945): 5–26.

Mathisen, Ralph W. 'Caesarius of Arles, Prevenient Grace, and the Second Council of Orange'. In *Grace for Grace: The Debates after Augustine and Pelagius*, ed. Alexander Hwang et al., 208–34. Washington, DC: The Catholic University of America Press, 2014.

Mathisen, Ralph W. *Ecclesiastical Factionalism and Religious Controversy in Fifth-Century Gaul*. Washington, DC: The Catholic University of America Press, 1989.

Mathisen, Ralph W. Introduction and Notes to *Ruricius of Limoges and Friends: A Collection of Letters from Visigothic Gaul*. Trans. Ralph Mathisen. TTH 30. Liverpool: Liverpool University Press, 1999.

Mattei, Paul. 'Le Fantôme Semi-Pélagien: Lecture du Traité *De Gratia* de Fauste de Riez', *Augustiniana* 60 (2010): 87–117.

Maxwell, David R. 'Christology and Grace in the Sixth-Century Latin West: The Theopaschite Controversy'. Ph.D. Dissertation, University of Notre Dame, 2003.

Maxwell, David R. 'The Christological Coherence of Cassian's *On the Incarnation of the Lord*', *StPatr* 43 (2006): 429–33.

Maxwell, David R. 'Crucified in the Flesh: Christological Confession or Evasive Qualification?' *ProEccl* 13 (2004): 70–81.

216   BIBLIOGRAPHY

Maxwell, David R. 'What Was 'Wrong' with Augustine? The Sixth-Century Reception (or Lack Thereof) of Augustine's Christology'. In *In the Shadow of the Incarnation: Essays on Jesus Christ in the Early Church in Honor of Brian E. Daley, S.J.*, 212–227. Notre Dame, IN: University of Notre Dame Press, 2008.

Morel, Bruno. 'De Invloed van Leporius op Cassianus' Weerlegging van het Nestorianisme', *Bijdragen* 21 (1960): 31–52.

Newton, John Thomas, Jr. 'The Importance of Augustine's Use of the Neoplatonic Doctrine of Hypostatic Union for the Development of Christology', *AugSt* 2 (1971): 1–16.

Norris, Richard A., Jr. *Manhood and Christ: A Study in the Christology of Theodore of Mopsuestia.* Oxford: Clarendon Press, 1963.

O'Connor, William. 'Saint Vincent of Lérins and Saint Augustine: Was the *Commonitorium* of Saint Vincent of Lérins Intended as a Polemic against Saint Augustine and his Doctrine on Predestination?' *Doctor Communis* 16 (1963): 125–257.

Ogliari, Donato. *Gratia et Certamen: The Relationship Between Grace and Free Will in the Discussion of Augustine with the So-Called Semipelagians.* Leuven: Leuven University Press, 2003.

Ogliari, Donato. 'The Role of Christ and of the Church in the Light of Augustine's Theory of Predestination', *ETL* 79 (2003): 347–64.

O'Keefe, John J. 'Impassible Suffering? Divine Passion and Fifth-Century Christology', *TS* 58 (1997): 38–60.

O'Keeffe, Dunstan. 'The *Via Media* of Monastic Theology: The Debate on Grace and Free Will in Fifth-Century Southern Gaul', *DR* 112 (1994): 264–83; 113 (1995): 54–73.

Olphe-Galliard, Michel. 'Débat à propos de Cassien.' *RAM* 17 (1936): 181–91.

Olphe-Galliard, Michel. 'La purité de coeur d'après Cassien', *RAM* 17 (1936): 28–60.

Olphe-Galliard, Michel. 'La science spirituelle d'après Cassien', *RAM* 18 (1937): 141–60.

Olphe-Galliard, Michel. 'Vie contemplative et vie active d'après Cassien', *RAM* 16 (1935): 252–88.

Pelikan, Jaroslav. *The Christian Tradition: A History of the Development of Doctrine. Vol. 1: The Emergence of the Catholic Tradition (100-600).* Chicago: University of Chicago Press, 1971.

Pereira, Matthew J. 'Augustine, Pelagius, and the Southern Gallic Tradition'. In *Grace for Grace: The Debates after Augustine and Pelagius*, ed. Alexander Hwang et al., 180–207. Washington, DC: The Catholic University of America Press, 2014.

Pereira, Matthew J. 'From Augustine to the Scythian Monks: Social Memory and the Doctrine of Predestination', *StPatr* 70 (2013): 671–83.

Pierce, Alexander H. 'At the Crossroads of Christology and Grace: Augustine on the Union of *Homo* and *Verbum* in Christ (*c.*411–430)', *Augustinianum* 60 (2020): 453–77.

Pinheiro-Jones, Rossana. 'Em torno do conceito de heresia: o caso de João Cassiano (Provença, Século V)', *Antíteses* 10 (2017): 1041–62.

Plagnieux, Jean. 'Le grief de complicité entre erreurs nestorienne et pélagienne: d'Augustin à Cassien par Prosper d'Aquitaine?' *REAug* 2 (1956): 391–402.

Portalié, Eugène. *A Guide to the Thought of Saint Augustine.* Trans. Ralph J. Bastian. Library of Living Catholic Thought. Chicago: Henry Regnery Company, 1960.

Portalié, Eugène. 'Augustin (Saint)', *DTC* 1/2 (1909): 2268–472.

Price, Richard, and Michael Gaddis, eds./trans. *The Acts of the Council of Chalcedon.* Three Volumes. TTH 45. Liverpool: Liverpool University Press, 2005.

Price, Richard, and Thomas Graumann, eds./trans. *The Council of Ephesus of 431: Documents and Proceedings.* TTH 72. Liverpool: Liverpool University Press, 2020.

Pristas, Lauren. 'The Theological Anthropology of John Cassian', Ph.D. Dissertation, Boston College, 1993.

Pristas, Lauren. 'The Unity of Composition in Book V of Cassian's *De institutis*', *StPatr* 25 (1993): 438–43.

'Prosper 1'. In *PCBE* 4 (2013): 1553–6.

Ramsey, Boniface. Introduction to *John Cassian: The Conferences.* ACW 57.5–24. New York: Newman Press, 1997.

BIBLIOGRAPHY   217

Ramsey, Boniface. 'John Cassian and Augustine'. In *Grace for Grace: The Debates after Augustine and Pelagius*, ed. Alexander Hwang et al., 114–30. Washington, DC: The Catholic University of America Press, 2014.

Rea, Robert F. 'Grace and Free Will in John Cassian', Ph.D. Dissertation, St. Louis University, 1990.

Rémy, Gérard. 'La christologie d'Augustin: cas d'ambiguïté', *RechSR* 96 (2008): 401–25.

Rivière, Jean. 'Le dogme de la rédemption après Saint Augustin. Première partie: Saint Léon le Grand', *RevSR* 9 (1929): 17–42, 153–87.

Rousseau, Philip. *Ascetics, Authority, and the Church in the Age of Jerome and Cassian.* Oxford: Oxford University Press, 1978.

Sage, Athanase. 'De la grâce du Christ, modèle et principe de la grâce', *REAug* 7 (1961): 17–34.

Salzman, Michelle Renee. 'Reconsidering a Relationship: Pope Leo of Rome and Prosper of Aquitaine'. In *The Bishop of Rome in Late Antiquity*, ed. G. D. Dunn, 109–25. Farnham, UK: Ashgate, 2015.

Schaff, Philip. *History of the Christian Church. Vol. 3: Nicene and Post-Nicene Christianity from Constantine to Gregory the Great, A.D. 311–590.* New York: Charles Scribner's Sons, 1867. (Reprint of 5th edition, revised. Peabody, MA: Hendrickson, 1996.)

Scheel, Otto. *Die Anschauung Augustin über Christi Person und Werk: Unter Bertücksichtigung ihrer verschiedenen Entwicklungsstufen und ihrer dogmengeschichtlichen Stellung.* Tübingen: Drack von H. Laup Jr., 1900.

Schindler, Alfred. 'Gnade und Freiheit: Zum Vergleich zwischen den griechischen und lateinischen Kirchenvätern', *Zeitschrift für Theologie und Kirche* 62:2 (1965): 178–95.

Schwartz, Eduard. *Konzilstudien I: Cassian und Nestorius.* Schriften der Wissenschaftlichen Gesellschaft in Straßburg 20, 1–17. Straßburg: Karl J. Trübner, 1914.

Smith, Mark S. *The Idea of Nicaea in the Early Church Councils, AD 431–451.* OECS. Oxford: Oxford University Press, 2018.

Smith, Peter J. 'John Cassian's Royal Road: Discretion, Balance, and the Tradition of the Fathers', *DR* 139 (2021): 145–53.

Smith, Thomas A. 'Agonism and Antagonism: Metaphor and the Gallic Resistance to Augustine.' *StPatr* 38 (2001): 283–9.

Smith, Thomas A. 'Augustine in Two Gallic Controversies: Use or Abuse?' In *Augustine:* presbyter factus sum, ed. Joseph T. Lienhard et al., 43–55. Collectanea Augustiniana. New York: Peter Lang, 1993.

Smith, Thomas A. De gratia: *Faustus of Riez's Treatise on Grace and Its Place in the History of Theology.* South Bend, IN: University of Notre Dame Press, 1990.

Stewart, Columba. 'Another Cassian?' *JEH* 66 (2015): 372–6.

Stewart, Columba. *Cassian the Monk.* OSHS. Oxford: Oxford University Press, 1998.

Studer, Basil. 'Una Persona in Christo: Ein augustinisches Thema bei Leo dem Grossen', *Augustinianum* 25 (1985): 453–87.

Tzamalikos, Panagiotes. *The Real Cassian Revisited: Monastic Life, Greek Paideia, and Origenism in the Sixth Century.* SVigChr 112. Leiden: Brill, 2012.

Teselle, Eugene. 'The Background: Augustine and the Pelagian Controversy'. In *Grace for Grace: The Debates after Augustine and Pelagius*, ed. Alexander Hwang et al., 1–13. Washington, DC: The Catholic University of America Press, 2014.

Teske, Roland J. '1 Timothy 2:4 and the Beginnings of the Massalian Controversy'. In *Grace for Grace: The Debates after Augustine and Pelagius*, ed. Alexander Hwang et al., 14–34. Washington, DC: The Catholic University of America Press, 2014.

Teske, Roland J. 'The Augustinianism of Prosper of Aquitaine Revisited', *StPatr* 43 (2003): 491–504.

Teske, Roland J., and Dorothea Weber. Introduction to *Prosper: De uocatione omnium gentium.* CSEL 97.9–76. Berlin: De Gruyter, 2009.

Tibiletti, Carlo. 'Libero arbitrio e grazia in Fausto di Riez', *Augustinianum* 19 (1979): 259–85.

Tibiletti, Carlo. 'Fausto di Riez nei giudizi della critica', *Augustinianum* 21 (1981): 567–87.

Trapé, Agustín. 'Un caso de nestorianismo prenestoriano en Occidente resuelto por San Agustín', *CD* 155 (1943): 45–67.

BIBLIOGRAPHY

Tudorie, Ionuț-Alexandru. '*Cassianus, Natione Scytha*: Revisiting an Old Issue', *Revue d'histoire ecclésiastique* 115 (2020): 5–33.

Turner, Henry E. W. *Jesus the Christ*. London: A.W. Mowbray & Co., 1976.

Turner, Philip. 'John Cassian and the Desert Fathers: Sources for Christian Spirituality', *ProEccl* 13 (2004): 466–86.

van Bavel, Tarsicius J. *Recherches sur la christologie de Saint Augustin: L'humain et le divin dans le Christ d'après Saint Augustin*. Paradosis 10. Fribourg: Éditions Universitaires, 1954.

Vannier, Marie-Anne. Introduction to Jean Cassien, *Traité De L'incarnation Contre Nestorius: Introduction, traduction du latin et annotation par Marie-Anne Vannier*, 9–71. Sagesses chrétiennes. Paris: Les Éditions du Cerf, 1999.

Vannier, Marie-Anne. 'Jean Cassien a-t-il fait oeuvre de théologien dans le *De incarnatione Domini*?' *StPatr* 24 (1993): 345–54.

Vega, Angel C. '*Vidal y Tonancio* o un caso de nestorianismo en Espana', *CD* 152 (1936): 412–20.

Verwilghen, Albert. *Christologie et Spiritualité selon Saint Augustin: L'Hymne aux Philippiens*. Théologie historique 72. Paris: Beauchesne, 1985.

'Vincentius 4'. In *PCBE* 4 (2013): 1978–80.

Warfield, Benjamin B. 'Introductory Essay on Augustin and the Pelagian Controversy'. In *Augustin: Anti-Pelagian Writings*. NPNF[1] 5:xiii–lxxi, 1887.

Weaver, Rebecca Harden. *Divine Grace and Human Agency: A Study of the Semi-Pelagian Controversy*. PMS 15. Macon, GA: Mercer University Press, 1996.

Weaver, Rebecca Harden. 'Prosper's Theological Legacy and its Limits', *StPatr* 49 (2010): 381–94.

Weigel, Gustave. *Faustus of Riez: An Historical Introduction*. Philadelphia: Dolphin Press, 1938.

Weijenborg, R. 'Leo der Grosse und Nestorius: Erneuerung der Fragestellung', *Augustinanum* 16 (1976): 353–98.

Westra, Liuwe H. *The Apostles' Creed: Origin, History, and Some Early Commentaries*. Instrumenta patristica et medievalia 43. Turnhout: Brepols, 2002.

Wickham, Lionel R, ed./trans. *Cyril of Alexandria: Select Letters*. OECT. Oxford: Oxford University Press, 1983.

Wickham, Lionel R. 'Pelagianism in the East'. In *The Making of Orthodoxy: Essays in Honour of Henry Chadwick*, ed. Rowan Williams, 200–13. Cambridge: Cambridge University Press, 1989.

Williams, Rowan Douglas. 'Augustine's Christology: Its Spirituality and Rhetoric'. In *In the Shadow of the Incarnation: Essays on Jesus Christ in the Early Church in Honor of Brian E. Daley, S.J.*, 176–89. Notre Dame, IN: University of Notre Dame Press, 2008.

Wilson-Kastner, Patricia. 'Grace as Participation in the Divine Life in the Theology of Augustine of Hippo', *AugSt* 7 (1976): 135–52.

Wisse, Maarten. '"Pro salute nostra reparanda": Radical Orthodoxy's Christology of Manifestation versus Augustine's Moral Christology', *Neue Zeitschrift für Systematische Theologie und Religionsphilosophie* 49 (2008): 349–76.

General Index

For the benefit of digital users, indexed terms that span two pages (e.g., 52–53) may, on occasion, appear on only one of those pages.

Adam/first man
as a type of Christ, 36, 37
original state of, 140–41, 166, 191 *see also* grace
sin of, 9, 24–25, 29, 37, 128, 129, 138, 145–46, 155–56, 166 *see also* original sin
adoption, *see* salvation
Anthropotokos, 127–28
Antiochene Christology, *see* Christology
Apollinaris, 57n.27, 73, 102, 107–10
Arius/Arianism, 10, 73, 100, 107–9, 179, 182, 184–85
Arles, 83–84, 172
ascent, *see* soteriology
Ataulf (king of Gaul), 153
atonement, 141–43, 168, 195–96
Aurelius of Carthage, 49
authorship
of Cassianic corpus, 2n.3
of *De prouid. Dei*, 135n.1
of *De uoc.*, 58
of *Excerp.*, 102–3
of *Lib. emend.*, 49n.4
of *Obiec. Vincent.*, 103–4

balancing emphases
between deity and humanity in Christ, 73, 82, 154, 162–63, 186–87
between divine and human action in salvation, 11–12, 61–62, 68, 85–86, 97–98, 134, 135, 170–71, 173, 199 *see also* freedom; grace; *uia regia*
body
church as Christ's body, *see* church, the
human, 30–34, 35, 75, 118, 126–27, 181–82, 185

Caelestius (follower of Pelagius), 18–19, 107–9, 128, 129, 155–56
Caesarius of Arles, 8–9, 206
Carthage, 49
Council of, *see* Council
Cassian the Sabaite, 2n.3

Celestine (pope), 17–18, 105–6, 156–57, 160
charitology, *see* grace
chastity, 87–88, 91, 93–94, 95–96, 97
Christ
as a collective term, 16–17, 19, 111, 117 *see also* Christology
as an example of grace/predestination, 22, 23, 37, 38, 39–47 *see also* predestination
as an example to Christians, 19, 73–74, 76–83, 205
as head of his body (the church), 35, 44–45, 46–47, 159, 160, 161, 162, 165
Christological controversies, 6–7
Christology
of Augustine, 12, 13, 22–28, 35, 47, 66–67, 98–99, 106–7, 126–27, 133, 177, 178, 202–3
Anti-'Nestorian', 3–4, 21, 100, 109, 162, 168, 202–3
'Antiochene', 4, 10, 16–17, 20, 22–25, 32–34, 35, 66, 126–27, 182–83, 186–87, 199, 202–3
Cyrillian/Chalcedonian, 20, 21, 23–25, 47, 66, 126–27, 131, 155, 186–87, 188–89, 202–3
of divine descent, 12–13, 16, 19, 21, 30, 47–48, 54–55, 56, 61–62, 72–73, 81–82, 88–89, 131–32, 134, 188–89, 194–95, 199, 200–1
of indwelling, 16, 24–25, 27, 50n.6, 65–66, 76–77, 205
Latin, 3–4, 22–23, 31–32, 49–50, 61, 66, 202–3
Origenist, 24–25, 26–27, 35–36
Theodorean/Nestorian, 12, 20, 23–25, 32–34, 35–36, 39–40, 41, 55, 126–27
Christotokos, 17, 109–10, 112
Chrysostom, 70–71, 78, 92
church, the, as the body of Christ, 9, 25–26, 29–30, 44–45, 46–47, 159, 162, 165
Constantinople, 17–19, 22, 69–70, 156, 162, 163–64
consubstantial, 115, 120, 162–63
Council
of Arles (473), 172
of Carthage (418), 6–7, 165
of Chalcedon (451), 20n.77, 164, 177

220 GENERAL INDEX

Council (*cont.*)
  of Constantinople (home synod–448), 163–64
  of Ephesus (431), 12, 17n.71, 18–19, 50n.6, 108, 150–51, 157, 158–59, 160, 162
  of Ephesus (*latrocinium*–449), 162, 163–64
  of Lyons (474), 172
  Second, of Orange (529), 3, 205–6
Creed, the, 16–17, 81–82, 185
  Athanasian Creed, *see Quicunque Vult*
  Creed of Nicaea, 179
  Old Roman/Apostles' Creed, 185n.62
Cyril of Alexandria, 17–19, 20, 156
Cyrillian Christology, *see* Christology

Dardanus (recipient of a letter from Augustine), 33–34, 126–27
degrees of emphasis, *see* freedom; grace
descent, *see* soteriology
desert fathers, 7–8, 86–87
Dioscorus of Alexandria, 163–64

election, 136–37, 139–40, 142–43, 144–45, 146–47, 158–59, 199–200, 205 *see also* predestination
essentia, 119n.71, 193
Eutyches (the person and his actual thought), 150–53, 162–64, 177
'Eutyches'/'Eutychianism' (as understood by the Gallic monks), 21, 162–64, 176–77, 182–83, 199

Fall, the, *see* Adam; original sin
Flavian of Constantinople, 162, 163–64
Florentius of Hippo Diarrhytus, 49, 50–51
foreknowledge, 98–99, 133–34, 138, 139–40, 168–69, 197–98, 199–200
forgiveness, *see* salvation
freedom (human), 42, 98–99, 144, 161, 166, 189–90, 192–95, 197–98, 200
Fulgentius of Ruspe, 2–3, 8–9

Gallicans, 6–7, 8–9, 13, 134, 141, 165, 174, 180–81, 204, 205
Gaul, factional conflict in, 6–7
Gennadius of Marseilles, 49–50, 56–57, 58, 59–60, 66–67, 77, 104–5, 151, 156–57, 176–77, 180–81
grace
  degree of emphasis on, 4–6, 10, 100, 204
  general aspects/effects of, 21, 130, 145, 148–49, 199–200, 203–4, 205
  given to Adam, 40, 42, 174–75
  gratia Redemptoris, 194–95, 200

logic of, 3–4, 21, 47–48, 99, 100, 168–69, 196, 199, 200–1, 203–5, 206 *see also* reasoning
particular aspects/effects of, 13–14, 21, 47–48, 98–99, 142–43, 145, 147–49, 150, 169, 199–200, 205
prevenient, 8–9
prima gratia, 170, 174–75, 188–91, 192–93, 194–95, 196–97, 198, 200–1, 205
priority of, 48, 96–97, 198, 200–1
Theodorean/Nestorian emphases on, 12, 16–17, 35–36
Graecus (recipient of a letter from Faustus), 170–71, 175–78, 180–84, 185

Hadrumetum, monks of, 22, 40
head (of the body/church), *see* Christ
Heros of Arles, 6–7
historia salutis, 13–14, 132–33
Holy Spirit, 16, 37, 62–65, 76n.31, 76–77, 78–79, 114, 145–46, 150, 178, 186n.65, 192
home synod, *see* Council
homo (in reference to Christ)
  as a quasi-independent man, 22–23, 26, 29–30, 32–33, 34–36, 37, 38–40, 41, 45–46, 53, 59, 61, 63, 116, 122, 123, 126–28, 133, 181–83, 186, 199, 202–3
  as Christ's human nature, 22–23, 27–28, 30, 32–33, 38–39, 44, 62, 126–27, 131–33, 141–42, 153, 182–83, 186
  as the Word considered as a man (*qua homo*), 27–28, 38–39, 41, 43, 44–45, 47, 64, 79, 121, 126–28, 131–32, 182–83, 186, 199
homo assumptus, 16–17, 25, 26, 27–28, 30–31, 37, 66, 71, 72, 76, 77–78, 79, 81–82, 110, 111, 116, 117, 121, 122, 131–32, 156–57, 162, 199

initium bonae uoluntatis, 86–87, 91, 189–90
Innocent I (pope), 165–66
Italy/Italian, 2–3, 6–7

John of Antioch, 18–19, 74
John Chrysostom, *see* Chrysostom
Julian of Eclanum (follower of Pelagius), 108

latrocinium, *see* Council
Laurentius (recipient of Augustine's *Enchir.*), 37
Lazarus of Aix, 6–7
Leo (pope), 149, 150, 151–53, 163–64, 165
Lérins
  Faustus as abbot of, 170–71, 175
  monastery of, 84, 102, 173, 179, 204
  Vincent as abbot of, 102, 179
Lucidus (recipient of a letter from Faustus), 171, 172

GENERAL INDEX   221

Marcian (emperor), 164
Marius Mercator, 15–16
Marseilles
  Cassian as abbot of, 51, 204
  monastery of, 48, 51, 53–54, 67, 204
Mary, *see* Mother of God; *Theotokos*
merit
  no preceding merits of Christ (as basis for
    Christological union), 39–40, 47
  no preceding merits of humans (as basis for
    salvation), 27, 35–36, 39–40, 42, 47, 126–27,
    198, 205
Mother of God, 74, 109–10, 178–79, 185–86 *see
  also Theotokos*

natura, see also substantia
  in Christ, only one, 180, 181–82, 188
  in Christ, two, 60–61, 64–65, 108, 110, 114,
    115, 120–21, 136, 165, 178, 181–82, 184, 199
  divine, 79–80, 113, 114–15, 117, 119, 122, 193
  human, 22–23, 32, 37, 38–39, 41, 43–44, 45–
    46, 62, 63, 114–15, 117–18, 151, 162–63,
    165, 182–83
Nicene Creed, *see* Creed
North Africa, 1, 2–3, 19, 22, 49, 51, 67

ὁμοούσιος, 16, 81 *see also* consubstantial
Only-Begotten, 35–36, 40, 43–44, 60–63, 64–65,
  66, 79–80, 81
ordo salutis, 13–14, 132–33
Origen, 108, 128
  Origenist Christology, *see* Christology
  Origenist monastic tradition, 7–8
original sin, 8–9, 15–16, 37, 189 *see also* Adam
οὐσία, 162–63

papacy/papal see, 149, 150n.75, 150–51, 163–64,
  165–66, 168, 204
  Prosper as papal secretary, 151–53
perfection, *see* salvation
person (subject) of Christ
  a conjunction of Word and man, 16–17
  the Word/Son himself, 13, 35–36, 54–55, 66,
    82, 116, 119, 120, 124, 125, 154, 167, 180–
    82, 202–3
φύσις, 61, 72, 110, 113
pneumatology, 8–9, 76n.31, 146, 148 *see also*
  Holy Spirit
predestinarians in Gaul, 2n.8, 7, 85–86, 95–96,
  101–2, 129–30, 171, 172–74, 187–89, 195–
  97, 200
predestination of Christ's humanity, 43–47, 132–33
prima gratia, see grace
πρόσωπον, 14–15, 72, 110, 113, 117

of union, 14–15, 72, 73, 76, 97, 110, 111, 117,
  162, 182–83, 184

qua homo, see homo
quaternity (instead of Trinity), 32–33, 45,
  53, 112–13
Quicunque Vult, 102n.13, 133

rational soul(s), *see* soul(s)
reasoning, *see also* grace, logic of
  regarding grace, 4, 66–67, 165, 169, 202, 204
  from the Fall to creation through *prima gratia*,
    200
  from the Fall to predestination, 22, 47–48, 169,
    200, 205
  from the Fall to the Incarnation, 21, 134, 165–
    66, 168, 200, 205
redemption, *see* salvation
Roman see, *see* papacy/papal see
Rufinus (recipient of a letter from Prosper), 15

salvation
  as adoption, 79–80, 95, 96–97, 98, 155–56
  as forgiveness, 44–45, 46–47, 164
  as monastic perfection, 8, 15, 56, 86–88, 93,
    95–96 *see also* chastity
  salvific will of God, 95–96, 146–47, 165, 167, 204
    see also atonement
  limited/restricted, 94–95, 101–2
  universal, 8–9, 94–96, 135, 142–44, 146–47,
    158–59, 167–68, 197, 199–201, 205
Scythia Minor, 2–3, 69
Scythian monks, 2–3
Secundus (Numidian bishop), 49
Sixtus III (pope), 102–3, 140, 150n.75
soteriology, *see also* salvation
  of divine descent, 12–13, 16, 19, 21, 30, 47–48,
    54–55, 56, 61–62, 65n.45, 72–73, 81–82, 88–
    89, 131–32, 134, 188–89, 194–95, 199, 200–1
  of human ascent, 19, 30, 54–55, 56, 64, 65n.45,
    76–77, 80, 111–12, 194–95
soul(s), rational
  in Christ, 30–33, 38, 41, 120, 124
  pre-existent, 26
subject in Christ, *see* person (subject) of Christ
substantia, see also natura
  as a word for 'nature', 61, 63, 65–66, 113–15,
    116, 119, 121, 133, 151, 181–82
  in Christ, only one, 180, 188
  in Christ, two, 60–61, 64–65, 108, 110, 114,
    115, 120–21, 125, 165, 178, 181, 182–83,
    185, 188, 199
  divine, 114–15, 117, 122, 181, 193
  human, 114–15, 162–63, 165

222   GENERAL INDEX

Synod of Diospolis (415), 6–7

Tertullian, 28n.31, 108, 128
theodochos, 75, 79–80
Theodore of Mopsuestia, *see* Christology; grace
Theodosius II (emperor), 162, 164
Theotokos, 17, 19, 69–70, 74, 75n.28, 109n.47,
    109–10, 112, 118–19, 127–28, 151n.79, 179,
    181, 182–83, 186 *see also* Mother of God
Tonancio (Spanish monk), 50n.6
Trinity, the
    terminology about, 108, 119, 181
    heresies about, 107–8
    theology of, 106, 109, 112n.53, 114, 119
two ages, the, 15, 16–17 *see also* Christology of ascent

ὑπόστασις, 113
Vandals, 153
verbal symmetry (in describing Christ), 61, 62,
    119, 124, 125–27, 133, 182, 199, 202–3
uia regia, 170–71, 172–73, 174, 186–88, 199
Vidal (Spanish monk), 50n.6
Vincentian canon, 100n.1
Virgin Mary, *see* Mary
Visigoths, 153
Volusian (recipient of a letter from Augustine),
    30–31, 126–27

will of God, *see* salvific will

Zosimus (pope), 6–7, 165

Scripture Index

For the benefit of digital users, indexed terms that span two pages (e.g., 52–53) may, on occasion, appear on only one of those pages.

Old Testament

Gen.
  1:26, 192
  9:20–7, 106
Num. 21:22, 170–71
2 Sam. 14:14, 197
Ps.
  5:9, 89n.83
  12[13]:4, 89n.83
  16[17]:5, 89n.83
  50[51]:9, 89n.83
  50[51]:12, 89n.83
  93[94]:10, 89n.83
  145[146]:8, 89n.83
Prov.
  4:26, 89n.83
  4:27, 170–71
Is.
  1:19, 89n.83
  7:14, 78, 178–79
Jer.
  6:29, 197
  14:9, 89n.83
Ezek.
  1:19–20, 89n.83
  18:32, 197
  24:12, 197
  28:31, 89n.83
  33:11, 197
Hos. 10:12, 89n.83
Mic. 6:8, 197
Mal. 3:8, 78

New Testament

Mt.
  3:17, 78
  7:7–8, 129–30
  8:20, 184
  11:28, 94–95, 138
  16:16, 78
  23:27, 197
  26:38, 184
Mk. 9:24, 196
Lk.
  1:35, 178–79
  19:41, 197
  23, 184
  23:43, 33–34
Jn.
  1:1, 185
  1:14, 167
  1:17, 80
  3:1–21, 29
  3:13, 29–30
  6:44, 89n.83, 196
  10:28, 184
  10:30, 37–38, 184
  14:28, 37–38, 184
  16:15, 184
  17, 82–83
  20:28, 74, 78
Rom.
  1:16, 64–65
  1:18–23, 194
  2:6, 89n.83
  5:12, 189
  6:23, 189
  7:14–25, 88
  8:3, 185
  8:31–2, 40
  9:3, 88
  9:11–12, 27
  9:16, 89n.83
  9:21, 198
1 Cor.
  2:8, 118
  15:10, 198
  15:28, 121

224 SCRIPTURE INDEX

2 Cor. 13:4, 64–65
Gal. 4:4, 80, 123
Eph. 2:8–9, 89n.83,
   198
Phil.
  1:22, 88
  2, 37
  2:7, 192

2:13, 89n.83
Col. 2:9, 35
1 Tim.
  2:4, 94–96
  2:5, 43–44, 147
  4:10, 148
James 4:8, 89n.83
2 Pet. 3:9, 197